THE STANDARD OF REVIEW BEFORE THE INTERNATIONAL COURT OF JUSTICE

This book examines how the International Court of Justice (ICJ) reviews State behaviour through the prism of the standard of review.

It develops a novel rationale to support the ICJ's application of deferential standards of review as a judicial avoidance technique, based on strategic considerations. It then goes on to empirically assess all 31 decisions of the Court in which the standard of review was at issue, showing how the Court determines that standard, and answering the question of whether it varies its review intensity strategically.

As a result, the book's original contribution is twofold: establishing a new rationale for judicial deference (which can be applied to all international courts and tribunals); and providing the first comprehensive, empirical analysis of the ICJ's standards of review. It will be beneficial to all scholars of the Court and those interested in judicial strategy.

Volume 93 in the series Studies in International Law

Studies in International Law

Recent titles in this series

General Principles as a Source of International Law:
Art 38(1)(c) of the Statute of the International Court of Justice
Imogen Saunders

The Law of Humanity Project: A Story of International Law Reform
and State-making
Ukri Soirila

Extraterritoriality and Climate Change Jurisdiction: Exploring EU Climate
Protection under International Law
Natalie L Dobson

International Law and the War with Islamic State: Challenges for
Jus ad Bellum and Jus in Bello
Saeed Bagheri

Private Actors as Participants in International Law: A Critical Analysis
of Membership under the Law of the Sea
Armando Rocha

Truth and Transitional Justice: Localising the International Legal
Framework in Muslim Majority Legal Systems
Alice Panepinto

State Responsibility for Non-State Actors: Past, Present and Prospects for the Future
Richard Mackenzie-Gray Scott

International Agreements between Non-State Actors as a Source of International Law
Melissa Loja

Judicial Decisions in International Law Argumentation: Between
Entrapment and Creativity
Letizia Lo Giacco

South-South Migrations and the Law from Below: Case Studies on China and Nigeria
Oreva Olakpe

Territorial Status in International Law
Jure Vidmar

Marine Bioprospecting, Biodiversity and Novel Uses of Ocean Resources:
New Approaches in International Law
Edited by Niels Krabbe and David Langlet

The Standard of Review before the International Court of Justice:
Between Principle and Pragmatism
Felix Fouchard

For a complete list of titles in this series
see www.bloomsbury.com/uk/series/studies-in-international-law/

The Standard of Review before the International Court of Justice

Between Principle and Pragmatism

Felix Fouchard

•HART•

OXFORD • LONDON • NEW YORK • NEW DELHI • SYDNEY

HART PUBLISHING

Bloomsbury Publishing Plc

Kemp House, Chawley Park, Cumnor Hill, Oxford, OX2 9PH, UK

1385 Broadway, New York, NY 10018, USA

29 Earlsfort Terrace, Dublin 2, Ireland

First published in Great Britain 2024

A catalogue record for this book is available from the British Library.

A catalogue record for this book is available from the Library of Congress.

ISBN: HB: 978-1-50997-130-5
ePDF: 978-1-50997-132-9
ePub: 978-1-50997-131-2

Typeset by Compuscript Ltd, Shannon
Printed and bound in Great Britain

Acknowledgements

THIS BOOK IS a modified and updated version of my dissertation in law at the University of Münster, Germany, completed during my time there as research associate at the Chair for Public Law, International Law, European Union Law and Empirical Legal Studies. And while the book stands for itself, the author does not, being embedded in a network of institutions and people who have greatly influenced this work and played an invaluable part in its completion.

First and foremost, I am particularly indebted to my doctoral supervisor, Niels Petersen, who has conferred on me his trust by granting me true intellectual freedom, given me his generous support, always shown a critical, kind openness for my ideas, and encouraged and enabled me to pursue all my academic projects. I also owe many thanks to my second doctoral reviewer, Nora Markard, for her thorough engagement with my thesis and her helpful suggestions on how to improve it, as well as to James Fowkes, third member of my doctoral committee, for his useful advice during the publication process.

Further, at the University of Münster, my heartfelt thanks go to my colleagues at the Chair for their companionship and, in particular, to my *Doktorgeschwister* Patrick Wasilczyk and Isabel Lischewski, with whom I spent many hours and days discussing our projects, exchanging ideas, and providing solidarity and support.

I would also like to thank Geir Ulfstein and Andreas Føllesdal, Co-Directors of PluriCourts – Centre for the Study of the Legitimate Roles of the Judiciary in the Global Order at the University of Oslo, Norway, for kindly inviting me to conduct research for my doctoral thesis at the Centre, and for providing advice that shaped the orientation of my thesis.

I am also thankful for the fruitful feedback to the convenors and participants at the conferences where I had the opportunity to discuss my work, in particular the German ICON-S Chapter's virtual works-in-progress workshop 2020 for young academics, and ASIL's International Courts and Tribunals Interest Group's virtual Works-in-Progress Conference in February 2021. The same goes for the editors of the Hague International Tribunals section of the *Leiden Journal of International Law* for helping me to improve my article '"Allowing leeway to expediency, without abandoning principle"? The International Court of Justice's use of avoidance techniques', published in volume 33, issue 3, of which chapter three of this book is an updated and expanded version.

Finally, I would like to thank the two anonymous reviewers for their useful feedback on my book. My gratitude also goes to the collaborators at Hart

Publishing for their professionalism and assistance during the publication process of this book.

My doctoral project has received the generous support of the *Studienstiftung des deutschen Volkes*.

In the end, I would like to thank those without whom this work would not have been possible, for their encouragement, their advice, their trust, and their help at every stage of this project: my parents, my brothers – and Katrin.

Contents

List of Tables

Table of Cases

Committee against Torture

European Court of Human Rights

GATT & World Trade Organization

International Court of Justice

International Criminal Tribunal for the former Yugoslavia

International Military Tribunal

International Tribunal for the Law of the Sea

Permanent Court of International Justice

1

Introduction

THE APPROPRIATE ALLOCATION of powers between the International Court of Justice ('ICJ', 'Court') and the states is an ever-constant subject of dispute in international legal practice and scholarship. This also concerns the Court's control density for state behaviour, a debate led under labels such as 'standard of review', 'margin of appreciation', and 'discretion'. States regularly claim that international courts and tribunals such as the ICJ should show deference to them as the first-hand decision-makers when evaluating their behaviour. While this concept is known in many municipal law systems, it has gained specific prominence in international law, premised as it is on the notion of state sovereignty.

Thus, states have advanced before the Court that 'it must be obvious that the concept of self-defence … involves a necessary power of appreciation',[1] that 'it cannot be correct to interpret the text [of the pertinent norm] as depriving a State of the margin of appreciation',[2] and that the margin of appreciation 'must be an axiom of international law and relations'.[3] Other states and scholars have denied the existence of such a principle before the ICJ, observing that '[t]he margin of appreciation is, in international law, an aberration [and] [i]t is time we treated it as such',[4] that 'the margin of appreciation is neither a rule of international law nor a justifiable exercise of adjudicative authority',[5] and that the idea that there is 'a general "margin of appreciation" test' [is] latitudinarian'.[6] Those contrasting statements illustrate a profound disagreement about the degree of deference, if any, the Court should accord to the concerned states when evaluating their behaviour, or, put differently, what standard of review it should apply.

[1] *Armed Activities on the Territory of the Congo (the Congo v Uganda)*, ICJ, Rejoinder of Uganda of 6 December 2002, 269.

[2] *Interim Accord of 13 September 1995 (Macedonia v Greece)*, ICJ, Rejoinder of Greece of 27 October 2010, para 6.30.

[3] *Whaling in the Antarctic (Australia v Japan: New Zealand intervening)*, ICJ, Counter-Memorial of Japan of 9 March 2012, para 9.16.

[4] E Bjorge, 'Been There, Done That: The Margin of Appreciation and International Law' (2015) 4(1) *Cambridge Journal of International and Comparative Law* 181, 181.

[5] G Born, D Morris and S Forrest, '"A Margin of Appreciation": Appreciating Its Irrelevance in International Law' (2020) 61(1) *Harvard Journal of International Law* 65, 65.

[6] *Whaling in the Antarctic*, ICJ, Oral Proceedings of 26 June 2013, afternoon (CR 2013/8), 45, para 63 (Crawford).

Scholars have extensively addressed this question for other international courts and tribunals in the domain of international human rights law,[7] international trade law,[8] European Union law,[9] investment arbitration,[10] and in

[7] From the burgeoning literature, see for instance HC Yourow, *The Margin of Appreciation Doctrine in the Dynamics of European Human Rights Jurisprudence* (Kluwer Law International, 1996); Y Arai-Takahashi, *The Margin of Appreciation Doctrine and the Principle of Proportionality in the Jurisprudence of the ECHR* (Intersentia, 2002); A Legg, *The Margin of Appreciation in International Human Rights Law: Deference and Proportionality* (Oxford University Press, 2012); J Asche, *Die Margin of Appreciation: Entwurf einer Dogmatik monokausaler richterlicher Zurückhaltung für den europäischen Menschenrechtsschutz* (Springer, 2018); G Candia Falcón, 'Standard of Review: Inter-American Court of Human Rights' in R Wolfrum (ed), *Max Planck Encyclopedia of Public International Law* (Oxford University Press, 2012); M Goldmann and M Sonnen, 'Soft Authority Against Hard Cases of Racially Discriminating Speech: Why the CERD Committee Needs a Margin of Appreciation Doctrine' (2016) 7(1) *Goettingen Journal of International Law* 131; D McGoldrick, 'A Defence of the Margin of Appreciation and an Argument for its Application by the Human Rights Committee' (2016) 65(1) *International and Comparative Law Quarterly* 21; Y Shany, 'All Roads Lead to Strasbourg? Application of the Margin of Appreciation Doctrine by the European Court of Human Rights and the UN Human Rights Committee' (2018) 9(2) *Journal of International Dispute Settlement* 180; S Dothan, 'Margin of Appreciation and Democracy: Human Rights and Deference to Political Bodies' (2018) 9(2) *Journal of International Dispute Settlement* 145; S Bertelsen, 'A margin for the margin of appreciation: Deference in the Inter-American Court of Human Rights' (2021) 19(3) *International Journal of Constitutional Law* 887; SB Traore and PAA Leta, 'La marge nationale d'appreciation dans la jurisprudence de la Cour africaine des droits de l'homme et des peuples: entre effeurements et remises en cause' (2021) 31(3) *Swiss Review of International and European Law* 317.

[8] From the burgeoning literature, see for instance M Oesch, *Standards of Review in WTO Dispute Resolution* (Oxford University Press, 2003); C Button, *The Power to Protect: Trade, Health and Uncertainty in the WTO* (Hart, 2004); R Becroft, *The Standard of Review in WTO Dispute Settlement: Critique and Development* (Edward Elgar, 2012); SP Croley and JH Jackson, 'WTO Dispute Procedures, Standard of Review, and Deference to National Governments' (1996) 90(2) *American Journal of International Law* 193; C-D Ehlermann and N Lockhart, 'Standard of Review in WTO Law' (2004) 7(3) *Journal of International Economic Law* 491; MM Du, 'Standard of Review under the SPS Agreement after EC-Hormones II' (2010) 59(2) *International and Comparative Law Quarterly* 441; for a recent study not focused on a specific international dispute settlement body, but rather on a subject-matter (namely, tobacco control) see L Gruszczynski, 'Saving Regulatory Space for States Through the Standard of Review' in G Kajtár, B Çalı and M Milanović (eds), *Secondary Rules of Primary Importance in International Law: Attribution, Causality, Evidence, and Standards of Review in the Practice of International Courts and Tribunals* (Oxford University Press, 2022).

[9] H Schulte, *Zur Übertragbarkeit der Margin-of-appreciation-Doktrin des EGMR auf die Rechtsprechung des EuGH im Bereich der Grundfreiheiten* (Nomos, 2018); J Zglinski, *Europe's Passive Virtues* (Oxford University Press, 2020); JA Sweeney, 'A "Margin of Appreciation" in the Internal Market: Lessons from the European Court of Human Rights' (2007) 34(1) *Legal issues of economic integration* 27; J Gerards, 'Pluralism, Deference and the Margin of Appreciation Doctrine' (2011) 17(1) *European Law Journal* 80; A Rosas, 'Standard of Review: Court of Justice of the European Union' in R Wolfrum (ed), *Max Planck Encyclopedia of Public International Law* (Oxford University Press, 2012).

[10] C Henckels, *Proportionality and Deference in Investor-State Arbitration* (Cambridge University Press, 2015); WW Burke-White and A von Staden, 'Private Litigation in a Public Law Sphere: The Standard of Review in Investor-State Arbitrations' (2010) 35(2) *Yale Journal of International Law* 283; A Roberts, 'The Next Battleground: Standards of Review in Investment Treaty Arbitration' (2011) 16 *International Council for Commercial Arbitration Congress Series* 170; S Schill, 'Deference in Investment Treaty Arbitration: Re-conceptualizing the Standard of Review' (2012) 3(3) *Journal of International Dispute Settlement* 577; J Paine, 'Standard of Review: Investment Arbitration' in R Wolfrum (ed), *Max Planck Encyclopedia of Public International Law* (Oxford University Press, 2012); E Shirlow, 'Deference and Indirect Expropriation Analysis in International Investment Law: Observations on Current Approaches and Frameworks for Future Analysis' (2014) 29(3) *ICSID Review* 595.

comparative outlooks,[11] from both a normative and an empirical viewpoint. Scholars have also turned specifically to the ICJ – yet predominantly from a normative standpoint, or with a focus on selected decisions only.[12]

In contrast, a comprehensive empirical study on the use of the standard of review notion by the Court is still wanting. This book aims to fill that gap. It proposes a reading of deferential standards of review as a judicial avoidance technique – a technique 'to dispose of cases or issues within cases where a decision seems unnecessary, inappropriate, or perhaps simply too controversial'.[13] The book argues that the use of deferential standards of review as such an avoidance technique can be advantageous for the ICJ, in particular in comparison to the other avoidance techniques it has been using in the past.[14]

With this as background, the book then proceeds to analyse in depth whether and how the Court uses the standard of review notion – not only explicitly, but also implicitly – and whether it does so as a tool of judicial avoidance. To this end, it proposes a four-by-four matrix, grouping the analysed proceedings in two consecutive steps: first, based on the standard of review chosen by the ICJ on a four-tier scale, and second, based on four different subject-matter categories – national security, domestic measures, political determinations, and scientific assessments.

Contrary to what has at times been asserted in the literature, the book establishes that the Court has regularly been resorting to deferential standards of review. There are also grounds to conclude that it employs them as an avoidance technique. The remainder of this introduction will expand on the central term of the study, 'standard of review', before outlining the book's structure, the methodology of the empirical analysis, and finally presenting the key empirical results.

[11] See for instance the volume edited by L Gruszczynski and W Werner (eds), *Deference in International Courts and Tribunals: Standard of Review and Margin of Appreciation* (Oxford University Press, 2014); JH Fahner, *Judicial Deference in International Adjudication: A Comparative Analysis* (Hart, 2020); E Shirlow, *Judging at the Interface: Deference to State Decision-Making Authority in International Adjudication* (Cambridge University Press, 2021).

[12] See for instance Y Shany, 'Toward a General Margin of Appreciation Doctrine in International Law?' (2005) 16(5) *European Journal of International Law* 907, 931–38; SR Tully, '"Objective Reasonableness" as a Standard for International Judicial Review' (2015) 6(3) *Journal of International Dispute Settlement* 546; E Cannizzaro, 'Proportionality and Margin of Appreciation in the Whaling Case: Reconciling Antithetical Doctrines?' (2016) 27(4) *European Journal of International Law* 1061; A Garrido-Muñoz, 'Managing Uncertainty: The International Court of Justice, "Objective Reasonableness" and the Judicial Function' (2017) 30(2) *Leiden Journal of International Law* 457; focusing on *explicit* statements regarding the intensity of review by several international courts and tribunals, including the ICJ, Fahner, *Judicial Deference in International Adjudication* (n 11), 18; with a focus on private property claims decided by inter alia the ICJ, and looking at judicial deference generally, of which deferential standards of review are but one manifestation: Shirlow, *Judging at the Interface* (n 11), 2–3.

[13] WJ Davey, 'Has the WTO Dispute Settlement System Exceeded Its Authority? A Consideration of Deference shown by the System to Member Government Decisions and its Use of Issue-Avoidance Techniques' (2001) 4(1) *Journal of International Economic Law* 79, 96.

[14] Note, however, that the book does not try to make the point that judicial avoidance is per se preferable from the viewpoint of judicial strategy.

I. SIGNIFICANCE OF THE STANDARD OF REVIEW

How the ICJ determines the applicable standard of review in a proceeding is of both practical and theoretical interest.

At first glance, determining the appropriate standard of review in a proceeding seems to be a purely procedural question. Yet, procedure matters. Setting a more deferential standard of review significantly increases the chances for the state whose measures form the subject of judicial appreciation to prevail. This becomes most obvious for the maximum degree of deference. In such instances, the ICJ abstains entirely from forming its own opinion on the correctness of an assertion advanced by the concerned state,[15] and blindly accept it as a defensible one. As a result, that assertion – generally, the concerned state will only make claims in its favour – will stand, and that state thus prevail. The chances of success are also higher under less far-reaching forms of deference. Unless the disagreement of the Court with the state's claim is qualified, it will uphold that claim. The range of the permissible thus becomes greater, and the concerned state's chances of winning increase[16] – as does the decision-making autonomy of that state and states in a similar position.[17]

On the other hand, the way the Court determines the standard of review also tells us something about its own perspective on its role in the international legal order. From a doctrinal point of view, the appropriate standard of review should only depend on legal factors. However, the UN Charter and the ICJ Statute as the ICJ's constitutive instruments remain silent on the applicable standard of review. The same is true for other international courts and tribunals.[18] Likewise,

[15] In what follows, this state will also be referred to as the defendant or respondent state, even if, technically, this is not the correct denomination in advisory proceedings, for often enough, there is a de facto respondent state in those proceedings as well. *Wall in the OPT* and *Marshall Islands* are such cases in point.

[16] Eskridge's and Baer's study on the US Supreme Court's standard of review to evaluate statutory agency interpretations confirms this empirically for that court, W Eskridge and L Baer, 'The Continuum of Deference: Supreme Court Treatment of Agency Statutory Interpretations from *Chevron* to *Hamdan*' (2008) 96 *The Georgetown Law Journal* 1083, 1099. Their findings can be transposed to judicial decision-making in general.

[17] See on this point with respect to the WTO system J Bohanes and N Lockhart, 'Standard of Review in WTO Law' in DL Bethlehem and others (eds), *The Oxford Handbook of International Trade Law* (Oxford University Press, 2009), 381; see also *Certain Iranian Assets (Islamic Republic of Iran v United States of America)*, ICJ, Judgment (Merits), Separate Opinion of Judge Iwasawa, para 10.

[18] One could be led to think that Art 11 of the Understanding on Rules and Procedures Governing the Settlement of Disputes (DSU) prescribes a particular standard of review for WTO panels. This provision requires panels to 'make an objective assessment of the matter before it, including an objective assessment of the facts of the case and the applicability of and conformity with the relevant covered agreements'. However, a closer analysis shows that Art 11 does not determine a specific standard of review. As the Appellate Body held in *EC-Hormones*, under Art 11 DSU, 'the applicable standard is neither *de novo* review as such, nor "total deference"… Many panels have in the past refused to undertake *de novo* review, wisely … On the other hand, "total deference to the findings of the national authorities", it has been well said, "could not ensure an 'objective assessment' as foreseen by Article 11"', *EC – Measures Concerning Meat and Meat Products*, Report of

most international treaties do not pronounce upon this aspect.[19] This void requires the Court to look for other factors shaping its decision on the applicable standard of review.

Considerations of power-allocation as well as of expertise and legitimacy are such other factors.[20] Examining the way the ICJ determines the applicable standard of review thus reveals how it defines its own role vis-a-vis the states. A more intrusive standard of review betrays its conviction that it is the competent decision-maker on this point, that it has the requisite expertise to evaluate that question, and that it is legitimised to do so. In turn, the adoption of a deferential standard of review conveys the ICJ's acknowledgment of the fact that either it is not competent to decide the matter without any regard to the respective state, that it is ill-equipped to evaluate that question for itself, and/or that it lacks the legitimacy to do so. Accordingly, every single decision in that regard adds another mosaic stone to the bigger picture of the Court's self-perceived role.[21]

The absence of normative guidance also enables the ICJ to factor in another set of aspects when determining the applicable standard of review: policy considerations.[22] As has been appositely remarked, '[a]t the end of the day, the purview of adjudication is a matter of judicial choice'.[23] A central consideration for the Court is that like any court of law, it is highly dependent on institutional support. Most important, for the ICJ, is its dependence on the states as well as for the initiation of proceedings, the conferral of jurisdiction, as for the implementation of its decisions.

This observation about the institutional dependency of both international and national courts and tribunals has brought a part of the literature to explain their behaviour with strategical considerations, assuming that they try to avoid

the Appellate Body (16 January 1998) WT/DS26/AB/R and WT/DS48/AB/R, 117 (footnotes omitted). This makes clear that different standards of review can be subsumed under the term 'objective assessment'. Bohanes and Lockhart thus conclude that the term 'speaks more obviously to the fairness, impartiality, and even-handedness of panels' examination' than to the degree of deference to be applied, Bohanes and Lockhart, 'Standard of Review in WTO Law' (n 17), 383.

[19] As Garrid-Muñoz observed, 'the definition of [standards of judicial review] is frequently left vague or even avoided by lawmakers', Garrido-Muñoz, 'Managing Uncertainty' (n 12), 461 (with further references). The notable exception is Art 17.6 of the WTO's Anti-Dumping Agreement. According to this provision, 'in its assessment of the facts of the matter, the panel shall determine whether the authorities' establishment of the facts was proper and whether their evaluation of those facts was unbiased and objective. If the establishment of the facts was proper and the evaluation was unbiased and objective, even though the panel might have reached a different conclusion, the evaluation shall not be overturned'.

[20] *cf* Oesch, *Standards of Review in WTO Dispute Resolution* (n 8), 23; with further references Shirlow, 'Deference and Indirect Expropriation Analysis in International Investment Law' (n 10), 601–02.

[21] As Shirlow puts it, '[t]he selection of a particular standard of review will … be highly dependent upon the tribunal's understanding of its role within a particular system', Shirlow, 'Deference and Indirect Expropriation Analysis in International Investment Law' (n 10), 600.

[22] On this point in the context of WTO jurisprudence, see AT Guzman, 'Determining the Appropriate Standard of Review in WTO Disputes' (2009) 42(1) *Cornell International Law Journal* 45, 53.

[23] K Sulyok, *Science and Judicial Reasoning: The Legitimacy of International Environmental Adjudication* (Cambridge University Press, 2021), 59.

challenges by other actors.[24] As will be argued in more detail below, one way for the ICJ to do so is to accommodate the core preferences of states, and refrain from overstepping its expertise and intruding into the domain of national sovereignty. Avoiding to adjudicate upon such questions through the use of judicial avoidance techniques is one such method. The ICJ has resorted to several judicial avoidance techniques in the past.[25]

A deferential standard of review can also serve as one such tool, one that holds particular potential for the Court. It has been observed for the European Court of Human Rights (ECtHR) that the margin of appreciation doctrine has become 'an essential ingredient of [its] success in fashioning an effective system of adjudication'.[26] Adopting a deferential standard of review enables the ICJ to practice pinpoint avoidance, thereby allowing it to balance out the competing expectations it faces with particular precision.

II. DEFINITION OF THE TERM 'STANDARD OF REVIEW'

At this point, it is necessary to define what the book understands by 'standard of review' and 'deferential' standard of review, as well as to examine to what degree the terms 'margin of appreciation' and 'discretion', already referred to above, are congruent with the notion of standard of review, and to what extent they are not. The latter will also be contrasted with the standard of proof.

It has been observed that the standard of review notion is 'a notoriously elusive concept'.[27] This has led to many different and at times contradictory definitions of the term. A short example, adopted from a simple yet elegant

[24] From the wealth of literature on this for both national and international courts and tribunals, see for instance WF Murphy, *Elements of Judicial Strategy* (University of Chicago Press, 1964); G Vanberg, *The Politics of Constitutional Review in Germany* (Cambridge University Press, 2009); RH Steinberg, 'Judicial Lawmaking at the WTO: Discursive, Constitutional, and Political Constraints' (2004) 98(2) *American Journal of International Law* 247, with further references at 263; CJ Carrubba and Gabel, Matthew, Hankla, Charles, 'Judicial Behavior under Political Constraints: Evidence from the European Court of Justice' (2008) 102(4) *American Political Science Review* 435; N Petersen, 'The International Court of Justice and the Judicial Politics of Identifying Customary International Law' (2017) 28(2) *European Journal of International Law* 357; L Graham, 'Strategic Admissibility Decisions in the European Court of Human Rights' (2020) 69(1) *International and Comparative Law Quarterly* 79; Ø Stiansen and E Voeten, 'Backlash and Judicial Restraint: Evidence from the European Court of Human Rights' (2020) 64(4) *International Studies Quarterly* 770.

[25] Notably, in the domain of nuclear weapons, see below at ch 3, sections II.C, III.A and III.C.

[26] With further references LR Helfer, 'Adjudicating Copyright Claims Under the TRIPs Agreement: The Case for a European Human Rights Analogy' (1998) 39(2) *Harvard Journal of International Law* 357, 404. This does not imply that the ECtHR resorts to the margin of appreciation as a strategic tool. Such a claim has been made elsewhere, see for instance EF Delaney, 'Analyzing Avoidance: Judicial Strategy in Comparative Perspective' (2016) 66(1) *Duke Law Journal* 1, 40; S Dothan, 'Judicial Deference Allows European Consensus to Emerge' (2018) 18(2) *Chicago Journal of International Law* 393, 406–07.

[27] M Ioannidis, 'Beyond the Standard of Review: Deference Criteria in WTO Law and the Case for a Procedural Approach' in L Gruszczynski and W Werner (eds), *Deference in International Courts and Tribunals: Standard of Review and Margin of Appreciation* (Oxford University Press, 2014), 94.

explanation by Shirlow,[28] will set out to explain what is meant in this enquiry by the term 'standard of review':

> Treaty provision P requires States not to do X unless Y is satisfied. State R, accused before the Court to have breached P, could assert that it has not done X, or that Y is satisfied. The ICJ must determine what weight, if any, it will accord to R's respective subsumption. This is the Court's 'standard of review'. The ICJ could accord R complete deference by delegating to that State the prerogative to determine, without any evaluation of its own, the (non-)existence of X or Y. On the other hand, it could also determine the (non-)existence of X or Y itself, without any reference to R's respective determinations. A range of options exists between these two extremes.

Accordingly, the term 'standard of review' denotes to what degree the ICJ scrutinises the first-hand assessments and determinations of a state in proceedings in which the latter's compliance with obligations under international law is at issue. A 'deferential' standard of review denotes the idea that the Court assigns particular weight to these assessments and determinations, and refrains from examining that question entirely by itself. It does not express a specific weight, only that the state's claim carries *some* weight for the ICJ.

To evaluate the lawfulness of a given behaviour, any court of law will have to perform three consecutive steps. First, it will have to establish the pertinent facts. Second, it will have to identify and interpret the pertinent legal rules.[29] Third and finally, it will have to qualify the facts in relation to the norms, or, put differently, subsume the facts established in the first step of the judicial reasoning under the norm content as established in the second step. While there are interconnections between these three steps, the book focuses exclusively on the third step: law-application. Accordingly, it focuses on the claim advanced by states that their behaviour cannot be subsumed under the terms of a prohibition, respectively that it can be subsumed under the requirements of a right. Contrary to other understandings of term 'standard of review',[30] it thereby leaves aside the two prior steps of judicial reasoning.[31]

[28] Shirlow, 'Deference and Indirect Expropriation Analysis in International Investment Law' (n 10), 601.

[29] D'Aspremont refers to law-ascertainment (the establishment of the binding character of a rule), and content-determination (the attribution of meaning to a rule), J D'Aspremont, 'The Multidimensional Process of Interpretation: Content-Determination and Law-Ascertainment Distinguished' in A Bianchi, D Peat and M Windsor (eds), *Interpretation in International Law* (Oxford University Press, 2015), 112.

[30] For instance E-U Petersmann, 'Judicial Standards of Review and Administration of Justice in Trade and Investment Law and Adjudication' in L Gruszczynski and W Werner (eds), *Deference in International Courts and Tribunals: Standard of Review and Margin of Appreciation* (Oxford University Press, 2014), 19–20; C Ragni, 'Standard of Review and the Margin of Appreciation before the International Court of Justice' in L Gruszczynski and W Werner (eds), *Deference in International Courts and Tribunals: Standard of Review and Margin of Appreciation* (Oxford University Press, 2014), 319.

[31] How the Court has approached these two stages has already received extensive attention in the literature. On the former question, see only the following dedicated monographs: M Kazazi, *Burden of Proof and Related Issues: A Study on Evidence before International Tribunals* (Kluwer,

In conclusion, the term 'standard of review' will be used to denote what weight, if any, the ICJ accords to a defendant state's first-hand assessment that its behaviour in question can be subsumed under a norm, respectively that it cannot. It encompasses both whether the Court examines that first-hand assessment at all as well as if so, to what degree.

In turn, the notion of standard of proof describes 'the quantum or degree of proof, i.e. by what measure is what the claimant has to prove to be judged'.[32] Accordingly, the standard of review and the standard of proof concern different questions. The standard of review describes what it is exactly that the concerned state has to prove – that X or Y had in fact been fulfilled, or merely that it had reasonably concluded at the time that this had been the case, and so on. In turn, the standard of proof describes the degree of judicial conviction that is required for the Court to hold that the condition just identified has been satisfied. Both the choice of the applicable standard of review and standard of proof directly influence the likelihood that the respondent state will prevail in a given case.[33] Both can also range on a continuum.[34]

A short example taken from the Court's case law illustrates these last two observations. In *Oil Platforms*, one issue was whether the United States could successfully invoke the right to self-defence as justification for its use of force against Iran. Lawful self-defence inter alia requires that the response is directed against the attacker. In this regard, 'standard of review' concerns the question what it was the United States had to prove: that Iran had in fact been responsible for the prior attacks on U.S.-flagged vessels, or merely that the United States had been reasonable to conclude so at the time of its response, etc. In turn, 'standard of proof' concerns the question what degree of probability is required to convince the Court of this point: conviction beyond reasonable doubt, or merely preponderance of evidence, etc. The standards of review and of proof

1996); CF Amerasinghe, *Evidence in International Litigation* (Martinus Nijhoff, 2005); M Benzing, *Das Beweisrecht vor internationalen Gerichten und Schiedsgerichten in zwischenstaatlichen Streitigkeiten* (Springer, 2010); A Riddell and B Plant, *Evidence before the International Court of Justice*, Reprint 2011 (British Institute of International Comparative Law, 2009); JG Devaney, *Fact-Finding Before the International Court of Justice* (Cambridge University Press, 2016); likewise, for the latter, see: R Kolb, *Interprétation et création du droit international: Esquisses d'une herméneutique juridique moderne pour le droit international public* (Bruylant, 2006); A Orakhelashvili, *The Interpretation of Acts and Rules in Public International Law* (Oxford University Press, 2008); RK Gardiner, *Treaty Interpretation*, 2nd edn (Oxford University Press, 2015).

[32] Amerasinghe, *Evidence in International Litigation* (n 31), 232.

[33] On the practical importance of the latter see for instance Riddell and Plant, *Evidence before the International Court of Justice* (n 31), 123. Moreover, the standard of review and the standard of proof share the particularity that the legal bases for the Court's functioning remain silent on both of them, see above at section II and GM Farnelli, 'Consistency in the ICJ's Approach to the Standard of Proof: An Appraisal of the Court's Flexibility' (2022) 21(1) *The Law and Practice of International Courts and Tribunals* 98, 102–05.

[34] On some possible standards of proof, see Amerasinghe, *Evidence in International Litigation* (n 31), 235–45; Kazazi, *Burden of Proof and Related Issues: A Study on Evidence before International Tribunals* (n 31), 344.

can, in principle, be combined freely. For instance, under the strictest standard of review and a beyond reasonable doubt standard of proof, the United States would thus have had to show that there was no reasonable doubt that the attacks had been carried out by Iran. Under the same standard of review, but a preponderance of evidence standard of proof, the United States would in turn only have had to show that it was more likely than not that this had been the case.

The term 'deferential standard of review' is also often used interchangeably with 'discretion' in the literature,[35] and international courts and tribunals as well do not always differentiate between the two.[36] This is not entirely surprising, as the two terms are indeed closely interrelated. Notably, the policy rationales behind the two notions are similar.[37] Furthermore, they have – broadly speaking – the same effect: a decreased level of judicial scrutiny.[38] Nonetheless, it is important to distinguish between the two terms. The main distinguishing characteristic is that they intervene at different stages of the judicial decision-making process referred to above. Discretion is latitude recognised as a result of the interpretation of a given norm, while standard of review as understood here relates to the application of that law to the facts.[39] Accordingly, 'discretion' intervenes in the second step of the judicial reasoning process – establishment of the law. 'Standard of review' in turn does so in the third step – law-application.

Finally, 'standard of review' has to be distinguished as well from the 'margin of appreciation'. While the latter has also been invoked before other international courts and tribunals, including the ICJ, it has gained prominence especially through its use by the ECtHR. The ECtHR famously refers to the 'margin of appreciation' that it accords to national authorities in their consideration of derogations from or restrictions to Conventions rights, as it considers that they are better placed to decide on the necessity of such steps.[40]

[35] See for instance Bohanes and Lockhart, 'Standard of Review in WTO Law' (n 17), 379.

[36] Shany, 'Toward a General Margin of Appreciation Doctrine in International Law?' (n 12), 910.

[37] ibid.

[38] J Fahner, 'The Margin of Appreciation in Investor-State Arbitration: The Prevalence and Desirability of Discretion and Deference' in N Lavranos and RA Kok (eds), *Hague Yearbook of International Law* (Brill/Nijhoff, 2013), 440.

[39] Shany, 'Toward a General Margin of Appreciation Doctrine in International Law?' (n 12), 909–10. Shany chooses a slightly different wording by referring to 'normative flexibility' as opposed to 'judicial deference', but the essential distinction is the same. With regard to the ECtHR, Christoffersen distinguishes between 'pure discretion', which is 'purely a consequence of the norms' themselves, and the Court's subsidiary review, together resulting in 'enlarged discretion', J Christoffersen, *Fair Balance: Proportionality, Subsidiarity and Primarity in the European Convention on Human Rights* (Brill/Nijhoff, 2009), 236–37; finally, Fahner notes that '[i]n contrast to discretion, deference does not relate to the normative substance of the applicable norm, but to the institutional relationship between the Court on the one hand and national authorities on the other hand. Deference does not concern the normative content of the treaty standard itself', Fahner, 'The Margin of Appreciation in Investor-State Arbitration' (n 38), 433–34.

[40] See for instance *A. and Others v the United Kingdom (Merits and Just Satisfaction)*, ECtHR, 3455/05 (2009) ECHR 301; for an early example, see *Handyside v The United Kingdom*, ECtHR Series A no 24 (1976) 1 EHRR 737; and *Ireland v the United Kingdom (Merits and Just Satisfaction)*, ECtHR Series A no 25 (1978) 2 EHRR 25.

The margin of appreciation has been described as one of the ECtHR's 'most prominent methodological features',[41] and it has been observed to be 'at the heart of virtually all major cases that come before [it], whether the judgments refer to it explicitly or not'.[42] Protocol 15 to the European Convention on Human Rights (ECHR) has codified it, adding a new recital to the Preamble of the Convention that affirms the margin of appreciation that Member States enjoy vis-a-vis the ECtHR.

The 'margin of appreciation' and 'standard of review' seem to express similar ideas. Yet, the term 'margin of appreciation' presupposes a degree of deference, whereas the standard of review per se does not. This suggests that the 'margin of appreciation' could perhaps better be understood as a specific deferential standard of review. However, two major characteristics of the 'margin' caution against such an understanding. First, the ECtHR uses the term to denote several distinct concepts, among others also the Member States' discretion in how to implement their conventional obligations.[43] Second, and more crucially, the fact that *some* deference is due to the state in question does not determine *what* degree of deference exactly. While the ECtHR regularly refers to *the* 'margin of appreciation', the degree of deference varies from case to case under the 'margin', as it has made clear itself. Thus, it has held that while a 'margin of appreciation must be left to the competent national authorities … [t]he breadth of this margin varies and depends on a number of factors'.[44] This shows that the ECtHR does not refer to the 'margin of appreciation' as a *specific* standard of review itself, but rather as a shorthand that comprises different degrees of deference, or different standards of review.[45]

[41] Asche, *Die Margin of Appreciation* (n 7), 6 (own translation. In the German original: 'eine seiner markantesten methodologischen Charakteristika').

[42] RJ St Macdonald, 'The Margin of Appreciation in the Jurisprudence of the European Court of Human Rights', *Le droit international à l'heure de sa codification: études en l'honneur de Roberto Ago, Vol III* (Giuffrè, 1987), 187.

[43] Fahner, 'The Margin of Appreciation in Investor-State Arbitration' (n 38), 431–33.

[44] *S. and Marper v The United Kingdom (Just Satisfaction)*, ECtHR, 30562/04 and 30566/04 (2008) ECHR 1581; see also *Stummer v Austria*, ECtHR, 37452/02 (2011) ECHR 1096.

[45] This has been noted by many scholars, tellingly illustrated by the title chosen by G Itzcovich, 'One, None and One Hundred Thousand Margins of Appreciations: The Lautsi Case' (2013) 13(2) *Human Rights Law Review* 287; Arato, analysing five arbitral awards in which investment tribunals referred to the 'margin of appreciation', calls it an 'empty proxy', J Arato, 'The Margin of Appreciation in International Investment Law' (2014) 54(3) *Virginia Journal of International Law* 545, 552, see also at 558; Fukunaga speaks of its 'accordion-like nature', Y Fukunaga, 'Margin of Appreciation as an Indicator of Judicial Deference: Is It Applicable to Investment Arbitration?' (2019) 10(1) *Journal of International Dispute Settlement* 69, 74; finally, Born, Morris and Forrest observe that '[r]eference to a single margin of appreciation suggests that the same standard of deference and thus the same margin of appreciation applies in each of the various settings in which it is invoked. That is not … accurate', Born, Morris and Forrest, '"A Margin of Appreciation"' (n 5), 118.

III. STRUCTURE OF THE BOOK

Based on this understanding of the central term of the study, 'standard of review', the book takes both a conceptual and an empirical approach. Chapters two and three analyse the notion's roots and its specific potential for the ICJ. Chapters four to seven then examine how the Court determines its standard of review. Chapter eight summarises the key results.

Focusing on the states' articulated stance towards the standard of review notion before the ICJ, chapter two sets out to uncover the argumentative background of their pleas for a deferential standard of review. It will be seen that states urging the Court to adopt such a standard are relying on an argumentative basis already established in connection with the well-known doctrine of non-justiciability in the international order. From this perspective, deferential standards of review seem to be old wine in new skins, so that one may think that their invocation does not put the Court in a substantially new position. However, there is something that has changed in between the birth of the non-justiciability doctrine and the invocation of deferential standards of review: the international adjudication paradigm. It has changed from the consideration that disputes between sovereign states are generally unfit for adjudication to the consideration that in principle, all inter-state disputes are fit for adjudication. From this angle, the invocation of the non-justiciability doctrine can be seen as an attempt to curb a development – that of the international legal order – while the plea for a deferential standard of review is an attempt to turn back the clock. Accordingly, one may at least speak of a conceptual transformation. In practical terms, the ICJ has consistently rejected to recognise the doctrine of non-justiciability, and there seems to be little reason at first for it to proceed otherwise with the standard of review claims.

Despite this conceptual continuity, chapter three, turning to the Court's perspective, argues that adopting a deferential standard of review holds specific and unprecedented potential for the ICJ. Just as the finding of non-justiciability, adopting a deferential standard of review may serve as a judicial avoidance technique.[46] Often, states consider a matter to be unsuitable for a decision by the ICJ because they view such a decision as a transgression of their sovereignty, broadly construed. Employing a deferential standard of review gives the Court a tool to address these resurfacing claims in a way that enables it to balance out the need to acknowledge their underlying concerns with the need to uphold its mandate as foreseen by the UN Charter. Against the background of its institutional reality, namely its significant reliance on state support, taking into account

[46] As Brownlie has noted, '[u]ltimately justiciability is a matter of policy', I Brownlie, 'The Justiciability of Disputes and Issues in International Relations' (1967) 42 *British Yearbook of International Law* 123, 142.

the expectations and preferences of the states is a sheer necessity for the Court. Judicial avoidance is one way to do so. An analysis of selected proceedings indicates that the ICJ has indeed been practising avoidance in the past to dispose of thorny issues and proceedings in order to avoid a backlash from both individual states and the overall state community. From the standpoint of judicial policy, the adoption of deferential standards of review is often preferable to the use of these other avoidance techniques. It allows the Court to practise avoidance in a much more nuanced way without undermining its very mandate. Seen in this light, adopting deferential standards of review could thus contribute to protecting and even strengthening the ICJ's institutional foundations, and incidentally the global legal order.[47]

With this as the conceptual background, chapters four to seven then turn to the question whether the ICJ has been employing deferential standards of review, and if so, whether it has done so as judicial avoidance technique. Thirty-one ICJ proceedings form the basis of this analysis, identified with a concern for comprehensiveness. The order of these four chapters follows the proposed standard of review scale, ranging from most to least deferential: absence of judicial oversight (chapter four), good faith (chapter five), reasonableness (chapter six), and *de novo* (chapter seven).[48] Within these four chapters, in order to allow for cross-comparison and generalisable conclusions, the structure will be broken down further through the establishment of four categories, based on the central subject-matter of each of the proceedings: national security, domestic measures, and political as well as scientific determinations.

IV. METHODOLOGY

These three central predeterminations for the empirical analysis – the selection of the included proceedings, the four-tier standard of review scale, and the sorting of the proceedings in one of the four subject-matter categories – merit further explanation, before turning to the key empirical insights.

A. The Selection of Proceedings

The empirical enquiry is based on a detailed analysis of 31 ICJ proceedings in which the Court dealt with first-hand state assessments and pronounced upon

[47] The main ideas contained in ch 3 have already been published in F Fouchard, 'Allowing "leeway to expediency, without abandoning principle"? The International Court of Justice's use of avoidance techniques' (2020) 33(3) *Leiden Journal of International Law* 767.

[48] The enquiry proceeds on a within-case basis, scrutinising the individual questions within these proceedings. This has consequences for the presentation: The same proceeding may be discussed in several sections, depending on the particular approach the Court adopted for the particular question.

the legality of a state's behaviour, broadly speaking, by subsuming the measure in dispute under a norm of international law. These proceedings originate from the entire period of its activity, and were compiled in two steps.

The first step consisted in screening all proceedings which ended with a judgment or advisory opinion to identify those in which the standard of review notion could have received the Court's attention. As the book seeks to yield a comprehensive picture, allowing for more wide-reaching and generalisable conclusions, it comprises a set of proceedings as broad and meaningful as possible. Thus, for instance, both advisory and contentious proceedings were included. Both may more or less directly involve a review of first-hand state assessments, and advisory proceedings may even turn out to be what has been referred to as 'disguised contentious cases'.[49] *Peace Treaties* and *Wall in the OPT* are ample expression of this.

The empirical enquiry focuses on those proceedings that have reached the merits stage, ie where the ICJ has given a substantial answer on the questions involved. It is at this stage that the different institutional, strategic and conceptual premises and goals underlying the standard of review notion culminate and where they become most apparent.[50] This latter consideration also led to the exclusion of territorial as well as maritime delimitation disputes. Albeit important in number, these proceedings do not lend themselves to the logic underlying the standard of review notion. Granting one state decision-making space in the delimitation of its territory directly and invariably puts into question that of the opposed state. Any recognition of a grey area in this domain is thus inevitably a zero-sum game. Apart from these considerations, particular subject-matters, states participating in the proceedings, or procedural situations were not relevant for this first stage.

Second, out of the proceedings thus identified in which the standard of review notion could have played a role, the book identified only those in which this possibility was not merely theoretical, but real. To filter out those proceedings, the set comprises only those in which either a participating state, an individual member of the Court or a scholar advocated for the adoption of a deferential standard of review in relation to a particular question brought up in the proceeding. Accordingly, the study does not rely on a self-identification of the situations where the adoption of a deferential standard of review would have been possible. Rather, it relies on the respective judgment of those best acquainted with the proceedings and best motivated to identify this possibility. By privileging this approach, it excludes a potential source of error that would

[49] F Zarbiyev, 'Judicial Activism in International Law – A Conceptual Framework for Analysis' (2012) 3(2) *Journal of International Dispute Settlement* 1, 26.

[50] Accordingly, the empirical enquiry only addresses preliminary proceedings in connection with the respective merits stage. By themselves, preliminary proceedings are included only insofar as they pre-empt the merits stage on the particular point involved. *Norwegian Loans* and *South West Africa* are the two proceedings to be listed in this regard.

result from the introduction of the author's subjective judgment on the matter. This leads to the exclusion of six further cases, in which neither the ICJ nor any of the parties or judges discussed the standard of review question.[51]

In two more cases, *Guardianship of Infants* and *Interim Accord*, parties and/or judges had urged the Court to adopt a deferential standard of review for a particular question. Yet, the ICJ issued its respective judgments based on an analysis of preceding questions, and did not come to address the standard of review. These two cases were therefore also left out of the empirical analysis.

At the end of this second filtering stage, there are 31 proceedings in which the possibility of adopting a deferential standard of review was brought up, and in which the ICJ took a stance on this question. It is these 31 proceedings that form the heart of the empirical analysis.

Table 1 Overview of the ICJ proceedings included in the empirical study

#	Short title of the Proceedings	#	Short title of the Proceedings
1	1948, Admission of a State to the UN	17	2003, Oil Platforms
2	1949, Corfu Channel	18	2004, Wall in the OPT
3	1950, Asylum	19	2005, Armed Activities
4	1951, Reservations to the Genocide Convention	20	2007, Bosnian Genocide
5	1952, Rights of US Nationals in Morocco	21	2008, Mutual Assistance
6	1955, Nottebohm	22	2009, Navigational Rights
7	1957, Norwegian Loans	23	2010, Pulp Mills
8	1960, Right of Passage	24	2010, Diallo
9	1966, South West Africa	25	2012, Obligation to Prosecute or Extradite
10	1971, Namibia	26	2014, Whaling
11	1980, Hostage	27	2015, Certain Activities
12	1986, Nicaragua	28	2015, Construction of a Road
13	1989, ELSI	29	2019, Jadhav
14	1996, Nuclear Weapons	30	2020, Immunities and Criminal Proceedings
15	1997, Gabčíkovo-Nagymaros	31	2023, Certain Iranian Assets
16	2001, LaGrand		

[51] Namely, *Avena*, *Arrest Warrant*, *Request for Interpretation of the* Avena *Judgment*, *Jurisdictional Immunities of the State*, *Croatian Genocide*, and *Access to the Pacific Ocean*.

B. The Standard of Review Scale

As explained, the structure of chapters four to seven mirrors the identified four different standards of review: absence of review, good faith, reasonableness, and *de novo*. The chapter on the *de novo* standard of review thus contains all proceedings in which the ICJ opted for this particular standard, the chapter on the reasonableness standard all proceedings in which it chose this standard, and so on. While '[d]eference is not an all or nothing concept, rather, [it] is a concept measured by degrees',[52] this choice of four[53] standards of review is mainly based on pragmatic considerations, and takes into account the specific situation of the ICJ. This situation is characterised by judicial silence, judicial ambiguity, a smaller case load, and a broader subject variety in comparison to other international courts and tribunals.

First – and this is a striking parallel to many other international courts and tribunals[54] – the ICJ tends to evade explicit statements on this point. It has only employed the term 'standard of review' as such in very few proceedings. The *Whaling* case is perhaps the best-known example. This recurrent silence means that the categorisation of the Court's approach in these proceedings is more often than not subject to interpretation. Second, there is an occasional discrepancy between the standard of review the ICJ announces and the standard it

[52] Roberts, 'The Next Battleground' (n 10), 172; see also on this point C Henckels, 'Indirect Expropriation and the Right to Regulate: Revisiting Proportionality Analysis and the Standard of Review in Investor-State Arbitration' (2012) 15(1) *Journal of International Economic Law* 223, 238.

[53] Ioannidis, while pointing to the risks of studies such as the present one, proposes a very similar categorisation, Ioannidis, 'Beyond the Standard of Review' (n 27), 95; for other proposed scales, see for instance Becroft, *The Standard of Review in WTO Dispute Settlement* (n 8), 6–7; Arato, 'The Margin of Appreciation in International Investment Law' (n 45), 556; L Gruszczynski and W Werner, 'Introduction' in L Gruszczynski and W Werner (eds), *Deference in International Courts and Tribunals: Standard of Review and Margin of Appreciation* (Oxford University Press, 2014), 1–2; Tully, '"Objective Reasonableness" as a Standard for International Judicial Review' (n 12), 547; J Pauwelyn, 'Defences and the Burden of Proof in International Law' in L Bartels and F Paddeu (eds), *Exceptions and Defences in International Law* (Oxford University Press, 2020), 106; but expressing scepticism towards any attempt to categorise and distinguish between different (deferential) standards of review JH Fahner, 'The Limited Utility of Deference in International Dispute Settlement' (2022) 21(2) *The Law and Practice of International Courts and Tribunals* 467, 470–73.

[54] As Lapa observed in her discussion of the WTO Panel Report in *Traffic in Transit*, 'international courts and tribunals tend to avoid mentioning a precise standard of review and it is quite hard to attribute the discretion utilised to a specific standard of review', V Lapa, 'The WTO Panel Report in Russia – Traffic in Transit: Cutting the Gordian Knot of the GATT Security Exception?' (2020) 69 *Questions of International Law* 5, 26; similarly, Sulyok notes that '[e]ven though international adjudicators often use deference "as a mantra", they normally do not reveal the exact scheme of allocating competences between the state and the tribunal', Sulyok, *Science and Judicial Reasoning* (n 23), 319 (footnotes omitted); Vadi in turn notes that 'while arbitral tribunals rely on standards of review, they often do so implicitly', V Vadi, *Proportionality, Reasonableness and Standards of Review in International Investment Law and Arbitration* (Edward Elgar Publishing, 2018), 308; with regard to the European Court of Justice (ECJ), Zglinski, *Europe's Passive Virtues* (n 9), 42–43; finally, Judge Cot observed in the International Tribunal for the Law of the Sea's *Volga* case that '[i]nternational courts constantly use the concept of margin of appreciation, often implicitly or unwittingly', *The 'Volga' Case (Russian Federation v Australia)*, ITLOS, Separate Opinion of Judge Cot, ITLOS Reports 50, para 16.

actually applies. This problem has also been highlighted for other international courts and tribunals, for instance concerning the ECtHR's use of the margin of appreciation.[55] As *Fahner* puts it more generally, '[t]he assertion of a tribunal that it applies a lenient standard of review does not necessarily imply that it actually does so and vice versa', resulting in the fact that these instances 'require a careful reading'.[56] Third, in contrast to the other international courts and tribunals whose resort to the standard of review notion has received the most attention in the literature so far, the ICJ has a far smaller case load.[57] This makes it more difficult to identify trends and distinguish its approach in particular situations. So does, fourth, the broad variety of subjects brought before it. Against this backdrop, the choice of a four-tier standard of review scale is motivated by the desire to allow for sufficient precision while avoiding the fallacy of overinterpretation and overdifferentiation. In the following, the four standards on this scale will be explained consecutively.

i. *Absence of Judicial Oversight*

'Absence of judicial oversight' (also referred to as 'complete deference', or 'non-reviewability') means that the ICJ will entirely abstain from evaluating the respective first-hand assessment of the acting state. The immediate consequences of adopting this standard of review are clear: The initial assessment of that state will be accepted as correct without judicial examination, making this standard of review the most deferential one.

However, it is important to note that not every situation in which the Court ultimately abstains from evaluating a respondent state's assertions represents an application of this standard. Findings such as lack of jurisdiction, for instance due to the absence of an indispensable third party, the absence of a dispute, or mootness, also lead to the absence of substantive review, and thereby – incidentally – of judicial oversight. Yet, these grounds either relate to

[55] For instance, Gerards notes that 'there does not always appear to be a close correspondence between the language of deference and the actual test applied by the court. It all too often occurs that the court elaborately reasons that a wide margin of appreciation should be left to the state, but it then carefully assesses the facts of the case to find out which interests were at stake and what weight should be accorded to these interests', Gerards, 'Pluralism, Deference and the Margin of Appreciation Doctrine' (n 9), 106.

[56] Fahner, 'The Margin of Appreciation in Investor-State Arbitration' (n 38), 441; and Fahner, *Judicial Deference in International Adjudication* (n 11), 127.

[57] The Court whose resort to the notion of standard of review has been covered most extensively is certainly the ECtHR. From 2012 to 2022 alone, the ECtHR rendered close to 11,000 judgments, giving it abundant opportunity to refine and systematise its approach towards this notion, Council of Europe – European Court of Human Rights, 'Annual Report 2022 of the European Court of Human Rights' (2023), 141, www.echr.coe.int/documents/d/echr/annual_report_2022_eng-2. Concerning the GATT and WTO dispute settlement system, which has been widely covered in this regard as well, under the WTO regime alone, over 600 cases have been brought so far, www.wto.org/english/tratop_e/dispu_e/dispu_current_status_e.htm. Finally, international investment arbitration has also seen an ever-greater number of proceedings: here as well, over 600 cases have been concluded under the auspices of ICSID alone, isid.worldbank.org/cases/concluded.

the qualities of a party to the proceedings or to the specific nature of the question, and not to the qualities of the Court. However, as will be shown below, the essence of the concept of standard of review is based on a specific perception of the ICJ's role and institutional competence.[58] Thus, an instance of absence of judicial oversight will be assumed to exist whenever the ICJ refrains from evaluating a respondent state's assertions based on the consideration that it lacks the requisite expertise to do so, or on a specific conception of its role as a judicial institution. The use of language such as 'self-judging', 'exclusive power of appreciation', and 'automatic acceptance' are central markers in this regard.

ii. The Good Faith Standard of Review

Good faith is widely held to be a general principle of law as understood by Article 38(1)(c) ICJ Statute.[59] In the UN Friendly Relations Declaration, the General Assembly considered that 'the fulfillment in good faith of the obligations assumed by States … is of the greatest importance for the maintenance of international peace and security and for the implementation of the other purposes of the United Nations'.[60] In the same vein, the ICJ noted in the *Nuclear Tests* cases that good faith is '[o]ne of the basic principles governing the creation and performance of legal obligations, whatever their source'.[61] Finally, the obligation for states to perform their treaty-based obligations in good faith is also codified in Article 26 of the Vienna Convention on the Law of Treaties.

Good faith can also serve as a standard of review. The relevant question is whether at the time that the state had taken the decision now under scrutiny, it could believe in good faith that the reasons for it were valid or that the conditions for the legality of the measure were indeed present. This means that the ICJ scrutinises the result of the state's initial decision-making process, but only to a very limited extent. 'Arbitrariness and capriciousness' and 'manifest unreasonableness' represent equivalent standards of review.[62]

Accordingly, good faith is a *substantial* standard of review, in that the Court does not abstain entirely from evaluating the respondent state's behaviour.[63] Yet,

[58] See ch 2, sections II and III.

[59] See only with further references R Kolb, 'Article 2(2)' in B Simma and others (eds), *The Charter of the United Nations: A Commentary*, 3rd edn (Oxford University Press, 2012), 16.

[60] UN General Assembly, 'Declaration on Principles of International Law concerning Friendly Relations and Co-operation among States in accordance with the Charter of the United Nations' (24 October 1970) A/RES/2625(XXV).

[61] *Nuclear Tests (Australia v France)*, ICJ, Judgment of 20 December 1974, 46.

[62] See for instance Japan's assertion in the *Whaling* case, according to which the ICJ would only be in a position to ascertain that Japan's assessment that the whaling programme was 'for purposes of scientific research' was 'arbitrary or capricious', 'manifestly unreasonable' or made in bad faith, *Whaling in the Antarctic (Australia v Japan: New Zealand intervening)*, ICJ, Judgment of 31 March 2014, 65.

[63] As *Burke-White* and *von Staden* note in this respect, '[w]hile deferential to a state's own determinations, good faith review is not hollow', W Burke-White and A von Staden, 'The Need for Public Law Standards of Review in Investor-State Arbitrations' in SW Schill (ed), *International Investment Law and Comparative Public Law* (Oxford University Press, 2010), 706.

at the same time, it is also a highly deferential standard of review. If there is any basis for the respective state's evaluation or decision, the Court will find that assessment to be unassailable.[64] Whether the Court evaluates if a decision was taken in good faith, arbitrary and capricious, or manifestly unreasonable, all these three terminological variations of this standard of review put the primary focus on the respondent state's point of view.[65] The implication of this high degree of deference is that finding a state to be in violation of its obligations is very unlikely. Judicial recognition of 'very considerable discretion', or the use of terms such as 'manifest error of assessment' or 'honestly' are first indicators for its use of this standard.

Admittedly, the frontier between the good faith standard of review and the reasonableness standard of review is blurred. The existence of such blurred lines is perhaps even inherent in the concept of a sliding standard of review scale. At times, scholars, states and the Court itself did not even distinguish between the notion of good faith and the notion of reasonableness.[66] However, these two notions, in particular when applied as standards of review, can be distinguished, as is argued here.

iii. The Reasonableness Standard of Review

Reasonableness is another ubiquitous notion in international law.[67] As the ICJ stated in *Barcelona Traction*, 'in the field of diplomatic protection as in all other

[64] ibid.

[65] See also S Schill and R Briese, '"If the State Considers": Self-Judging Clauses in International Dispute Settlement' (2009) 13 *Max Planck Yearbook of United Nations Law* 61, 108.

[66] See for instance Burke-White and von Staden, 'Private Litigation in a Public Law Sphere' (n 10), 312; Ragni, 'Standard of Review and the Margin of Appreciation before the International Court of Justice' (n 30), 330. Parties before the Court have at times equally sought to equate both notions. For instance, in the *Whaling* case, New Zealand asserted that 'the discretion of a Contracting Government … is not a blank cheque – its exercise remains subject to review to ensure that it is exercised properly in light of the central obligation of good faith. That principle requires that it must be exercised … in a reasonable way', *Whaling in the Antarctic (Australia v Japan: New Zealand intervening)*, ICJ, Written Observations of New Zealand of 4 April 2013, 68 (footnotes omitted). The ICJ has also at times associated both notions. For instance, in the *Rights of US Nationals in Morocco* case, it held that '[t]he power of making the valuation rests with the Customs authorities, but it is a power which must be exercised *reasonably and in good faith*', *Rights of Nationals of the United States of America in Morocco (France v United States of America)*, ICJ, Judgment of 27 August 1952, 212 (emphasis added); see also *ELSI (United States of America v Italy)*, ICJ, Judgment of 20 July 1989, 124; *Immunities and Criminal Proceedings (Equatorial Guinea v France)*, ICJ, Judgment (Merits) of 11 December 2020, para 73.

[67] O Corten, *L'utilisation du "raisonnable" par le juge international: Discours juridique, raison et contradictions* (Bruylant, 1997), 671; somewhat surprisingly against this background, there are but few other studies besides Corten's on reasonableness in public international law. But for an earlier example, see J Salmon, 'Le concept du "raisonnable" en droit international public', *Le Droit international, unité et diversité: Mélanges offerts à Paul Reuter* (A. Pedone, 1981); see also S Jovanović, *Restriction des compétences discrétionnaires des Etats en droit international* (A. Pedone, 1988), ch V, 'Le principe de l'exercice raisonnable des compétences', 147–68; for a study on reasonableness in international investment law, Vadi, *Proportionality, Reasonableness and Standards of Review in International Investment Law and Arbitration* (n 54).

fields of international law, it is necessary that the law be applied reasonably'.[68] In particular, international courts and tribunals have been resorting to the notion of reasonableness to review a state's exercise of what would otherwise be an unfettered right.[69] Judge Read's dissenting opinion in *Norwegian Loans* serves as an instructive example. Dealing with the question of whether a state may rely on a 'self-judging' national jurisdiction reservation in a declaration under Article 36(2) ICJ Statute by way of reciprocity, he notes that that state 'must establish that there is a genuine understanding, i.e. *that the circumstances are such that it would be reasonably possible to reach the understanding that the dispute was essentially national*'.[70] Thus employed, reasonableness can be operationalised as a standard of review. Reliance on reasonableness as a standard of review results in granting room for manoeuvre to the rule-applier. As Corten noted, 'the introduction of the qualifier [of reasonableness] leaves a margin of appreciation to the States, allowing them to adapt the notion to the circumstances of the situation'.[71]

Yet, at first sight, the notion remains vague. Perelman observed that 'is unreasonable what is deemed inadmissible in a community'[72] – and what is inadmissible in a community is inevitably subject to evolution, and disagreement. Jovanovic in turn explains that reasonableness 'implies a certain connection between the measure and the objective situation at its root'.[73] Finally, the ICJ itself observed that 'what is reasonable and equitable in any given case must depend on its particular circumstances'.[74] To flesh out this standard of review, it is useful to turn to the practice of GATT and WTO dispute settlement bodies, which have considerable experience in handling this notion.

[68] *Barcelona Traction (Belgium v Spain)*, ICJ, Judgment (Second Phase) of 5 July 1970, 93.

[69] Corten, *L'utilisation du "raisonnable" par le juge international* (n 67), 112–15; see also the Court's finding in *Certain Iranian Assets* that '[r]easonableness is one of the considerations that limit the exercise of the governmental powers', *Certain Iranian Assets (Islamic Republic of Iran v United States of America)*, ICJ, Judgment (Merits) of 30 March 2023, para 186.

[70] *Certain Norwegian Loans (France v Norway)*, ICJ, Judgment (Preliminary Objections), Dissenting Opinion of Judge Read, 94 (emphasis added).

[71] Corten, *L'utilisation du 'raisonnable' par le juge international* (n 67), 130 (own translation, in the original: 'l'introduction du qualificatif [du raisonnable] maintient une marge d'appréciation pour les États, en leur permettant d'adapter la notion aux circonstances de l'espèce'); see also at 131; Perelman makes a similar observation when he notes that 'reasonable does not imply one unique solution, but a multitude of different solutions' (own translation, in the original: 'le raisonnable ne renvoie pas à une solution unique, mais implique une pluralité de solutions possibles'), C Perelman, *Le raisonnable et le déraisonnable en droit: Au-delà du positivisme juridique* (Librairie générale de droit et de jurisprudence, 1984), 15; see also Salmon, 'Le concept du "raisonnable" en droit international public' (n 67), 450; and *The Volga Case*, Separate Opinion of Judge Cot (n 54), para 18.

[72] Perelman, *Le raisonnable et le déraisonnable en droit* (n 71), 15 (own translation, in the original: 'est déraisonnable ce qui est inadmissible dans une communauté').

[73] Jovanović, *Restriction des compétences discrétionnaires des Etats en droit international* (n 67), 158 (own translation, in the original: 'implique un certain rapport entre l'acte et la situation objective qui est à sa base').

[74] *Continental Shelf (Tunisia/Libyan Arab Jamahiriya)*, ICJ, Judgment (Merits) of 24 February 1982, para 72.

For instance, in *Korea – Anti-Dumping Duties on Imports of Polyacetal Resins from the United States*, the Panel observed that its task 'was not to make its own independent evaluation of the facts … but to review the determination as made by the [Korean Trade Commission] for consistency with the Agreement, *bearing in mind that in a given case reasonable minds could differ as to the significance to be attached to certain facts*'.[75] In turn, in *United States – Softwood Lumber II*, the Panel stated that 'the review to be applied in the present case required consideration of *whether a reasonable, unprejudiced person could have found, based upon the evidence relied upon by the United States at the time … , that sufficient evidence existed*' for the presence of the claimed situation.[76] Finally, in *Dominican Republic – Import and Sale of Cigarettes*, the WTO Panel observed that 'the ordinary meaning of the word "reasonable", refers to notions such as "in accordance with reason", "not irrational or absurd", "proportionate", "having sound judgement", "sensible", "not asking for too much", "within the limits of reason, not greatly less or more than might be thought likely or appropriate", "articulate"'.[77]

This makes clear that the reasonableness standard does not permit the reviewing entity to declare a measure taken by a state unlawful merely because it would have taken a different decision or arrived at a different conclusion. Thus, it is a (moderately) deferential standard of review.[78] In other words, the Court will sanction a measure if, while ultimately disagreeing with the state, it concludes that a rational actor could have arrived at the same assessment as that state.[79] In contrast, under a good faith standard, the measure will already

[75] *Korea – Anti-Dumping Duties on Imports of Polyacetal Resins from the United States*, Report of the Panel (2 April 1993) ADP/92, 227 (emphasis added).

[76] *United States – Measures Affecting Imports of Softwood Lumber from Canada*, Report of the Panel (19 February 1993) SCM/162, 335 (emphasis added). The issue at hand was whether the US could self-initiate 'an investigation to determine the existence, degree and effect of any alleged subsidy' according to Article 2:1 Agreement on Subsidies and Countervailing Measures (1979); see also *European Communities – Countervailing Measures on Dynamic Random Access Memory Chips from Korea*, Report of the Panel (17 June 2005) WT/DS299/R, 7.6.

[77] *Dominican Republic – Measures Affecting The Importation and Internal Sale of Cigarettes*, Report of the Panel (26 November 2004) WT/DS302/R, 7.385 (references omitted). The dispute involved Art X:3(a) GATT 1994, which requires all contracting parties to administer certain laws, regulations, decisions and ruling inter alia in 'a *reasonable* manner' (emphasis added); cited by *United States – Certain Country of Origin Labelling (COOL) Requirements*, Report of the Panel (18 November 2011) WT/DS384/R, WT/DS386/R, 7.850. For an overview over the use of the term 'reasonableness' in WTO jurisprudence, see G Cook, *A Digest of WTO Jurisprudence on Public International Law Concepts and Principles* (Cambridge University Press, 2015), 221–32.

[78] As Judge Ammoun remarked in the *North Sea Continental Shelf* cases, 'the reasonable … has an element of subjectivity, or even of relativity', *North Sea Continental Shelf (Germany v Denmark; Germany v Netherlands)*, ICJ, Judgment, Separate Opinion of Judge Ammoun, 36.

[79] Shany equates the reasonableness standard of review with the margin of appreciation. Discussing the *Oil Platforms* case, he posits that 'a margin of appreciation analysis would ask not whether US operations were necessary and proportional, but whether the US's conclusions on the aforementioned questions were *reasonable*', Shany, 'Toward a General Margin of Appreciation Doctrine in International Law?' (n 12), 937 (emphasis added). However, as has been argued above, in the jurisprudence of the ECtHR as the judicial body most closely concerned with the notion of 'margin of appreciation', this notion is merely a shorthand for various deferential standards of review.

be declared valid if there is *any* rational basis for the measure in question, and invalid only if that assessment is arbitrary or capricious. Consequently, there is a line between reasonableness and good faith as standards of review, even if it is a fine one. Besides explicit reference to the notion of reasonableness, language such as 'convincing' or 'serious' reasons are likewise indicative of the reasonableness standard of review.

iv. De Novo *Review*

Finally, the *de novo* standard of review leaves no room for acceptable deviation from the correct assessment or best possible decision. Under this standard, the Court scrutinises the state's assessments and measures without leaving any room for lawful deviation. Consequently, the ICJ will conduct its own, fully independent assessment of the situation. Thereby, this standard represents the most intrusive standard of review, leaving the lowest changes of success to the defendant state.

In practice, when the parties in a proceeding do not argue that the Court ought to apply a deferential standard of review, it will implicitly apply this *de novo* standard. It is thus the default standard of review before the Court.[80] The default character of this standard of review is mirrored by the fact that it is – with the exception of *Oil Platforms* – not the explicit rejection of deference, but rather the *absence* of statements recognising a margin of manoeuvre to the concerned state that betrays the Court's application of this standard. In general, under this standard, the ICJ will simply state in objective terms whether or not the subsumption advanced by the concerned state is correct.

C. The Categorisation of Proceedings

Finally, within chapters four to seven, the proceedings are categorised in one of four categories, according to their main thematic focus: national security, domestic measures, political determinations, and scientific determinations. As will be seen in chapter two, it is in these four domains that states have been advancing claims for the adoption of a deferential standard of review before the Court.

The first two of those domains, national security and domestic measures, touch upon issues close to the core of state sovereignty. States have regularly been claiming a degree of deference before the Court by arguing that the latter would lack the authority to interfere with their alleged prerogatives in these matters. Likewise, states have been claiming that the ICJ should adopt a deferential standard of review in proceedings revolving around allegedly political as

[80] See ch 8, section I.

well as scientific determinations, this time focusing on an alleged lack of expertise of the ICJ for these matters.

The first category, 'National Security Interests' comprises all proceedings in which the concerned states justified their measures with national security considerations, broadly understood. Matters of national security go to the heart of state sovereignty, as they implicate that state's internal stability and order, and at times even its very existence. This category is made up of 12 contentious cases and advisory proceedings: *Corfu Channel*, *Right of Passage*, *Nicaragua*, *Nuclear Weapons*, *Oil Platforms*, *Wall in the OPT*, *Armed Activities*, *Mutual Assistance*, *Diallo*, *Construction of a Road*, *Jadhav*, and *Certain Iranian Assets*. This category comprises both 'inward-looking' measures, ie measures taken on the state's own territory, and 'outward-looking' measures, for instance attacks on other states.

The second category, 'Domestic Measures', comprises all proceedings in which the emphasis laid on the domestic aspect of the dispute, ie in which the respondent argued with its inherent right to manage its internal affairs as it best sees fit. This includes, among others, the conferral of nationality, the organisation of criminal justice, and domestic infrastructure projects. This makes this category the most diverse one, containing ten contentious cases: *Norwegian Loans*, *Rights of US Nationals in Morocco*, *Nottebohm*, *Hostage*, *ELSI*, *LaGrand*, *Obligation to Prosecute or Extradite*, *Navigational Rights*, *Certain Activities*, and *Immunities and Criminal Proceedings*.

The third category, 'Political Determinations', comprises all proceedings in which the concerned states pointed to the allegedly inherently political nature of the decisions under judicial examination to argue why the Court should, due to its lack of expertise, defer to their respective decisions. These decisions would be inherently incapable of forming the object of an independent judicial appreciation. This category contains five proceedings: *Conditions of Admission to the UN*, *Reservations to the Genocide Convention*, *Asylum*, *South West Africa*, and *Namibia*.

The fourth and final category, 'Scientific Determinations' also contains proceedings in which the respondents relied on considerations of relative institutional expertise to back their claim that the ICJ should refrain from evaluating their respective subsumptions *de novo*. It contains three contentious cases in which the assessment of scientific information in environmental matters was at the heart of the dispute: *Gabčíkovo-Nagymaros*, *Pulp Mills*, and *Whaling*.

Admittedly, the sorting of the proceedings into these four categories has its limitations. For instance, there are several proceedings which could also be sorted into another category. This is true for *Corfu Channel*, *Right of Passage*, *Diallo*, and *Construction of a Road* as well as *Pulp Mills*, which all implicate domestic measures and in which the respective respondents at times also explicitly emphasised this aspect. Yet, national security respectively scientific assessments were arguably at the heart of these cases. Furthermore, there is one case which does not fit neatly into any of the proposed categories: *Bosnian Genocide*. This is in part due to the fact that the respondent in that case, Serbia and Montenegro, did not make a claim for a deferential standard of review. Consequently, it did not invoke considerations of sovereignty, nor of institutional expertise. However, as will be seen in chapter five, the Court's choice for the good faith standard of review in that case was also not based on such considerations.

V. KEY EMPIRICAL INSIGHTS

The empirical analysis laid out in chapters four to seven shows that the standard of review notion has been part and parcel of the ICJ's decision-making practice from its early days until today. States have regularly been invoking the application of deferential standards of review, though not necessarily by employing the term as such. The Court has reacted to these invocations, sometimes tacitly, at other times explicitly, and laid down a deferential standard of review in a significant number of proceedings. Accordingly, and despite the common roots of the invocations of deferential standards of review and the non-justiciability doctrine in the international legal order, the ICJ has shown more openness towards the standard of review notion than it did towards the non-justiciability doctrine.

As chapter four demonstrates, the Court has almost invariably rejected to apply the most deferential standard of review, complete deference, and thus to abstain from a substantive review on the substance of the issues in question altogether. In 12 out of 14 proceedings where the respondent states had pleaded for non-reviewability, it rejected that claim. This is in line with its near-constant rejection of the non-justiciability doctrine,[81] as shown in chapter two. Thereby, the ICJ has consistently denied that it would be lacking the requisite legitimacy or expertise to evaluate the correctness of a state's first-hand determinations at all. In principle, there is no subject-matter which it acknowledged to be beyond its purview merely by virtue of the proximity to the core of national sovereignty or the close link to extra-judicial considerations. This portrays the Court as a confident and self-assertive institution.

This finding is also in line with the fact that, as chapter five shows, the ICJ has only applied the highly deferential good faith standard of review in very few, namely three, proceedings. Furthermore, these three instances can be explained with particular and not readily generalisable concerns pertaining to each of them. The adoption of the good faith standard in these three proceedings does therefore not signal the Court's general endorsement of this standard of review.

In turn, chapter six reveals that the ICJ has resorted to the moderately deferential reasonableness standard of review in a significant number of proceedings. It has done so in 12 proceedings in total, and thus in over a third of all instances

[81] See on the role of this doctrine before the ICJ also A John, 'Inarticulate and Unconscious: Non-Justiciability before the International Court of Justice' (2021) 20(1) *The Law and Practice of International Courts and Tribunals* 77, 82–104.

in which it took a stance on the standard of review question. This demonstrates that the reasonableness standard is an important feature of the Court's decision-making practice. It has in particular laid down this standard of review in proceedings involving measures justified with national security interests, and based on a scientific appreciation. It is also noteworthy that the ICJ has mostly adopted the reasonableness standard of review as 'middle ground' between the positions of the respective applicants and respondents on this question.

Finally, the analysis conducted in chapter seven shows that the least deferential, the *de novo* standard of review, is nonetheless the ICJ's default standard, chosen (at least partially) in 17 proceedings. It has privileged this standard in particular for state actions purportedly taken in exercise of the customary right of self-defence. In the particularly noteworthy *Oil Platforms* case, it has even done so explicitly, presumably with the intention to uphold the effectiveness of the prohibition of the use of force. Yet, apart from this exception, the Court did not deem it necessary to disclose its choice of the *de novo* standard. Furthermore, there is a conspicuous absence of justification on its part for the choice of this standard. This dearth of justification particularly catches the reader's eye in those proceedings in which the participants had extensively argued for or against the adoption of a deferential standard of review. This leaves the impression of a Janus-faced Court. First, by not addressing the arguments about its purportedly limited capabilities and legitimacy behind the claims for a deferential standard of review, it avoids visibly recognising any merit to them, and leaves the impression of an institution that silently but confidently assumes its judicial role. On the other hand, by not doing away with these arguments openly – perhaps in order to avoid antagonising the states making these claims? – it leaves the impression of a somewhat constrained institution.

Taken together, chapters four to seven prove that the Court rarely applies a deferential standard of review out of its own initiative, but rather only when the defendant state has urged it to do so. On the other hand, this does not mean that even then, it automatically follows that state's preferences – to the contrary, it usually adopts a stricter standard of review than invoked by the concerned state. Furthermore, one can discern patterns in the ICJ's standard of review determination in some of the four subject-matter categories, most notably in a specific group of national security measures: measures allegedly taken in self-defence. Finally, there are grounds to conclude that the Court resorted to deferential standards of review as a judicial avoidance tool on several occasions. First and foremost, to the respondents' benefit in proceedings in which the adoption of such a standard of review either led to an overall or at least partially favourable outcome for them. Second, even if without immediate consequences for the outcome of the proceeding at hand, as a signal for the Court's readiness to recognise some room of manoeuvre to the states – especially regarding essential state interests such as national security measures.

2

Old Wine in New Skins?

THE DOCTRINE OF non-justiciability in the international order has a long pedigree. It has especially been invoked before the International Court of Justice and the Permanent Court of International Justice (PCIJ) in the first half of the twentieth century. While state invocations of the doctrine have since then become less frequent in the face of its steadfast rejection by the ICJ, the considerations at its root have not disappeared. Some of them have resurfaced under a different guise, namely as part of the claim that the Court should defer to the defendant state's first-hand assessment in certain matters. Ultimately, a similar perception of the ICJ's judicial role lies at the base of the non-justiciability doctrine and the plea for deferential standards of review, as this chapter will show.

For this purpose, it will first lay out the background of the non-justiciability doctrine in the international order, relying primarily on Lauterpacht's seminal *The Function of Law in the International Community*, and highlight how states have relied on this doctrine in their proceedings before the Court (section I). In a second step, the analysis will focus on the argumentation advanced by states to advocate for the adoption of a deferential standard of review in selected ICJ proceedings (section II). It will become clear that states have been arguing for a deferential standard of review both with regard to the ICJ's alleged lack of expertise, and its alleged lack of mandate. The common denominator of both strands is the better-placed assertion: that there is another entity in a better position than the Court to deal with the matter.

Precisely this denominator is also at the heart of two of the strands of the non-justiciability doctrine identified by Lauterpacht. This juxtaposition suggests that the invocation of deferential standards of review does not put the Court in a substantially new position, and that it is merely old wine in new skins (section III). Yet, from the ICJ's perspective, such an assessment would overlook the specific potential of the determination of the applicable standard of review: The (state) concerns underlying both notions have not gone away, and the standard of review notion allows the Court to deal with these concerns in a much more nuanced way than the non-justiciability doctrine does (section IV).

I. THE DOCTRINE OF NON-JUSTICIABILITY IN THE INTERNATIONAL ORDER

The doctrine of non-justiciability in the international order is the doctrinal expression of the idea that certain types of disputes involving states are by their very nature beyond the ambit of international judicial settlement. It is based in great part on a very broad conception of the notion of state sovereignty. According to this doctrine, the international judicial settlement of a certain category of disputes would inevitably encroach upon this sovereignty, as states must remain the ultimate judges for their own affairs in those matters.[1] International courts and tribunals may thus only take cognisance of these categories of disputes with the explicit and concrete authorisation of the state(s) concerned on a case-by-case basis.

Lauterpacht traced the origins of the non-justiciability doctrine in the international order back to Vattel. Vattel explained in 1758 that a duty for states to seek legal settlement would only exist for disputes regarding 'less important' or 'non-essential' rights. In turn, they could not be required to submit disputes involving their essential interests to judicial settlement, such as those involving their security.[2] To justify this differentiation, Vattel distinguished between duties towards oneself and duties towards others, with the former generally prevailing. Based on a balance of interests, he concluded that there was a duty for states to submit disputes to judicial settlement whenever non-essential interests or disputes of little consequence were involved. In those situations, the balance of interests would tip in favour of the 'welfare of human society', ie the 'inestimable blessing of peace', realised through the judicial settlement of disputes. In contrast, for essential rights, to submit to such settlement, and thus '[t]o listen to any terms at all is to risk everything' and would go against a state's duties towards itself. Here, the balance of interests would tip in favour of the concerned state's interests, outweighing the aspiration of peace.[3]

According to Lauterpacht, the contemporary roots of the non-justiciability doctrine go back to the second half of the nineteenth century.[4] He identified two major motivations behind what he qualifies as 'first and foremost [a] work

[1] H Lauterpacht, *The Function of Law in the International Community* (Oxford University Press, 1933, Reprint 2011), 4.

[2] E de Vattel, *Le Droit des gens, ou Principes de la loi naturelle appliqués à la conduite et aux affaires des nations et des souverains: Translation of the Edition of 1758* (Carnegie Institution of Washington, 1916), § 332. Vattel introduced a further caveat, namely that 'clear, certain and indisputable' cases had not to be submitted to judicial settlement, but only 'doubtful' cases, at § 331. For a contemporary perspective on Vattel's position on the judicial settlement of international disputes, see L Caflisch, 'Vattel and the Peaceful Settlement of International Disputes' in V Chetail and P Haggenmacher (eds), *Vattel's International Law from a XXIst Century Perspective/ Le Droit International de Vattel vu du XXIe Siècle* (Brill/Nijhoff, 2011).

[3] Vattel, *Le Droit des gens, ou Principes de la loi naturelle appliqués à la conduite et aux affaires des nations et des souverains* (n 2), § 332.

[4] Lauterpacht, *The Function of Law in the International Community* (n 1), 9–10.

of international lawyers':[5] one relating to the strengthening of international dispute settlement, and the other relating to strengthening the conception of international law as law.

First, as he described, the idea of international judicial dispute settlement was still novel at the time. States were highly sceptical of ceding authority to a third party to settle their disputes.[6] Against this background, in Lauterpacht's view, one can read the introduction of the non-justiciability doctrine in the international order as an attempt to 'help to overcome the general unwillingness of Governments to submit their disputes to international adjudication'.[7] The doctrine helped to alleviate their fear that their high-stakes matters would end up being adjudicated by a third entity, thereby reducing their room for manoeuvre and exposing them to the risk of adverse rulings. Seen in this light, the creation of the non-justiciability doctrine toned down the radicalness of the transition from a scattered practice to a system of international judicial dispute settlement, and enabled states to go along with this development instead of combatting it. From this angle, the non-justiciability doctrine in the international order can be seen as a device of pragmatism.

Second, at the time, Lauterpacht explained, the character of international law as law was still doubtful (and by some accounts, still is today[8]). As he observed, '[lending] the authority of a legal principle to an attitude of Governments inimical to any real recognition of the sovereignty of law' might have been seen by contemporaries as a way 'to represent that situation as compatible with the rule of law in international society'.[9] Seen in this light, the creation of the doctrine of non-justiciability in the international order was an attempt to incorporate what ultimately were political considerations of states into a legal order which lawyers

[5] ibid, 6.

[6] Russia's remarks in the Explanatory Note concerning Art 10 of its Draft to the First Hague Conference are emblematic in this regard. According to Russia, '[i]n introducing international arbitration into the international life of States, we must proceed with extreme care in order not to extend unreasonably its sphere of application so as to shake the confidence which may be inspired therein, or discredit arbitration in the eyes of Governments and peoples.' Specifically, in its view, 'obligatory arbitration could not and should not be applied to disputes ... arising in connexion with political treaties which concern the vital interests and national honour of States. Obligatory arbitration in these cases would tie the hands of the interested Power, and reduce it to a passive state when dealing with questions upon which its security in large part depends; that is to say, questions of which none but the sovereign Power can be the judge', reprinted in JB Scott, 'The Reports to the Hague Conferences of 1899 and 1907' (Oxford, 1917), 99.

[7] Lauterpacht, *The Function of Law in the International Community* (n 1), 5.

[8] Not least evidenced by the fact that the American Society of International Law chose 'International Law as Law' as the theme for its yearly conference in 2009. As noted by Guzman, this title 'evidences a certain kind of insecurity or concern that maybe some people ... have doubts about whether it is law. One would not, after all, hold a conference with the theme "American Law as Law"', AT Guzman, 'Rethinking International Law as Law' (2009) 103 *Proceedings of the Annual Meeting (American Society of International Law)* 155, 155.

[9] Lauterpacht, *The Function of Law in the International Community* (n 1), 6. Lauterpacht also calls this an 'attempt at embellishment' and adds that the doctrine's purpose since its creation 'has been to supply a legal cloak for, or explanation of, the traditional claim of the sovereign State to remain the ultimate judge of disputed legal rights in its controversies with other States', ibid at 6, 7.

were eager to portray as a coherent system. The non-justiciability doctrine thus served as a tool to defend – or rather, not threaten – the idea of the doctrinal coherence of international law. According to this view, the doctrine can also be seen as part of a juridification attempt.

Lauterpacht identified four different characteristics that, according to the traditional view at the time, allegedly made disputes non-justiciable: the absence of a pertinent rule of international law, the implication of a major interest for one of the involved states, the better suitability of another method of dispute settlement, and the fact that the dispute amounts to a conflict of interests rather than to a conflict of rights.[10] Two of these strands merit particular attention here: if a state's major interests are involved, and if there are other, more suitable modes of dispute settlement. As will be seen, both these strands of the non-justiciability doctrine in the international order are based on a specific conception of the role of international adjudication vis-a-vis the states. In the following, they will be referred to as 'major interest strand' and 'settlement method strand'.

Highly critical of the doctrine of non-justiciability in the international order, Lauterpacht set out to refute all four strands of the doctrine. Ultimately, he observed, '[i]t is not the nature of an individual dispute which makes it unfit for judicial settlement, but the unwillingness of a state to have it settled by the application of law'.[11] His arguments for rejecting the doctrine have yet to be disproved.[12] Nonetheless, the doctrine of non-justiciability has been making regular appearances in international judicial fora.

Generally, in contentious proceedings, the Court will address the justiciability question in the evaluation of admissibility, where it ponders whether 'even if [it] has jurisdiction, … there are reasons why [it] should not proceed to an examination of the merits'.[13] In advisory proceedings, the Court may deal with considerations of justiciability while examining whether or not to exercise its discretion to decline to accede to the request.[14] As Brownlie noted, this discretion 'is a matter which obviously permits of formulation in terms of justiciability'.[15]

Brownlie also observed that the non-justiciability doctrine 'may hide behind a variety of categories and judicial tactics'.[16] With this in mind, he established a list of so-to-speak procedural manifestations of the doctrine. Among those,

[10] Three in H Lauterpacht, 'The Doctrine of Non-Justiciable Disputes in International Law' (1928) 24 *Economica* 277, 315; and a fourth in Lauterpacht, *The Function of Law in the International Community* (n 1), 359–90.

[11] Lauterpacht, *The Function of Law in the International Community* (n 1), 377.

[12] What is more, *Milanov* makes the point that Lauterpacht greatly influenced the ICJ in this respect, M Milanov, 'A Lauterpachtian Affair: Security Exceptions as "Self-Judging Obligations" in the Case Law of the International Court of Justice and Beyond' (2021) 22(4) *The Journal of World Investment & Trade* 509.

[13] *Oil Platforms (Iran v United States of America)*, ICJ, Judgment (Merits) of 6 November 2003, 29.

[14] Art 65(1) ICJ Statute.

[15] I Brownlie, 'The Justiciability of Disputes and Issues in International Relations' (1967) 42 *British Yearbook of International Law* 123, 136.

[16] ibid.

Brownlie listed the assertion that a more suitable forum for the settlement of the dispute would be available, that a judgment on the merits would prejudice the political settlement of the dispute, that the question would only be open to political and not to judicial appreciation, and that the question would be one of domestic jurisdiction and thus be beyond the ICJ's reach.[17]

These assertions follow along the lines of the 'major interest' strand and the 'settlement method' strand of the non-justiciability doctrine. The first three, the 'more suitable forum', the 'judicial pronouncement as impairment to a political settlement', and the 'impossibility of judicial appreciation' assertions belong to the 'settlement method' strand. In turn, the 'domestic jurisdiction' assertion relates to the 'major interest' strand. Typically, it is the domain of essential interests that states consider to be part of their domestic jurisdiction.

The two following subsections will illustrate how states have been relying on those two strands of the non-justiciability doctrine in their proceedings before the Court.

A. The Settlement Method Strand of the Non-Justiciability Doctrine

The assertion that a more suitable forum for the settlement of the dispute is available overlaps with the assertion that a judgment would prejudice the political settlement of the dispute. For the latter implies that a political resolution of the dispute is more appropriate than resolution by an international judicial body, and that there exists such a political arena. Thus, both these assertions rest on the assumption that a judicial body is not the optimal dispute-resolver in certain situations. An example for this argumentation can be found in the *Nicaragua* case.

There, the United States contended that the ICJ would not be the right forum to hear the case. In its view, the UN Charter clearly assigned the competence to intervene in situations of ongoing armed conflicts to the UN Security Council,

[17] ibid, 124–33. The link between the 'domestic jurisdiction' assertion and the standard of review question becomes apparent in the *Belgian Linguistic* case before the ECtHR, which *Brownlie* cites as an example for the former. In the case, Belgium had argued in the preliminary objection phase that the question under review 'form[s] part of the reserved domain of the Belgian legal order; that the linguistic and educational legislation is to a large extent an integral part of the State's political and social structure, which belongs pre-eminently to the reserved domain' and that 'therefore, there is in this case an inherent limit to the exercise of the Court's jurisdiction', *Certain Aspects of the Laws on the Use of Languages in Education in Belgium (Preliminary Objection)*, ECtHR Series A no 5 (1967) 1 EHHR 241. The Court, having joined this objection to the merits, held that it could proceed to a review of the measure in question while recognising that it 'cannot disregard those legal and factual features which characterise the life of the society in the State which, as a Contracting Party, has to answer for the measure in dispute. In so doing it cannot assume the rôle of the competent national authorities, for it would thereby lose sight of the subsidiary nature of the international machinery of collective enforcement established by the Convention', and that review by the Court would therefore be limited, *Certain Aspects of the Laws on the Use of Languages in Education in Belgium (Merits)*, ECtHR Series A no 6 (1968) 1 EHHR 252. The case is also one of the first before the Court in which the margin of appreciation was invoked (in this case, by the now-obsolete Commission on Human Rights).

leaving no room for a Court pronouncement.[18] Furthermore, the United States pointed to the Contadora process, an initiative by several Latin American countries aimed at resolving the conflicts in the Central American region by diplomatic means. The Contadora process initially continued to run in parallel to the *Nicaragua* proceedings. Any decision on the merits of the case, the United States argued, would disturb the balance of that process, and jeopardise its functioning and chances for success. Thus, the United States asserted that a judgment on the merits would prejudice the political settlement of the dispute, implying also that the Contadora process would be a more suitable forum for the settlement of the dispute. Accordingly, it argued for the predominance of the political over the judicial process.[19]

Finally, there is the claim that a matter would only be open for political, and not for judicial appreciation. This assertion also rests on the assumption that it would not be appropriate for the Court as a judicial organ to interfere in inherently 'non-judicial' questions. Specifically, this claim implies that the ICJ would be lacking the institutional expertise to address such matters.[20] The United Kingdom's position in the *Chagos Islands* advisory opinion is illustrative for this kind of assertion. The United Kingdom argued that even if the Court were to find that the decolonisation of the Chagos archipelago had not been lawfully completed, it should not pronounce upon when and how this transfer of sovereignty should take place. The United Kingdom alleged that '[i]t is not for the Court, as a court of law, to lay down such timescale and modalities'.[21] In the oral phase of the proceedings, it affirmed this claim, adding that 'it could not be for the Court, a judicial body … to tell the Parties when the Islands should be returned. That is a matter of policy, not law … Many non-legal factors need to be taken into account when determining the timing of decolonization'.[22]

[18] *Military and Paramilitary Activities in and against Nicaragua (Nicaragua v United States of America)*, ICJ, Counter-Memorial of the United States of America (Questions of Jurisdiction and Admissibility) of 17 August 1984, 450–57 and 493–97.

[19] The United States reasserted this position in a statement accompanying its announcement of withdrawal from the proceedings in the case. There, it stated that '[t]he conflict in Central America … is not a narrow legal dispute; it is an inherently political problem that is not appropriate for judicial resolution …. The International Court of Justice was never intended to resolve issues of collective security and self-defence', reprinted in 'U.S. Withdrawal From the Proceedings Initiated by Nicaragua in the International Court of Justice' *New York Times* (19 January 1985), www.nytimes.com/1985/01/19/world/text-of-us-statement-on-withdrawal-from-case-before-the-world-court.html.

[20] In the *Wall* Advisory Proceedings, South Africa also raised this point. Referring to the contention of several states that the matter should be addressed by political organs rather than the ICJ due to its 'political' nature, counsel for South Africa observed that '[t]his approach implies an inability of the Court to address matters with a political complexion', *Legal Consequences of the Construction of a Wall in the Occupied Palestinian Territory*, ICJ, Oral Proceedings of 23 February 2004, afternoon (CR 2004/2), 22, para 38 (Madlanga).

[21] *Legal Consequences of the Separation of the Chagos Archipelago from Mauritius in 1965*, ICJ, Written Comments of the United Kingdom of 14 May 2018, para 5.10.

[22] *Legal Consequences of the Separation of the Chagos Archipelago from Mauritius in 1965*, ICJ, Oral Proceedings of 3 September 2018 (CR 2018/21), 59, paras 19–20 (Wood).

B. The Major Interest Strand of the Non-Justiciability Doctrine

Second, the assertion that the question is one of domestic jurisdiction and thus beyond the ICJ's reach also rests on the assumption that the Court is not the appropriate forum to settle the matter. This assertion lays emphasis on the fact that questions of domestic jurisdiction – regularly involving essential state interests – are unsuitable for international judicial determination. Only the concerned state could authoritatively make the respective assessments and take the respective decisions in such matters. If only indirectly, India's position in the *Right of Passage* case picks up on this assertion, even if India couched its argument in jurisdictional terms. In its view, '[t]he exclusive right of every State by reason of its sovereignty to regulate and control persons and things within its own boundaries is a fundamental doctrine of international law'. Thus, it asserted, a state had 'complete power and discretion to deal with matters within its boundaries as it alone thinks fit' in this domain.[23] Accordingly, India's claim that the Court would be lacking jurisdiction amounts to a claim that the dispute would not be open to judicial review, as it touched upon its own exercise of territorial sovereignty.

Iran's position in the *Hostage* case is a further example for such an assertion. It did not participate in the proceedings, but voiced its rejection of the Court's involvement in two letters. Therein, Iran argued that the issues brought before the ICJ could not be dissolved from an appreciation of the Islamic Revolution. Among others due to the 'deep-rootedness' and 'essential character' of this revolution, 'any examination of the numerous repercussions thereof [would be] a matter essentially and directly within the national sovereignty of Iran'.[24]

As will be seen next, states have also started to invoke the ideas behind the 'major interest' and the 'settlement method' strands of the non-justiciability doctrine not (necessarily) to have a matter excluded from the Court review altogether, but to convince it to apply a deferential standard of review. The following section will address this aspect.

II. STATE ARGUMENTS FOR A DEFERENTIAL STANDARD OF REVIEW

When states urge the Court to apply a deferential standard of review, they base this contention on the idea that there are assessments only they themselves can meaningfully make and decisions only they themselves can meaningfully take. This idea goes hand in hand with their diagnosis of a respective deficiency on the ICJ's part. First, they contend that the Court would be lacking the requisite

[23] *Right of Passage over Indian Territory (Portugal v India)*, ICJ, Preliminary Objection of India of April 1957, 161; see also *Right of Passage over Indian Territory (Portugal v India)*, ICJ, Counter-Memorial of India of March 1958, 288.

[24] Printed in *United States Diplomatic and Consular Staff in Tehran (United States of America v Iran)*, ICJ, Order (Provisional Measures) of 15 December 1979, 8.

abilities to arrive at a well-informed, autonomous decision on certain matters. Second, this idea is based on a specific consideration of the allocation of powers between states and the international judiciary, according to which certain matters would be inherently beyond the purview of the latter. States use both contentions to argue that the ICJ should apply a deferential standard of review.

Ultimately, both these assertions have a common denominator: the better-placed assertion. According to this assertion, on the one hand, there are institutions that are better placed to deal with the matter under review, because they have superior expertise in comparison to the Court. Often enough, in the states' view, it will be themselves and their institutions that possess that comparative advantage.[25] On the other hand, according to this assertion, there are certain domains where select entities have a special prerogative. This second branch is not so much concerned with the correctness of the respective decisions taken, but rather with the authority of the entity to take these decisions in the first place. Based on a specific conception of sovereignty, states thereby argue that it is them having to answer certain questions and decide on certain measures, not the ICJ.

States have made statements to that effect in proceedings involving what they refer to as essential interests and domestic matters, in proceedings concerning matters allegedly reserved to 'political' decision-making, and in proceedings revolving around questions of science. While the expertise consideration underlies the claims for deference in all four domains, the sovereignty consideration only underlies the domains of essential interests, domestic matters and political considerations. Because of this overlap, both considerations often appear in parallel.

A. Proceedings Concerning Essential State Interests

First, invocations of a deferential standard of review have appeared in proceedings involving measures based on purported essential interests of the respective state. States have urged the Court on a regular basis to apply a deferential standard of review regarding their assessment that essential interests such as their national security or their public order would be involved, and what measures the protection of those interests would require. It would be beyond the ICJ's purview to define by itself what a state's essential interests are, and whether measures taken for the protection of those interests were justified or not. One such particular measure is the use of force in a purported exercise of the right

[25] Note that states do not invariably contend that an institution better equipped to deal with the question than the Court would exist, as the analysis under the header 'Proceedings concerning Scientific Questions' below will show. Sometimes, states simply assert that the ICJ would be lacking the requisite characteristics. In those situations, it would be more accurate to speak of the 'ill-placed assertion'.

of self-defence. This line of argumentation appears for instance in the *Nuclear Weapons* advisory proceedings, and in the *Diallo* case.

In the words of counsel for the Solomon Islands, the *Nuclear Weapons* advisory proceedings were 'such for which one could predict that they would make history for the Court, if not history altogether'.[26] Numerous states tried to persuade the ICJ that it was not in a position to deal with the request, and accordingly should decline to issue an opinion. In support for their position, they pointed to the fact that second-guessing their first-hand assessments in the matter before the Court would violate their sovereignty. Additionally, they also referred to the ICJ's alleged lack of institutional expertise.

On the one hand, Germany observed that issuing an opinion would presuppose the analysis of 'extremely complex' aspects.[27] Likewise, the United Kingdom stated that the questions posed 'touch on what the Court will certainly recognize are immense and complex subjects'.[28] Finland discerned a lack of institutional expertise on the ICJ's part for the analysis of such 'extremely complex and controversial pieces of technical, strategic and scientific information'.[29]

On the other hand, Australia linked the themes of sovereignty and expertise. In the parallel proceedings involving the WHO's request, it asserted that the matter would be unsuitable for adjudication because it 'enters into the wider realms of policy and security doctrines of States'.[30] It would 'rest on a set of very complex strategic judgements which go beyond the traditional competence of a body such as the Court', and in consequence, the matter would be 'one to be resolved by national security judgments rather than legal opinion. Most pertinent to these judgements are individual countries' assessments of their security position in the world'.[31] Thereby, Australia asserted that the question of the possession and use of nuclear weapons would involve an appreciation of factors beyond the grasp of a judicial body. Furthermore, Australia thereby also alluded to the central importance of the question for each state's core interests, arguing that it would pertain to the (exclusive) purview of each state.

Several states followed this second line of argumentation. For instance, Germany asserted that since the purpose of nuclear weapons would be to 'help prevent any kind of war' – and thus ultimately be a political one – '[t]heir use cannot be assessed using the norms of international law without such an

[26] *Legality of the Threat or Use of Nuclear Weapons*, ICJ, Oral Proceedings of 14 November 1995 (CR 95/32), 33 (Salmon, own translation. In the original: 'de celles dont on peut prédire qu'elles feront date dans l'histoire de la Cour sinon dans l'histoire tout court.').

[27] *Legality of the Threat or Use of Nuclear Weapons*, ICJ, Written Statement of Germany of 20 June 1995, 5.

[28] *Legality of the Threat or Use of Nuclear Weapons*, ICJ, Oral Proceedings of 15 November 1995 (CR 95/34), 21 (Lyell).

[29] *Legality of the Threat or Use of Nuclear Weapons*, ICJ, Written Statement of Finland of 13 June 1995, 1.

[30] *Legality of the Use by a State of Nuclear Weapons in Armed Conflict*, ICJ, Written Statement of Australia of 20 September 1994, 8; referred to in *Legality of the Threat or Use of Nuclear Weapons*, ICJ, Oral Proceedings of 30 October 1995 (CR 95/22), 29, para 3 (Griffith).

[31] *Nuclear Weapons in Armed Conflict*, Written Statement of Australia (n 30), 9.

assessment turning from a judicial into a political one'.[32] Furthermore, Germany observed that '[t]he subject of the assessment would, in the final analysis, be key security policy elements of today's global order'[33] and 'touch upon issues of fundamental political importance, ones where States' vital interests are involved',[34] thereby implying that it would be improper for the Court to conduct such an assessment. Thus, Germany stressed the Court's inability to deal with matters central to the world order and involving key state security concerns.

Finally, France asserted that decisions about disarmament and arms control would be part of the exclusive domain of the states.[35] It would be improper for the ICJ to weigh in on a question going to the heart of the national defence policy of – and consequently of vital importance to – a considerable number of states.[36] Furthermore, France argued that in order to answer the request, the Court could be led to make appreciations of a military, political, moral and strategic nature – something 'evidently foreign' to its mission and something that it had allegedly excluded from its competence in *Nicaragua*.[37]

The *Diallo* case serves as the second example for the invocation of a deferential standard of review based on the notion of essential interests. The respondent, the Democratic Republic of the Congo (DRC), had arrested, detained and expelled Ahmadou Sadio Diallo, a Guinean national, who had established himself in the DRC. On behalf of its national, Guinea brought forward charges against the DRC, among others alleging violations of the International Covenant on Political and Civil Rights (ICCPR). Specifically, it alleged that the DRC had violated Mr Diallo's right under Article 13 of the Covenant by not allowing him to challenge his expulsion. According to Article 13, an alien 'shall, except where compelling reasons of national security otherwise require, be allowed to submit the reasons against his expulsion and to have his case reviewed'.

The DRC objected to any review by the ICJ of its decision not to allow Mr Diallo to challenge the expulsion measure. It contended that 'the compelling reasons of national security are left to the sovereign appreciation of each State'. In these circumstances, the DRC asserted, its government 'had judged, in a discretionary manner, that it was imperative for reasons of national security and public order to remove him from the territory'.[38] The usage of the terms 'sovereign appreciation' and 'discretionary' make clear that the DRC insisted

[32] *Nuclear Weapons*, Written Statement of Germany (n 27), 2; see also *Legality of the Threat or Use of Nuclear Weapons*, ICJ, Oral Proceedings of 2 November 1995 (CR 95/24), 31, at paras 12, 14 (Hillgenberg).

[33] *Nuclear Weapons*, Written Statement of Germany (n 27), 3.

[34] *Nuclear Weapons*, Oral Proceedings of 2 November 1995, 29 at para 3 (Hillgenberg).

[35] *Legality of the Threat or Use of Nuclear Weapons*, ICJ, Written Statement of France of 20 June 1995, 17–18.

[36] ibid, 20; *Legality of the Threat or Use of Nuclear Weapons*, ICJ, Oral Proceedings of 1 November 1995 (CR 95/23), 57, para 20 (Pellet).

[37] ibid, 56, paras 19, 22 (Pellet).

[38] *Ahmadou Sadio Diallo (Guinea v the Congo)*, ICJ, Counter-Memorial of the Congo of 27 March 2008, 1.28 (own translation. In the original: 'les raisons impérieuses de sécurité nationale

that the Court should accord it deference concerning its decision not to grant Mr Diallo the possibility of appeal against his expulsion. This amounts to the claim that certain subject matters are exempted from judicial oversight due to their importance and corresponding link to the core of state sovereignty.

B. Proceedings Concerning Domestic Matters

Second, states have invoked their sovereignty to convince the Court to apply a deferential standard of review in proceedings involving matters they deem to be domestic. In such matters, by virtue of its sovereignty, the ICJ would have to defer to the concerned state. Besides the *Guardianship of Infants* case, such a claim has for instance been made in *Obligation to Prosecute or Extradite*.

In *Guardianship of Infants*, Sweden, the respondent, invoked its national *ordre public* to justify its purported interference with the Dutch guardian's effective exercise of guardianship over a Dutch minor residing in Sweden. First, Sweden doubted the ability of international courts and tribunals to second-guess a state's qualification of a law as part of the national *ordre public*: 'the *ordre public* is different from country to country, and, to make things worse, the *ordre public absolu* is almost never affirmed in a text, it is the tribunals … which attribute it [such a character]'. Sweden thereby alluded to the superior expertise of the concerned state itself for such a determination. Because of this superior expertise, international judicial bodies, less able to answer these questions, should adjust their enquiry of that qualification to a good faith standard of review.[39] Furthermore, Sweden argued that the ICJ should not try to redo its first-hand assessment that the conditions for the application of the law qualified as *ordre public* had been met. This would go beyond the Court's task as envisioned in its Statute and encroach upon Sweden's national sovereignty.[40]

A second example for an invocation of a deferential standard of review justified with the consideration that domestic matters fall into the sovereign decision-making space of the concerned state can be found in *Obligation to Prosecute or Extradite*. The case involved the question to what extent the Court could scrutinise Senegal's compliance with its obligations under the Convention against Torture (CAT) to conduct criminal proceedings against an alleged human rights offender on its territory. Senegal maintained that '[h]ow a State fulfils an international obligation, particularly in a case such as that before the

sont laissées à l'appréciation souveraine de chaque Etat', and 'a jugé, de manière discrétionnaire, qu'il était urgent et impérieux, pour des raisons de sécurité nationale et de maintien de l'ordre public, de l'éloigner du territoire.').

[39] *Guardianship of Infants*, ICJ, Oral Pleadings of 30 September 1958, afternoon, 220 (Rolin, own translation. In the original: 'l'ordre public est différent de pays à pays, et, pour comble de malheur, l'ordre public absolu n'est presque jamais affirmé dans un texte, ce sont les tribunaux qui … lui attribuent un caractère d'ordre public absolu.').

[40] *Guardianship of Infants*, ICJ, Oral Pleadings of 1 October 1958, morning, 234–35 (Rolin).

Court, where the State must take internal measures of application, is to a very large extent left to the discretion of that State'.[41] In its view, the involvement of its domestic judiciary called for deference on the ICJ's part. Accordingly, Senegal asserted that the Court should defer to some extent to its own first-hand assessment what measures had been feasible and appropriate on the way to the criminal prosecution. A violation could only be found to exist if it were to be found that Senegal had not acted in good faith.[42]

C. Proceedings Concerning Political Decisions

Third, states have regularly advanced claims for a deferential standard of review with regard to the domain of allegedly 'political' decisions. Assertions of this kind have already been made in the first proceeding before the Court, *Admission of a State to the UN*.[43] Further, the *South West Africa* case will be analysed in more detail.

Admission of a State to the UN concerned the admission process for new UN Members, which had come to a standstill in connection with the Cold War. Against this background, the UN General Assembly had requested an opinion from the ICJ on two questions. It enquired whether a UN Member State generally could make its consent to the admission of a new state dependent on conditions not expressly laid down by Article 4(1) UN Charter. Specifically, it also asked whether a state could subject its consent to the simultaneous admission of other states. This is in effect what the Soviet Union had been doing, thus blocking the admission of two states.[44]

Several states urged the ICJ not to accede to the request due to its allegedly political nature. They asserted that the decision to vote on the admission of a state to the UN would only be subject to political considerations, which the ICJ would not be able to control. In support for this position, Yugoslavia for instance argued that 'the admission of a new Member is a political question, it concerns the security of the international order … It also involves appreciating the future consequences of this act on the general international stability and peace … For these reasons, a discretionary power has to be recognized for the members of the Security Council'.[45]

[41] *Obligation to Prosecute or Extradite (Belgium v Senegal)*, ICJ, Counter-Memorial of Senegal of 23 August 2011, 235.

[42] *Obligation to Prosecute or Extradite*, ICJ, Oral Proceedings of 21 March 2012, morning (CR 2012/7), 26, paras 42–43 (Thiam).

[43] While the ICJ issued its judgment on preliminary objections in the *Corfu Channel* case before this opinion, the judgment on the merits only came on 9 April 1949.

[44] See the Statement of the Representative of the Soviet Union at the 206th meeting of the UN Security Council, United Nations, 'Official Records from the 206th Meeting of the Security Council' (1 October 1947) UN Doc. S/PV.206, 2476–2477, undocs.org/en/S/PV.206.

[45] *Admission of a State to the United Nations (Charter, Art 4)*, ICJ, Oral Statements, 82 (own translation. In the original: 'l'admission d'un nouveau Membre est une question politique, il s'agit de la sécurité de l'ordre international … Il s'agit également d'apprécier les conséquences futures

In the same vein, counsel for Poland advanced that:

> The reasons upon which [states] base their judgment [under Article 4 UN Charter] are political, and, therefore not subject to judicial control … [I]f one uses a right it should be used in the interest of what it is meant for … You may ask me who is to judge whether [the right to vote upon the admission of new Members] is used for these purposes [ie, 'in the interest of peace and security, in the interest of the Organization']. The reply that I give is: those who are primarily politically responsible for the wellbeing of the Organization; because there are no legal criteria for security, and the criteria are undoubtedly political.[46]

From these states' perspective, the questions before the ICJ were inherently political, and thus not amenable to a judicial appreciation.[47]

The *South West Africa* case serves as the second example for an invocation of a deferential standard of review based on the 'political decision' argument. The proceedings revolved around South Africa's actions under the League of Nations mandate over what was then South West Africa, and is today Namibia. According to Article 2(2) of the Mandate, South Africa had an obligation to 'promote to its utmost the material and moral well-being and the social progress of the inhabitants' of the administered territory. Liberia and Ethiopia inter alia alleged that South Africa had breached this obligation. South Africa urged the ICJ to apply a deferential standard of review for its compliance with this obligation. It advanced two contentions in this respect: first, that the Court would be lacking the necessary institutional expertise to review its behaviour, and second, that the applicable norm had been laid down in such broad terms as to be devoid of any standards amenable to judicial appreciation.

In South Africa's view, any review of its exercise of the mandate would entail an evaluation of—

> decisions of a purely political nature. The functions of Courts of Law do not normally extend to the realm of politics; and where a legislature or an administrative body acts within the scope of powers conferred upon it, it is not the function of Courts of Law to enquire into the policy or soundness of its acts.[48]

de cet acte sur la stabilité internationale générale et sur la paix … Pour les raisons indiquées, c'est le pouvoir discrétionnaire qui doit être reconnu aux membres du Conseil de Sécurité.').

[46] ibid, 109.

[47] Not only states from the Eastern Bloc had argued in such a way. France had advanced that while the question was justiciable, it was, 'indeed, a political question to ask from States to be peaceful, to be peace-loving States … It is an essentially political condition, it is an essential condition, but it is already a condition that implies diverse elements of appreciation.' Additionally, it had asserted that 'the organs … have the right to rely on considerations of expediency in the appreciation of the very broad content of the conditions laid down in Article 4' (own translation, in the original: 'en effet, une question d'ordre politique que d'exiger des États qu'ils soient pacifiques, qu'ils soient des *peace-loving States*…. C'est une condition essentiellement politique, c'est une condition essentielle, mais c'est déjà une condition qui implique des éléments d'appréciation divers', and 'les organes … ont le droit de faire intervenir des conditions d'opportunité dans l'appréciation du très large contenu des conditions posées à l'article 4' ibid, 68 and 73–74 respectively.

[48] *South West Africa (Ethiopia v South Africa; Liberia v South Africa)*, ICJ, Preliminary Objections of South Africa of 30 November 1961, 386–87; reasserted in the oral arguments by G van

Courts, including the ICJ, would be lacking the necessary institutional expertise to review such acts, 'consist[ing] of people versed in the law, who may not necessarily possess any expert knowledge of ethnology, sociology, economics, administration, etc'.[49] Such knowledge, South Africa argued, would be necessary to review legislative or administrative acts as those at issue. Therefore, it concluded, 'an international court is in many ways an unsuitable body to review the exercise of administrative and legislative powers by organs or officials of a State'.[50]

Additionally, the relevance of this alleged lack of institutional expertise would be reinforced by the nature of Article 2(2). According to South Africa, if its compliance with this provision were found to be subject to review, this would place upon the Court 'a task of judicial review in respect of so wide and essentially political a function as the government of a territory, with no more precise formulation or criteria than the broad and general one … that the powers of legislation and government are to be exercised with a view to promoting to the utmost the well-being and progress of the inhabitants'.[51] Thus, it asserted that the exercise of this kind of political power could not be reviewed by courts, but only of technical bodies such as the (by then already defunct) Permanent Mandates Commission.

D. Proceedings Concerning Scientific Questions

Fourth and finally, pleas for the application of a deferential standard of review have been made in proceedings revolving around state assessments and measures with a scientific background. Several proceedings brought before the ICJ prominently featured such questions, namely *Gabčíkovo-Nagymaros*, *Pulp Mills*, and *Whaling*. In all these three cases, the respondents urged the Court to adopt a deferential standard of review. As a judicial institution, it would be lacking the expertise and abilities to conduct that appreciation, and thus to second-guess the respective determinations made by scientists from the state or independent entities. For this reason, it should defer to their respective first-hand assessment. The respondents' assertions to that effect in *Gabčíkovo-Nagymaros* and *Whaling* are good examples for this argumentation.

Gabčíkovo-Nagymaros posed intricate questions of environmental protection and ecological risk assessment. Among others, Hungary invoked a state

R Muller, Public hearing of 10 October 1962, morning, *South West Africa*, ICJ, Oral Arguments (Preliminary Objections) of 1962, 210. See also DP De Villiers, who asserted for South Africa that passing to the merits would mean 'passing judgment on policies which are in many respects the subject of red-hot controversy, emotional and political, in the international political arena', Public hearing of 19 October 1962, morning, 330; see also *South West Africa (Ethiopia v South Africa; Liberia v South Africa)*, ICJ, Rejoinder of South Africa of 22 December 1964, 384.

[49] ibid, 153–54.

[50] ibid, 154.

[51] ibid, 153.

of 'ecological necessity'[52] to justify its suspension and later abandonment of the joint Hungarian-Slovakian Gabčíkovo-Nagymaros dam project that was at the heart of the dispute. In its counter-memorial, under the header 'the task of the Court', Hungary pointed to the outcome-determinative nature of 'scientific and technical issues'. Further, it noted that 'the assessment of complex risks in a large unimplemented project of this type is extremely difficult, with many uncertainties', and that '[r]isks and damage can seldom be proved with 100% certainty … Clearly no one can be absolutely certain about the long-term scientific and technical prognosis for a major project such as this'.[53] Thereby, it alluded to the limitations of its own expertise and abilities, limitations that would hinder it from establishing an irreproachable and definitive factual basis and drawing unassailable conclusions therefrom. Significantly, it not only drew attention to its own limitations, but, by trying to portray the matter as a dispute among experts, it also alluded to the respective limitations on the Court's part. Accordingly, in its view, as no one could provide a definitive answer to these questions, the ICJ should refrain from attempting to do so.

In *Whaling*, Japan resorted to this argument in a slightly different way. The case revolved around the question whether the Japanese JARPA II whaling programme qualified as being 'for purposes of scientific research' and was therefore exempt from the whaling moratorium by virtue of Article VIII of the Whaling Convention (ICRW).[54] *Whaling* has gained prominence for the extensive focus on the applicable standard of review. While it was not the first case where a state had invoked the 'margin of appreciation' as a standard of review before the Court, it was certainly the one where this received most attention in the literature so far.[55]

[52] At the time, the Draft Articles on Responsibility of States for Internationally Wrongful Acts had not yet been submitted to the UN General Assembly. Yet, both Hungary and Slovakia were in agreement that Art 33 of the ILC's Draft Articles was to constitute the legal yardstick for Hungary's state of necessity claim, *Gabčíkovo-Nagymaros (Hungary v Slovakia)*, ICJ, Judgment of 25 September 1997, 50.

[53] *Gabčíkovo-Nagymaros (Hungary v Slovakia)*, ICJ, Counter-Memorial of Hungary of 5 December 1994, 1.44–6; a point repeated during the oral stage, *Gabčíkovo-Nagymaros*, ICJ, Oral Proceedings of 4 March 1997 (CR 97/3), 35, para 44 (Wheater).

[54] Art VIII(1) ICRW: 'Notwithstanding anything contained in this Convention any Contracting Government may grant to any of its nationals a special permit authorizing that national to kill, take and treat whales for purposes of scientific research subject to such restrictions … and … conditions as the Contracting Government thinks fit, and the killing, taking and treating of whales in accordance with the provisions of this Article shall be exempt from the operation of this Convention.'

[55] See, for instance, E Bjorge, 'Been There, Done That: The Margin of Appreciation and International Law' (2015) 4(1) *Cambridge Journal of International and Comparative Law* 181; E Cannizzaro, 'Proportionality and Margin of Appreciation in the Whaling Case: Reconciling Antithetical Doctrines?' (2016) 27(4) *European Journal of International Law* 1061; A Garrido-Muñoz, 'Managing Uncertainty: The International Court of Justice, "Objective Reasonableness" and the Judicial Function' (2017) 30(2) *Leiden Journal of International Law* 457; and the contributions in M Fitzmaurice and D Tamada (eds), *Whaling in the Antarctic: Significance and Implications of the ICJ Judgment* (Brill/Nijhoff, 2016).

Japan did not argue that no one could determine the scientific questions with the requisite certainty, as Hungary had done in *Gabčíkovo-Nagymaros*. Instead, it asserted that it could, but not the ICJ. The most revealing passage in Japan's written submissions reads as follows:

> It is doubtful that the Court can make its own enquiry into the facts .... The facts are not the only issue. When the facts have been gathered, how is the Court, as a non-technical body, to appraise them? This is not a case of the kind that may arise in the WTO, where the issue takes the form of the technical question whether there are any 'less restrictive' measures that may achieve the chosen aim. That may be a technical question to which there is a clear technical answer. In the present case, however, the question is one of the propriety of the research aims themselves, which is a matter of science policy, and science policy is neither a technical nor a legal question.[56]

As it further observed, even the then-Chairman of the International Whaling Commission's Scientific Committee had once reported that the Committee 'felt that ... the only people who could judge whether the project of research would justify a special permit would be the Contracting Government'.[57] If not even the Scientific Committee, a technical body comprised of scientists, was in a position to review Japan's decision to grant a whaling licence under Article VIII, how could the Court affirm its competency to do so?

Specifically, reviewing JARPA II

> would require a survey of the existing data, an analysis of the questions left unanswered by that data and of the importance of that data and of the alternative ways in which that data might be obtained, and of the levels of accuracy needed. It would involve the determination of the necessary sample size, and of the frequency and duration of the data collection. Crucially, it would be premised upon a determination of what are the proper questions that ... biologists, oceanographers, ecologists, resource managers, environmentalists or whatever ... should be asking, or perhaps are entitled to ask ... [W]ith respect, it is not obvious that the Court has the necessary expertise to enable it to analyse such information.[58]

As a judicial institution, the ICJ would be no more in a position to 'impose a line separating science from non-science than it could decide what is and what is not "Art"'.[59] Instead, 'the Court is the "organ" of "international law"; it has the utmost authority to settle the legal disputes submitted to it. However ... *it cannot decide between opposing scientific views*... [I]t is not our responsibility, as jurists to pass judgment on the substantive merits of particular scientific

[56] *Whaling in the Antarctic (Australia v Japan: New Zealand intervening)*, ICJ, Written Observations of Japan on New Zealand's Written Observations of 31 May 2013, 57–58.

[57] Quoted after *Whaling in the Antarctic (Australia v Japan: New Zealand intervening)*, ICJ, Counter-Memorial of Japan of 9 March 2012, 417, para 9.20.

[58] *Whaling in the Antarctic*, ICJ, Oral Proceedings of 4 July 2013, morning (CR 2013/15), 19, paras 25–26 (Lowe).

[59] *Whaling in the Antarctic*, ICJ, Oral Proceedings of 15 July 2013, afternoon (CR 2013/22), 60, para 20 (Lowe).

positions: this is not the medieval Inquisition'.[60] Instead of conducting its own assessment, Japan alleged, by reason of its institutional inability to deal with those matters, the Court should defer to the actor's assessment who had the capabilities to do so – Japan.

III. A COMMON DENOMINATOR: THE BETTER-PLACED CONTENTION

The above analysis has shown that states have been urging the Court to adopt a deferential standard of review predominantly in proceedings involving four domains: essential interests, domestic measures, 'political' decisions, and scientific determinations. On the one hand, the associated questions would be beyond the ICJ's grasp because of their inherent complexity, scale, or their emphasis on technical and non-legal aspects. The Court's lack of abilities to deal with such aspects would inevitably come to bear during its appreciation of them, and vitiate the result of the law-application process. Namely, it inevitably would fail to apprehend the meaning of concepts such as essential state interests (including national security), or science, or oversee essentially political considerations. Due to its inherently limited toolbox, the ICJ as a judicial institution would be unable to grasp these matters as would be required.

This underlying conception appears clearly in *South West Africa*, where South Africa observed that the ICJ only 'consists of people versed in the law, who may not necessarily possess any expert knowledge of ethnology, sociology, economics, administration, etc'.[61] It also constituted the foundation for Australia's remark in *Nuclear Weapons* that 'very complex strategic judgements … go beyond the traditional competence of a body such as the Court'.[62] Finally, Japan's (rhetorical) question in the *Whaling* case is emblematic: 'When the facts have been gathered, how is the Court, as a non-technical body, to appraise them?'[63]

On the other hand, states have also asserted that the Court would be lacking the mandate to intervene in matters of the highest importance to them. This conception can be discerned in Germany's observation in *Nuclear Weapons* that '[t]he subject of the assessment would … be key security policy elements of today's global order'[64] and 'touch upon issues of fundamental political importance, ones where States' vital interests are involved'.[65] Furthermore, this contention appears in *Diallo*, when the DRC categorically asserted that

[60] *Whaling in the Antarctic*, ICJ, Oral Proceedings of 16 July 2013, morning (CR 2013/23), 22, paras 18 and 21 (Pellet, references omitted).

[61] *South West Africa*, Rejoinder of South Africa (n 48), 154–55.

[62] *Nuclear Weapons in Armed Conflict*, Written Statement of Australia (n 30), 9.

[63] *Whaling*, Written Observations of Japan on New Zealand's Written Observations (n 56), para 58.

[64] *Nuclear Weapons*, Written Statement of Germany (n 27), 3.

[65] *Nuclear Weapons*, Oral Proceedings of 2 November 1995, 29 at para 3 (Hillgenberg).

'the compelling reasons of national security are left to the sovereign appreciation of each State'.[66] It is interesting to note that the respective states largely forwent expanding upon this assertion to justify why this should specifically persuade the Court to apply a deferential standard of review. Instead, reference to national sovereignty was generally made in the form of apodictic statements.

Ultimately, both these assertions – sovereignty, and expertise – have a common denominator: the better-placed assertion. These two branches of the better-placed assertion are often invoked in parallel. Thus, states regularly make the argument that both their superior expertise in matters of national security and their sovereign prerogative to decide upon those questions call for the adoption of a deferential standard of review by the Court. The statements made by Australia, France and Germany in *Nuclear Weapons* are emblematic in this respect.

Especially the expertise-based contention has also found support in the literature concerned with the adjudicatory role of international courts and tribunals. For instance, for Shany, a central argument in favour of a deferential standard of review 'is that national actors have superior law-application capabilities to those of international courts', because the decision-making process of international courts 'suffers from chronic deficiencies that support the delegation of decision-making powers to non-judicial decision-makers'.[67] Among those deficiencies would be the—

> constrain[ed] judicial perspectives, limit[ed] ... sources of information and ... a circumscribed time-frame for the decision-making process. By contrast, state bureaucracies continually monitor situations and address them utilizing a variety of inter-disciplinary tools, incorporating a variety of short-term and long-term interests. Hence, they seem to be better situated to adopt general policies and to anticipate the entire gamut of implications deriving from specific decisions.[68]

With respect to the WTO adjudicatory system, Ioannidis likewise noted that '[s]tate authorities, having much greater capabilities with regard to information gathering and assessment, might reasonably claim that they are in a better position than a WTO panel to evaluate issues such as whether the import of certain product can cause "serious injury" to the domestic industry'.[69] With regard to the review of 'non-precluded measures' clauses by ICSID tribunals, Burke-White and von Staden have argued that—

> the members of an ICSID panel are often very distant, physically, politically, culturally, and socially, from the particular state or circumstances in question. They often

[66] *Diallo*, Counter-Memorial of the Congo (n 38), para 1.28 (own translation. In the original: 'les raisons impérieuses de sécurité nationale sont laissées à l'appréciation souveraine de chaque Etat').

[67] Y Shany, 'Toward a General Margin of Appreciation Doctrine in International Law?' (2005) 16(5) *European Journal of International Law* 907, 918.

[68] ibid.

[69] M Ioannidis, 'Beyond the Standard of Review: Deference Criteria in WTO Law and the Case for a Procedural Approach' in L Gruszczynski and W Werner (eds), *Deference in International Courts and Tribunals: Standard of Review and Margin of Appreciation* (Oxford University Press, 2014), 102 (footnotes omitted).

> lack the fact-finding capacity to fully appreciate the context of government policies. Without the kind of deep connection to the state, society, and community impacted by the dispute, such *ad hoc* panels are poorly positioned to engage in full substantive review of critical state policies ... Such tribunals are, therefore, ill positioned to undertake substantive review that essentially second-guesses core governmental policy.[70]

Most famously, perhaps, Alexy has coined the term 'epistemic discretion'[71] to describe the idea that primary decision-makers are to be granted some degree of deference by judicial bodies based on considerations of expertise. He differentiates between epistemic empirical and epistemic normative deference. The former refers to the limits of empirical knowledge, and thus to the knowledge of facts. The latter refers to the limits of normative knowledge, and thus to the uncertainty as to the weight to be accorded to certain normative values.[72] The claim that the ICJ would be lacking the necessary expertise to evaluate especially decisions based on scientific knowledge and certain technical or strategic decisions overlaps with what Alexy calls epistemic empirical deference. In turn, the claim that the ICJ would lack the abilities to make value assessments about the importance of certain policy goals, state interests, or decisions whether and what measures are advisable to protect those interests broadly overlaps with what Alexy calls epistemic normative deference.[73]

[70] WW Burke-White and A von Staden, 'Investment Protection in Extraordinary Times: The Interpretation and Application of Non-Precluded Measures Provisions in Bilateral Investment Treaties' (2008) 48(2) *Virginia Journal of International Law* 307, 372.

[71] R Alexy, *A Theory of Constitutional Rights* (Oxford University Press, Reprint 2010), 393. What Alexy refers to as 'discretion' will from hereon be referred to as 'deference', as this is the term that, in my view, better captures the idea of deferential standards of review. With a similar approach ADP Brady, *Proportionality and Deference under the UK Human Rights Act: An Institutionally Sensitive Approach* (Cambridge University Press, 2012), 62, at fn 71.

[72] Alexy, *A Theory of Constitutional Rights* (n 71), 414–15; see also C Henckels, 'The Role of the Standard of Review and the Importance of Deference in Investor-State Arbitration' in L Gruszczynski and W Werner (eds), *Deference in International Courts and Tribunals: Standard of Review and Margin of Appreciation* (Oxford University Press, 2014), 115–16.

[73] On expertise as a factor for judicial restraint, see also J King, *Judging Social Rights* (Cambridge University Press, 2012), 211–49. Further reasons, not necessarily related to considerations of expertise, are being invoked for the adoption of a deferential standard of review by (international) courts, see for instance A Kavanagh, 'Deference or Defiance? The Limits of the Judicial Role in Constitutional Adjudication' in G Huscroft (ed), *Expounding the Constitution: Essays in Constitutional Theory* (Cambridge University Press, 2008), 188. Not least, Alexy himself refers to structural discretion, Alexy, *A Theory of Constitutional Rights* (n 71), 395–414. A presentation of these arguments would go beyond the scope of this enquiry. For instance, Shany emphasises democratic accountability, 'fairness in attributing responsibility', and 'inter-institutional comity' as arguments for the application of a deferential standard of review, Shany, 'Toward a General Margin of Appreciation Doctrine in International Law?' (n 67), 919–22; in turn, von Staden focuses on the democratic legitimacy of judicial review as an argument for the application of a deferential standard of review, A von Staden, 'The democratic legitimacy of judicial review beyond the state: Normative subsidiarity and judicial standards of review' (2012) 10(4) *International Journal of Constitutional Law* 1023, 1033–39; Ioannidis briefly discusses the argument of superior democratic accountability of national authorities vis-a-vis international judicial bodies, Ioannidis, 'Beyond the Standard of Review' (n 69), 101–02; on the 'democratic argument', further JH Fahner, *Judicial Deference in International Adjudication: A Comparative Analysis* (Hart, 2020), 161–71.

In the context of the UK Human Rights Act, Brady has described the reasoning behind the fact-related uncertainty justification for a deferential standard of review in more detail. He observed that there are certain decisions governments take that 'involve educated guesswork of one form or another', such as in the field of national security. In these situations, '[i]t may not always be possible to accurately assess the nature and extent of a particular problem', '[n]or will it always be possible to measure precisely how much a particular measure will go towards solving that problem. Where questions such as this arise it may be appropriate to afford the decision-maker empirical deference'.[74] Vadi and Gruszczynski have specifically addressed the fact-related uncertainty rationale for a deferential standard of review with respect to scientific questions. For them, 'multiple reasons speak in favour of the deferential approach … of any international court or tribunal … with respect to evaluation of scientific facts. Probably the most important one is the limited epistemic competence of such bodies to assess the correctness of scientific evidence'.[75] As they note further, the WTO Appellate Body explicitly recognised this when it held that 'a [WTO] panel is not well suited to conduct scientific research and assessment itself'.[76]

With respect to the value-related uncertainty rationale for a deferential standard of review in the WTO dispute settlement system, Guzman has noted for instance that 'as compared to a national government[,] the [WTO] panel … is poorly positioned to evaluate the preferences and attitudes of individuals, and is less skilled at evaluating political, cultural, and other factors relevant to a decision'.[77] Similar concerns seem to have motivated Jennings to remark over sixty years ago that '[n]ational security is a matter of which the government is sole trustee. It is eminently a matter on which an international court can have no useful opinion and is probably not entitled to an opinion … [I]t is not a category capable of any kind of juridical assessment'.[78]

In contrast, the literature has accorded little merit, if any, to the contention that states are better placed to assess certain questions and decide on certain measures as a ground for the application of a deferential standard of review merely by virtue of state sovereignty. For instance, Oesch has remarked in the context of the WTO dispute settlement system that absent a constitutional framework such as those found in domestic settings, the balance of powers consideration would not apply with equal force in the international setting.

[74] Brady, *Proportionality and Deference under the UK Human Rights Act* (n 71), 113.

[75] V Vadi and L Gruszczynski, 'Standard of Review and Scientific Evidence in WTO Law and International Investment Arbitration' in L Gruszczynski and W Werner (eds), *Deference in International Courts and Tribunals: Standard of Review and Margin of Appreciation* (Oxford University Press, 2014), 165 (footnotes omitted).

[76] *Australia – Measures Affecting the Importation of Apples from New Zealand*, Report of the Appellate Body (29 November 2010) WT/DS367/AB/R, 225.

[77] AT Guzman, 'Determining the Appropriate Standard of Review in WTO Disputes' (2009) 42(1) *Cornell International Law Journal* 45, 46.

[78] RY Jennings, 'Recent Cases on "Automatic" Reservations to the Optional Clause' (1958) 7(2) *International and Comparative Law Quarterly* 349, 362.

To the contrary, if panels and the appellate body were to apply a deferential standard of review merely out of concern for national sovereignty, this would go against the WTO's contractual nature.[79] Ioannidis in turn noted that 'the sovereignty criterion begs the question of *why* domestic sovereignty deserves respect by an international adjudicator'.[80]

This cursory overview has illustrated that states have repeatedly relied on the expertise-based better-placed contention to convince the ICJ to apply a deferential standard of review. To a lesser extent, they have also invoked the sovereignty-based better-placed assertion. While there are several instances of states relying exclusively on the expertise-based better-placed assertion (especially in the domain of science), there are fewer examples where states have exclusively relied on the sovereignty-based better-placed assertion. Instead, in those cases, they have often invoked it in conjunction with the expertise-based better-placed assertion. The final section of this chapter will conclude by highlighting that there is a considerable overlap between these two groups of arguments invoked before the Court for the application of a deferential standard of review, and some of the state arguments invoked for the application of the non-justiciability doctrine.

IV. STANDARD OF REVIEW CLAIMS AS OLD WINE IN NEW SKINS?

The analysis conducted in the two preceding sections of this chapter has demonstrated that states have pointed both to an alleged lack of expertise on the part of the ICJ and have relied on a specific conception of sovereignty to justify why the Court should accord them deference and apply a deferential standard of review. These two argumentative bases are also at the heart of two strands of the non-justiciability doctrine in the international order as identified by Lauterpacht: the 'settlement method'-strand with the assertions that there is a more suitable forum for resolution than the Court, that a judicial pronouncement would impair political settlement, and that judicial appreciation is impossible, and the 'major interest' strand with the assertion that the ICJ cannot adjudicate over essential interests and domestic matters. This becomes apparent through two observations.

First, the assertions put in the spotlight in the previous parts of this chapter reveal this parallelism. For instance, in the two analysed cases that involved

[79] M Oesch, *Standards of Review in WTO Dispute Resolution* (Oxford University Press, 2003), 29–30. However, Oesch notes, from a pragmatic policy perspective, adopting a deferential standard of review out of consideration for state sovereignty might be justified on some occasions, ibid, 30–31; on this point, see SP Croley and JH Jackson, 'WTO Dispute Procedures, Standard of Review, and Deference to National Governments' (1996) 90(2) *American Journal of International Law* 193, 211–13.

[80] Ioannidis, 'Beyond the Standard of Review' (n 69), 101; on the sovereignty argument for deference in international adjudication, see also Fahner, *Judicial Deference in International Adjudication* (n 73), 171–74.

questions of science, *Gabčíkovo-Nagymaros* and *Whaling*, the respective respondent states asserted that crucial aspects of the matter before the Court would be beyond its province. On closer view, this is but a modified version of the 'impossibility of judicial appreciation' assertion. While states have been contending under that header that an issue would only be open to a *political* appreciation, in these three proceedings, the respondents contended that the issue would only be open to a *scientific* appreciation, and that the Court should accordingly defer to their first-hand assessment.

The political appreciation theme in turn reappeared directly in the *Nuclear Weapons* advisory proceedings, accompanied by a technical appreciation theme. The underlying argument was invariably related to the nature of the respective decisions: the ICJ as a court of law would be ill-equipped to conduct an evaluation on its own in domains beyond its institutional expertise, and should for this reason defer to the states' respective assessments. The political appreciation theme appears most clearly in Australia's contention that the matter 'enters into the wider realms of policy and security doctrines of states' and 'rests on a set of very complex strategic judgements which go beyond the traditional competence of a body such as the Court'.[81] The second theme – technical appreciation – surfaces for instance in Finland's statement, where it observed that the Court would be lacking expertise for the analysis of 'extremely complex and controversial pieces of technical, strategic and scientific information'.[82] Finally, the major interest strand of the non-justiciability doctrine also reappeared in the course of standard of review invocations. Although in a less developed form, it is clearly at the base of the pleas for the adoption of a deferential standard of review in *Guardianship of Infants* and *Diallo*, and one of the bases for the respective plea in *Nuclear Weapons*.

Second, there are the proceedings in which states have relied on the conceptions behind the settlement method strand both to urge the ICJ to recognise the non-justiciability of the matter *and* to adopt a deferential standard of review. The *Admission of a State to the UN* proceedings are a first case in point. There, Yugoslavia asserted that in order to decide whether to admit a state to the UN, it would be necessary 'to appreciate the future consequences of this act on the general international stability and peace'. Because of the resulting discretionary decision-making space that had to be recognised to the current Member States, the very question before the ICJ would be no longer a legal question.[83] Thus, as Yugoslavia argued, the fact that the ICJ would have to accord a decision-making space to the states for this question – and thus apply a deferential standard of review – would render the entire matter non-justiciable, because the very essence

[81] *Nuclear Weapons in Armed Conflict*, Written Statement of Australia (n 30), 8–9.
[82] *Nuclear Weapons*, Written Statement of Finland (n 29), 1.
[83] *Admission of a State to the UN*, Oral Statements (n 45), 82–84. (Own translation. In the original: 'apprécier les conséquences futures de cet acte sur la stabilité internationale générale et sur la paix').

of the question would be removed from its purview. Accordingly, Yugoslavia chose to frame the question as one of non-justiciability, but effectively made a standard of review claim.[84]

A similar approach can be identified in the *South West Africa* case. There, South Africa tried to convince the ICJ to drop the case in the first stage of the proceedings. In the second stage, it made the same claim, but now framed as a standard of review assertion proper. Both assertions rested on the same base: that the question would only be capable of political appreciation and be outside of the Court's province. Finally, the *Nuclear Weapons* proceedings demonstrate this point as well. Here, states such as Australia, Germany and France all tried to demonstrate that answering the request would exceed the ICJ's expertise as a judicial institution to convince it to decline the request. Again, they asserted that their respective assessments on the central question could not be second-guessed by the Court, and that this fact would make the entire request non-justiciable.

Both these observations demonstrate that one and the same consideration underlies the non-justiciability doctrine and the pleas for the adoption of a deferential standard of review. Accordingly, there is a line of continuity between certain arguments advanced for the non-justiciability of a matter and the arguments invoked for the application of a deferential standard of review for a certain question. That line of continuity is based upon a specific conception of the Court's role in the international legal order. From this perspective, the invocation of deferential standards of review merely appears to be a newly wrapped, less offensive way for the states to advance yet the same ideas. *Lauterpacht* once stated that states invoke the non-justiciability doctrine mainly because they are eager to evade a judicial pronouncement, while still 'professing to remain within the pale of the law'.[85] Ultimately, the same may be said of states arguing for the adoption of a deferential standard of review. On this basis, it seems as if the standard of review invocation is just old wine in new skins.

Yet, two observations caution against such a reading. On the one hand, it is important not to lose sight of the context in which the two respective claims have been and are being advanced. What has fundamentally changed from the era where the non-justiciability doctrine in the international order was conceived to the era of the standard of review-invocations is the premise underlying

[84] Poland's argumentation, referred to above at II.C., is a further example for this.

[85] Lauterpacht, *The Function of Law in the International Community* (n 1), 167; also generally R Higgins, 'Policy Considerations and the International Judicial Process' (1968) 17(1) *International and Comparative Law Quarterly* 58. But see Judge Lachs, who observed in the *Nicaragua* case that '[a]lmost all disputes arising between States have both political and legal aspects; politics and law meet at almost every point on the road … This does not mean that all disputes arising out of them are suitable for judicial solution. Need I recall that in the last century and the beginning of the present, those concerning "vital interests" of States, or their "honour", were viewed as political, and thus not subject to third-party settlement? Even a very minute dispute may be viewed as touching the vital interests of a State … the world we live in is one where certain notions, though part of the vocabulary of law, continue to be controlled by subjective evaluations', *Military and Paramilitary Activities in and against Nicaragua (Nicaragua v United States of America)*, ICJ, Judgment (Merits), Separate Opinion of Judge Lachs, 168.

international adjudication. Especially in the early days of the non-justiciability doctrine in the international order, the common perception was that in principle, inter-states disputes were unfit for international adjudication. Accordingly, no established compulsory system for the settlement of inter-state disputes yet existed. The doctrine of non-justiciability was invented precisely to transpose parts of this conception into an era where this underlying perception had undergone a fundamental change. However, over time, the room that international judicial bodies such as the PCIJ and the ICJ have accorded to this doctrine has been significantly reduced. Especially the Court's steadfast rejection of the non-justiciability doctrine is a clear expression that it is not willing to recognise any merit in the underlying conception. The new aspiration of the international legal order is that in principle, all inter-state disputes are fit for international adjudication.[86] It was in this changed environment that states increasingly began to call for the application of deferential standards of review before international judicial bodies. Accordingly, the conception underlying the non-justiciability doctrine has been profoundly reframed. It has changed from a rejection in principle to an acceptance in principle of international adjudication. So to speak, the invocations of the non-justiciability doctrine were an attempt to curb a development, while the invocations of a deferential standard of review are an attempt to turn back the clock. From this perspective, one may speak of a transformation with a continuity in terms of functions.[87] In the same vein, *Allan* commented on the doctrine of judicial deference in UK constitutional law that it 'turns out, on close inspection, to be non-justiciability dressed in pastel colours'.[88]

On the other hand, and what matters for the purposes of this enquiry, is that precisely this 'pastel colour' of the standard of review notion is its main advantage. The (state) concerns underlying both the non-justiciability doctrine and the standard of review notion have not gone away (and it is unlikely that they ever will). Against this background, the notion of deferential standard of review permits the ICJ to define its approach in a much more nuanced way than the application of the non-justiciability doctrine does. It may turn both findings, the establishment of the applicable standard of review, and the finding of non-justiciability, into judicial avoidance techniques. It is at this point that it

[86] In his dissenting opinion in the *Anglo-Iranian Oil case*, Judge Alvarez observed a parallel development for the *domaine reservé*, noting that that while initially, the 'reserved domain covered a very wide field', 'from the middle of the 19th century … the traditional *individualistic* regime of the absolute sovereignty of States began to give place to a new regime, … [which] resulted in the beginning of the total or partial internationalization of … matters … within the reserved domain', *Anglo-Iranian Oil Co. (United Kingdom v Iran)*, ICJ, Judgment (Preliminary Objections), Dissenting Opinion of Judge Alvarez, 127–28.

[87] Arguably, there is a parallel to the domestic context. McGoldrick observed with regards to the UK domestic courts that 'the modern judicial trend is to find that issues are justiciable and focus instead on the degree and intensity of the review exercised', D McGoldrick, 'The Boundaries of Justiciability' (2010) 59(4) *International and Comparative Law Quarterly* 981, 981.

[88] TRS Allan, 'Human Rights and Judicial Review: A Critique of "Due Deference"' (2006) 65(3) *Cambridge Law Journal* 671, 689.

becomes clear that the finding on the applicable standard of review holds more potential for the Court. The finding permits it to adapt the degree of consequentiality and thereby to escape the black-or-white logic underlying the doctrine of non-justiciability. This makes the finding of the applicable standard of review a particularly versatile avoidance technique superior to others the ICJ has been resorting to. The following chapter will expand upon this point.

3

Something New under the Sun: Standards of Review as a Judicial Avoidance Technique

THE COMMON ROOTS of the non-justiciability assertion and the invocation of deferential standards of review suggest that, for the Court, the latter is just old wine in new skins. However, this chapter argues that such a reading would be premature. The notion of standard of review holds specific potential for the ICJ: It may function as a particularly balanced, and thus particularly useful, judicial avoidance technique. From this perspective, the notion of standard of review is something new under the sun.

First, this chapter will outline why the use of judicial avoidance techniques is dubious for any court of law, yet is a practical necessity. This holds true especially for international courts and tribunals such as the ICJ. Then, in a second and third step, the chapter will turn to the Court's use of such avoidance techniques. It will be shown that it has regularly relied on such techniques to dispose of thorny questions.[1] However, the majority of these techniques are problematic,

[1] This chapter builds on and expands upon ideas developed elsewhere, see F Fouchard, 'Allowing "leeway to expediency, without abandoning principle"? The International Court of Justice's use of avoidance techniques' (2020) 33(3) *Leiden Journal of International Law* 767. Others have also already analysed the use of such avoidance techniques by international courts and tribunals. Most notably, Odermatt provides an overview over some of the avoidance strategies used by the ECJ, the ICJ, and the East African Court of Justice, J Odermatt, 'Patterns of avoidance: political questions before international courts' (2018) 14(2) *International Journal of Law in Context* 221; focusing on the WTO dispute settlement system, WJ Davey, 'Has the WTO Dispute Settlement System Exceeded Its Authority? A Consideration of Deference shown by the System to Member Government Decisions and its Use of Issue-Avoidance Techniques' (2001) 4(1) *Journal of International Economic Law* 79; on the ECJ's use of 'passive virtues', notably judicial deference, in the context of free movement law, J Zglinski, *Europe's Passive Virtues* (Oxford University Press, 2020); likewise with respect to the ECJ, Helfer and Slaughter have observed that the ECJ 'is also discovering the "passive virtues" of rulings that dispose of contentious issues on grounds of jurisdiction (admissibility) and justiciability', LR Helfer and A-M Slaughter, 'Toward a Theory of Effective Supranational Adjudication' (1997) 107(2) *Yale Law Journal* 273, 316; on the ECtHR's use of the finding of non-admissibility as a 'strategic utility' tool to avoid confrontation with the United Kingdom, particularly with the UK judiciary, L Graham, 'Strategic Admissibility Decisions in the European Court of Human Rights' (2020) 69(1) *International and Comparative Law Quarterly* 79; on the ICJ's use of avoidance techniques, see also AF Perez, 'The Passive Virtues and the World Court: Pro-Dialogic Abstentation by the International Court of Justice' (1997) 18(3) *Michigan Journal of International Law* 399; and A John, 'Inarticulate and Unconscious: Non-Justiciability before the International Court of Justice' (2021) 20(1) *The Law and Practice of International Courts and Tribunals* 77.

for they lack the nuance to establish the best balance between considerations of practical expediency and respect for the Court's mandate as a judicial institution. Fourth, it will be shown that in contrast to these techniques, the use of deferential standards of review as an avoidance technique holds a distinctive potential for the ICJ. Resort to this technique enables it to rebalance the fragile equilibrium between asserting its role and avoiding to antagonise those on whose support it is dependent: the states. Such a rebalancing might be particularly needed in times of contestation and resistance against international courts and tribunals.

I. JUDICIAL AVOIDANCE: DUBIOUS FROM AN ORTHODOX POINT OF VIEW, YET A PRACTICAL NECESSITY

With hindsight, the last seven decades, and especially those since the end of the Cold War, might be described as the golden age of international law. They have seen the creation of a host of international organisations, an equally marked growth of international rules addressing state conduct, and an ever-growing number of rulings from the numerous international judicial bodies set up to enforce these rules.[2] All of this activity has contributed to a considerable narrowing of the space for manoeuvre by states. One of the most notable developments has been the judicialisation of international relations, the increasing involvement of judicial bodies in the realm of international politics.[3]

Lately, however, the pendulum seems to be on the cusp of swinging back. States increasingly argue for re-nationalisation, especially in 'sovereignty-sensitive' areas, and recent changes in the ECHR,[4] the ongoing debates about the role and propriety of international investment arbitration[5] and new treaty designs in international economic law[6] illustrate that some states have already

[2] On this development, see with further references CPR Romano, 'The Proliferation of International Judicial Bodies: The Pieces of the Puzzle' (1999) 31 *International Law and Politics* 709, 709.

[3] See for instance KJ Alter, 'Judicialization of International Relations' in B Badie, D Berg-Schlosser and L Morlino (eds), *International Encyclopedia of Political Science* (Sage, 2011), 1378.

[4] Notably, the adoption of Protocol 15, already referred to in the Introduction. For further details, see for instance I Cram, 'Protocol 15 and articles 10 and 11 ECHR – The partial triumph of political incumbency post-Brighton?' (2018) 19 *International and Comparative Law Quarterly* 1, 1–2 and 4–7.

[5] From the wealth of literature on this subject, with further references SW Schill, 'International Investment Law and Comparative Public Law – an Introduction' in SW Schill (ed), *International Investment Law and Comparative Public Law* (Oxford University Press, 2010), 6.

[6] See for instance T Broude, YZ Haftel and A Thompson, 'Legitimation Through Modification: Do States Seek More Regulatory Space in Their Investment Agreements?' in D Behn, OK Fauchald and M Langford (eds), *The Legitimacy of Investment Arbitration: Empirical Perspectives* (Cambridge University Press, 2022); basing themselves on the UN Conference on Trade and Development database, *Bahmaei* and *Sabzevari* observe that since 2005, states have been including 'self-judging clauses', thereby trying to preserve room for manoeuvre in sovereignty-sensitive areas, in 148 investment agreements, M-A Bahmaei and H Sabzevari, 'Self-Judging Security Exception Clause as a Kind of Carte Blanche in Investment Treaties: Nature, Effect and Proper Standard of Review' (2023) 13(1) *Asian Journal of International Law* 97, 97.

begun to act accordingly. International courts and tribunals have become the target of criticism from those who lament that state conduct is being overly constrained and that courts are overstepping the boundaries of national sovereignty.[7] Such criticism is not new for the ICJ, and it has had the opportunity to develop a toolkit to meet such criticism.

As the 'principal judicial organ' of the UN, the ICJ shares the organisation's purposes,[8] including maintaining international peace and security (Article 1 (1) UN Charter). Accordingly, the Court's primary aim is to promote the peaceful settlement of disputes among the states.[9] Furthermore, as any court does, it strives to promote norm-compliance[10] and the realisation of justice.[11] As the ICJ mainly acts through its decisions, contributing to these objectives presupposes that it *issues* decisions in the first place. This underlying idea, that the Court needs to issue decisions in order to fulfil its role, is what arguably motivated the UN General Assembly to recommend, on several occasions, that states refer their disputes to the Court.[12] The ICJ also participates in the activities of the UN by issuing advisory opinions. Accordingly, in principle, it should not decline to do so when its opinion is requested. The Court's recognition of this principle manifests itself in its pronouncement that only 'compelling reasons' may lead it to refuse to issue an advisory opinion once it has found it has jurisdiction.[13]

The Court's ability to issue decisions, however, depends on the states. Its jurisdiction for contentious proceedings is based on consent, 'even if one might regret this state of affairs'.[14] So does its ability to issue advisory

[7] For an overview over the forms of state resistance, see MR Madsen, P Cebulak and M Wiebusch, 'Backlash against international courts: explaining the forms and patterns of resistance to international courts' (2018) 14(2) *International Journal of Law in Context* 197; C Hillebrecht, *Saving the International Justice Regime: Beyond Backlash against International Courts* (Cambridge University Press, 2021).

[8] See S Rosenne, *The Law and Practice of the International Court, 1920-2005: Volume I, The Court and the United Nations,* 4th edn (Martinus Nijhoff, 2006), 104–06.

[9] As expressed at the San Francisco Conference, 'the First Committee ventures to foresee a significant role for the new Court in the international relations in the future. The judicial process will have a central place in the plans of the United Nations for the settlement of international disputes', Draft Report of the Rapporteur of Committee IV/1, Doc. 875, IV/1/74, June 9, 1945, *Documents of the United Nations Conference on International Organization, 1945, Volume XIII: Commission IV, Judicial Organization*, 315.

[10] *cf* Y Shany, *Assessing the Effectiveness of International Courts* (Oxford University Press, 2014), 164–66, together with R Giladi.

[11] *cf* the Preamble of the UN Charter. With the term 'justice', the Preamble refers to natural law, R Wolfrum, 'Preamble' in B Simma and others (eds), *The Charter of the United Nations: A Commentary*, 3rd edn (Oxford University Press, 2012), 9.

[12] See for instance United Nations General Assembly Resolutions 171 (II), 37/10, and 60/1.

[13] For a recent affirmation of this principle, see with further references *Legal Consequences of the Separation of the Chagos Archipelago from Mauritius in 1965*, ICJ, Advisory Opinion of 25 February 2019, 65.

[14] *Legality of Use of Force (Serbia and Montenegro v United Kingdom)*, ICJ, Order (Provisional Measures), Separate Opinion of Judge Higgins, 26; Alter speaks of a Court 'hobbled by design', KJ Alter, 'The ICJ in Comparison: Understanding the ICJ's Limited Influence' (2021) 21(3) *Melbourne Journal of International Law* 1, 3; see also A Coleman, 'The International Court of Justice and Highly Political Matters' (2003) 4(1) *Melbourne Journal of International*

opinions: it is the states that ultimately stand behind the requests made by UN organs or authorised agencies. Furthermore, absent formalised effective enforcement mechanisms,[15] the Court depends on the states' willingness to implement its decisions.[16] Whether a state is willing to submit to the Court's jurisdiction or to comply with its decisions depends on several factors.

First, a state's perception of the Court's legitimacy is potentially important.[17] The more the state perceives the Court as a legitimate institution, the more likely it is to consent to its jurisdiction and comply with its decisions (conversely, the less so, the less likely this becomes).

Second, Goodman and Jinks have argued that acculturation may be a factor in compliance: Actors adopt the beliefs and behaviours of their surrounding culture, regardless of their normative assessment of that pattern.[18] Applied to the situation of states[19] dealing with the ICJ, this means that if there is a strong social norm among states to follow the Court's decisions, an individual state will be inclined to comply as well. This mechanism would also work in favour of widespread consent to the Court's jurisdiction, if such a norm were to exist.

A third factor is the outcome of a cost-benefit analysis. A multitude of variables may be relevant in this regard, such as whether and to what extent the state views the ICJ as a useful institution. The more that is the case, the more likely will that state support the Court in order to retain the (perceived) advantages of its activity for the future.[20] Another variable in this cost-benefit analysis is the stance taken by a state's internal actors. The higher the pressure to cooperate with the ICJ exercised, for instance, by domestic political actors, civil society and the judiciary, the more likely that state's cooperation becomes.[21]

Law 29, 37. Note that the degree of dependence varies according to how its jurisdiction may be established, see EA Posner and JC Yoo, 'Judicial Independence in International Tribunals' (2005) 93(1) *California Law Review* 1, 36.

[15] The enforcement mechanism provided by Art 94(2) UN Charter has yet to be used successfully.

[16] Note that jurisdiction and compliance are by far not the only means for states to influence the ICJ, see LR Helfer and A-M Slaughter, 'Why States Create International Tribunals: A Response to Professors Posner and Yoo' (2005) 93(3) *California Law Review* 899, 905 and 942–953, advancing a 'theory of constrained independence'.

[17] Commonly described by the term 'sociological legitimacy'. For US constitutional law, Fallon Jr furthermore distinguishes legal and moral legitimacy, RH Fallon, Jr , 'Legitimacy and the Constitution' (2005) 118(6) *Harvard Law Review* 1787, 1794–1801.

[18] R Goodman and D Jinks, 'How to Influence States: Socialization and International Human Rights Law' (2004) 54(3) *Duke Law Journal* 621, 638 and 643.

[19] Goodman and Jinks explicitly advance that this dynamic also applies to states, ibid, 646.

[20] This might apply with more force to states with lower prospects to successfully settle their disputes through diplomatic negotiations, such as weaker states in disputes with more powerful states.

[21] Note that the presence of strong national preferences speaking against compliance might influence the stance of domestic actors as well. On the role of domestic factors influencing state compliance with decisions of international courts and tribunals, see with further references A Huneeus, 'Compliance with Judgments and Decisions' in C Romano and others (eds), *The Oxford Handbook of International Adjudication* (Oxford University Press, 2014), 453–56.

Finally, the stance taken by the international community matters in this analysis.[22] Not cooperating despite a general expectation to do so would signal unreliability and disrespect for international law. States perceived as unreliable will likely face repercussions in the form of higher 'costs' for future transactions with other states, or even be confronted with the latters' unwillingness to conclude transactions in the first place. On the other hand, if there is a general expectation of cooperation among states, a state will reap the benefits if it lives up to this expectation. Cooperation will enhance its reputation among the international community, making advantageous transactions more likely.[23] Accordingly, the higher the peer pressure exercised by other states, the more likely a state's cooperation with the ICJ becomes.[24]

Whether the mechanism of acculturation works, and whether the cost-benefit analysis made by the states tilts in the ICJ's favour, depends on whether there is a general rule or expectation to cooperate with the Court by submitting to its jurisdiction and complying with its decisions in the first place.[25] Thus, the key for the Court is to create (and maintain) an atmosphere in which state cooperation with it becomes widespread and regular.[26] It can strengthen this cooperation expectation by working on the states' perception of its legitimacy, such as by relying on recognised methods of interpretation or by issuing 'morally right' decisions. What matters for the purposes of this study is that it may also do so by lowering the perceived cost of cooperation. In this regard, it is important for states to see that the ICJ sufficiently takes into account their (individual and shared) preferences.[27]

[22] HL Jones, 'Why Comply: An Analysis of Trends in Compliance with Judgments of the International Court of Justice since Nicaragua' (2012) 12(1) *Chicago-Kent Journal of International and Comparative Law* 57, 60–62.

[23] See on this in detail AT Guzman, *How international Law Works: A Rational Choice Theory* (Oxford University Press, 2008), 71–117.

[24] This is only a cursory presentation. Many factors influence whether a state will cooperate with international courts, and there is a vast body of literature on this, mostly on compliance, both with international law generally and decisions of international courts in particular. For instance, *Guzman* focuses on the 'three Rs of compliance': reputation, retaliation and reciprocity, ibid; in turn, *Llamzon* argues that the way in which the ICJ acquired jurisdiction is less relevant for the prospects of the parties' compliance, AP Llamzon, 'Jurisdiction and Compliance in Recent Decisions of the International Court of Justice' (2007) 18(5) *European Journal of International Law* 815.

[25] Dyevre also points out that 'international courts need the support of, at least, some state actors in order to secure … compliance', A Dyevre, 'Uncertainty and international adjudication' (2019) 32(1) *Leiden Journal of International Law* 131, 132.

[26] Similarly, JI Charney, 'Disputes Implicating the Institutional Credibility of the Court: Problems of Non-Appearance, Non-Participation, and Non-Performance' in LF Damrosch (ed), *The International Court of Justice at a Crossroads* (Brill Nijhoff, 1987), 303.

[27] See also in this regard *Posner* and *Yoo*, who have sparked a debate about the influence of an international tribunal's independence on its effectiveness. They posit that dependent tribunals are more likely to follow state interests, and therefore states rely on them more often and comply, Posner and Yoo, 'Judicial Independence in International Tribunals' (n 14), 27–28. While their hypothesis concerns a tribunal's institutional set-up, the point here concerns a tribunal's behaviour.

Among the preferences states have, the most important one is that the Court respects their national sovereignty. Visibly taking into account this concern may set in motion a self-reinforcing process. First, it is more likely that a state will cooperate with the ICJ when the Court respects this central value. Each instance of cooperation would further strengthen the dynamics of acculturation, and tilt the cost-benefit analysis more in the Court's favour.[28] Accordingly, each individual instance of cooperation would induce more states to cooperate with the Court in the future. However, this process also works the other way.[29]

Consequently, it is crucial that the Court adequately acknowledges sovereignty. Defining such a concept is difficult, but it is likely to be common ground among states that core national interests, as for instance national security, fall under that term. One way for the ICJ to acknowledge these interests would be to resort to judicial avoidance techniques whenever they are at stake. While 'avoidance [is often seen] as something that should be avoided',[30] the use of avoidance techniques enables the Court to not pass judgment on certain questions and thus to not antagonise the state(s) in question.[31] Perhaps, Judge Oda's observation in the *Nicaragua* case is the clearest expression of this rationale from the bench: '[I]t would in my view have been prudent for the Court, in the light of the merits of the present case, to find it a matter of judicial propriety not to proceed with a case so highly charged with issues central to the sensitive political relations of many States'.[32]

Of course, this is a fragile equilibrium to achieve. States do not invariably expect the ICJ to pay respect to sovereignty in such a substantial way, particularly

[28] Focusing on compliance with the ICJ's decisions, Schulte speaks of a 'self-fulfilling prophecy' in this regard, C Schulte, *Compliance with Decisions of the International Court of Justice* (Oxford University Press, 2004), 438; Jones makes a similar point, Jones, 'Why Comply' (n 22), 86.

[29] Considerations of this type presumably led *Janis* to conclude in 1987 that the ICJ should 'contemplate a doctrine of judicial restraint' when the likelihood of compliance seems slim. To him, instances of non-compliance 'display the Court in its weakest … role' and cause a 'loss in respect', MW Janis, 'Somber Reflections on the Compulsory Jurisdiction of the International Court' (1987) 77(1) *American Journal of International Law* 144, 146; see also Charney, 'Disputes Implicating the Institutional Credibility of the Court' (n 26), 305–06. Writing in 1991, Hahn draws the connection between the ICJ's loss of importance as 'World Court' and its consistent rejection of doctrines such as the political question doctrine, non-justiciability of disputes, or the distinction between legal and political disputes: 'States do walk away from international judicial proceedings when they perceive that their vital interests are not sufficiently appreciated … [W]hile the ICJ has – some think in a rather cavalier fashion – never accepted those concepts in its case law, it has, perhaps not coincidentally, lost much of its importance as a "World Court"', MJ Hahn, 'Vital Interests and the Law of GATT: An Analysis of GATT's Security Exception' (1991) 12(3) *Michigan Journal of International Law* 558, 613. Focusing on courts' strategies to improve compliance, Dothan speaks of their 'reputational capital', S Dothan, *Reputation and Judicial Tactics: A Theory of National and International Courts* (Cambridge University Press, 2015), 3, 7–10.

[30] Odermatt, 'Patterns of avoidance' (n 1), 224.

[31] EF Delaney, 'Analyzing Avoidance: Judicial Strategy in Comparative Perspective' (2016) 66(1) *Duke Law Journal* 1, 10; see also Odermatt, 'Patterns of avoidance' (n 1), 227. Borrowing from the political question debate in US constitutional law, he refers to these considerations as 'pragmatic' reasons, at 224. See also T Schultz and N Ridi, 'Comity and International Courts and Tribunals' (2017) 50(3) *Cornell International Law Journal* 577, 596–97, 604–06.

[32] *Military and Paramilitary Activities in and against Nicaragua (Nicaragua v United States of America)*, ICJ, Judgment (Merits), Dissenting Opinion of Judge Oda, 18.

when they appear before the Court as applicants. Relying too heavily on avoidance techniques may make states seeking resolution of their disputes reluctant to initiate proceedings before the Court.[33] In addition, it would put the ICJ at odds with its important role as enshrined in the UN Charter. Accordingly, overuse of avoidance techniques would result in a loss of relevance and credibility, also inducing states to settle their disputes elsewhere. Crawford addressed this issue in his role as counsel for Iran in the *Oil Platforms* case:

> [N]o doubt international law has to be applied realistically, and I suppose a court might hesitate before a major power which is invoking essential security interests to justify its behaviour. But for this Court the fundamental value is the rule of international law. States can hardly be expected to comply with international law – as they are constantly enjoined by the powerful to do – unless the powerful can themselves be called to account for their own actions by the same standards before a tribunal which has jurisdiction.[34]

Above all, these considerations make clear that the choice whether to resort to avoidance techniques requires strategic judicial considerations in each case. There is no magic formula.[35]

The following sections present some avoidance techniques available to the ICJ that may help it to achieve this equilibrium. At the outset, they can be divided into merits-avoidance techniques (section II) and issue-avoidance techniques (section III).[36] Merits-avoidance techniques enable the Court to avoid a pronouncement on the entire substance of a case (or request) and are available in the first phase of the proceedings.[37] Issue-avoidance techniques in turn enable the Court to give a decision on the substance or merits but to avoid a

[33] The hiatus in the Court's activities in the aftermath of the 1966 *South West Africa* judgment is a case in point.

[34] *Oil Platforms*, ICJ, Oral Proceedings of 17 February 2003, afternoon (CR 2003/5), 43, para 34 (Crawford).

[35] '[B]oth principle and pragmatism are necessary', Delaney, 'Analyzing Avoidance' (n 31), 8. Several scholars argue that in certain circumstances, international courts may even enhance their legitimacy by taking up highly politicised/controversial cases, see for instance S Caserta, 'Regional International Courts in Search of Relevance: Adjudicating Politically Sensitive Disputes in Central America and the Caribbean' (2017) 28(1) *Duke Journal of Comparative & International Law* 59. On the dangers of resorting (too readily) to a deferential standard of review, see for instance CE Foster, 'Adjudication, Arbitration and the Turn to Public Law 'Standards of Review': Putting the Precautionary Principle in the Crucible' (2012) 3(3) *Journal of International Dispute Settlement* 525, 557–58; E Bjorge, 'Been There, Done That: The Margin of Appreciation and International Law' (2015) 4(1) *Cambridge Journal of International and Comparative Law* 181, 190; see also, critical of the ICJ's avoidance of 'big cases' A Bianchi, 'Choice and (the Awareness of) its Consequences: The ICJ's "Structural Bias" Strikes Again in the Marshall Islands Case' (2017) 111 *AJIL Unbound* 81, 86.

[36] See already Davey, 'Has the WTO Dispute Settlement System Exceeded Its Authority?' (n 1), 96; Delaney in turn distinguishes three 'timeframes': ex ante, merits phase, and ex post avoidance mechanisms, Delaney, 'Analyzing Avoidance' (n 31), 5; finally, distinguishing avoidance of 'adjudication altogether' and the attempt to 'minimise the [decision's] political impact', Odermatt, 'Patterns of avoidance' (n 1), 222.

[37] ie, the preliminary objections phase in contentious proceedings, and the examination of jurisdiction and discretion to issue an opinion in advisory proceedings. The Court may also dispose of preliminary questions in contentious proceedings within the merits, Art 79 (10) Rules of Court.

pronouncement on certain issues during that examination. A third category will then be suggested, comprised of one avoidance technique: the use of deferential standards of review (section IV).[38]

II. PRONOUNCEMENTS SERVING AS MERITS-AVOIDANCE TECHNIQUES

Merits-avoidance techniques concern the question of whether the Court proceeds to a review of the merits at all, and tend to follow a binary, black-or-white logic. Resorting to a merits-avoidance technique enables the ICJ to clearly acknowledge that the matter be best settled in another (political) forum. Examples of merits-avoidance techniques include the denial of jurisdiction, the denial of standing, and the denial that there is a dispute to adjudicate upon.

According to Article 36(6) ICJ Statute, it is the Court that ultimately decides whether it has jurisdiction. As a result of this '*Kompetenz-Kompetenz*',[39] it enjoys a certain amount of factual latitude in this regard inasmuch as this provision puts the decision in the hands of the Court alone. This latitude creates the possibility of taking into account considerations of expediency.[40]

The two other examples of merits-avoidance techniques are available when the Court examines whether a claim is admissible. There, it evaluates whether 'even if [it] has jurisdiction … there are reasons why [it] should not proceed to an examination of the merits'.[41] Questions of admissibility relate directly to the Court's judicial character, of which it is the sole guardian.[42] Protecting this integrity can only be done on a case-by-case basis, again resulting in some leeway for the Court. As Shany observes: 'There may be occasions … when the exercise of jurisdiction would be undesirable from the viewpoint of an international court … Hence, international courts may prefer to avoid to adjudicate certain cases, and the rules of admissibility provide them with a legally valid method to [do so].'[43]

[38] On the use of avoidance techniques by other international courts and tribunals, see also the references at n 1.

[39] C Tomuschat, 'Article 36' in A Zimmermann and others (eds), *The Statute of the International Court of Justice: A Commentary*, 3rd edn (Oxford University Press, 2019), 109.

[40] Here defined as considerations of aspects going beyond what is part of the strictly legal realm. As Bedjaoui notes: 'A decision dictated by expediency is … one which, while remaining legal, is inspired by feelings of appropriateness, wisdom or prudence', M Bedjaoui, 'Expediency in the Decisions of the International Court of Justice' (2001) 71(1) *British Yearbook of International Law* 1, 3.

[41] *Oil Platforms (Iran v United States of America)*, ICJ, Judgment (Merits) of 6 November 2003, 29.

[42] *Northern Cameroons (Cameroon v United Kingdom)*, ICJ, Judgment (Preliminary Objections) of 2 December 1963, 29.

[43] Y Shany, *Questions of Jurisdiction and Admissibility before International Courts* (Cambridge University Press, 2016), 52, see also at 155, and 158–63.

A. Denying Jurisdiction

The judgment in the *Aerial Incident of 27 July 1955* case illustrates how a negative finding on jurisdiction[44] can serve as a merits-avoidance technique.[45]

Bulgarian fighter planes had shot down an Israeli civil aircraft that had intruded into Bulgarian airspace. All 58 people aboard the plane were killed, including American, British, Canadian, French, South African, and Israeli citizens. Many Western nations protested; the United States, the United Kingdom and Israel instituted proceedings against Bulgaria. Israel sought the Court's declaration that Bulgaria was responsible for the aircraft's destruction and the resulting loss of life and all other damage.[46]

The Court, however, accepted Bulgaria's claim that it did not have jurisdiction to adjudicate. It held that Bulgaria's declaration accepting the PCIJ's jurisdiction from 1921 had ceased to be in force with that court's dissolution, and that accordingly Article 36(5) ICJ Statute[47] could not confer jurisdiction on the Court when Bulgaria had joined the Statute by virtue of becoming a member of the UN in 1955. Furthermore, it drew a distinction between the signatory states present at the San Francisco conference in 1945, and all other states, to which Bulgaria belonged. According to the ICJ, Article 36(5) could not maintain

[44] Fitzmaurice pointed to 'the solution which such a finding [of lack of jurisdiction] may provide in those cases where the necessity of giving a decision on the merits would involve unusual difficulty or embarrassment for the tribunal', G Fitzmaurice, 'The Law and Procedure of the International Court of Justice, 1951–1954: Questions of Jurisdiction, Competence and Procedure' (1958) 34 *British Yearbook of International Law* 1, 12, at fn 3.

[45] Note that the finding on jurisdiction can also be used as an *issue*-avoidance technique: Excluding only one of several jurisdictional bases enables the Court to avoid certain issues. The *Immunities and Criminal Proceedings* case is an apt illustration of this point. In the case, the Court found in its judgment on the preliminary objections that it did not have jurisdiction over several of Equatorial Guinea's claims, thereby discarding a (substantial) part of the application. In consequence, it did not have to address whether France had violated international law by initiating criminal proceedings against the then Vice-President of Equatorial Guinea on charges of money laundering in its 2020 judgment on the merits. While the Palermo Convention does not expressly refer to the customary rules on diplomatic immunity from criminal jurisdiction, Equatorial Guinea had argued that Art 4 (1) of the Convention, which imposes on states parties a duty to 'carry out their obligations under this Convention in a manner consistent with the (principle) of sovereign equality', incorporated these rules. The Court, however, rejected this argument, *Immunities and Criminal Proceedings (Equatorial Guinea v France)*, ICJ, Judgment (Preliminary Objections) of 6 June 2018, 93–102. In a Joint Dissenting Opinion, Vice-President Xue, Judges Sebutinde and Robinson and Judge *ad hoc* Kateka asserted that the Court had jurisdiction also for this part of the claims, *Immunities and Criminal Proceedings (Equatorial Guinea v France)*, ICJ, Judgment (Preliminary Objections), Joint Dissenting Opinion of Vice-President Xue, Judges Sebutinde and Robinson and Judge *ad hoc* Kateka, 13–14, and 18–49. They stated that 'the majority have failed to identify or have avoided identifying the relevant criteria for determining whether the dispute falls within the provisions of the Palermo Convention' (para 9), thereby alluding to a possible desire of avoidance that might have motivated the majority's approach. Because denying jurisdiction had the effect of excluding certain issues only, it might more properly be categorised as an issue-avoidance technique in this context.

[46] *Aerial Incident of July 27th, 1955 (Israel v Bulgaria)*, ICJ, Judgment (Preliminary Objections) of 26 May 1959, 130.

[47] 'Declarations made under Article 36 of the Statute of the [PCIJ] and which are still in force shall be deemed, as between the parties to the present Statute, to be acceptances of the compulsory jurisdiction of the [ICJ] for the period which they still have to run and in accordance with their terms'.

the latter states' declarations in force and was not intended to. Consequently, the Court did not have to address Bulgaria's other preliminary objections, nor the merits of the case.[48]

However, the Court's reasoning is not entirely convincing, as a joint dissenting opinion by three judges indicates. For instance, had the Court considered the equally authentic French version of the ICJ Statute, it should have concluded that Article 36(5) indeed conferred jurisdiction upon the Court. The French version of Article 36 (5) reads: 'Les déclarations faites en application de l'Article 36 du Statut de la Cour permanente de Justice internationale *pour une durée qui n'est pas encore expirée*',[49] and thus only refers to the element of time – and not to other causes of termination, as the majority held.[50] Furthermore, the dissenting judges objected to the majority's position that the provision contained a distinction between the original signatory states and those that later acceded to the Statute.[51] During a time of tension and strained relations between the Western powers and the Eastern Bloc, however, proceeding the way it did enabled the Court to avoid adjudicating upon the merits of a politically sensitive case.[52]

B. Denying Standing

The Court also can turn a negative finding on standing into a merits-avoidance technique, as the *South West Africa* case[53] and the *NATO* cases show. In the

[48] *Aerial Incident of July 27th, 1955 (Israel v Bulgaria)*, ICJ, Judgment (Preliminary Objections) (n 46), 145.

[49] Emphasis added.

[50] *Aerial Incident of July 27th, 1955 (Israel v Bulgaria)*, ICJ, Judgment (Preliminary Objections), Joint Dissenting Opinion of Judges Sir Hersch Lauterpacht, Wellington Koo and Sir Percy Spender, 161–65; see also C Shachor-Landau, 'The Judgment of the International Court of Justice in the Aerial Incident Case between Israel and Bulgaria' (1960) 8(3) *Archiv des Völkerrechts* 277, 280–85; and AM Weisburd, *Failings of the International Court of Justice* (Oxford University Press, 2016), 113–15. It is also worth noting that in the *Nicaragua* case, the ICJ did recognise its jurisdiction based on Art 36(5) ICJ Statute, despite the fact that Nicaragua's declaration accepting the Permanent Court's jurisdiction never entered into force. It seems that the Court deliberately chose not to rely on a negative finding on jurisdiction as a means of avoidance in that case, *Military and Paramilitary Activities in and against Nicaragua (Nicaragua v United States of America)*, ICJ, Judgment (Jurisdiction and Admissibility) of 26 November 1984, 397–413; critical *Military and Paramilitary Activities in and against Nicaragua (Nicaragua v United States of America)*, ICJ, Judgment (Jurisdiction and Admissibility), Dissenting Opinion of Judge Schwebel, 11–47. Judge Oda spoke of 'the questionable loophole which the Court drilled into Article 36, paragraph 5', *Nicaragua (Merits)*, Judgment (n 32), Dissenting Opinion of Judge Oda, 70.

[51] *Aerial Incident of July 27th, 1955*, Judgment (Preliminary Objections) (n 50), Joint Dissenting Opinion of Judges Sir Hersch Lauterpacht, Wellington Koo and Sir Percy Spender, 175–86.

[52] See with a further reference Weisburd, *Failings of the International Court of Justice* (n 50), 325–26; Shany, *Questions of Jurisdiction and Admissibility before International Courts* (n 43), 123–24. On the potential of the finding of jurisdiction as an avoidance technique for the ECtHR, see S Dothan, 'Judicial Deference Allows European Consensus to Emerge' (2018) 18(2) *Chicago Journal of International Law* 393, 407–08.

[53] In the *South West Africa* case, despite the fact that the Court had dismissed all of South Africa's preliminary objections in 1962, inter alia that Ethiopia and Liberia would be lacking *locus standi*, it

latter cases, Serbia and Montenegro[54] had asked the Court to find that several NATO Member States had violated among others the prohibition of the use of force by bombing several targets on its territory.[55] In addition, it had requested the indication of provisional measures. To establish the jurisdiction of the ICJ, Serbia and Montenegro had invoked both Article 36(2) ICJ Statute and Article IX of the Genocide Convention.[56] The Court, however, refused to issue provisional measures, observing the lack of prima facie jurisdiction *ratione temporis* under Article 36(2) and the lack of prima facie jurisdiction *ratione materiae* under Article IX.[57]

However, when the Court went on to decide on the preliminary objections, it chose to rely on another finding to dismiss the cases: It held that Serbia and Montenegro did not possess standing under Article 35(1) ICJ Statute. The ICJ found that at the time of the filing of the applications, Serbia and Montenegro had not been a member of the UN and accordingly had not been a party to the

held in 1966 that the Applicants did not possess standing 'regarding the subject-matter of their claim' and rejected all claims without further enquiry, *South West Africa (Ethiopia v South Africa; Liberia v South Africa)*, ICJ, Judgment (Preliminary Objections) of 21 December 1962, 327; *South West Africa (Ethiopia v South Africa; Liberia v South Africa)*, ICJ, Judgment (Second Phase) of 18 July 1966, 4, 74–76, 99. Many believed that this approach had been motivated by the majority's desire to avoid pronouncing upon the highly politicised issues of the case, see for instance *South West Africa (Ethiopia v South Africa; Liberia v South Africa)*, ICJ, Judgment (Second Phase), Dissenting Opinion of Judge Jessup, 325; R Higgins, 'The International Court and South West Africa: The Implications of the Judgment' (1966) 42(4) *International Affairs* 573, 589–90; remarkably frank Bedjaoui, 'Expediency in the Decisions of the International Court of Justice' (n 40), 17; more recently, Kattan, looking specifically at President Sir Percy Spender, who had cast the decisive vote in 1966, has argued that Sir Percy had wanted to avoid the merits of the case 'at all costs' because of the self-determination 'elephant in the court room', V Kattan, '"There was an elephant in the court room": Reflections on the role of Judge Sir Percy Spender (1897–1985) in the South West Africa Cases (1960–1966) after half a century' (2018) 31(1) *Leiden Journal of International Law* 147, 147.

[54] During the proceedings, the applicant, Yugoslavia, changed its name to Serbia and Montenegro. For the sake of simplicity, and following the approach taken by the ICJ, the applicant will be referred to by that name in the discussion of this and the further cases involving that state.

[55] *Legality of Use of Force (Serbia and Montenegro v Belgium)*, ICJ, Judgment (Preliminary Objections) of 15 December 2004; *Legality of Use of Force (Serbia and Montenegro v Canada)*, ICJ, Judgment (Preliminary Objections) of 15 December 2004; *Legality of Use of Force (Serbia and Montenegro v France)*, ICJ, Judgment (Preliminary Objections) of 15 December 2004; *Legality of Use of Force (Serbia and Montenegro v Germany)*, ICJ, Judgment (Preliminary Objections) of 15 December 2004; *Legality of Use of Force (Serbia and Montenegro v Italy)*, ICJ, Judgment (Preliminary Objections) of 15 December 2004; *Legality of Use of Force (Serbia and Montenegro v Netherlands)*, ICJ, Judgment (Preliminary Objections) of 15 December 2004; *Legality of Use of Force (Serbia and Montenegro v Portugal)*, ICJ, Judgment (Preliminary Objections) of 15 December 2004; *Legality of Use of Force (Serbia and Montenegro v United Kingdom)*, ICJ, Judgment (Preliminary Objections) of 15 December 2004. Serbia and Montenegro had also filed applications against Spain and the United States. The Court, however, removed these two cases from the List due to a manifest lack of jurisdiction. As the Court's reasoning regarding the aspects at issue here is essentially the same in all the remaining decisions, for sake of simplicity, the following analysis will only refer to the case against the Netherlands.

[56] Note that Serbia and Montenegro had invoked additional grounds for jurisdiction in the proceedings against Belgium and the Netherlands based on bilateral treaties.

[57] *Legality of Use of Force (Yugoslavia v Netherlands)*, ICJ, Order (Provisional Measures) of 2 June 1999, 22–30, and 34–41.

ICJ Statute by virtue of Article 93(1) UN Charter.[58] Furthermore, it held that the Genocide Convention could not give Serbia and Montenegro access to the Court by virtue of Article 35(2) ICJ Statute.[59] Consequently, the Court held that Serbia and Montenegro did not have access to the Court at the time of its applications, and dismissed all of them.

While the result, ie that the cases were discarded at this stage, did not come as a surprise, the justification employed by the Court in order to reach this result is conspicuous. Presumably, these cases would not have reached the merits stage in any event – the jurisdictional basis (both *ratione temporis* and *ratione materiae*) was too weak. However, while the decisions were issued unanimously, seven of the 15 judges criticised the majority for relying on this particular ground for dismissing the cases, among others because of its implications for other proceedings pending before the Court at the time, namely the *Bosnian* and the *Croatian Genocide* cases.[60] These cases had been brought by Bosnia and Herzegovina and by Croatia against Serbia and Montenegro in 1993 and 1999, respectively. The necessary implication of the finding in the *NATO* cases that Serbia and Montenegro did not have access to the Court between 1992 and 2000 normally would have been that the Court could not review the merits in those two proceedings as well.[61]

Thus, while the negative finding on standing in the *NATO* cases was not used as a merits-avoidance technique in this instance, it seems that the ICJ relied on this finding as a forward-looking avoidance technique – an avoidance technique that it could resort to in the *Bosnian* and the *Croatian Genocide* cases.[62] It needs to be mentioned, however, that when the Court eventually addressed the question of Serbia and Montenegro's access to the Court in the *Bosnian* and *Croatian Genocide* cases in 2007 and 2008, it refused to resort to this avoidance technique – it even went to considerable lengths to overcome this hurdle. In the *Bosnian Genocide* case, it did so in its merits judgment by basing itself on the principle of *res judicata*, having already concluded in its 1996 judgment on preliminary objections that it had jurisdiction.[63] In the *Croatian Genocide* case, the Court overcame this hurdle

[58] *Legality of Use of Force (Serbia and Montenegro v Netherlands)*, Judgment (Preliminary Objections) (n 55), 44–78, 90.

[59] ibid, 91–113.

[60] *Legality of Use of Force (Serbia and Montenegro v Netherlands)*, ICJ, Judgment (Preliminary Objections), Joint Declaration of Vice-President Ranjeva, Judges Guillaume, Higgins, Kooijmans, Al Khasawneh, Buergenthal and Elaraby, 13; *Legality of Use of Force (Serbia and Montenegro v Netherlands)*, ICJ, Judgment (Preliminary Objections), Separate Opinion of Judge Higgins, 18.

[61] See also S Olleson, '"Killing Three Birds with One Stone"? The Preliminary Objections Judgments of the International Court of Justice in the Legality of Use of Force Cases' (2005) 18(2) *Leiden Journal of International Law* 237, 243.

[62] For Olleson, 'the adoption of that particular chain of reasoning … has itself to be seen as the exercise of a conscious choice by the majority … fully aware of the potential implications for other pending cases', ibid, 254.

[63] *Application of the Convention on the Prevention and Punishment of the Crime of Genocide (Bosnia and Herzegovina v Serbia and Montenegro)*, ICJ, Judgment (Merits) of 26 February 2007, 80–141.

by invoking that it had in the past shown 'realism and flexibility in certain situations in which the conditions governing the Court's jurisdiction were not fully satisfied when proceedings were initiated but were subsequently satisfied, before the Court ruled on its jurisdiction', and argued that it was appropriate to apply this principle here because in 2000, Serbia and Montenegro had become a member of the UN and accordingly of the ICJ Statute.[64]

C. Denying that there is a Dispute

The finding that there is no dispute between the parties to adjudicate upon constitutes a third merits-avoidance technique available to the Court. One example for this can be found in the *Marshall Islands* cases. Other examples for dispute-related avoidance techniques can be found in the *Nuclear Tests* cases[65] and the *Georgia v Russia* case.[66]

In the *Marshall Islands* cases, the Marshall Islands brought forward claims against India, Pakistan and the United Kingdom, alleging that they were in violation of customary international law (in the case of the United Kingdom, also of Article VI of the Treaty on Non-Proliferation of Nuclear Weapons) because they had 'not pursued in good faith negotiations to cease the nuclear arms race' and

[64] *Convention on the Prevention and Punishment of the Crime of Genocide (Croatia v Serbia)*, ICJ, Judgment (Preliminary Objections) of 18 November 2008, 73–91.

[65] The *Nuclear Tests* cases revolved around French atmospheric nuclear weapon testing in the South Pacific region. The Court had already ordered France to refrain from any further tests. However, it did not reach a decision on the merits. Adopting a very narrow understanding of the dispute, the ICJ held that a dispute between the parties no longer existed and that the case was moot, *Nuclear Tests (Australia v France)*, ICJ, Judgment of 20 December 1974, 55–56, 59, 62; *Nuclear Tests (New Zealand v France)*, ICJ, Judgment of 20 December 1974, 58–59, 62, 65. Thereby, it avoided deciding whether or not nuclear atmospheric tests were in accordance with international law, Weisburd, *Failings of the International Court of Justice* (n 50), 326. For a discussion of the narrow definition of the dispute by the Court, see section III.A. below.

[66] *International Convention on the Elimination of All Forms of Racial Discrimination (Georgia v Russian Federation)*, ICJ, Judgment (Preliminary Objections) of 1 April 2011. This case can also be understood as an example for a dispute-related avoidance technique, if only indirectly. Properly speaking, the Court found it did not have jurisdiction because the prerequisite to have fruitless negotiations before being able to submit a dispute to the Court (Art 22 CERD) had not been fulfilled. It held that it is only possible to have those negotiations once a dispute had arisen. Ultimately, however, the ICJ reached its negative decision on jurisdiction because of its narrow way to construe the existence of a dispute. It held that no dispute relating to the CERD had existed from the period of 1990 to July 2008, and only had arisen in August 2008, immediately before Georgia had filed its application. Therefore, negotiations could have only taken place in a very short period, which the Court did not find to have been the case. Several individual judges were highly critical of this approach, pointing out that despite the 'thorny questions' on the merits raised by the application, the Court should have found that a dispute had existed much earlier and accordingly not have rejected the objection based on Art 22 CERD, *Application of the International Convention on the Elimination of All Forms of Racial Discrimination (Georgia v Russian Federation), Preliminary Objections*, ICJ, Judgment, Joint Dissenting Opinion of President Owada, Judges Simma, Abraham and Donoghue and Judge *ad hoc* Gaja, 4.

'negotiations leading to nuclear disarmament in all its aspects'.[67] Thus, over 40 years after the *Nuclear Tests* cases, and 20 after the *Nuclear Weapons* Opinion, the Court was again asked to pronounce on the thorny topic of nuclear arms.

However, as in previous proceedings, the ICJ 'decided not to decide'.[68] It held that a dispute between the parties did not exist, and accordingly dismissed the Marshall Islands' applications. Two points in the Court's reasoning were crucial for this finding. First, it introduced a new subjective criterion for a dispute to exist: The Marshall Islands needed to show that 'the respondent *was aware, or could not have been unaware*, that its views were 'positively opposed' by the applicant'.[69] Second, while the ICJ initially referred to its traditional flexibility by holding that '*[i]n principle*, the date for determining the existence of a dispute is the date on which the application is submitted', it then factually contradicted this position.[70] The majority's desire to avoid having to adjudicate on the merits was arguably the cause for both those findings.[71]

The doctrinal inconsistency of the majority's approach serves as an indicator for this. Contrary to the Court's position that the awareness criterion was already 'reflected in previous decisions', it arguably amounts to the creation of an entirely new jurisdictional precondition not based in previous case law.[72] What is more, the *Marshall Islands* cases mark a departure from the Court's

[67] *Negotiations relating to Cessation of the Nuclear Arms Race and to Nuclear Disarmament (Marshall Islands v India)*, ICJ, Judgment (Preliminary Objections) of 5 October 2016, 1; *Negotiations relating to Cessation of the Nuclear Arms Race and to Nuclear Disarmament (Marshall Islands v Pakistan)*, ICJ, Judgment (Preliminary Objections) of 5 October 2016, 1; *Negotiations relating to Cessation of the Nuclear Arms Race and to Nuclear Disarmament (Marshall Islands v United Kingdom)*, ICJ, Judgment (Preliminary Objections) of 5 October 2016, 1.

[68] TM Franck, 'Word made Law: The Decision of the ICJ in the Nuclear Test Cases' (1975) 69(3) *American Journal of International Law* 612, 613.

[69] *Marshall Islands (Marshall Islands v India)*, Judgment (Preliminary Objections) (n 67), 38; *Marshall Islands (Marshall Islands v Pakistan)*, Judgment (Preliminary Objections) (n 67), 38; *Marshall Islands (Marshall Islands v United Kingdom)*, Judgment (Preliminary Objections) (n 67), 41 (own emphasis).

[70] *Marshall Islands (Marshall Islands v India)*, Judgment (Preliminary Objections) (n 67), 39–40; *Marshall Islands (Marshall Islands v Pakistan)*, Judgment (Preliminary Objections) (n 67), 39–40; *Marshall Islands (Marshall Islands v United Kingdom)*, Judgment (Preliminary Objections) (n 67), 42–43 (own emphasis).

[71] Casas, while ultimately defending the Court's decision, argues that the reliance on the dispute requirement could be qualified 'as an escape device or, perhaps more accurately, a technique of functional non-justiciability' – 'a technique that allows the Court to reach the results usually produced by non-justiciability doctrines without having to expressly admit that it is deliberately declining jurisdiction over a case due to its subject matter. In other words, it is a technique that allows the Court to engage in the principled avoidance of a dispute without having to expressly admit to it', M Casas, 'Functional Justiciability and the Existence of a Dispute: A Means of Jurisdictional Avoidance?' (2019) 10(4) *Journal of International Dispute Settlement* 599, 611.

[72] Representative in this regard: *Negotiations relating to Cessation of the Nuclear Arms Race and to Nuclear Disarmament (Marshall Islands v United Kingdom)*, ICJ, Judgment (Preliminary Objections), Dissenting Opinion of Judge Yusuf, 20–23; *Negotiations relating to Cessation of the Nuclear Arms Race and to Nuclear Disarmament (Marshall Islands v India)*, ICJ, Judgment (Preliminary Objections), Dissenting Opinion of Judge Robinson, 23–40; but, coming to the opposite assessment, A Kulick, 'Let's (Not) (Dis)Agree to Disagree!? Some Thoughts on the "Dispute" Requirement in International Adjudication' (2020) 19(1) *The Law and Practice of International Courts and Tribunals* 79, 89–92.

'tradition of flexibility'[73] in jurisdictional aspects.[74] The Court had found in the past on several occasions that a dispute did exist, even if that dispute only 'clearly manifest[ed] itself during the proceedings', as long as there was a 'start or … onset of [the] dispute prior to the filing of [the] application'.[75] On this occasion, however, it chose instead to 'artificially stop the time of law and analysis at the date of submission of the request'.[76] Thereby, the ICJ refused to apply the established principle that it should overlook preliminary defects in an application if a new one would not be vitiated by the same defect, so as to avoid a circularity of procedure.[77]

Instead, it may have been the subject-matter that was ultimately behind the majority's approach.[78] The Marshall Islands' applications had posed a momentous challenge to the Court, a challenge to enter dangerous waters. Had the Court pronounced on the merits, it would have had to review the policy of nuclear deterrence, a cornerstone of the global security system. Furthermore, the application against the United Kingdom had involved the only Permanent Member of the UN Security Council that still accepted the Court's jurisdiction under Article 36(2) of the ICJ Statute. By dismissing the cases at the jurisdictional stage,

[73] *Negotiations relating to Cessation of the Nuclear Arms Race and to Nuclear Disarmament (Marshall Islands v United Kingdom)*, ICJ, Judgment (Preliminary Objections), Dissenting Opinion of Judge Crawford, 10.

[74] Judge Cançado Trindade observed that the ICJ thereby made '*tabula rasa* of the requirement that "in principle" the date for determining the existence of the dispute is the date of filing of the application', *Negotiations relating to Cessation of the Nuclear Arms Race and to Nuclear Disarmament (Marshall Islands v India)*, ICJ, Judgment (Preliminary Objections), Dissenting Opinion of Judge Cançado Trindade, 29.

[75] *Marshall Islands (Marshall Islands v United Kingdom)*, Judgment (Preliminary Objections) (n 72), Dissenting Opinion of Judge Yusuf, 39, see in general at paras 34–40; see also with further references to the Court's case law and the literature *Marshall Islands (Marshall Islands v United Kingdom)*, Judgment (Preliminary Objections) (n 73), Dissenting Opinion of Judge Crawford, 11–19.

[76] *Negotiations relating to Cessation of the Nuclear Arms Race and to Nuclear Disarmament (Marshall Islands v India)*, ICJ, Judgment (Preliminary Objections), Dissenting Opinion of Judge Bennouna, 315.

[77] *Croatian Genocide*, Judgment (Preliminary Objections) (n 64), 85; with further references *Negotiations relating to Cessation of the Nuclear Arms Race and to Nuclear Disarmament (Marshall Islands v United Kingdom)*, ICJ, Judgment (Preliminary Objections), Separate Opinion of Judge Tomka, 17–18; Judge Crawford calls this the 'Mavrommatis principle', *Marshall Islands (Marshall Islands v United Kingdom)*, Judgment (Preliminary Objections) (n 73), Dissenting Opinion of Judge Crawford, 9. Tellingly, the Court did not refer to the *Croatian Genocide* case in this decision. *Becker*, on the other hand, argues that three recent decisions before the *Marshall Islands* cases had indicated that the Court had already begun to embrace a more formalistic approach concerning the dispute requirement. Thus, in his view, the *Marshall Islands* cases 'did not mark a sharp break with recent practice', MA Becker, 'The dispute that wasn't there: judgments in the Nuclear Disarmament cases at the International Court of Justice' (2017) 6(1) *Cambridge International Law Journal* 4, 13. On the other hand, he also notes 'a gap between the rationale for the dispute requirement and how the Court enforces it', *ibid* 14; see 14–20.

[78] See Judge Xue, who, while voting with the majority, makes the broader point by expressing doubts whether questions such as the cessation of the nuclear arms race and the negotiation process on nuclear disarmament are at all justiciable, *Negotiations relating to Cessation of the Nuclear Arms Race and to Nuclear Disarmament (Marshall Islands v United Kingdom)*, ICJ, Judgment (Preliminary Objections), Declaration of Judge Xue, 16.

the ICJ avoided dealing with these sensitive issues, and avoided antagonising powerful states. In the eyes of several commentators, the Court made 'a deliberate choice not to entertain the case',[79] 'and [hid] its evasion behind a façade of formalist legal reasoning'.[80] The *Marshall Islands* decisions are regarded as an expression of the 'ICJ's trepidation to take jurisdiction over the "big cases"'.[81]

D. Conclusion on Merits-Avoidance Techniques

In the *Nicaragua* case, while dealing with contentions that the dispute was inadmissible, the ICJ observed that '[i]t must … be remembered that, as the *Corfu Channel* case … shows, the Court has never shied away from a case … merely because it had political implications'.[82] This statement implies that the ICJ has steadily rejected all claims for restraint that were based on the political nature of the matter. However, the cases discussed above represent instances in which it seems at least plausible that considerations of expediency and the desire to avoid hostile state reactions indeed motivated the Court to practise avoidance.[83]

Shany argues that such behaviour is not illegitimate per se, pointing out that 'case selection' serves as an 'important tool' for international courts: It enables them to secure support from the relevant stakeholders.[84] In the same vein, Prott observes that '[i]t would be rash to claim that … factual considerations play no part at all in the judges' processes of reasoning. Of course they do, and any organization which completely disregards the views of persons on which its continued existence as a functioning institution depends, is likely to destroy the social acceptance and support which alone confer authority and power on it'.[85]

Not relying on merits-avoidance techniques might be interpreted by the respondent as the Court's outright rejection of its (more or less) legitimate

[79] Bianchi, 'Choice and (the Awareness of) its Consequences: The ICJ's "Structural Bias" Strikes Again in the Marshall Islands Case' (n 35), 82; see also J von Bernstorff and others, 'Courts as Rhetorical Actors: A Rhetorical Analysis of Judicial Conflict Avoidance' (2021) 81(4) *Zeitschrift für ausländisches öffentliches Recht und Völkerrecht* 1001, 1021–22.

[80] N Krisch, 'Capitulation in The Hague: The Marshall Islands Cases' (2016), www.ejiltalk.org/capitulation-in-the-hague-the-marshall-islands-cases/; Alvarez-Jimenez infers that formalist reasoning 'was utilized as a dispute-avoidance technique', A Alvarez-Jimenez, 'The ICJ's Marshall Islands (Mis)judgments on Nuclear Disarmament' (2017) 45(1) *Syracuse Journal of International Law and Commerce* 1, 7.

[81] V-J Proulx, 'The Marshall Islands Judgments and Multilateral Disputes at the World Court: Whither Access to International Justice?' (2017) 111 *AJIL Unbound* 96, 101.

[82] *Nicaragua (Jurisdiction and Admissibility)*, Judgment (Jurisdiction and Admissibility) (n 50), 96.

[83] That being said, there are many further instances where the Court would probably have preferred to 'shy away', but nonetheless issued a decision on the merits, or acceded to the request for an advisory opinion. Besides the above-mentioned *Nicaragua* and *Croatian* and *Bosnian Genocide* cases, one can for instance point to the *Wall in the OPT* and the *Chagos* Advisory Opinions as an illustration of this, or to the *Oil Platforms* case.

[84] Shany, *Questions of Jurisdiction and Admissibility before International Courts* (n 43), 125.

[85] LV Prott, 'Avoiding a Decision on the Merits in the International Court of Justice' (1976) 7(3) *Sydney Law Review* 433, 444.

sovereignty concerns, and trigger adverse reactions on that state's part. The decision in the *Nicaragua* case serves an illustrative example of what a refusal to employ merits-avoidance techniques may trigger.[86]

On the other hand, the cases just discussed also highlight the inherent limitations of this set of avoidance techniques. Resorting to these techniques merely permits the Court to avoid a matter entirely, therefore forcing it to operate in a binary, black-or-white logic. Relying on them implicates the Court's institutional credibility to a significant extent and displeases the applicant side. Furthermore, other states might be less inclined to resort to the ICJ in the future. The Court's reliance on a merits-avoidance technique in the *South West Africa* case is a case in point. While some applauded this decision, it drew the 'far more vociferous displeasure of the other States and the rest of international opinion'.[87] The Court suffered from this instance of avoidance for several years, with only few states willing to bring new cases to the ICJ.

This shows that the all-or-nothing outcome associated with merits-avoidance techniques does not give the Court the flexibility it needs. Indeed, the resulting (rather crude) balancing act between state expectations and the ICJ's goals seems bound to leave one side dissatisfied – a feeling that might quickly become dangerous for the Court. Thus, the use of merits-avoidance techniques not only seems less suitable to help the Court garner support and strength, but rather risks leading to the opposite outcome.

III. PRONOUNCEMENTS SERVING AS ISSUE-AVOIDANCE TECHNIQUES

Even when proceeding to the substantial review of a case,[88] the ICJ may still exclude certain issues from its evaluation. Avoidance techniques in that stage include the restriction of the scope of review, practising economy of argument, and the finding of *non liquet*.

A. Restricting the Scope of Review

The *Kosovo* advisory opinion as well as the *Land and Maritime Boundary between Cameroon and Nigeria* and the *Certain Activities* cases show how the ICJ can use the restriction of the scope of review as an issue-avoidance

[86] Namely, withdrawal from the Court's compulsory jurisdiction. In *Crawford*'s view, '[t]he Court's authority and the system of the optional clause were shaken by the case – so far as the US was concerned, profoundly shaken', JR Crawford, 'Military and Paramilitary Activities in and against Nicaragua Case (Nicaragua v United States of America)' in R Wolfrum (ed), *Max Planck Encyclopedia of Public International Law* (Oxford University Press, 2012), 41.

[87] Bedjaoui, 'Expediency in the Decisions of the International Court of Justice' (n 40), 16.

[88] In contentious proceedings, this corresponds to the merits, in advisory proceedings, to giving an answer to the request.

technique. In the *Kosovo* opinion, the deeply divided UN General Assembly had asked the ICJ whether 'the unilateral declaration of independence by the Provisional Institutions of Self-Government of Kosovo [was] in accordance with international law'.[89] This embroiled the Court in highly controversial questions of self-determination, remedial secession, territorial integrity, and statehood. With the aim of asserting its judicial authority, it held that possible political implications did not constitute a reason to refuse to respond.[90] However, one may speculate whether such concerns did not in fact influence the Court majority: The opinion remained silent on self-determination and secession.

First, the ICJ did not expand the scope of the already narrowly framed question (despite several suggestions to that end),[91] which was however ambiguous in itself and would have allowed for a broader reading.[92] In addition, it is noteworthy that in the past, the Court had already affirmed its freedom to go beyond the strict terms of the question. In the *Certain Expenses* opinion (which the ICJ cited, albeit in a different context), in a very similar situation,[93] it had asserted that it 'must have full liberty to consider all relevant data … in forming an opinion'.[94] Self-determination and secession were highly relevant aspects of the *Kosovo* request. Second, the Court read the question in an even more constrained way, understanding 'in accordance with' as 'not in violation of'.[95] This made it possible to focus exclusively on the violation of negative prohibitions and to dodge the more salient issues, most notably the self-determination entitlement and the issue of remedial secession.[96]

The reactions to this silence have been varied. For several commentators, the narrow answer given by the Court was the only legitimate answer it could give. For instance, Pellet, analysing the Serbian choice to submit what was at face value a very narrow question, observed that '[t]he risk of playing a game is that

[89] *Accordance with International Law of the Unilateral Declaration of Independence in Respect of Kosovo*, ICJ, Advisory Opinion of 22 July 2010, 1.

[90] ibid, 35. It is noteworthy in this connection that the ICJ has so far never declined to respond to a request for an advisory opinion, P D'Argent, 'Article 65' in A Zimmermann and others (eds), *The Statute of the International Court of Justice: A Commentary*, 3rd edn (Oxford University Press, 2019), 35. In the recent *Chagos Islands* opinion, the ICJ also confidently rejected arguments that it should decline to issue the opinion requested by the UN General Assembly. Among others, the United Kingdom had argued that issuing the opinion would be improper because advisory proceedings would be unsuitable to resolve complex factual questions, and because the request would circumvent the principle of state consent. The Court also resisted calls to restrict the scope of review to provide a more limited response, *Chagos Islands*, Advisory Opinion (n 13), 63–91 and 133–37.

[91] *Kosovo*, Advisory Opinion (n 89), 49–56.

[92] See on this also Bernstorff and others, 'Courts as Rhetorical Actors' (n 79), 1014.

[93] In both instances, a majority of states had rejected attempts by individual states to enlarge the question submitted (France in *Certain Expenses*, Serbia in *Kosovo*).

[94] *Certain Expenses of the United Nations*, ICJ, Advisory Opinion of 20 July 1962, 157; see further *Arrest Warrant of 11 April 2000 (the Congo v Belgium)*, ICJ, Judgment, Joint Separate Opinion of Judges Higgins, Kooijmans and Buergenthal, 13–15.

[95] *Kosovo*, Advisory Opinion (n 89), 56 and 83.

[96] R Wilde, 'Kosovo (Advisory Opinion)' in R Wolfrum (ed), *Max Planck Encyclopedia of Public International Law* (Oxford University Press, 2012), 14; T Burri, 'The Kosovo Opinion and Secession: The Sounds of Silence and Missing Links' (2010) 11(8) *German Law Journal* 881, 885–86.

you may be taken at your own word. This is exactly what happened in this case. The Court strictly kept to the question asked – and rightly so.'[97] Others have taken issue with the decision, criticising that the Court 'answer[ed] the question asked in the most direct manner, and via the shortest available route'.[98] Several judges also criticised the Court for not dealing with the underlying issues of the request.[99] One commentator called the opinion 'a masterpiece of avoidance', achieved by 'stupefying formalism'.[100]

Several commentators explained the ICJ's approach with its general reluctance to delve into unsolved issues of 'high politics', where the Court faces a dilemma: It has to assert its authority without deciding in a way that might not find the states' acceptance.[101] Answering the question but sidestepping the major issues might just have been the way out for the Court. Whether the opinion issued was appropriate or not, it is clear that a more assertive answer would not have been legally precluded. The ICJ had a choice, and it made a choice.[102]

By focusing on what it identifies as the central aspect of the dispute, the Court may also avoid dealing with purportedly secondary, but potentially sensitive issues, as the *Nuclear Tests* cases have already illustrated. Here, Australia and New Zealand had asked the Court to 'adjudge and declare that … the carrying out of further atmospheric nuclear weapon tests in the South Pacific Ocean is not consistent with … international law' and to order 'that the French Republic shall not carry out any further such tests', respectively to 'adjudge and declare … [t]hat the conduct by the French Government of nuclear tests in the South Pacific region … constitutes a violation of New Zealand's rights … , and that these rights will be violated by any further such tests'. The ICJ, however, observed with respect to Australia that 'although the Applicant has … used the traditional formula of asking the Court "to adjudge and declare" … the original

[97] A Pellet, 'Kosovo – The Questions Not Asked' in M Milanovic and M Wood (eds), *The Law and Politics of the Kosovo Advisory Opinion* (Oxford University Press, 2015), 269; for Hannum, the Court's answer was 'certainly a plausible (if not inevitable) response to the question actually posed', H Hannum, 'The Advisory Opinion on Kosovo: An Opportunity Lost, or a Poisoned Chalice Refused?' (2011) 24(1) *Leiden Journal of International Law* 155, 155–56.

[98] M Weller, 'Modesty Can Be a Virtue: Judicial Economy in the ICJ Kosovo Opinion?' (2011) 24(1) *Leiden Journal of International Law* 127, 130; in the same vein, Shany speaks of the Court's 'choice of a narrow as possible reading of [its] jurisdiction over the request', Shany, *Questions of Jurisdiction and Admissibility before International Courts* (n 43), 60.

[99] *Accordance with International Law of the Unilateral Declaration of Independence in Respect of Kosovo*, ICJ, Advisory Opinion, Declaration of Judge Simma, 1, 4–6, 10; *Accordance with International Law of the Unilateral Declaration of Independence in Respect of Kosovo*, ICJ, Advisory Opinion, Separate Opinion of Judge Sepúlveda-Amor, 33–35; *Accordance with International Law of the Unilateral Declaration of Independence in Respect of Kosovo*, ICJ, Advisory Opinion, Separate Opinion of Judge Yusuf, 4–5.

[100] TW Waters, 'Misplaced Boldness: The Avoidance of Substance in the International Court of Justice's *Kosovo* Opinion' (2013) 23 *Duke Journal of Comparative & International Law* 267, 270.

[101] Weller, 'Modesty Can Be a Virtue' (n 98), 133–34; with a similar explanation Waters, 'Misplaced Boldness' (n 100), 327–28.

[102] *cf* A Nollkaemper, 'The Court and its Multiple Constituencies' in M Milanovic and M Wood (eds), *The Law and Politics of the Kosovo Advisory Opinion* (Oxford University Press, 2015), 221.

and ultimate objective of the Applicant was and has remained to obtain a termination of those tests; thus its claim cannot be regarded as being a claim for a declaratory judgment', and chose a similar path in the case of New Zealand.[103] Thus, the ICJ construed the true subject of the dispute as merely relating to the termination of the nuclear tests.[104] The *Land and Maritime Boundary between Cameroon and Nigeria* and the *Certain Activities* cases are more recent examples for such an approach. While both these cases mainly concerned the boundary delimitation between the respective parties, the issue of a party's use of force was brought up in each of them as well. For instance, in *Cameroon v Nigeria*, Cameroon had also sought the Court's declaration that Nigeria had breached the prohibition of the use of force by invading and occupying parts of the disputed territory. In turn, Nigeria had inter alia submitted that it had acted in self-defence.[105] The ICJ, however, focused almost exclusively on the border delimitation issue. With respect to the use of force issue, it merely held that 'by the very fact of the present Judgment and of the evacuation of the Cameroonian territory occupied by Nigeria, the injury suffered by Cameroon by reason of the occupation of its territory will in all events have been sufficiently addressed. The Court will not therefore seek to ascertain whether and to what extent Nigeria's responsibility to Cameroon has been engaged as a result of that occupation'.[106] As *Gray* observes, the Court might have been sympathetic to Nigeria's argument that '[t]his case is not essentially about state responsibility: it is about title to territory'.[107] However, given the fact that both parties sought a declaration on this issue, the Court's succinct justification leaves something to be desired. Either way, the ICJ thereby avoided dealing with the potentially sensitive question of a state's international responsibility for the violation of the prohibition to use force.

Similarly, in the *Certain Activities* case, Costa Rica had alleged that Nicaragua had violated the prohibition of the use of force in the disputed territories, and had dedicated extensive attention to this issue in its pleadings.[108] Mirroring Nigeria's position, Nicaragua alleged that the dispute was essentially

[103] *Nuclear Tests (Australia v France)*, Judgment (n 65), 11, 30; *Nuclear Tests (New Zealand v France)*, Judgment (n 65), 11, 31.

[104] Also making the case for this instance being one of avoidance: John, 'Inarticulate and Unconscious' (n 1), 87–89.

[105] *Land and Maritime Boundary between Cameroon and Nigeria (Cameroon v Nigeria: Equatorial Guinea intervening)*, ICJ, Judgment (Merits) of 10 October 2002, 27, submission (e), and at para 311, respectively.

[106] ibid, 319.

[107] *Land and Maritime Boundary between Cameroon and Nigeria (Cameroon v Nigeria: Equatorial Guinea intervening)*, ICJ, Rejoinder of Nigeria of 3 January 2001, 15.2; C Gray, 'The Use and Abuse of the International Court of Justice: Cases concerning the Use of Force after Nicaragua' (2003) 14(5) *European Journal of International Law* 867, 883.

[108] *Certain Activities Carried Out by Nicaragua in the Border Area (Costa Rica v Nicaragua) and Construction of a Road in Costa Rica along the San Juan River (Nicaragua v Costa Rica)*, ICJ, Judgment of 16 December 2015, para 49 (2) (ii).

about the border question.[109] Quoting its holding in *Cameroon v Nigeria*, the Court seems to have agreed with Nicaragua. It found that 'given that the unlawful character of these activities has already been established, the Court need not dwell any further on this submission'.[110] Several judges criticised this silence on the use of force issue. For instance, Judge Robinson noted that it was 'the Court's responsibility, as the "principal judicial organ of the United Nations", to take on the sometimes difficult and sensitive task of identifying the contours of international law's prohibition of the use of force', quoting the Court's dictum in *Nicaragua* that 'the Court has never shied away from a case brought before it merely … because it involved serious elements of the use of force'.[111]

Thus, both the *Land and Maritime Boundary between Cameroon and Nigeria* and the *Certain Activities* cases are further examples for how the Court can turn the restriction of the scope of review into an issue-avoidance technique.

B. Economy of Argument

Another way to engage in issue-avoiding is through resort to 'economy of argument': The ICJ draws upon one specific issue or argument to decide the case, and leaves aside other issues raised without relevance for the outcome of the proceedings. Apart from the question of whether the Court may or should delve into these 'other' issues at all,[112] it is clear that one effect of this approach is that the ICJ avoids dealing with these – potentially sensitive – questions. One example for this is the *Arrest Warrant* case,[113] brought by the DRC against Belgium.

Asserting universal jurisdiction, Belgium had issued an arrest warrant for the then incumbent Congolese minister for foreign affairs. This prompted the DRC to turn to the ICJ, asking it to declare that Belgium should annul the warrant.

[109] *Certain Activities Carried Out by Nicaragua in the Border Area (Costa Rica v Nicaragua) and Construction of a Road in Costa Rica along the San Juan River*, ICJ, Oral Proceedings of 17 April 2015, afternoon (CR 2015/7), 49, para 23 (Pellet).

[110] *Certain Activities & Construction of a Road*, Judgment (n 108), para 97.

[111] *Certain Activities Carried Out by Nicaragua in the Border Area (Costa Rica v Nicaragua) and Construction of a Road in Costa Rica along the San Juan River (Nicaragua v Costa Rica)*, ICJ, Judgment, Separate Opinion of Judge Robinson, para 31, see also at paras 3, 30 and 64. Judge Robinson further diagnosed a 'reluctance of the Court in recent times to determine certain issues relating to the use of force', *ibid* at fn 42; see also *Certain Activities Carried Out by Nicaragua in the Border Area (Costa Rica v Nicaragua) and Construction of a Road in Costa Rica along the San Juan River (Nicaragua v Costa Rica)*, ICJ, Judgment, Declaration of Vice-President Yusuf; and *Certain Activities Carried Out by Nicaragua in the Border Area (Costa Rica v Nicaragua) and Construction of a Road in Costa Rica along the San Juan River (Nicaragua v Costa Rica)*, ICJ, Judgment, Separate Opinion of Judge Owada, paras 9–12.

[112] As Zarbiyev points out, the answer to this question depends on whether one sees the ICJ as a mere 'dispute-settler' or, borrowing an expression from Judge Lachs, rather as a 'guardian of legality for the international community as a whole', F Zarbiyev, 'Judicial Activism in International Law – A Conceptual Framework for Analysis' (2012) 3(2) *Journal of International Dispute Settlement* 1, 11–13; *Aerial Incident at Lockerbie (Libyan Arab Jamahiriya v United Kingdom)*, ICJ, Order (Provisional Measures), Separate Opinion of Judge Lachs, 26.

[113] *Arrest Warrant of 11 April 2000 (the Congo v Belgium)*, ICJ, Judgment of 14 February 2002.

Initially, the DRC had based its submissions on two different arguments – first, that the exercise of universal jurisdiction violated international law, and second, that the arrest warrant violated the diplomatic immunity of the accused. Its final submissions, however, only included the second strand, on which the Court exclusively based its judgment.[114]

Concerning the first stand, the ICJ held that the *non ultra petita* rule barred it from addressing this point in the operative part of the judgment. However, the Court noted that it could have addressed this issue in its reasoning if 'necessary or desirable', and also that it was logically prior to the question of immunity[115] – a point also stressed by several individual judges. In a plea to the Court to take up its role and provide guidance to the international community, three judges argued that indeed, addressing this issue would have been 'necessary'.[116] At the very least, the ICJ was not barred from addressing the issue of universal jurisdiction, and indeed did not think it was.

However, a pronouncement on this question could have produced unwanted consequences from the Court's perspective. Indicating that universal jurisdiction could be lawfully exercised could have destabilised the conduct of international relations and antagonised states with leaders under threat by this principle. In turn, the opposite would have dealt a serious blow to the enforcement of human rights and disappointed others. Perhaps fittingly, Cot finds the Court's decision to be an expression of 'judicial politics'.[117]

[114] ibid, paras 45, 51–55, 78(2). It is worth mentioning that political pressure exercised by further states whose officials had been the subject of criminal complaints has since then prompted Belgium to revise its universal jurisdiction legislation. It has thereby significantly limited the possibility to lodge further such complaints before its courts, see SR Ratner, 'Belgium's War Crimes Statute: A Postmortem' (2003) 97(3) *American Journal of International Law* 888, 889–92.

[115] *Arrest Warrant*, Judgment (n 113), para 46; Zarbiyev, 'Judicial Activism in International Law' (n 112), 12.

[116] *Arrest Warrant*, Judgment (n 94), Joint Separate Opinion of Judges Higgins, Kooijmans and Buergenthal, paras 3–5. The judges furthermore emphasised their view that 'the Court should not, *because one or more of the parties finds it more comfortable for its position*, forfeit necessary steps on the way to the finding it does make in the *dispositif*', para 13 (emphasis added); *Arrest Warrant of 11 April 2000 (the Congo v Belgium)*, ICJ, Judgment, Separate Opinion of President Guillaume, para 1. It is worth noting that the Court has on several occasions quite openly chosen not to follow this restrictive approach. The *Oil Platforms* case, discussed below, is an illustrative example.

[117] J-P Cot, 'Eloge de l'Indécision: La Cour et la Compétence Universelle' (2002) 35(1–2) *Revue belge de droit international* 546, 550 (own translation, in the original: 'politique judiciaire'). Wouters in turn speculates that '[t]he real reason may be that the judges were very much divided on this controversial issue', J Wouters, 'The Judgement of the International Court of Justice in the Arrest Warrant Case: Some Critical Remarks' (2003) 16(2) *Leiden Journal of International Law* 253, 263. The Court explicitly reserved itself the freedom to rely on this economy of argument in the *Guardianship of Infants case*, where it held that '[i]t retains its freedom to select the ground upon which it will base its judgment, and is under no obligation to examine all the considerations advanced by the Parties if other considerations appear to it to be sufficient for its purpose', *Guardianship of Infants (Netherlands v Sweden)*, ICJ, Judgment of 28 November 1958, 62. The Court thereby justified that it did not deal with a question relating to the existence of an *ordre public* exception in the 1902 Convention and the question whether the relevant Swedish law qualified as such. Several judges criticised the majority's silence on these questions, see for instance *Guardianship of Infants (Netherlands v Sweden)*, ICJ, Judgment, Separate Opinion of Judge Moreno Quintana, 102.

C. *Non Liquet*

A holding of *non liquet* – that a court cannot decide a question because there is a gap in the law[118] – can also serve as an issue-avoidance technique, as illustrated by the *Nuclear Weapons* Advisory Opinion. The UN General Assembly had asked whether 'the threat or use of nuclear weapons [was] in any circumstances permitted under international law'.[119] The Court did not decline to deal with this request (as it was urged to do),[120] and thus did not rely on a merits-avoidance technique to avoid a review entirely.

Core security concerns were at stake for virtually all states. For several of them, nuclear weapons were the cornerstone of their defence strategy, and they would have most likely ignored a Court decision finding that the use of these weapons was unlawful. Many other states in turn regarded nuclear weapons as their ultimate menace. Discarding the request was not a feasible option for the Court, with the *South West Africa* judgment still looming in the background.[121] There seemed no good way out. In short, this 'momentous'[122] question had the ICJ 'caught between a rock and a hard place'.[123]

It finally resolved the issue with its first ever finding of *non liquet*. The Court held that 'the threat or use of nuclear weapons would *generally* be contrary to the rules of international law', but that it '[could not] conclude *definitively* whether the threat or use of nuclear weapons would be lawful or unlawful in an extreme circumstance of self-defence, in which the very survival of a State would be at stake'.[124]

This pronouncement made it possible for both sides to claim their victory. As Chesterman pointed out, the decision might best be explained with judicial prudence exercised by a Court struggling to preserve its legitimacy vis-a-vis the states.[125] Koskenniemi observed in the same vein that '[t]he Court felt both the law *and its own authority* to be insufficient' for reaching a definite conclusion.[126]

[118] D Bodansky, 'Non Liquet' in R Wolfrum (ed), *Max Planck Encyclopedia of Public International Law* (Oxford University Press, 2012), para 1.

[119] *Legality of the Threat or Use of Nuclear Weapons*, ICJ, Advisory Opinion of 8 July 1996, para 1.

[120] ibid, paras 14–19. None of the nuclear weapon states supported the request. See also above ch 2, II.A.

[121] S Chesterman, 'The International Court of Justice, Nuclear Weapons and the Law' (1997) 44(2) *Netherlands International Law Review* 149, 161.

[122] R Falk, 'Nuclear Weapons, International Law, and the World Court: An Historic Encounter' (1996) 71(3) *Die Friedens-Warte* 235, at 248.

[123] D Akande, 'Nuclear Weapons, Unclear Law? Deciphering the Nuclear Weapons Advisory Opinion of the International Court' (1998) 68(1) *British Yearbook of International Law* 165, at 217.

[124] *Nuclear Weapons*, Advisory Opinion (n 119), para 105(2)E. (emphasis added).

[125] Chesterman, 'The International Court of Justice, Nuclear Weapons and the Law' (n 121), 161 and 167.

[126] M Koskenniemi, 'The Silence of Law/The Voice of Justice' in L Boisson de Chazournes and P Sands (eds), *International Law, the International Court of Justice, and Nuclear Weapons* (Cambridge University Press, 1999), 508 (emphasis added).

The opinion showcases another tool the ICJ can use to avoid an issue in order to preserve its authority as a 'political institution in a world of sovereign states'.[127]

D. Conclusion on Issue-Avoidance Techniques

While these three decisions can all be endorsed from a strictly legal point of view, the introduction of a certain measure of expediency in each of them is palpable. They also illustrate the specific potential of issue-avoidance techniques: They enable the ICJ to take on the case or request, while at the same time avoiding certain isolated issues (which may however lie at the very heart of the matter). Thus, rather than functioning in the binary, black-or-white logic of merits-avoidance techniques, they allow the Court to proceed with a more subtle distinction between those questions to be treated and those to be discarded from its scrutiny.

IV. DEFERENTIAL STANDARDS OF REVIEW AS A JUDICIAL AVOIDANCE TECHNIQUE

The use of both merits- and issue-avoidance techniques brings certain benefits for the ICJ. However, on a balance, these benefits are in most situations outweighed by the significant risks associated with them. The Court's use of them has often been perceived as an abdication of its role as the principal judicial organ of the UN, and has provoked negative reactions from various states, scholars, and civil society alike. The central deficiency of these avoidance techniques is that they do not generally allow the ICJ to strike a balance between the contradictory expectations of the UN Charter, the states, and civil society as delicately as would be necessary. In contrast, resorting to deferential standards of review renders this fine balancing possible. Additionally, this particular avoidance technique presents two further advantages: It allows the Court to reveal the policy behind the use of avoidance techniques, which contributes to building up trust among its constituency, and can form part of a strategy of judicial incrementalism, of particular use to gradually expand its jurisdictional reach.

First, resorting to deferential standards of review permits the ICJ to adjust the division of decisional power among the states and itself in a nuanced way. The standard of review ranges on a continuum and can take any form from *de novo* to complete deference towards the respondent state's assertions. Applying a deferential standard of review does not rule out a substantive review of the entire case or of the request a priori. Rather, it determines how this review should be carried out with regard to a specific issue. By adopting a deferential standard

[127] PW Kahn, 'Nuclear Weapons and the Rule of Law' (1999) 31 *NYU Journal of International Law and Politics* 349, 272.

of review, the Court may thus pronounce on a certain aspect, without however having to follow through to the last detail of it. Accordingly, resort to this notion allows it to make pronouncements on a certain aspect while still acknowledging the respondent state's assertions and concerns for its decision-making space. As a consequence, the ICJ may approach even sensitive questions while still avoiding findings that could prove damaging for its institutional stability.

By relying on this particular avoidance technique, the Court leaves some of the decisional power to the concerned state(s). This may for instance concern the question what measures are best suited to realise a certain policy goal, whether and what reaction is necessary to protect essential security interests, or how to best secure one's borders. Adopting a deferential standard of review, and thus to defer to the respective state's first-hand assessment to a certain extent, allows the Court to avoid getting involved with questions states see as forming part of their sovereign prerogatives without however having to flatly reject the application or request as a whole. Leaving space for assessment and manoeuvre to the (respondent) states signals the ICJ's respect for their prerogatives in certain, especially sensitive areas, and its recognition of the inherent limitations of its mandate.

This makes it possible to use deferential standards of review as a judicial avoidance technique that allows the Court not to avoid entire issues, but rather *issues within issues*. Because of this characteristic, resorting to this particular avoidance technique can preserve the benefits of using such a technique in the first place, while mitigating the risk of adverse reactions from the ICJ's larger constituency at the same time. It is a way for the Court to finely balance out the competing demands associated with its activity. Certainly, this avoidance technique is not a catch-all solution. There might be situations when the use of other, less balanced avoidance techniques is called for, just as the scalpel is not always the surgeon's first choice. At times, outright avoidance might thus be more sensible from the ICJ's institutional point of view. Yet, often enough, it is precisely the sort of fine balancing that would best serve the Court's interests.

As noted in chapter two, the states' concerns for their sovereignty are no less, if not even more acute today than they have been in the past. Adopting deferential standards of review represents a pragmatic way to address these concerns. Resorting to deferential standards of review allows the ICJ to introduce (legitimate) concerns of sovereignty into the equation – and indeed so in a much more balanced way than the other categories of judicial avoidance techniques, as it enables the Court to fine-tune the weight given to state sovereignty. Deferential standards of review introduce the possibility for gradations in tone and thus for leaving zones of legality for the state(s) while still allowing the ICJ to give answers that provide guidance for the international community. Thereby, the Court can follow its mandate and avoid the states' outright rejection at the same time.[128] Ultimately, a well-considered use of this avoidance technique might help

[128] On this point, see also Y Shany, 'Toward a General Margin of Appreciation Doctrine in International Law?' (2005) 16(5) *European Journal of International Law* 907, 922. Note that data suggests

to secure their support.[129] Expanding its jurisdictional reach and increasing its case load will enable the ICJ to take a more active role on the world stage, thus strengthening the global legal order as a whole.

Second, resorting to deferential standards of review as opposed to the other judicial avoidance techniques brings the possibility of publicity. This publicity is crucial for practising effective state expectation management. Even merely discussing whether to adopt a deferential standard of review could be beneficial. As seen above, the other avoidance-techniques tend to be rather opaque, and the Court often hides the motives for their (non-)application behind legalistic pretexts. Additionally, the way it applies these techniques is inconsistent. Both these factors make it difficult for states to anticipate the Court's use of these techniques in future proceedings. In contrast, the rationales for applying deferential standards of review have already been systematised by scholars and other international courts and tribunals. The arguments for and against deferential standards of review more openly acknowledge their normative roots, their link to the principle of sovereignty, and to the role and expertise of international judicial bodies.

By building on this edifice of ideas, the Court could lay out more openly its perspective on its own role. It could demonstrate political consciousness, rather than insisting on an artificial (and not very credible) distinction between the 'political' and the 'legal', and make its decisions more transparent.[130] This transparency is a key factor in making the Court's decisions more predictable for states. Better predictability in turn enables states to better assess the costs for cooperating with the ICJ. States will likely be more inclined to refer to the ICJ and submit to its jurisdiction if they can reasonably predict its behaviour.[131]

the ECtHR is increasingly using the margin of appreciation in such a way, MR Madsen, 'Rebalancing European Human Rights: Has the Brighton Declaration Engendered a New Deal on Human Rights in Europe?' (2018) 9(2) *Journal of International Dispute Settlement* 199; on the strategic potential of the margin of appreciation doctrine Dothan, 'Judicial Deference Allows European Consensus to Emerge' (n 52), 406–07; see further A Kavanagh, 'Deference or Defiance? The Limits of the Judicial Role in Constitutional Adjudication' in G Huscroft (ed), *Expounding the Constitution: Essays in Constitutional Theory* (Cambridge University Press, 2008), 203–04; on strategic considerations influencing investment tribunals when determining the standard of review C Henckels, *Proportionality and Deference in Investor-State Arbitration* (Cambridge University Press, 2015), 184–86.

[129] Making a similar argument for the use of the 'margin of appreciation' by the African Court on Human and Peoples' Rights with a view to securing more widespread Member State acceptance of the decisions of this jurisdiction, whose authority and legitimacy are, according to the authors, yet to be established, SB Traore and PAA Leta, 'La marge nationale d'appreciation dans la jurisprudence de la Cour africaine des droits de l'homme et des peuples: entre effeurements et remises en cause' (2021) 31(3) *Swiss Review of International and European Law* 317, 421, 439–45; on the possible use of deference by adjudicators as a 'tool of legitimation to build, maintain or defend their legitimacy', including for 'new adjudicator[s] or [those] whose decisions are under particular scrutiny', see also E Shirlow, *Judging at the Interface: Deference to State Decision-Making Authority in International Adjudication* (Cambridge University Press, 2021), 31–32.

[130] Corresponding to the legal dictum that 'justice should not only be done, but should … be seen to be done', *R v Sussex Justices* [1924] 1 KB 256, 259.

[131] On this point, see already CW Jenks, *The Prospects of International Adjudication* (Stevens & Sons, 1964), 106.

Thus, the transparency associated with resorting to the notion of standard of review can help the Court to build up trust and secure crucial state support.[132]

Third and finally, resort to deferential standards of review holds particular potential as a building block of a strategy of incrementalism.[133] An incremental approach is characterised by a gradual step-by-step instead of a rapid disruptive process. Simulating whether constitutional courts are more likely to build power through 'big breaks', ie, through deciding against the preferences of the political branch in high-profile cases from early on, or through 'baby steps', ie by proceeding cautiously in the beginning and gradually becoming more assertive vis-a-vis the political branch as the record of compliance improves, Schwartz finds that incrementalism 'is the best long-term strategy for building judicial power'.[134] Madsen argues that the ECtHR became the central institution for the enforcement of human rights that it is today precisely because of such an incremental approach. In his view, it exercised 'legal diplomacy' at a time when the Member States were still reluctant about the idea of a strong adjudicative human rights body, thereby managing to set in motion a process of legitimisation. Only later, under more favourable conditions, did the ECtHR take on a more assertive role vis-a-vis the Member States.[135] European law scholars have equally identified a strategy of incrementalism as one reason for the ECJ's success.[136] Finally, turning to the ICJ, Miles has noted that it has resorted to 'a certain incrementalism' with respect to provisional measures,[137] potentially in a similar attempt.

As outlined in the introductory part of this chapter, the Court is in many ways highly dependent on the states' goodwill and cooperation. Against this background, adopting an incremental approach to gradually build its power and gain the trust of the states, and thereby to expand its jurisdictional reach over

[132] Also arguing for transparency in connection with the standard of review determination, V Lanovoy, 'Standards of Review in the Practice of International Courts and Tribunals' in G Kajtár, B Çalı and M Milanović (eds), *Secondary Rules of Primary Importance in International Law: Attribution, Causality, Evidence, and Standards of Review in the Practice of International Courts and Tribunals* (Oxford University Press, 2022), 60; in turn, on the (un-)desirability of judicial candour about avoidance Delaney, 'Analyzing Avoidance' (n 31), 12–16; and second-guessing the conventional wisdom that judicial candour is both a virtue and a requirement, SC Idleman, 'A Prudential Theory of Judicial Candor' (1995) 73 *Texas Law Review* 1307.

[133] See already Shany, 'Toward a General Margin of Appreciation Doctrine in International Law?' (n 128), 922.

[134] A Schwartz, 'An Agent-based Model of Judicial Power' (2019) 9(1) *Journal of Law (Journal of Legal Metrics)* 21, 53; but see the aforementioned Caserta, 'Regional International Courts in Search of Relevance' (n 35), 95.

[135] MR Madsen, 'The Protracted Institutionalization of the Strasbourg Court: From Legal Diplomacy to Integrationist Jurisprudence' in J Christoffersen and MR Madsen (eds), *The European Court of Human Rights between Law and Politics* (Oxford University Press, 2011).

[136] See with further references Alter, 'The ICJ in Comparison' (n 14), 7; however, *Zglinski* makes the contradicting observation that 'the European judges are gradually scaling down their control of Member State acts and behave in an increasingly deferential manner in free movement law' instead of the other way around, Zglinski, *Europe's Passive Virtues* (n 1), 93.

[137] CA Miles, 'Provisional Measures and the "New" Plausibility before the International Court of Justice' (2018) 88 *British Yearbook of International Law*, 37.

them is a strategy worth of consideration. Because of the possibility to scale back the degree of deference in small steps along the continuum of deference, resort to the notion of standard of review fits an incremental approach particularly well. Following Burke-White and von Staden, the question which standard of review should be adopted in the absence of respective treaty or customary law is 'essentially a question of the *appropriateness* of such standard of review *for the specific institutional context in which the court or tribunal operates*'.[138] As the Court becomes stronger as an institution, nothing prevents it from gradually reducing the degree of deference over time when determining the applicable standard of review.

Consequently, in an 'ideal' world, resorting to avoidance techniques would not be necessary for the ICJ. In such a world, the Court would be respected, and its decisions would be implemented simply on the basis of its status in the UN system. However, reality is different. Due to the ICJ's institutional design, states have a decisive influence on its effectiveness, and this situation is highly unlikely to change in the future. In this environment, relying on deferential standards of review as an avoidance technique may be a pragmatic way for the Court to adapt to that reality.

To these observations, two caveats are in order. For one, one must not lose sight of the fact that this strategic argument in favour of deferential standards of review as a judicial avoidance technique does not amount to a claim that practicing judicial avoidance is always preferable for the ICJ in the first place.[139] First of all, strategic-institutional considerations themselves do not invariably call for deference. There may be situations where the exact opposite, (visible) self-assertion, would be advisable for the Court also from this perspective. *South West Africa (Second Phase)*, discussed elsewhere in this book,[140] is a case in point. The avoidance practised by the Court in that case led to a significant loss of trust in the Court especially among the newly-formed states at the time.[141] Visible self-assertion could have led to the opposite outcome. Another example pointing in this opposite direction is that of the Inter-American Court of Human Rights (IACtHR), which has been observed to have applied a rather strict standard of review overall from its early days on,[142] without destabilising effects. Second,

[138] W Burke-White and A von Staden, 'The Need for Public Law Standards of Review in Investor-State Arbitrations' in SW Schill (ed), *International Investment Law and Comparative Public Law* (Oxford University Press, 2010), 711.

[139] On the risks of overly avoidance for the judicial institution itself, see also Bernstorff and others, 'Courts as Rhetorical Actors' (n 79), 1031–32.

[140] See section II.B. above, and ch 4, section III.C.

[141] JR Crawford, '"Dreamers of the Day": Australia and the International Court of Justice' (2013) 14(2) *Melbourne Journal of International Law* 520, 536–37.

[142] G Candia Falcón, 'Standard of Review: Inter-American Court of Human Rights' in R Wolfrum (ed), *Max Planck Encyclopedia of Public International Law* (Oxford University Press, 2012), paras 7–13; see also P Contreras, 'National Discretion and International Deference in the Restriction of Human Rights: A Comparison Between the Jurisprudence of the European and the Inter-American Court of Human Rights' (2012) 11(1) *Northwestern Journal of International Human*

practising judicial deference is not a catch-all solution for international courts and tribunals for ensuring their continued stability. For instance, scholars have noted the 'marked self-restraint and deference to the states' exercised by the WTO Appellate Body.[143] And yet, in hindsight, this approach has been to no avail, with the Appellate Body now being defunct.

Furthermore, this strategic argument leaves aside considerations of a strictly legal nature. Ensuring rule effectiveness is a key factor in any judicial interpretation and application exercise. The aim to uphold the effectiveness of a legal rule may thus lead the Court to adopt a strict standard of review, thereby opposing strategic considerations pointing towards avoidance, lest to avoid abetting rule erosion. The ICJ's stance on the prohibition of the use of force is arguably a case in point for this overall weighing in operation.[144]

Nevertheless, if used with strategic wisdom, the use of deferential standards of review does little damage to the Court's standing, and leaves the effectiveness of the concerned rule intact. As such, it may prove particularly useful as a power-balancing tool, as a state expectation management device, and as an important building block of a strategy of incrementalism. Judicious resort to deferential standards of review thus seems to be one of the most promising options available for the ICJ to acknowledge states' interests in order to win their support and reconcile this concern with the fulfilment of its mandate as envisaged in the UN Charter in the medium and long term. To borrow an expression from *Bickel*: the use of deferential standards of review is a technique that allows the Court to '[grant] leeway to expediency without abandoning principle'.[145]

The following four chapters will turn to whether and how the ICJ resorts to such deferential standards of review, including as an avoidance technique.

Rights 28, 57–60, 82; and A Legg, *The Margin of Appreciation in International Human Rights Law: Deference and Proportionality* (Oxford University Press, 2012), 31–32.

[143] A Gattini, 'Judicial Discretion' in R Wolfrum (ed), *Max Planck Encyclopedia of Public International Law* (Oxford University Press, 2012), para 19.

[144] See the discussion especially of *Nicaragua* and *Oil Platforms*, ch 7, section I.A.

[145] AM Bickel, *The Least Dangerous Branch: The Supreme Court at the Bar of Politics*, 2nd edn (Yale University Press, 1986), 71.

4

Absence of Judicial Oversight

THIS MOST DEFERENTIAL standard of review is set apart from the other three – good faith, reasonableness, and *de novo* – in two regards: by its categorical nature, and by how the Court applied it. First, complete deference concerns the 'if', and the other three the 'how' of judicial evaluation. Accordingly, this standard of review raises a question logically prior to the manner of evaluation, one which cannot be answered by degrees. Second, for reasons to be laid out below, it plays but a very marginal role in the ICJ's jurisprudence. The Court only employed this standard in three proceedings, and it has since then revised its respective stance in two of these three instances. This is so even despite the fact that states regularly plead for complete deference, especially in the early stages of the proceedings, and thus that the Court should not evaluate their first-hand assessment in question at all.

This gap between the number of invocations of this most lenient standard of review and its very limited acceptance by the Court tells us something about its self-perception and the image it is trying to convey. To uncover this, this chapter operates a change of perspective. In contrast to chapters five to seven, it contains all proceedings in which states pleaded for the adoption of this standard of review, regardless of whether they were successful with that claim or not.[1]

As the analysis in this chapter shows, as a first rule, the Court is reticent to accept any inherent, unwritten limitations of its mandate: Rejection of complete deference constitutes the rule, not the exception. In 12 out of the 14 proceedings in which a state had pleaded for complete deference – thus in more than one-third of the proceedings open for standard of review arguments – the ICJ refused to accord that degree of deference. It did so without distinguishing between the claims based on a specific notion of state sovereignty and those based on considerations of relative institutional expertise. This proves that for the Court, there are in principle no matters inherently beyond its purview.

What is even more noteworthy is that it generally rejected the complete deference assertion explicitly. This was the case in nine out of the 12 instances of

[1] Incidentally, this means that the proceedings in which states unsuccessfully pleaded for the absence of judicial oversight standard of review will appear twice in the following presentation: in this chapter, and in the chapter on the standard of review the ICJ ultimately adopted. For the sake of brevity, the respective positions of the concerned states will not be laid out in full again on that second occasion.

rejection, and thus is the rule among the instances of affirmation of judicial oversight. The existence of this second rule manifests the ICJ's desire to send a clear signal of self-assertion to the states. It projects an image of strength and unwillingness to accept any unwritten limitations of its mandate. In the remaining three proceedings where it rejected the non-reviewability claim – *Corfu Channel*, *South West Africa (First Phase)*, and *Wall in the OPT* – the Court did not address the states' respective claims, but proceeded to a substantive evaluation nonetheless. Accordingly, here, one can speak of an implicit opposition of complete deference. This choice could among others be explained with the Court's desire not to confer legitimacy upon far-fetched non-reviewability claims.

However, a caveat is in order. The fact that the ICJ has almost always rejected the plea for complete deference does not mean that it discarded the underlying argument altogether. Thus, rejection of complete deference does not automatically translate to the subsequent adoption of the *de novo* standard of review. On the contrary, on several occasions, the Court incorporated the arguments underlying the non-reviewability claim to adopt a *somewhat* deferential standard of review – either good faith, or, more often, reasonableness. Thus, the ICJ has repeatedly accepted the underlying argument, yet refused to attach the same consequentiality to it as the respective states. The analysis of this phenomenon will be the subject of the two ensuing chapters.

Finally, there are three exceptional instances in which the Court did recognise that it could not review a state's first-hand assessment or measure: *Norwegian Loans*, *South West Africa (Second Phase)*, and *Nuclear Weapons*. These instances merit special attention, for their existence could suggest that the first conclusion above – that the ICJ recognises no inherent limitations of its mandate – has to be nuanced to a certain extent. Yet, as the analysis below shows, the significance of these three instances should not be overstated. The Court's almost abashed application of complete deference in these three proceedings does not challenge the existence of the rule that it finds no matter to be inherently beyond its purview. Furthermore, the ICJ has reversed its *Norwegian Loans* and *South West Africa (Second Phase)* non-reviewability findings in subsequent proceedings, where it held that it could examine the pertinent questions, despite a similar procedural situation. Thus, on the contrary, these three exceptions ultimately even corroborate the interpretation that the Court is eager to convey the impression of a self-assertive international judicial institution.

The following presentation will be structured in four sections. It deals first with state pleas for complete deference in the domain of national security interests (section I), before turning second to allegedly domestic matters (section II), third to allegedly political determinations (section III), and fourth and finally to allegedly scientific determinations (section IV). Where applicable, each of those four sections will be further broken down into the presentation of all occurrences of explicit rejection, implicit rejection, and the exception to the rule. This presentation will be followed by section V, summing up the conclusions to be drawn from this chapter.

I. NATIONAL SECURITY INTERESTS

The first category includes the seven proceedings in which the Court dealt with claims that it neither could nor should exercise judicial oversight over a state's determinations and assessments in matters concerning national security interests: *Corfu Channel*, *Nicaragua*, *Nuclear Weapons*, *Oil Platforms*, *Wall in the OPT*, *Mutual Assistance*, and *Diallo*.

A. Explicit Rejection

In four proceedings, the ICJ explicitly refuted the states' claims for complete deference. Among them, the *Nicaragua* and the *Oil Platforms* cases as well as the *Mutual Assistance* case stand out. The first two concerned the question of self-defence. As will become evident through a joint analysis of the pertinent passages in this and in the *de novo* chapter, what arguably motivated the Court's clear and conclusive rejection of any degree of deference was the desire to uphold the effectiveness of the prohibition of the use of force. In turn, the *Mutual Assistance* case concerned the application of a so-called 'self-judging' clause. Even there, the ICJ found that it could exercise oversight over France's application of that norm. At the same time, this finding signals a reversal of its position taken in the *Norwegian Loans* case.

i. Nicaragua

Taking the General Treaty for the Renunciation of War[2] as an example, Lauterpacht illustrated the tendency among states to argue that questions of self-defence would be incapable of judicial appreciation. As he explained, states had been claiming an exclusive right to decide for themselves whether the requirements of self-defence were met, and thus whether the notion of self-defence could justify their use of force in a given situation.[3] This phenomenon has persisted into the era of the ICJ. *Nicaragua* is a case in point. In an argument later picked up by France in *Nuclear Weapons*,[4] the United States advanced that

[2] General Treaty for Renunciation of War as an Instrument of National Policy, League of Nations Treaty Series 1929 (vol XCIV), no 2137, p 57.

[3] H Lauterpacht, *The Function of Law in the International Community* (Oxford University Press, First Published 1933, Reprint 2011), 186. Lauterpacht points to the US and the French declarations to the General Treaty for the Renunciation of War. Both had therein stated that every sovereign state 'alone is competent to decide whether circumstances require recourse to war in self-defence', see at 186, fn 1. As pointed out by Judge Koroma in his dissenting opinion in the *Nuclear Weapons* proceedings, the International Military Tribunal at Nuremberg had rejected the same contention, voiced by Germany in these proceedings, *Legality of the Threat or Use of Nuclear Weapons*, ICJ, Advisory Opinion, Dissenting Opinion of Judge Koroma, 561; *Trial of the Major War Criminals before the International Military Tribunal*, Vol I (1947–1949), 208.

[4] See ch 2, section II.A.

'the plea of collective self-defence … requires the Court to determine whether the United States was legally justified in adjudging itself under a necessity, because its own security was in jeopardy, to use force … Such a determination … involves a pronouncement on political and military matters, not a question of a kind that a court can usefully attempt to answer'. Questions relating to a state's security would 'fall outside the limits of the kind of questions a court can deal with', and not be capable of judicial appreciation.[5]

Judge Schwebel subscribed to this reasoning, if only with a certain reserve. He expressed doubts whether the ICJ really was 'in a position to adjudge the necessity of continued United States recourse to measures of collective self-defence'[6] and whether it could 'really judge, *by legal criteria*, whether the United States was right or wrong to reject [the "belated" affirmation of Nicaragua that it would not support the rebellion in El Salvador]'. While this would be a 'reasonable question', he doubted that it would be a 'justiciable question'.[7]

The Court majority declined to accede to this assertion. While not without its ambiguities, in sum, its approach makes clear that in its view, at least parts of the self-defence justification were open to a judicial appreciation. The ICJ observed that its examination of the reaction taken to a purported armed attack would not 'necessarily involve it in any evaluation of military considerations. Accordingly the Court can at this stage confine itself to a finding that, in the circumstances of the present case, the issues raised of collective self-defence are issues which it has competence, and is equipped, to determine'.[8] On the one hand, the ICJ thereby asserted its competence to evaluate whether the invocation of self-defence was justified. On the other hand, this observation may be read as implying that an 'evaluation of military considerations' would be beyond its purview.

Weisburd consequently views this statement as the ICJ's recognition of the difficulties associated with judicial review of self-defence.[9] However, as he further notes, the Court did proceed to evaluate military considerations when assessing whether Nicaragua's purported involvement in arms-trafficking could justify the United States' exercise of self-defence. There, the ICJ remarked 'in passing' that if the United States had had any evidence to prove such an involvement, it 'could be expected to have taken advantage of it in order to forestall

[5] *Military and Paramilitary Activities in and against Nicaragua (Nicaragua v United States of America)*, ICJ, Judgment (Merits) of 27 June 1986, para 34; see also Weisburd, who argues that the significance of certain facts in cases involving the use of force might not be apparent to individuals lacking military expertise. According to him, '[i]f decisions in such cases are made by persons lacking the necessary specialized knowledge, the results may be doubtful', AM Weisburd, 'Use of Force: Justiciability and Admissibility' in M Weller (ed), *The Oxford Handbook of the Use of Force in International Law* (Oxford University Press, 2015), 332.

[6] *Military and Paramilitary Activities in and against Nicaragua (Nicaragua v United States of America)*, ICJ, Judgment (Merits), Dissenting Opinion of Judge Schwebel, para 69.

[7] ibid, para 71 (emphasis added).

[8] *Nicaragua*, Judgment (Merits) (n 5), para 35.

[9] Weisburd, 'Use of Force: Justiciability and Admissibility' (n 5), 332, at fn 14.

or disrupt the traffic observed; it could presumably for example arrange for the deployment of a strong patrol force in El Salvador and Honduras, along the frontiers of these States with Nicaragua'.[10] Indirectly, this serves as proof of its conviction that it was not precluded from evaluating a state's respective considerations.[11]

Finally, and most importantly, the Court addressed the reviewability question through the prism of jurisdiction. Specifically, it pondered whether Article XXI para 1(d) of the US-Nicaragua Treaty of Friendship excluded its jurisdiction for 'the application of measures … necessary to protect [a Party's] essential security interests'. The ICJ rejected the contention that this provision was self-judging, and that in consequence, it would be precluded from evaluating a Party's reliance on that norm. Contrasting the norm with Article XXI GATT, it held that the fact that it—

> ha[d] jurisdiction to determine whether measures taken by one of the Parties fall within such an exception, is also clear *a contrario* from the fact that … the Treaty does not employ the wording which was already to be found in Article XXI [GATT]. This provision … contemplating exceptions to the normal implementation of the General Agreement, stipulates that the Agreement is not to be construed to prevent any contracting party from taking any action which it 'considers necessary for the protection of its essential security interests'… The 1956 Treaty, on the contrary, speaks simply of 'necessary' measures, not of those *considered* by a party to be necessary.[12]

Later, in the course of its evaluation of the lawfulness of the US trade embargo, it affirmed this point, observing that 'by the terms of the Treaty itself, whether a measure is necessary to protect the essential security interests of a party *is not… purely a question for the subjective judgment of the party*; the text does not refer to what the party "considers necessary" for that purpose'.[13] On the other hand, it thereby followed along the lines of the earlier *Norwegian Loans*

[10] *Nicaragua*, Judgment (Merits) (n 5), para 156.

[11] According to Judge Oda, the Court should have found the dispute to be non-justiciable because it 'is one which does not fall into the category of "legal" disputes within the meaning and intention of Article 36, paragraph 2, of the Statute' and because '[u]nder the United Nations system, where the maintenance of international peace and security falls within the functions of the Security Council … a dispute in which use of force is resorted to is in essence and *in limine* one most suitable for settlement by a political organ such as the Security Council', and 'not necessarily a justiciable dispute such as falls within the proper functions of the judicial organ.' In contrast, he asserts, '[i]t is definitely not [his] intention to have the Court declare, as a matter of principle, that disputes relating to use of force or intervention are non-justiciable, nor to contend that the Court is incapable of dealing with the present dispute once it is properly entertained', *Military and Paramilitary Activities in and against Nicaragua (Nicaragua v United States of America)*, ICJ, Judgment (Merits), Dissenting Opinion of Judge Oda, paras 17, 58 and 53 respectively.

[12] *Nicaragua*, Judgment (Merits) (n 5), para 222 (emphasis added).

[13] ibid, para 282 (emphasis added). Nicaragua shared this position. In its memorial on the merits, it stated that '[o]ne party to a treaty … cannot absolve itself of all responsibility for violations of the provisions of the treaty by simply invoking an exculpatory provision. *It is for the Court and not for the Parties to determine the validity of such assertions*', *Military and Paramilitary Activities in and against Nicaragua (Nicaragua v United States of America)*, ICJ, Memorial of Nicaragua (Merits) of 30 April 1985, 113 (emphasis added).

case in suggesting that states were due complete deference in their application of so-called 'self-judging clauses'[14] – a finding only reversed later in the *Mutual Assistance* case.

Accordingly, the ICJ rejected both manifestations of the non-reviewability contention in *Nicaragua*. It implicitly rejected the 'military considerations' assertion, and, more remarkably, it explicitly rejected the jurisdictional non-reviewability assertion.[15]

ii. Oil Platforms

Just as the *Nicaragua* case, *Oil Platforms* revolved around the question whether the ICJ could evaluate a state's measures purportedly taken to protect its

[14] See also in that sense S Schill and R Briese, '"If the State Considers": Self-Judging Clauses in International Dispute Settlement' (2009) 13 *Max Planck Yearbook of United Nations Law* 61, 98–99.

[15] In 2019, the first WTO panel report on the security exception in the GATT, Art XXI, was issued, which revolved around very similar questions. *Russia – Traffic in Transit* concerned the question whether Russia could invoke Art XXI (b) GATT. According to this provision, '[n]othing in this Agreement shall be construed … to prevent any contracting party from taking any action which it considers necessary for the protection of its essential security interests … taken in time of war or other emergency in international relations'. Russia, and the United States as an intervening party, had argued that the invocation of the security exception could not be subject to review by the panel. The panel refused to accede to this assertion, and instead opted for a differentiated standard of review. It applied a *de novo* standard when evaluating whether the measures in dispute had been taken in time of war or other emergency in international relations. In turn, for the question whether those measures were necessary for the protection of Russia's essential security interests, it applied a good faith standard of review. Accordingly, Russia had to 'articulate the essential security interests … sufficiently enough to demonstrate their veracity', and its measures had to 'meet a minimum requirement of plausibility in relation to the proffered essential security interests, i.e. that they are not implausible as measures protective of these interests', *Russia – Measures Concerning Traffic in Transit*, Report of the Panel (5 April 2019) WT/DS512/R, paras 7.134, and 7.138. On the standard of review for the requirement under Art XXI (b) (iii), see ibid, paras 7.53–7.126, on the chapeau of Art XXI (b), see generally ibid, paras 7.127–7.148. A detailed discussion on this case and the appropriate standard of review under Art XXI GATT is beyond the scope of this work. For a discussion of the case, see C Wang, 'Invocation of National Security Exceptions under GATT Article XXI: Jurisdiction to Review and Standard of Review' (2019) 18(3) *Chinese Journal of International Law* 695; D Boklan and A Bahri, 'The First WTO's Ruling on National Security Exception: Balancing Interests or Opening Pandora's Box?' (2020) 19(1) *World Trade Review* 123; V Lapa, 'The WTO Panel Report in Russia – Traffic in Transit: Cutting the Gordian Knot of the GATT Security Exception?' (2020) 69 *Questions of International Law* 5. Since *Russia – Traffic in Transit*, the security exception has been the subject of several other WTO disputes, for instance in *Saudi Arabia – Measures concerning the Protection of Intellectual Property Rights*, Report of the Panel (16 June 2020) WT/DS567/R, paras 7.229–7.294; and *United States – Certain Measures on Steel and Aluminium Products*, Report of the Panel (9 December 2022) WT/DS544/R, paras 7.102–7.149. For further discussions on the appropriate standard of review for the GATT security exception clause, see S Mantilla Blanco and A Pehl, *National Security Exceptions in International Trade and Investment Agreements: Justiciability and Standards of Review* (Springer, 2020); and the contributions referred to in MJ Menkes, 'The Legality of US Investment Sanctions against Iran before the ICJ: A Watershed Moment for the Essential Security and Necessity Exceptions' (2019) 56 *Canadian Yearbook of international Law/Annuaire canadien de droit international* 328, 353, fn 116 and 117; DA Desierto, *Necessity and National Emergency Clauses: Sovereignty in Modern Treaty Interpretation* (Brill/Nijhoff, 2012), 142, fn 67; finally, for the history of the GATT security exception, see M Pinchis-Paulsen, 'Trade Multilat-

security essential interests. The United States extensively addressed the applicable standard of review under Article XX (1)(d) of the US-Iran Treaty of Amity, a parallel provision to that at issue in *Nicaragua*, arguing that its attacks on Iran's oil platforms at issue could be justified as measures 'necessary to protect … essential security interests'. However, there was a marked difference between its position in the preliminary and in the merits stage. While the United States urged the Court to apply what essentially amounts to the application of a good faith standard in the merits phase, it argued for the (partial) non-reviewability of its invocation of Article XX(1)(d) in the preliminary objections phase.

Specifically, at this stage, the United States asserted that the ICJ could only evaluate whether the United States had used force in reaction to an actual threat to its national security interests. If that was the case, under Article XX (1)(d), the subject-matter would already be excluded from the reach of the Treaty of Amity, and thus beyond the Court's jurisdiction. Thus, according to the United States, the invocation of this provision should only be open to a partial judicial review. The ICJ could review whether the United States' assessment that its national security interests had been under threat had been well-founded. In contrast, this implies that the United States' first-hand assessment as to the necessity of the measures taken in response could not form the subject of its appreciation.[16]

The Court did not explicitly address this aspect in its judgment on the preliminary objections, as it held that Article XX(1)(d) did not per se exclude matters relating to the use of force from the Treaty. Accordingly, it concluded that it had jurisdiction.[17] Consequently, it did not have to deal with the standard of review-contention the United States had made. However, in its judgment on the merits, the Court returned to the non-reviewability assertion, and rejected it expressly, yet on a different normative level. It held that the interpretation of Article XX(1)(d) had to follow the customary law on self-defence.[18] Whether the invocation of the right to self-defence was justified, in turn, *was* subject to judicial review.[19]

eralism and U.S. National Security: The Making of the GATT Security Exceptions' (2020) 41(1) *Michigan Journal of International Law* 109.

[16] *Oil Platforms (Iran v United States of America)*, ICJ, Preliminary Objection of the United States of America of 16 December 1993, paras 3.36–3.42; Vice-President Schwebel seemed to agree with this standard of review, see *Oil Platforms (Iran v United States of America)*, ICJ, Judgment (Preliminary Objection), Dissenting Opinion of Vice-President Schwebel, 877–81; in the oral stage of the proceedings, the United States seems to have modified this position slightly, now arguing that all cases involving the use of force would be excluded from the ICJ's jurisdiction under the Treaty of Amity, *Oil Platforms*, ICJ, Oral Proceedings, of 17 September 1996, morning (CR 96/13), 55 (Chorowsky).

[17] *Oil Platforms (Iran v United States of America)*, ICJ, Judgment (Preliminary Objection) of 12 December 1996, paras 18–21; subsequently affirmed in *Alleged Violations of the 1955 Treaty of Amity, Economic Relations, and Consular Rights (Islamic Republic of Iran v United States of America)*, ICJ, Judgment (Preliminary Objections) of 3 February 2021, paras 109–10; and in *Certain Iranian Assets (Islamic Republic of Iran v United States of America)*, ICJ, Judgment (Preliminary Objections) of 13 February 2019, paras 45–47.

[18] *Oil Platforms (Iran v United States of America)*, ICJ, Judgment (Merits) of 6 November 2003, paras 39–42.

[19] ibid, para 73.

Accordingly, the ICJ left unanswered whether reliance on Article XX(1)(d) was beyond its purview in situations not involving the use of armed force. In turn, it explicitly rejected the idea that a state's exercise of the right to self-defence was.

iii. Mutual Assistance

As noted above, after the *Norwegian Loans* case, *Mutual Assistance* was the second ICJ case revolving around the question of whether the invocation of a norm formulated as a 'self-judging' clause could be subject to its review, and if so, by what standard. The term 'self-judging' describes clauses conferring a degree of discretion upon a state to determine whether certain circumstances are met, thereby triggering the possibility to exercise a certain right. Usually, this concerns the right not to comply with certain international legal obligations.[20]

Djibouti had unsuccessfully requested the transmission of a record in a criminal investigation from France. In consequence, Djibouti alleged, France had breached the bilateral Convention on Mutual Assistance in Criminal Matters by not complying with its request to execute its international letter rogatory. France, in turn, justified its refusal by reference to the 'self-judging' Article 2 c) of the Convention, according to which each party may refuse to execute a letter rogatory if it 'considers that [doing so] is likely to prejudice its sovereignty, security, *ordre public* or other of its essential interests'.[21] France claimed that national intelligence reports were contained in the records, the transmission of which would, even after their declassification, fall under this provision.[22] It asserted that its reliance on Article 2 c) could not form the subject of the ICJ's review, asserting that this provision assigned an 'exclusive power of appreciation' to the state invoking it, making it judge in its own cause.[23] Accordingly, it would solely be up to France to define its essential interests, and to decide whether these interests likely would be prejudiced by the execution of the request.[24]

In support, it pointed to the wording of the provision, further emphasised by the contrast to that in Article 2 b) of the Convention.[25] France further stressed the particular sensitivity attached to questions of criminal law and the close

[20] See R Briese and S Schill, 'Djibouti v France: Self-Judging Clauses before the International Court of Justice' (2009) 10 *Melbourne Journal of International Law* 308, 308; on self-judging clauses in investment arbitration, see M-A Bahmaei and H Sabzevari, 'Self-Judging Security Exception Clause as a Kind of Carte Blanche in Investment Treaties: Nature, Effect and Proper Standard of Review' (2023) 13(1) *Asian Journal of International Law* 97.

[21] Own translation, in the original: 'estime que l'exécution de la demande est de nature à porter atteinte à sa souveraineté, à sa sécurité, à son ordre public ou à d'autres de ses intérêts essentiels'.

[22] *Mutual Assistance in Criminal Matters (Djibouti v France)*, ICJ, Judgment of 4 June 2008, para 137.

[23] *Mutual Assistance in Criminal Matters*, ICJ, Oral Proceedings of 25 January 2008, morning (CR 2008/5), 10, para 9 (Ascensio. Own translation, in the original: 'pouvoir d'appréciation exclusif').

[24] *Mutual Assistance in Criminal Matters (Djibouti v France)*, ICJ, Counter-Memorial of France of 13 July 2007, paras 3.39–40.

[25] *Mutual Assistance*, Oral Proceedings of 2 November 1995, 10, para 9 (Ascensio).

nexus to national sovereignty, security and *ordre public*.[26] Finally, it addressed the ICJ's previous jurisprudence. First, it purported to show that Article 2 c) could be read in parallel with the self-judging reservation contained in its compulsory declaration that had been at issue in *Norwegian Loans*.[27] Second, France discarded the relevance of the *Rights of US Nationals in Morocco* case. It recognised that the Court had therein indeed laid down certain limits for the exercise of a right falling under a decision-making space. Yet, it noted that that case had concerned the execution of a treaty, and not the non-execution of a treaty, as was the case here. Furthermore, unlike the present case, *Rights of US Nationals in Morocco* would not have involved essential state interests.[28] Accordingly, France justified its non-reviewability contention by reference to three aspects: first, the self-judging wording of Article 2 c), second, the close nexus to national security and core state concerns, and third the Court's jurisprudence concerning comparable clauses, namely the *Norwegian Loans* case.

Despite France's partial retreat from this position in the final stage of the proceedings,[29] the ICJ addressed the non-reviewability assertion – and rejected it expressly. Referring to its previous judgments in *Nicaragua* and *Oil Platforms*, it concluded that it could oversee France's invocation of Article 2 c).[30] What is noteworthy is the tangible absence of any substantial justification for this. In addition, the Court's reference to *Nicaragua* is self-contradictory, for it seems to have departed from this jurisprudence rather than followed it. As explained above, in *Nicaragua*, the ICJ had contrasted the pertinent provision with Article XXI GATT and argued that it had jurisdiction because unlike Article XXI GATT, the provision in the US–Nicaragua Treaty of Friendship was not couched in self-judging terms. Article 2 c), in contrast, is formulated as a self-judging clause. Accordingly, following *Nicaragua*, one would have expected a non-reviewability finding for France's invocation of Article 2). On the other hand, as two commentators conclude, the finding that the application of self-judging clauses can be reviewed is in line with the jurisprudence of other international courts and tribunals.[31]

iv. Diallo

As already noted above, in *Diallo*, the respondent also argued with a specific conception of national security to invoke the non-reviewability standard of review.[32] What was at issue here was whether the DRC had violated Article 13

[26] ibid, 10, para 9, and 11, para 12 (Ascensio).

[27] ibid, 13, para 18 (Ascensio). For a discussion of that case, see below at section II.B.

[28] ibid, 12, para 15 (Ascensio).

[29] *Mutual Assistance in Criminal Matters*, ICJ, Oral Proceedings of 29 January 2008, afternoon (CR 2008/7), 57, at paras 15–18 (Belliard).

[30] *Mutual Assistance*, Judgment (n 22), para 145.

[31] Schill and Briese, '"If the State Considers"' (n 14), 96–113; to their examples, one may add the position of the WTO Panel in the *Russia – Traffic in Transit case*, already referred to above at fn 15.

[32] Ch 2, section II.A.

ICCPR by not allowing Mr Diallo, a Guinean national, to challenge his expulsion. According to Article 13 ICCPR, an alien 'shall, except where compelling reasons of national security otherwise require, be allowed to submit the reasons against his expulsion and to have his case reviewed'. The DRC objected to any review by the ICJ of its decision not to allow Mr Diallo such a challenge.[33] Effectively, it claimed that certain subject matters would be beyond the Court's purview due to their importance and corresponding link to the core of state sovereignty. The matter at hand would be such a case.

Not surprisingly, Guinea opposed this position. It argued that the *Nicaragua* case had shown that the Court had the power to control whether there had really been a threat to the DRC's national security. Guinea further observed that unlike the pertinent provision in the *Mutual Assistance* case, Article 13 ICCPR was not cast in self-judging terms. Accordingly, the security exception in Article 13 could not grant the DRC *carte blanche*.[34]

The ICJ decided in Guinea's favour. It recognised that '[i]n principle, it is doubtless for the national authorities to consider the reasons of public order that may justify the adoption of one police measure or another'. On the other hand, 'when this involves setting aside an important procedural guarantee provided for by an international treaty, *it cannot simply be left in the hands of the State in question* to determine the circumstances which, exceptionally, allow that guarantee to be set aside'.[35] This passage is noteworthy for what it does say, and for what it does not say.

First, what does it say? The ICJ recognises that in principle, there may be domains where it has no or a reduced role to play. Measures taken for reasons of public order or national security may be such domains. Two criteria for evaluating whether a specific decision is excluded from the Court's review can be discerned in this passage. The first is whether the national decision in question is subject to international regulation. The second criterion is the importance of the right protected by the international rule.

Second, what does it not say? The Court does not mention the subject-matter of the decision as defining factor for the degree of judicial deference. Contrary to what states have asserted on numerous occasions, the *Diallo* judgment implicitly makes clear that no national decision is beyond the Court's purview merely because of its subject-matter. Despite their close link to the core of state sovereignty, the Court does not hold itself to be precluded per se from reviewing decisions involving national security or public order.[36]

[33] *Ahmadou Sadio Diallo*, ICJ, Oral Proceedings of 26 April 2010 (CR 2010/3), 35, para 67 (Kalala).

[34] *Ahmadou Sadio Diallo*, ICJ, Reply of Guinea of 19 November 2008, paras 1.69 and 1.128.

[35] *Ahmadou Sadio Diallo*, ICJ, Judgment (Merits) of 30 November 2010, para 74 (emphasis added).

[36] Judge Cançado Trindade observes that the Court's rejection of the DRC's non-reviewability argument is in line with the relevant jurisprudence of international human rights bodies such as the Human Rights Committee, *Ahmadou Sadio Diallo (Guinea v the Congo)*, ICJ, Judgment (Merits),

The rejection of the DRC's respective argument becomes even clearer when one contrasts it with the separate opinion of Judge *ad hoc* Mampuya, who joined the DRC in arguing that certain categories of decisions would be removed from the ambit of judicial review solely by virtue of their subject-matter. He compared the security exception of Article 13 ICCPR with the parallel provision of the ECHR, Article 1 of Protocol 7, which would show 'that territorial authorities are recognised to enjoy a certain latitude … specifically, of [*sic*] a prerogative of a discretionary nature, which cannot be implicitly restricted, even by a suggestion that it is "arbitrary"'. Furthermore, in his view, 'only the territorial State is in a position to say what is and what is not "necessary in the interests of public order" or required for its "national security"'.[37]

B. Implicit Rejection

The Court only chose to refute the plea for complete deference concerning security-related judgments of the concerned states implicitly in *Corfu Channel* and *Wall*. Its choice for a tacit rejection in these two instances could be explained by its desire not to confer legitimacy upon the concerned state's non-reviewability arguments by addressing them in the first place.

i. Corfu Channel

The complete deference-claim already made its appearance in the very first contentious case decided by the ICJ: *Corfu Channel*. It opposed Albania and the United Kingdom in proceedings revolving among others around the right of foreign warships to pass through the Corfu Channel, part of Albania's territory. Albania claimed a right to prohibit that passage in 'exceptional circumstances', and asserted that its assessment that such circumstances had existed in the present case could not form the subject of the Court's review. While it did not detail what sort of 'special circumstances' it had found to exist, the context at the time makes clear that it alluded to considerations of national security.[38] Thus, Albania claimed that no one but itself could evaluate its own security needs and decide how to protect them. Consequently, the Court would have to defer to its respective assessment. Namely, Albania stated that it 'could rightfully invoke exceptional circumstances, and that *the right to assess whether these circumstances indeed existed rested with the*

Separate Opinion of Judge Cançado Trindade, paras 149–52. See on this point also the recent study on the application of the public policy exception by courts and arbitral tribunals in various international law regimes by Z Prodromou, *The Public Order Exception in International Trade, Investment, Human Rights and Commercial Disputes* (Wolters Kluwer, 2020), 206–07.

[37] *Ahmadou Sadio Diallo (Guinea v the Congo)*, ICJ, Judgment (Merits), Separate Opinion of Judge *ad hoc* Mampuya, para 13.

[38] *Corfu Channel (United Kingdom v Albania)*, ICJ, Judgment (Merits) of 9 April 1949, 29.

Albanian government'.[39] Its counsel made this point even more clearly in the oral proceedings, when he asserted that 'it is clear that *it is the State and the State only* that can evaluate whether there are exceptional circumstances'.[40]

The United Kingdom understood this for what it was: a claim to a self-judgment entitlement. During the oral proceedings, counsel rejected 'Albania's contention … that it is the sole judge of the "exceptional circumstances" on which it bases its claim to subject the passage of warships … to its prior permission. The decision whether to issue such special regulation is, of course, the sole decision of Albania; but others are entitled to complain and protest if that decision is an arbitrary cancellation of the right of innocent passage'.[41] Thereby, the United Kingdom seems to have argued that the Court could (at least) apply a good faith-type standard of review. Furthermore, it asserted that, notwithstanding the question whether coastal states had a right to prohibit the passage of foreign warships at all, such a right must, 'in any case … be a strictly limited one'.[42] This assertion lends further support to the conclusion that the United Kingdom opposed the non-reviewability standard invoked by Albania. The idea that the right of prohibition of passage could be exercised without the possibility of judicial supervision does not sit well with its puportedly 'strictly limited' character.

The Court rejected Albania's justification for its restriction of access to the strait even before addressing the non-reviewability assertion. It held that '[u]nless otherwise prescribed in an international convention, there is no right for a coastal state to prohibit [innocent] passage [of foreign warships] through straits in time of peace'. No such convention was identified by the ICJ. Consequently, it held that Albania did not have the right to prohibit the passage of UK warships through the Corfu Strait, regardless of the specific circumstances.[43]

Significantly, however, the Court also recognised that in principle, states have a right to issue regulations for such passage short of prohibitions or an authorisation requirement. In this connection, it implicitly dealt with – and rejected – Albania's non-reviewability contention. Pointing to the tensions prevailing between Greece and Albania at the time, it observed that 'Albania, *in view of these exceptional circumstances*, would have been justified in issuing regulations in respect of the passage of warships through the Strait'.[44] Had it held complete deference appropriate for regulations of passage, it would not have referred to

[39] *Corfu Channel (United Kingdom v Albania)*, ICJ, Counter-Memorial of Albania of 15 June 1948, 133–34 (emphasis added, own translation. In the original:' était bien fondé de se réclamer des circonstances exceptionnelles, dont le droit de juger de l'existence appartenait d'ailleurs bien au Gouvernement albanais').

[40] *Corfu Channel*, ICJ, Oral Proceedings (Merits), First Part, 380 (Pierre Cot, 18.11.1948, morning session. Emphasis added, own translation. In the original: 'il est bien évident que c'est l'État et l'État seul qui peut apprécier si l'on est en présence de circonstances exceptionnelles').

[41] ibid, 276 (Sir Beckett, 11.11.1948, morning session).

[42] *Corfu Channel (United Kingdom v Albania)*, ICJ, Memorial of the United Kingdom of 30 September 1947, 45.

[43] *Corfu Channel*, Judgment (Merits) (n 38), 28.

[44] ibid, 29 (emphasis added).

the exceptional circumstances as justification for them, for in that case, any qualification of Albania's assessment of that situation at the time would have been precluded. Rather, the Court would have either explicitly recognised that Albania's decision to issue regulations would (or could) not form the subject of its review, or it would not have examined the underlying situation at all. Yet, it chose to refer to – and assess – the situation that Albania had been facing at the time. Thereby, the ICJ made clear that it would assert the competence to evaluate whether a state could lawfully regulate the access to international straits.

ii. Wall in the Occupied Palestinian Territories

In the *Wall* proceedings, Israel took the position that its construction of the wall was justified as a means to halt terrorist attacks from the West Bank.[45] Yet, primarily, it argued that the situation would be beyond the Court's purview because of its exceptional complexity. Specifically, the ICJ would be lacking the necessary expertise to assess complex security threats and the appropriate reactions thereto. Yet, such an assessment would be indispensable to be able to answer the request by the UN General Assembly.

Namely, Israel asserted, answering the question would 'require an assessment of the nature and scale of terrorist attacks, the continuing nature of the threat, and the likely nature and scale of future attacks', 'an assessment of the specific nature of the threat to the Israeli population at different sections of the fence', 'an assessment of the routing of the fence', the evaluation of alternative routes and the resulting level of threat for Israel, and various questions pertaining to the alleged violation of certain human rights of Palestinians.[46] It contended that it would be simply impossible for the ICJ to answer such questions 'of such a complex and highly politicised character'. As a consequence, the Court would have to defer to its first-hand security assessment.[47] Simply put, in Israel's view, there would be certain questions a court of law cannot 'usefully attempt to answer' for lack of abilities – thereby echoing the position of another state invoking complete judicial deference in security-related domains: that of the United States in *Nicaragua*.[48]

Other participants in the proceedings opposed the non-reviewability standard as inappropriate. For instance, Madagascar 'refuse[d] to consider discretionary power one and the same as arbitrary power. A political decision freely and

[45] *Legal Consequences of the Construction of a Wall in the Occupied Palestinian Territory*, ICJ, Advisory Opinion of 9 July 2004, para 116.

[46] *Legal Consequences of the Construction of a Wall in the Occupied Palestinian Territory*, ICJ, Written Statement of Israel on Jurisdiction and Propriety of 30 January 2004, paras 8.3–8.4.

[47] Israel advocated this position especially with reference to advisory proceedings. Significantly, however, it also put in doubt the Court's capacity to address such questions in contentious proceedings. This makes clear that Israel wanted to make a general point not limited to a particular type of proceedings, ibid, para 8.7.

[48] See above at section I.A.

sovereignly taken must be implemented in a way which does not violate the rules of international law.'[49] This statement implies the possibility of international judicial review. Similarly, counsel for the League of Arab States emphasised that '[s]ecurity concerns are not a catch-all, sweeping consideration'.[50] Finally, counsel for Palestine asserted that it 'is not a matter within Israel's domestic jurisdiction and not a matter on which it has a sovereign privilege to act'. In its view, 'States cannot cast off all legal and moral constraints by merely calling on the name of "security interests"'.[51]

The Court agreed with these states. It observed that it disposed of extensive factual material and sufficient evidence to render the requested opinion.[52] In contrast, it apparently did not deem it necessary nor appropriate to deal with Israel's complexity-assertion properly speaking. The fact that it spelled out this evidentiary consideration yet left the main thrust of Israel's complexity/expertise-argument unaddressed is conspicuous. In the following, it proceeded to a substantive analysis of the legality of the construction of the wall, which further demonstrates that it attributed no merit to Israel's non-reviewability assertion. Arguably, one can interpret this silence as a manifestation of judicial self-assertion. By refusing to wade into a discussion about the limitations of its institutional competency, the Court could have wanted to signal that this discussion was without merit and did not deserve its attention.

C. The Exception: Implicit Acceptance in Nuclear Weapons

There is only one proceeding involving national security interests in which the ICJ – arguably – acceded to the plea for complete deference: the *Nuclear Weapons* advisory opinion. At the same time, this is the only one of the three proceedings in which it did so with implications beyond the individual proceeding.

As detailed in chapter two, several states had argued that the Court should exercise its discretion and decline to exercise its jurisdiction. Among others, they had claimed that the matter would be unsuitable for the ICJ because it would enter 'into the wider realms of policy and security doctrines of States' and be based 'on a set of very complex strategic judgements which go beyond the traditional competence of a body such as the Court',[53] because it would 'touch upon

[49] *Legal Consequences of the Construction of a Wall in the Occupied Palestinian Territory*, ICJ, Oral Proceedings of 24 February 2004, afternoon (CR 2004/4), 18, para 31 (Rambeloson).

[50] *Legal Consequences of the Construction of a Wall in the Occupied Palestinian Territory*, ICJ, Oral Proceedings of 25 February 2004, morning (CR 2004/5), 29 (Bothe).

[51] *Legal Consequences of the Construction of a Wall in the Occupied Palestinian Territory*, ICJ, Oral Proceedings of 23 February 2004, morning (CR 2004/1), 35, para 25 (Crawford), and 51, para 24 (Lowe).

[52] *Wall in the OPT*, Advisory Opinion (n 45), paras 57–58.

[53] *Legality of the Use by a State of Nuclear Weapons in Armed Conflict*, ICJ, Written Statement of Australia of 20 September 1994, paras 8–9; referred to in *Legality of the Threat or Use of Nuclear Weapons*, ICJ, Oral Proceedings of 30 October 1995 (CR 95/22), 29, para 3 (Griffith).

issues of fundamental political importance, ones where States' vital interests are involved'[54] and could not be properly assessed 'without such an assessment turning from a judicial into a political one',[55] and because the ICJ would be lacking the institutional expertise for analysing the 'extremely complex and controversial pieces of technical, strategic and scientific information'.[56] On the substance, several states had argued for the application of a somewhat deferential standard of review, especially in the proportionality assessment.[57]

At first sight, the addressee of these arguments largely appears to have ignored them. It concluded that the question was indeed a legal one, and that it was not concerned with the political implications of its opinion.[58] Turning to its discretion whether or not to issue an opinion, it only addressed – and rejected – contentions other than those just referred to.[59] Thus, again, the ICJ did not directly react to the assertion that the matter would be inherently unfit for judicial appreciation. This gives the appearance of another tacit rejection of the assertion that there are matters for whose consideration the Court would be lacking institutional expertise and legitimacy.

However, there are grounds to believe that ultimately, it did subscribe to these arguments. As discussed above, it found that it could not provide a definitive answer to the request, arriving at a *non liquet*. Effectively, the ICJ's reticence to establish concrete guidelines concerning the use of nuclear weapons made every

[54] *Legality of the Threat or Use of Nuclear Weapons*, ICJ, Oral Proceedings of 2 November 1995 (CR 95/24), 29 at para 3 (Hillgenberg).

[55] *Legality of the Threat or Use of Nuclear Weapons*, ICJ, Written Statement of Germany of 20 June 1995, 2; see also *Nuclear Weapons*, Oral Proceedings of 2 November 1995, 31, at paras 12, 14 (Hillgenberg).

[56] *Legality of the Threat or Use of Nuclear Weapons*, ICJ, Written Statement of Finland of 13 June 1995, para 1.

[57] For instance, India noted that 'reprisals must remain *within reasonable bounds of proportionality* to the effect created by the original act', *Legality of the Threat or Use of Nuclear Weapons*, ICJ, Written Statement of India of 20 June 1995, 2 (emphasis added); New Zealand observed that reprisals 'which lack a *reasonable* connection to legitimate objectives are inconsistent with international law', *Legality of the Threat or Use of Nuclear Weapons*, ICJ, Written Statement of New Zealand of 20 June 1995, para 70 (emphasis added); France in turn noted that the 'criterion of proportionality does not itself permit to rule out in principle the utilization … of any particular weapon whatsoever, particularly a nuclear weapon, provided that such use responds to an attack and appears to be the most appropriate means of doing so.' The usage of the word 'appears' also implies a somewhat deferential standard of review, *Legality of the Threat or Use of Nuclear Weapons*, ICJ, Written Statement of France of 20 June 1995, 29 (own translation, in the original: 'critère de proportionnalité ne permet pas en lui-même d'exclure par principe l'utilisation … de quelque arme déterminée que ce soit, et notamment de l'arme nucléaire, dès lors que cet emploi vise à faire face à une agression, et qu'il apparaît comme le moyen adéquat pour faire face à celle-ci'); finally, Nauru asserted that '[o]nly such amount of violence is permissible *as is reasonably proportionate* to the legitimate military objective sought to be achieved in the given military operation', *Legality of the Threat or Use of Nuclear Weapons*, ICJ, Written Comments of Nauru of 13 July 1995, 17 (emphasis added).

[58] *Legality of the Threat or Use of Nuclear Weapons*, ICJ, Advisory Opinion of 8 July 1996, para 13.

[59] Namely, that the question was vague and abstract, that the opinion would serve no useful purpose to the requesting organ, and that the opinion could undermine disarmament negotiations, ibid, paras 14–19.

state the (initial) judge in its own cause in an 'extreme circumstance of self-defence, in which the very survival of a state would be at stake'.[60] It is doubtful whether these conditions are at all amenable to judicial appreciation.[61] Several judges' individual statements furnish further indications that the majority felt the question to go beyond the Court's purview.

First, Judge Fleischhauer, while generally agreeing with the majority, observed that the judgment 'could ... and in [his] view should – have gone further'. Specifically, he emphasised that the 'principles and rules of the humanitarian law and the other principles of law applicable in armed conflict ... and the inherent right of self-defence ... [are not] above the law .... They are justiciable'.[62] The fact that he clarified this point shows that for him, the advisory opinion was at least ambiguous in this respect.

Judge Shahabuddeen in turn noted the conceptual overlap of the notion of 'an extreme circumstance of self-defence, in which the very survival of a State would be at stake' and the notion of 'vital security interests'.[63] This second term has historically been associated with questions deemed unsuitable for judicial appreciation.[64] Judge Shahabuddeen further explained that 'the inference could be that the Court is saying that there is a possibility that the use of nuclear weapons could be lawful in certain circumstances and *that it is up to States to decide whether that possibility exists in particular circumstances*, a result which would give me difficulty'.[65]

Finally, for Judge Koroma, the finding of *non liquet* amounted to recognising the states' non-reviewability arguments: 'That the Court cannot decide definitively whether the use of nuclear weapons would be lawful or unlawful when the survival of the State is at stake is a confirmation of the assertion that the survival of that State is not ... a matter for the law'.[66]

[60] ibid, para 105, (2)E. Concerning the finding of *non liquet*, see above at ch 3, section III.C.

[61] See also *Legality of the Threat or Use of Nuclear Weapons*, ICJ, Advisory Opinion, Dissenting Opinion of Judge Weeramantry, 435.

[62] *Legality of the Threat or Use of Nuclear Weapons*, ICJ, Advisory Opinion, Separate Opinion of Judge Fleischhauer, para 5. Judge Fleischhauer also states that in his view, '[f]or a recourse to nuclear weapons to be lawful, however, not only would the situation have to be an extreme one, but the conditions on which the lawfulness of the exercise of self-defence generally depends would also always have to be met. These conditions comprise ... that there must be proportionality ... The margin that exists for considering that a particular threat or use of nuclear weapons could be lawful is therefore extremely narrow', at para 6.

[63] *Legality of the Threat or Use of Nuclear Weapons*, ICJ, Advisory Opinion, Dissenting Opinion of Judge Shahabuddeen, 376.

[64] See above at ch 2, section I.

[65] *Legality of the Threat or Use of Nuclear Weapons*, ICJ, Dissenting Opinion of Judge Shahabuddeen (n 63), 376 (emphasis added).

[66] *Nuclear Weapons*, Advisory Opinion (n 3), Dissenting Opinion of Judge Koroma, 561. Judge Koroma also remarked that '[t]o suggest that [the right of self-defence] exists outside or above the law is to render it probable that force may be used unilaterally by a State when it by itself considers its survival to be at stake.... the Court's finding would appear to be tantamount to according to each State the exclusive right to decide for itself to use nuclear weapons when its survival is at stake as that State perceives it – a decision subjected neither to the law nor to third party adjudication', at 560.

Thus, in conclusion, there is some ground to believe that the ICJ ultimately adhered to the position of several states that the use of nuclear weapons would be incapable of judicial appreciation. By declaring that the law was lacking, it avoided the need to declare that it would be lacking the requisite institutional expertise and legitimacy for an evaluation itself.

D. Conclusion for National Security Interests

Taken together, these seven proceedings demonstrate two things: first of all, that the Court is unwilling to accord complete deference to a state's judgment in the domain of national security. In six out of the seven proceedings, it rejected doing so. The only exception is *Nuclear Weapons*.

Table 2 ICJ treatment of complete deference claims in proceedings relating to national security interests

Rejection of the claim for complete deference	Recognition of the claim for complete deference
• Corfu Channel	• Nuclear Weapons
• Nicaragua	
• Oil Platforms	
• Wall in the OPT	
• Mutual Assistance	
• Diallo	

The *Nuclear Weapons* opinion was, by all accounts, an exceptional case.[67] Its outcome disappointed many states who had hoped for a judicial ban of nuclear weapons, and was found to 'reflect … the precarious status of the Court in the international community generally and among the major powers in particular'.[68] The bench was divided on the substantial question, and the *non liquet* the product of this division.[69] Yet, at the same time, the opinion stands in a longer line together with *Nuclear Tests*, the parallel *Legality of the Use by a state of Nuclear Weapons in Armed Conflict* initiated by the WHO, and the *Marshall Islands* cases. Together, they convey the impression

[67] As Akande remarked, '[t]he Court … seemed destined to lose favour with a number of States. It was giving an opinion on what some States regarded as their ultimate security assurance and what others regarded as the ultimate menace and threat to humanity', D Akande, 'Nuclear Weapons, Unclear Law? Deciphering the Nuclear Weapons Advisory Opinion of the International Court' (1998) 68(1) *British Yearbook of International Law* 165, 217.

[68] S Chesterman, 'The International Court of Justice, Nuclear Weapons and the Law' (1997) 44(2) *Netherlands International Law Review* 149, 167.

[69] See R Falk, 'Nuclear Weapons, International Law, and the World Court: An Historic Encounter' (1996) 71(3) *Die Friedens-Warte* 235, 239.

that the ICJ considers itself ill-equipped and/or ill-legitimised to exercise judicial oversight over a domain of most eminent concern to states worldwide: the possession and use of nuclear weapons.[70]

Second, among those proceedings in which the Court refuted the non-reviewability plea, it chose to do so explicitly in four, and implicitly only in two proceedings (*Corfu Channel*, and *Wall*). Most notably, the ICJ chose explicit over implicit rejection in *Nicaragua*, *Oil Platforms*, and *Mutual Assistance*. The ICJ's rejection of complete deference for the right of self-defence in *Nicaragua* and *Oil Platforms* has to be read together with its subsequent adoption of the *de novo* standard in both cases. This combined analysis suggests that the ICJ was motivated by a desire to uphold the effectiveness of the prohibition of the use of force and the strictly limited character of the exception to that prohibition, the right of self-defence. To that end, it made its rejection of non-reviewability in *Nicaragua* and its adoption of the *de novo* standard of review in *Oil Platforms* explicit.

The *Mutual Assistance* case, on the other hand, is noteworthy in that even the 'self-judging' wording of a national security clause could not convince the ICJ to abstain from exercising judicial oversight. Accordingly, not even the combined forces, as it were, of subjective wording and the close nexus to core sovereignty concerns suffice to exclude a matter from its judicial purview. Furthermore, the case is a reversal of the *Norwegian Loans* and the *Nicaragua* judgments. By holding that the application of the 'self-judging' clause remained subject to its evaluation, the Court made clear that contrary to that earlier jurisprudence, it would not blindly accept the respective state's first-hand determinations.

Finally, there is the implicit rejection of the plea for non-reviewability in *Corfu Channel* and *Wall*. First of all, the Court could have chosen this way of rejection simply because the non-reviewability arguments and assertions were not the main points upon which Albania and Israel relied. Specifically, its silence regarding Albania's non-reviewability assertion could be explained by the fact that Albania failed to justify and develop its claim. In that situation, the Court might have deemed it unnecessary to address this mere assertion. Second, and speaking more generally – and this consideration is valid for *Wall* as well – the Court's choice for an implicit rejection could also be due to the fact that it did not want to participate in the discussion about its institutional limitations, as doing so could have weakened its standing. Addressing such an assertion – even if only to refute it – could send the signal that one gives at least some credit to it. Understood in that light, the ICJ's reticence to address these assertions and arguments appears as a silent but unequivocal rejection of the underlying assumption about its limitations.

[70] *cf* S Ranganathan, 'Nuclear Weapons and the Court' (2017) 111 *AJIL Unbound* 88.

II. DOMESTIC MATTERS

The second category concerns non-reviewability claims for measures that allegedly fall within the state's sovereign decision-making prerogative. The *Hostage* case is the only case in which the respondent made such a claim. In the *Norwegian Loans* case, the respondent, Norway, did not make a non-reviewability claim, and even explicitly recognised that the Court could oversee its invocation of the French 'self-judging' proviso contained in its declaration of compulsory acceptance. Yet, the ICJ implicitly adopted the non-reviewability standard. However, that case is an isolated incident for two reasons: First, it is the sole case where the Court acted on its own initiative in according complete deference to the concerned state, and second, and more importantly, it has since then reversed its non-reviewability finding for self-judging clauses in *Mutual Assistance*, discussed above.

A. Explicit Rejection: *Hostage*

In the wake of the Iranian Revolution, a militant group had attacked the US embassy and two of its consulates in Iran, and had taken US personnel and two private citizens hostage. Subsequently, the United States initiated proceedings before the ICJ, alleging among others that Iran had violated the Vienna Conventions on Diplomatic and Consular Relations, and the 1955 US–Iran Treaty of Amity.[71] As noted above, Iran, for its part, refused to take part in the proceedings. Nonetheless, it voiced its rejection of the Court's involvement in two letters addressed to the Court, wherein it effectively made a non-reviewability claim.[72]

The Court confidently rejected these superficial objections in the provisional measures stage. It held that while—

> it is no doubt true that the Islamic revolution of Iran is a matter 'essentially and directly within the national sovereignty of Iran'[,] a dispute which concerns diplomatic and consular premises and the detention of internationally protected persons, and involves the interpretation or application of multilateral conventions codifying the international law governing diplomatic and consular relations, is one which by its very nature falls within international jurisdiction.[73]

Thus, it treated the Islamic Revolution and the attacks as analytically separable, and held that it could evaluate Iran's conduct during the attacks on the US embassy and consulates.

[71] *United States Diplomatic and Consular Staff in Tehran (United States of America v Iran)*, ICJ, Judgment of 24 May 1980, 6–7, for the factual background see paras 12–18.

[72] See above at ch 2, section I.B.

[73] *United States Diplomatic and Consular Staff in Tehran (United States of America v Iran)*, ICJ, Order (Provisional Measures) of 15 December 1979, para 25.

In its judgment, the ICJ returned to the 'political character' of the dispute. It noted that 'legal disputes between sovereign states by their very nature are likely to occur in political contexts, and often form only one element in a wider and longstanding political dispute between the states concerned. Yet never has the view been put forward before that, because a legal dispute submitted to the Court is only one aspect of a political dispute, the Court should decline to resolve for the parties the legal questions at issue between them. Nor can any basis for such a view of the Court's functions or jurisdiction be found in the Charter or the Statute of the Court; if the Court were, contrary to its settled jurisprudence, to adopt such a view, it would impose a far-reaching and unwarranted restriction upon the role of the Court in the peaceful solution of international disputes'.[74] After *Admission of a State to the UN*, this can be read as a further affirmation that political aspects of a dispute do not render it unreviewable.

B. The Exception: Implicit Acceptance in *Norwegian Loans*

As noted above, *Norwegian Loans* was the first case in which the Court had to apply a clause couched in self-judging terms. The French compulsory declaration contained the so-called *Connally* reservation: The declaration did 'not apply to differences relating to matters which are essentially within the national jurisdiction *as understood by the Government of the French Republic*'.[75] Norway relied on this proviso by virtue of reciprocity and claimed that it understood the matter before the Court to be falling within its domestic jurisdiction. France challenged this point, and purported to show that Norway's invocation of the *Connally* reservation was objectively unjustified.[76]

Norway rejected this *de novo* standard of review, but did not argue that the reservation would make it the sole judge in its own cause. Rather, it accepted that the ICJ could evaluate its invocation of the clause, and proposed the good faith standard of review.[77] Thus, there was no dissent among the parties about the reviewability of Norway's invocation of that clause as such, but rather about the intrusiveness of that review.

[74] *Hostage*, Judgment (n 71), para 37.

[75] *Certain Norwegian Loans (France v Norway)*, ICJ, Judgment (Preliminary Objections) of 6 June 1957, 21 (emphasis added).

[76] ibid, 24; *Certain Norwegian Loans*, ICJ, Oral Arguments, Reply of the French Republic of 24 May 1957, afternoon, 181 (Gros).

[77] *Certain Norwegian Loans (France v Norway)*, ICJ, Preliminary Objections of Norway of 20 April 1956, para 26; Judge Basdevant also points out in his dissenting opinion that Norway's expression of its *conviction* that the matter fell within its domestic jurisdiction 'would have been unnecessary … if it had purported to confer upon its own understanding of the nature of the dispute a decisive character taking it outside the control of the Court'. In this case, it would have sufficed for Norway merely to state that it *asserted* that the matter fell within its domestic jurisdiction, *Certain Norwegian Loans (France v Norway)*, ICJ, Judgment (Preliminary Objections), Dissenting Opinion of Judge Basdevant, 73.

The ICJ did not address this difference of opinions. Instead, it merely held in a succinct statement that because of Norway's reliance on the *Connally* reservation, it lacked jurisdiction.[78] It does not become immediately apparent what led it to this conclusion. This silence could mean either of three things. First, the Court could have reached its conclusion by silently applying a *de novo* standard – as France had argued – and finding that Norway's reliance on the reservation was objectively well-founded. Or, second, the ICJ could have reached this conclusion by silently applying a good faith standard – as Norway had suggested – and come to the same result. Or, third, the Court could have reached this finding by completely deferring to Norway's assessment without any evaluation of its own, taking Norway's mere invocation of the reservation as decisive.

The better arguments speak for the third interpretation, as individual opinions by four judges make clear. The separate opinion by Vice-President Badawi, who voted with the majority, serves as a first demonstration in this regard. He held Norway's objection to be 'subjective in character', and remarked that it was 'conclusive' and 'ha[d] a formal and direct character *which precludes any argument*'.[79] These formulations are clear indicators that for him, Norway's mere invocation of the reservation automatically deprived the ICJ of jurisdiction, the 'subjective' invocation not being open to judicial review. Judge Lauterpacht viewed the French reservation in the same light, referring to it as an 'automatic reservation', that is, 'by virtue of it, the function of the Court is *confined to registering the decision made* by the defendant Government and *not subject to review by the Court*'.[80] This passage makes clear that he also understood the clause to leave no possibility of review.

Judge Basdevant's dissenting opinion lends further support to this interpretation. Concurring with Vice-President Badawi on this point, he observed that Norway's mere invocation of the French reservation 'was regarded by the Court as sufficient to preclude the compulsory jurisdiction of the Court'.[81] Finally, there is Judge Read's dissenting opinion. In his view, it would have been—

> necessary, for Norway to succeed, to establish that the Norwegian Government *understands* that the dispute relates to matters which are essentially within the Norwegian national jurisdiction. It is not sufficient to establish that the Norwegian Government *pretends to understand, or declares that it understands* that the dispute comes essentially within the scope of Norwegian national law. The text … does use language that suggests that it had in mind a genuine understanding.[82]

[78] *Norwegian Loans*, Judgment (Preliminary Objections) (n 75), 27.

[79] *Certain Norwegian Loans (France v Norway)*, ICJ, Judgment (Preliminary Objections), Separate Opinion of Vice-President Badawi, 29 (emphasis added).

[80] *Certain Norwegian Loans (France v Norway)*, ICJ, Judgment (Preliminary Objections), Separate Opinion of Judge Sir Lauterpacht, 34 (emphasis added).

[81] *Norwegian Loans*, Judgment (Preliminary Objections) (n 77), Dissenting Opinion of Judge Basdevant, 71.

[82] *Certain Norwegian Loans (France v Norway)*, ICJ, Judgment (Preliminary Objections), Dissenting Opinion of Judge Read, 94.

Rather, as Judge Read observed,

> the wording of the reservation … properly construed means that the respondent State, in invoking the reservation, must establish that there is a genuine understanding, i.e. that the circumstances are such that it would be *reasonably* possible to reach the understanding that the dispute was essentially national. *Whether the circumstances are such is not a matter for decision by a respondent Government, but by the Court.* But, assuming that such circumstances existed, the conclusion reached by a respondent Government could not be reviewed by the Court.[83]

In contrast to the ICJ majority, Judge Read thus concluded that the Court *could* review the invocation of the French reservation (namely by resort to the reasonableness standard).[84]

Consequently, the better reasons indicate that the ICJ chose not to evaluate Norway's invocation of the *Connally* reservation at all, and that it implicitly accepted it as it stood.[85] It did so even though Norway had conceded that it could conduct such a review. Thereby, the Court implicitly held that a clause granting the state a right to define for itself what it would regard as a matter of domestic jurisdiction in subjective language barred it from evaluating that assessment.[86]

[83] ibid, 94 (emphasis added).

[84] see also ibid, 95.

[85] Several contemporary writers also were of the opinion that the invocation of self-judging clauses such as the *Connally* clause was not subject to judicial review, see for instance A Larson, 'The Facts, the Law, and the Connally Amendment' (1961) 10(1) *Duke Law Journal* 74, 116; J Dixon, Jr. 'The Connally Amendment: The Conflict Between Nationalism and an Effective World Court' (1964) 53(1) *Kentucky Law Journal* 164, 170. There is yet one more indication for the correctness of this reading – a subsequent interpretation of this judgment by the Court itself, as it were. On the second occasion that the ICJ had to apply a self-judging clause, the *Mutual Assistance* case, it adopted the good faith standard of review. If the members of the bench at that time had estimated that the Court in the *Norwegian Loans* case had equally applied this standard, it stands to reason that they would have tried to bolster their stance by (approvingly) referring to the *Norwegian Loans* case, as is regular practice at the ICJ. However, no reference at all is made to this case in the *Mutual Assistance* judgment. Presumably, therefore, the judges felt that *Norwegian Loans* did not constitute a precedent supporting their position. Note that there are also other interpretations of the Court's standard of review. For instance, Corten argues that the ICJ *did* review Norway's invocation of the clause, and that it applied a resonableness standard of review, O Corten, *L'utilisation du "raisonnable" par le juge international: Discours juridique, raison et contradictions* (Bruylant, 1997), para 114; in the *Mutual Assistance* case, Djibouti also viewed the case in this light. However, this may be due to strategic considerations, for the adoption of the opposite reading would have harmed the case Djibouti was trying to make, *Mutual Assistance in Criminal Matters*, ICJ, Oral Proceedings of 28 January 2008, morning (CR 2008/6), 33, para 16 (Condorelli).

[86] A *Connally* clause-type reservation was invoked again only two years later in the *Interhandel* case. There, the respondent, the United States, invoked it in response to one of the Swiss claims. It asserted that its determination that the aspect was one 'essentially within its domestic jurisdiction' was 'not subject to review or approval by any tribunal.' Consequently, this claim would not be justiciable before the ICJ, the United States argued, *Interhandel (Switzerland v United States of America)*, ICJ, Preliminary Objections of United States of America of June 1958, 320. The United States did provide some background for its determination that the matter would fall within its domestic jurisdiction, but 'only for the information of the Court; their submission does not in any way modify the conclusion that the determination of the United States is not subject to review or approval by this Court', at 320. Presumably, the United States presented this as a fall-back mechanism in case that the Court were to reject the United States' non-reviewability argument and conduct

C. Conclusion for Domestic Matters

The fact that there are only two proceedings in this category limits the generalisability of any conclusions. First, Iran arguably failed to provide even a remotely convincing justification for its non-reviewability assertion in the *Hostage* case, making it easy for the ICJ to refute it. Second, the *Norwegian Loans* case, potentially of broader concern, was an isolated case in many respects. For one, it concerned the application of the *Connally* reservation, the use of which has since then greatly declined and is not very likely to reappear in Court proceedings.[87] Furthermore, in the only case since then where the ICJ had to evaluate a state's invocation of a self-judging clause, *Mutual Assistance*, it found that it *could* exercise its review. Thus, the *Norwegian Loans* non-reviewability finding has been reversed, as it were. Finally, in that case, the Court applied a more deferential standard than even the respondent had argued for – an approach since then only repeated in the *Bosnian Genocide* case, in a particular situation as well.[88]

III. POLITICAL DETERMINATIONS

The third category comprises a broader set of measures and assessments. Their connecting feature is that the respective states deemed them to be of a

its own review of the well-foundedness of the determination. In the oral proceedings, counsel for the United States asserted that '[o]ur use of the automatic reservation … is not arbitrary; the Court has never examined and we assume will not examine into the motives which lead nations to exercise the automatic reservation. Suffice it to say, any examination would nevertheless reveal the reasonableness of the United States position', *Interhandel*, ICJ, Oral Proceedings of 14 November 1958, morning, 610 (Becker). This came in reaction to the comments of Switzerland, which, not surprisingly, had rejected the United States' position and instead argued for the reviewability of its decision to invoke the *Connally* reservation. At a minimum, Switzerland argued, the Court could apply an arbitrariness standard of review, *Interhandel*, ICJ, Oral Proceedings of 12 November 1958, morning, 578–79 (Guggenheim); *Interhandel*, ICJ, Oral Proceedings of 17 November 1958, morning, 632 (Guggenheim). The Court, however, rejected Switzerland's application already on another ground, *Interhandel (Switzerland v United States of America)*, ICJ, Judgment (Preliminary Objections) of 21 March 1959, 25–26; Judge Sir Percy Spender's separate opinion can be read as suggesting that this course of action was motivated by a desire to avoid the thorny questions associated with the *Connally* reservation, *Interhandel (Switzerland v United States of America)*, ICJ, Judgment (Preliminary Objections), Separate Opinion of Sir Percy Spender, 54. Finally, the *Connally* reservation was invoked again by virtue of reciprocity by Bulgaria in the *Aerial Incident of 27 July 1955 (United States of America v Bulgaria)* case. While the United States initially contended that the Court *could* review whether a state's invocation of that reservation was arbitrary, it later returned to its stance in *Interhandel*, arguing now that the application of the clause could not be subject to the ICJ's review. Consequently, it recognised Bulgaria's invocation of the clause, and the case was discontinued on its initiative, thus depriving the Court of the occasion to decide once more on the appropriate standard of review for the *Connally* clause. For an instructive overview and with further references, L Gross, 'Bulgaria Invokes the Connally Amendment' (1962) 56(2) *American Journal of International Law* 357, 357–58, 366–72. Since then, the clause has not been invoked again before the ICJ.

[87] B McGarry, 'Nicaragua's Impacts on Optional Clause Practice' in E Sobenes Obregon and B Samson (eds), *Nicaragua Before the International Court of Justice: Impacts on International Law* (Springer, 2018), 204.

[88] For an analysis of that case, see below at ch 5, section II.

'political' nature, and asserted that, by that virtue, they would be removed from the Court's ambit. Such claims have mostly been made in the earlier years of the ICJ's existence: 1948 in *Admission of a State to the UN*, 1950 in *Asylum*, 1951 in *Reservations to the Genocide Convention*, and 1962 in the *South West Africa* proceedings. An analysis of the *South West Africa* case would be incomplete without the second stage – one of the three seeming exceptions to the rule that the Court finds no matters to be inherently beyond its purview. Yet, as the conclusion will show, the significance of that finding is limited in light of the ICJ's subsequent rejection of any degree of deference in the 1971 *Namibia* advisory proceeding.

A. Explicit Rejection

In most proceedings in which the ICJ has rejected the non-reviewability claims in this domain, it has done so openly. Thereby, it has emphatically rejected the contention that it would be ill-equipped and -legitimised to assess 'political' determinations through the prism of law.

i. Admission of a State to the UN

As shown above, in the *Admission of a State to the UN* advisory proceedings, several states had argued for the application of complete deference as standard of review.[89] The questions were whether a UN Member State could make its consent to the admission of a state to the UN dependent on conditions not expressly laid down by Article 4(1) UN Charter, and, specifically, whether it could subject its consent to the condition that other states be admitted at the same time.[90]

The states opposing the request argued that it was only up to the state in question to consider whether and which further conditions beyond Article 4(1) would be appropriate. The question whether further criteria were appropriate would only be amenable to political and not to judicial appreciation. Poland made this point most clearly when its representative asserted that—

> The reasons upon which [states] base their judgment [under Article 4 UN Charter] are political, and, therefore not subject to judicial control … [I]f one uses a right it should be used in the interest of what it is meant for … You may ask me who is to judge whether [the right to vote upon the admission of new Members] is used for these purposes [ie, 'in the interest of peace and security, in the interest of the Organization']. The reply that I give is: those who are primarily politically responsible for the wellbeing of the Organization; because there are no legal criteria for security, and the criteria are undoubtedly political.[91]

[89] See above at ch 2, section II.C.

[90] *Admission of a State to the United Nations (Charter, Art 4)*, ICJ, Advisory Opinion of 28 May 1948, 58.

[91] *Admission of a State to the United Nations (Charter, Art. 4)*, ICJ, Oral Statements, 109.

A group of judges agreed. In their view—

> [i]f the request for an opinion involved the Court in approving or disapproving the desire ... by a Member of the United Nations to procure the admission of other States at the same time as the applicant State, it would only be possible to assess this political consideration from a political point of view. But such an assessment is not within the province of the Court ... It is one thing to ask the Court whether a Member is legally entitled to rely on political considerations in voting upon the admission of new Members ... It is quite another thing to ask the Court to assess the validity of any particular political consideration upon which a Member relies; that is a political question and must not be answered.[92]

Thereby, these judges held that judicial review of the reasons laid down by a state for its decision whether to consent to the admission of a new state was inappropriate.

The majority, however, decided otherwise. It held that the request was of a legal nature, and that there were no reasons why the Court should decline to issue the opinion.[93] Thereby, the ICJ rejected the assertion that the inclusion of additional criteria in the voting decision on the admission of a new UN member would not be amenable to judicial appreciation. While it rejected this assertion during its evaluation of whether to accede to the request for its opinion, by the same token, it also deprived the complete deference claim of its argumentative foundation. However, as will be seen below, this rejection was only one of degree – for the Court did ultimately apply a (moderately) deferential standard of review, reasonableness.[94]

ii. Asylum

The *Asylum* case was the first in a series of cases involving Haya de la Torre, a Peruvian politician who had been granted asylum in the Colombian embassy in 1949 shortly after a military junta had taken over the Peruvian government. The central question in *Asylum* was whether Colombia had a right to request safe-conduct for him from Peru under the 1928 Havana Convention on Asylum. Peru in turn sought a declaration that the grant of asylum was not in conformity with international law.[95] The relevant provisions were Articles 1 and 2 of the 1928 Convention. According to Article 1(1), '[i]t is not permissible for States to grant asylum ... to persons accused or condemned for common crimes'. Article 2 (2) stipulates that '[a]sylum may not be granted except in urgent cases and for the

[92] *Admission of a State to the United Nations (Charter, Art. 4)*, ICJ, Advisory Opinion, Dissenting Opinion of Judges Basdevant, Winiarski, Sir Arnold McNair and Read, para 24; see also in this regard *Admission of a State to the United Nations (Charter, Art 4)*, ICJ, Advisory Opinion of 28 May 1948, Individual Opinion of Judge Alvarez, 71; and *Admission of a State to the United Nations (Charter, Art 4)*, ICJ, Advisory Opinion, Dissenting Opinion of Judge Zoričić, 95.

[93] *Admission of a State to the UN*, Advisory Opinion (n 90), 61–62.

[94] See below at ch 6, section III.

[95] *Asylum (Colombia v Peru)*, ICJ, Judgment of 20 November 1950, 271–73.

period of time strictly indispensable for the person who has sought asylum to ensure in some other way his safety'.

In the words of Peru, the decisive question of the case was whether Colombia's qualification of Haya de la Torres' purported crimes as 'political', as opposed to 'common crimes', 'was definitive, conclusive, and must be considered as having equal force to *res iudicata*, that it to say, to be beyond challenge by anyone and in particular by the government of which the criminal is a national'.[96] Specifically, Colombia claimed a right of unilateral and definitive qualification under Article 1(1). It asserted that Article 2(1) implicitly recognised its prerogative to decide whether Haya de la Torre had been charged with common or with political crimes.[97] The right of unilateral and definitive qualification would be 'a sovereign right', 'a sovereign act of State'.[98] Colombia recognised that the provision did not lay down such a right explicitly, but argued that this would be implicitly so. Otherwise, the goal of the institution of asylum would be compromised: protecting an individual from prosecution. Without a right of unilateral qualification, the effectiveness of the right of asylum would be reduced to vanishing point.[99] In contrast, it did not argue that its qualification of Haya de la Torre's case as 'urgent' under Article 2 would be beyond the Court's purview.

The ICJ explicitly declined to defer to Colombia's qualification both under Articles 1(1) and 2. It observed that any 'interpretation [that] would lead … to the conclusion that Colombia would be entitled to decide alone whether the conditions provided by Articles 1 and 2 of the Convention for the regularity of asylum are fulfilled' would 'obviously … be incompatible with the legal situation created by the Convention'.[100] Furthermore, it noted with respect to Colombia's qualification under Article 1(1) that the appreciation of the Colombian ambassador who had granted asylum to Haya de la Torre 'is not the relevant element in the decision which the Court is called upon to take'.[101] Thus, it declined to take Colombia's perspective as the relevant one and to accord it complete deference. It justified this position with reference to the object and purpose of the 1928 Convention, which would be undermined, were judicial oversight excluded.

[96] *Asylum (Colombia v Peru)*, ICJ, Counter-Memorial by Peru of 21 March 1950, 141 (own translation, in the original: '[t]out le problème est de savoir si cette qualification est définitive, irréfragable, et doit être considérée comme ayant une force égale à la force juridique de la chose jugée, c'est-à-dire, comme ne pouvant plus être contestée par personne et en particulier par le gouvernement dont le criminel est le ressortissant'); see also *Asylum*, ICJ, Oral Proceedings of 9 October 1950, morning, 186 (Scelle).

[97] *Asylum (Colombia v Peru)*, ICJ, Reply by Colombia of 20 April 1950, 349.

[98] *Asylum (Colombia v Peru)*, ICJ, Memorial of Colombia of 20 January 1950, 29 (own translation, in the original: 'une faculté souveraine', 'un acte souverain de la part d'un Etat').

[99] *Asylum*, ICJ, Oral Proceedings of 27 September 1950, morning, 65 (Vasquez); *Asylum*, ICJ, Oral Proceedings of 6 October 1950, morning, 164 (Vasquez); *Asylum*, Memorial of Colombia (n 98), 29, see also at 30; *Asylum*, Reply by Colombia (n 97), 342 and 350.

[100] *Asylum*, Judgment (n 95), 279. Judge *ad hoc* Caicedo Castilla disagreed with this position and sided with Colombia, arguing that only a right of unilateral and definitive qualification by the asylum state could guarantee the effectiveness of asylum, *Asylum (Colombia v Peru)*, ICJ, Judgment, Dissenting Opinion by Judge *ad hoc* Caicedo Castilla, 364.

[101] *Asylum*, Judgment (n 95), 287.

iii. Reservations to the Genocide Convention

Properly speaking, the request for the Court's opinion in the *Reservations to the Genocide Convention* advisory proceedings did not ask it to evaluate whether a given reservation to an international treaty was compatible with that treaty. Rather, it posed the question whether a 'reserving state [can] be regarded as being a party to the Convention while still maintaining its reservation if the reservation is objected to by one or more of the parties to the Convention but not by others'.[102] Indirectly, however, this raised the question whether the Court could evaluate a reservation's compatibility with the treaty (in future proceedings) and decide whether a state's accession coupled with its reservation could produce the effects desired by that state.

Among others, Poland and the Soviet Union had claimed that no state would have the right to object to a reservation, and thereby prevent another state's accession to a treaty. Every state would have the 'incontestable' right to make any reservation it wished when acceding to a multilateral convention. Accordingly, that treaty would enter into force between this state and the other parties exactly as desired by the acceding state.[103] These states justified their claim by reference to the principle of state sovereignty. This claim necessarily entailed the impossibility for the Court to invalidate – save, evaluate – a state's decision to accede to an international treaty with certain reservations.

The ICJ, however, held that such an unlimited possibility for every state to accede to a treaty with any reservation it wished did not exist. There was a standard by which to decide whether a state could still be considered a party to a treaty despite its reservation: the treaty's object and purpose.[104] The Court thus found indirectly that judicial review of a reservation would be possible, and that the principle of state sovereignty could not exclude such a review.[105] Accordingly, once more, it justified the reviewability of a certain state measure with the object and purpose of the respective treaty.

B. Implicit Rejection: *South West Africa (First Phase)*

Taken together, the two *South West Africa* judgments in 1962 and 1966 and the *Namibia* Advisory Opinion in 1971 certainly form one of the most debated

[102] *Reservations to the Convention on Genocide*, ICJ, Advisory Opinion of 28 May 1951, 16.

[103] *Reservations to the Convention on Genocide*, ICJ, Written Statements, Written Statement of the Soviet Union of 13 January 1951, at 21; Written Statement of Poland of 13 January 1951, at 285; see also Written Statement of Romania of 20 January 1951, at 291.

[104] *Reservations to the Genocide Convention*, Advisory Opinion (n 102), 24.

[105] The United States specifically emphasised the possibility of judicial review of reservations, noting that '[i]t would not be beyond the province of a court to find that a seeming ratification together with its seeming accompanying reservation were futile and fraudulent devices, and without legal effect. There is no greater intrinsic difficulty in distinguishing such a fraudulent reservation than in distinguishing reasonable declarations of understanding from the category of true reservations',

chapters of the Court's history. The divide did not only run between two camps of international commentators, but also between the members of the bench (composed differently in all three instances). This divide also concerned the determination of the applicable standard of review. On each occasion, the Court adopted a different stance. In 1962, it implicitly rejected South Africa's non-reviewability arguments.

The central question in the *South West Africa* case was whether South Africa had violated Article 2(2) of the Mandate for South West Africa. According to that provision, South Africa had the obligation to 'promote to its utmost the material and moral well-being and the social progress of the inhabitants' of the administered territory. In both the first and second stages of the *South West Africa* proceedings, South Africa's principal claim[106] was that the Court could not evaluate its compliance with this provision. It argued that the Court would be lacking the necessary institutional expertise to undertake this assessment,[107] and that Article 2(2) was formulated in such broad terms that it would be devoid of any standards amenable to a judicial appreciation.[108]

Several judges shared this position. In 1962, this was the case for Judges Sir Percy Spender and Sir Gerald Fitzmaurice. In their joint dissenting opinion, they asserted that the 'considerations of a non-juridical character, social, humanitarian and other, which underlie this case … are matters for the political rather than for the legal arena', and that South Africa's compliance with Article 2(2) was not capable of 'objective legal appreciation'. Thus, the task of controlling its compliance, 'in the final analysis, hardly appears to be a judicial one'. Like South Africa, they justified this assessment with the purportedly special character of the obligation contained in Article 2(2). They noted that—

> There is hardly a term [in that provision] which would not require prior objective definition, or redefinition … [or] which could not be applied in widely different ways to the same situation or set of facts, according to differing subjective views as to what it meant, or ought to mean in the context; and it is a foregone conclusion that, in the absence of objective criteria, a large element of subjectivity must enter into any attempt to apply these terms to the facts of a given case … [In consequence, the application of Article 2(2) would inevitably] involve questions of appreciation rather than of objective determination.[109]

Written Statement of the United States of America, *Reservations to the Genocide Convention*, Written Statements (n 103), 43.

[106] South Africa argued in the alternative that, if the Court were not to find the question to be non-reviewable, it could only apply a good faith standard of review to assess South Africa's compliance with Art 2(2) of the Mandate, *South West Africa (Ethiopia v South Africa; Liberia v South Africa)*, ICJ, Rejoinder of South Africa of 22 December 1964, 157–58. In the 1971 *Namibia* proceedings, this argument was South Africa's principal claim.

[107] *South West Africa (Ethiopia v South Africa; Liberia v South Africa)*, ICJ, Preliminary Objections of South Africa of 30 November 1961, 386–87; *South West Africa*, Rejoinder of South Africa (n 106), 153–54.

[108] ibid, 153. See above at ch 2, section II.C.

[109] *South West Africa (Ethiopia v South Africa; Liberia v South Africa)*, ICJ, Judgment (Preliminary Objections), Joint Dissenting Opinion of Sir Percy Spender and Sir Gerald Fitzmaurice, 465–67.

The majority rejected these assertions, if only tacitly. It did not specifically address the non-reviewability arguments advanced by South Africa and the two individual judges. However, significantly, it concluded that it had jurisdiction to address the merits of the dispute.[110] As South Africa and Judges Spender and Fitzmaurice had argued, the non-reviewability of the latter's compliance with Article 2(2) should have led the ICJ to find that the question was non-justiciable, and thus to decline to proceed to the merits. Against this background, the majority's decision to proceed to the merits presupposes that it also held South Africa's conduct under Article 2 (2) to be reviewable in the first place.

C. The Exception: Implicit Acceptance in *South West Africa (Second Phase)*

Just as the composition of the bench had changed in the second phase of the *South West Africa* proceedings, so did the majority's stance on the reviewability of South Africa's compliance with its obligation under Article 2(2) of the Mandate. Despite the Court's implicit rejection of its non-reviewability contention in 1962, South Africa kept insisting on this assertion. Only in the alternative did it urge the ICJ to apply the good faith standard of review. The Court, however, did not reach this question: It found that the applicants had failed to establish their standing, and left the substance of the case unaddressed.[111] Thus, it did not adopt the non-reviewability standard properly speaking. Yet, it is submitted here that the ICJ did accede to South Africa's respective argument, if only indirectly. Arguably, the negative decision on standing merely served as proxy for the – now procedurally unavailable – decision that the question was beyond the Court's purview.

First, on the part of the majority itself, there is the eloquent silence of Sir Percy Spender, now President of the Court. In his individual statement to the 1966 judgment, he remained silent on the questions revolving around Article 2(2), arguing that any such expression would be improper for any judge. However, he also noted that 'there are grounds other than as stated in the Judgment upon which the Applicants' claims or certain of them could have been rejected'.[112] It is fair to assume that in his view, one such ground was the alleged non-reviewability of South Africa's conduct.[113]

[110] *South West Africa (Ethiopia v South Africa; Liberia v South Africa)*, ICJ, Judgment (Preliminary Objections) of 21 December 1962, 347.

[111] *South West Africa (Ethiopia v South Africa; Liberia v South Africa)*, ICJ, Judgment (Second Phase) of 18 July 1966, para 99. As noted above, this finding was likely used as a merits-avoidance technique, see at ch 3, section II.B.

[112] *South West Africa (Ethiopia v South Africa; Liberia v South Africa)*, ICJ, Judgment (Second Phase), Declaration of President Sir Percy Spender, para 5.

[113] It is unlikely that this 'other ground' was that the mandate had lapsed, for he notes that it would have been 'entirely proper' for a concurring judge 'to base a separate opinion wholly or in part' on this ground, ibid, paras 30–31. Thus, had this been the reason for his vote, he would most likely have explained so. It seems likely, then, that with this 'other ground', he is referring

Second, it is significant that despite the President's call to abstain from any pronouncements on any questions of substance, several of the dissenting judges explicitly argued that South Africa's behaviour *could* be subject to the ICJ's evaluation.[114] The fact that these judges all deemed this question worthy of attention suggests that the bench must have grappled with the question. For instance, Judge Tanaka expressed his agreement in principle with Judges Fitzmaurice and Spender's position in 1962 that '[i]f the dispute ... is political, administrative, technical or otherwise in character, and not of legal character, the Court will have no power to exercise its jurisdiction over it'. However, he argued that this consideration would not apply in the present case, and concluded that South Africa's compliance with Article 2(2) was amenable to the Court's review.[115]

Finally, Judge Jessup made this connection explicitly. For him, '[t]he intimation in the Judgment that the Applicants' interest in, for example, the practice of apartheid in the mandated territory of South West Africa, is only political and not legal, harks back to the joint dissent of 1962'. The thesis advanced therein 'that the interpretation of Article 2 ... is more political than legal is in effect another way of saying as today's Judgment says, that the interest of Applicants ... is political rather than legal'.[116] Judge Jessup dedicated more than five pages to the applicable standard of review, concluding that the 'task which ... confronted this Court ... is not beyond its capabilities'.[117]

D. Conclusion for Political Determinations

As was the case in the first category, national security interests, the five proceedings analysed under this header demonstrate that the Court is unwilling to accord complete deference when concerned with a state's allegedly political determinations. In four out of the five proceedings, it rejected doing so. The only exception is *South West Africa (Second Phase)*.

to the non-reviewability of South Africa's compliance with Art 2(2), for which he had already argued in his joint dissenting opinion with Sir Gerald Fitzmaurice in the first phase of the proceedings.

[114] See for instance the dissenting opinions of Vice-President Wellington Koo and Judge Forster, *South West Africa (Ethiopia v South Africa; Liberia v South Africa)*, ICJ, Judgment (Second Phase), Dissenting Opinion of Vice-President Wellington Koo, 235; *South West Africa (Ethiopia v South Africa; Liberia v South Africa)*, ICJ, Judgment (Second Phase), Dissenting Opinion of Judge Forster, 480–81.

[115] *South West Africa (Ethiopia v South Africa; Liberia v South Africa)*, ICJ, Judgment (Second Phase), Separate Opinion of Judge Tanaka, 279, and 284–87.

[116] *South West Africa (Ethiopia v South Africa; Liberia v South Africa)*, ICJ, Judgment (Second Phase), Dissenting Opinion of Judge Jessup, 425.

[117] ibid, 438.

Table 3 ICJ treatment of complete deference claims in proceedings relating to political determinations

Rejection of the claim for complete deference	Recognition of the claim for complete deference
• Admission of a State to the UN	• South West Africa (Second Phase)
• Asylum	
• Reservations to the Genocide Convention	
• South West Africa (First Phase)	

The significance of this sole exception to that rule is limited. Both in 1962 and in 1971, the majority of the Court held that it could evaluate South Africa's compliance with its obligation under Article 2(2) of the Mandate for South West Africa, including the associated political choices. It did so implicitly in the *South West Africa (First Phase)* judgment, and explicitly in the *Namibia* advisory opinion in 1971, where it even chose to apply the most intrusive standard of review, *de novo*.[118] Consequently, the ICJ also reversed its non-reviewability position in this case, so to speak. Furthermore, the 1966 decision had caused a significant backlash, and led to a notable dent in the number of new applications to the Court in the following years, with especially the newly formed states refusing to bring cases.[119]

The presentation of these four proceedings makes clear that the Court is not ready to refrain from exercising judicial oversight over state decisions of an allegedly political nature or allegedly decisively shaped by political considerations. Accordingly, it refuses to attach the same consequentiality to the expertise-based arguments as the states that have been relying on them to urge it to apply a completely deferential standard of review. Not only in that respect, there are major parallels and overlaps between the way the Court has dealt with claims for complete deference for states in their political determinations and the way it has treated claims that it would be lacking jurisdiction for a dispute or that it should decline to answer a request because it was non-legal. Indeed, states have often made both claims simultaneously, as *Admission of a State to the UN* and *South West Africa* demonstrate.[120]

IV. SCIENTIFIC DETERMINATIONS: EXPLICIT REJECTION IN *WHALING*

Finally, in the *Whaling* case, prominent for its focus on the 'margin of appreciation', the respondent, Japan, equally relied on considerations of relative institutional

[118] See above at section III.B and below at ch 7, section III.B, respectively.

[119] See for instance JR Crawford, '"Dreamers of the Day": Australia and the International Court of Justice' (2013) 14(2) *Melbourne Journal of International Law* 520, 536–37.

[120] On this point, see above at ch 2, section IV.

expertise to justify its claim for complete judicial deference. Specifically, it argued with the Court's lack of expertise to evaluate first-hand assessments made by states in the domain of science to convince the Court to apply a deferential standard of review in the evaluation of its own assessment that the JARPA II whaling programme was 'for purposes of scientific research' under Article VIII ICRW, and thereby excluded from the whaling moratorium. Initially, Japan even argued for complete deference.[121]

As further arguments, it pointed to the wording of Article VIII and the absence of substantive obligations on the state granting the permit.[122] Yet, as explained above, the emphasis was on the ICJ's alleged lack of expertise to deal with scientific questions. Japan thus pleaded at first for a non-reviewable decision-making space both concerning the question whether JARPA II constituted 'scientific research' and whether that programme was 'for purposes of' scientific research.[123]

Australia and New Zealand as applicant respectively intervening party explicitly opposed this conclusion.[124] They did not try to rebut Japan's expertise-based arguments. Instead, they focused on other considerations. Namely, they advanced that the report and review procedure set up by Article VIII ICRW and Article 30 of the Schedule would show that Article VIII was not self-judging.[125] In addition, Australia distinguished the provision from national

[121] Only later did it concede that its determination regarding the applicability of Art VIII was 'not entirely beyond question. It can be reviewed by the Court', *Whaling in the Antarctic (Australia v Japan: New Zealand intervening)*, ICJ, Written Observations of Japan on New Zealand's Written Observations of 31 May 2013, para 53; or, in the words of counsel during the oral proceedings, Japan's reliance on these arguments 'is not to say … that Japan is claiming a "carte blanche"', *Whaling in the Antarctic*, ICJ, Oral Proceedings of 15 July 2013, morning (CR 2013/21), 48 para 36 (Pellet).

[122] For instance, Japan asserted that 'the ordinary meaning of the terms of Article VIII in their context and in the light of the object and purpose of the Convention is clear and unequivocal: a Contracting Government authorizing a special permit has discretion to do so "[n]otwithstanding anything contained in" the ICRW, and to set the conditions as it thinks fit. Under the ICRW, no-one else is given the right to challenge that exercise of the discretion', *Whaling in the Antarctic (Australia v Japan: New Zealand intervening)*, ICJ, Counter-Memorial of Japan of 9 March 2012, 18, para 50, see also at 21, para 61; *Whaling*, Written Observations of Japan on New Zealand's Written Observations (n 121), para 31; and *Whaling in the Antarctic*, ICJ, Oral Proceedings of 3 July 2013, morning (CR 2013/13), 62, paras 7–10, and 67, para 22 (Pellet).

[123] See above at ch 2, section II.D.

[124] Australia: 'The application of Article VIII is to be determined on an objective basis – it is not self-judging. That is, a Contracting Government is not entitled to determine unilaterally that it is free to issue special permits according to its own asserted view that the killing, taking or treating of whales under those permits is "for purposes of scientific research"', *Whaling in the Antarctic (Australia v Japan: New Zealand intervening)*, ICJ, Memorial of Australia of 9 May 2011, para 4.5; see also *Whaling in the Antarctic*, ICJ, Oral Proceedings of 26 June 2013, afternoon (CR 2013/8), 46, para 67 (Crawford); New Zealand: 'Whether Article VIII has been applied properly in a particular case is a question … open for the judicial determination of this Court', *Whaling in the Antarctic*, ICJ, Oral Proceedings of 8 July 2013, morning (CR 2013/17), 34, para 66 (Finlayson).

[125] *Whaling*, Memorial of Australia (n 124), paras 4.16, 4.24; *Whaling in the Antarctic (Australia v Japan: New Zealand intervening)*, ICJ, Written Observations of New Zealand of 4 April 2013, para 53.

security exceptions, 'couched in subjective terms, and intended to reserve core rights of sovereignty against international incursion'. Instead, what would be at issue here was 'of public interest occurring outside the jurisdiction of any single State, and not the prerogative of any single State'.[126] New Zealand further highlighted that the wording of Article VIII would be 'clearly distinguishable from classic "self-judging" provisions'.[127] The adoption of the complete deference standard of review by the ICJ would be 'entirely inconsistent' with and undermine the ICRW system of collective regulation of whaling,[128] and have negative impacts in other domains as well.[129]

The Court rejected Japan's non-reviewability arguments, and only acceded to one of its contentions pro forma. Namely, Japan had noted that the question whether JARPA II was 'for purposes of' scientific research would require the ICJ to address 'the propriety of the research aims themselves, which is a matter of science policy'. Yet, 'science *policy* is neither a technical nor a legal question', and therefore none of the kind the Court could answer.[130] The Court indeed acknowledged that it was 'not called upon to resolve matters of scientific or whaling policy. [It] is aware that members of the international community hold divergent views about the appropriate policy towards … whaling, but it is not for [it] to settle these differences'.[131] Yet, this statement has to be juxtaposed with the rejection of Japan's more far-reaching non-reviewability assertions. Against this background, the recognition of the non-reviewability of 'scientific policy' seems to be mere lip-service. This statement did not stop the ICJ from examining (and evaluating the correctness of) Japan's assertions that JARPA II involved 'scientific research' and that it was 'for purposes of' such research.

Namely, the Court held that whether a whaling programme falls under Article VIII 'cannot depend simply on that State's perception'.[132] Furthermore, the ICJ remarked that this evaluation encompassed both the question whether it involved 'scientific research' and whether it was 'for purposes of' scientific research. That way, it made clear that it would not

[126] *Whaling in the Antarctic*, ICJ, Oral Proceedings of 10 July 2013, morning (CR 2013/19), 66, para 25 (Crawford).

[127] *Whaling*, Written Observations of New Zealand (n 125), para 51.

[128] ibid, para 54; speaking of 'black holes', *Whaling*, Oral Proceedings of 10 July 2013, 59, para 7 (Crawford); see further at 63, para 15.

[129] *Whaling in the Antarctic*, ICJ, Oral Proceedings of 27 June 2013, morning (CR 2013/9), 14, para 2 (Sands).

[130] *Whaling*, Written Observations of Japan on New Zealand's Written Observations (n 121), para 58. As one commentator remarked, '[t]his argument seems to introduce the distinction between political and legal disputes by transposing it to the field of fact finding', qualifying this as an attempt 'to limit the adjudicator's control over the purely formal aspects of the problem', G Gros, 'The ICJ's Handling of Science in the Whaling in the Antarctic Case: A Whale of a Case?' (2015) 6(3) *Journal of International Dispute Settlement* 578, 596.

[131] *Whaling in the Antarctic (Australia v Japan: New Zealand intervening)*, ICJ, Judgment of 31 March 2014, para 69.

[132] ibid, para 61.

completely defer to Japan's respective assessments.[133] Incidentally, it also rejected the proposition that its alleged lack of institutional expertise for scientific questions would force it to accord complete deference to the concerned state. Even if such a lack of expertise were to exist, it would not justify this degree of deference.

In conclusion, the Court hinted at the fact that it was not its task to settle scientific controversies. Arguably, this was motivated by the consideration that it would be lacking the requisite expertise to do so. Yet, it only conceded this for a minor aspect of the dispute. Concerning the main issue, namely the subsumption of JARPA II under Article VIII ICRW, it dismissed Japan's plea, and thereby also the argumentation at its base, including the expertise consideration for scientific questions. Thus, the Court also refused to recognise substantial merit to the second manifestation of the expertise-based argument for complete deference – the domain of scientific determinations.

V. CONCLUSION FOR THE ABSENCE OF JUDICIAL OVERSIGHT

The final part of this chapter will conclude by highlighting three aspects: the clear pattern of rejection of non-reviewability assertions, possible reasons for the Court's choice of their explicit or implicit rejection, and the question whether the ICJ resorted to the finding of non-reviewability as an avoidance technique.

A. A Clear Pattern of Rejection

The above analysis has yielded a clear pattern of how the Court deals with assertions of non-reviewability: In 12 out of 14 proceedings, it has rejected them. Thus, it has consistently denied that it would be lacking the requisite legitimacy or expertise to evaluate the correctness of a state's first-hand determinations. In principle, there is no subject-matter which it acknowledged to be beyond its purview merely by virtue of the proximity to the core of national sovereignty or the close link to extra-judicial considerations. This holds true for such diverse matters as the regulation of access of warships to a state's territorial waters, the use of force purportedly taken in self-defence, expulsion measures justified with national security concerns, the granting of asylum to an allegedly political offender, the pursuance of the best interests of a population by political means, and the assessment of an allegedly scientific matter. The three exceptions discussed in this chapter do not put that conclusion into doubt.

[133] ibid, para 67.

Table 4 ICJ rejection vs acceptance of complete deference claims

Rejection of the claim for complete deference	Accordance of complete deference
• Admission of a State to the UN	• Norwegian Loans
• Corfu Channel	• South West Africa (Second Phase)
• Asylum	• Nuclear Weapons
• Reservations to the Genocide Convention	
• South West Africa (First Phase)	
• Hostage	
• Nicaragua	
• Oil Platforms	
• Wall in the OPT	
• Mutual Assistance	
• Diallo	
• Whaling	

Table 4 shows that the Court accorded complete deference to Norway in *Norwegian Loans*, and that it further (arguably) recognised the respective states' claims for complete deference in *South West Africa (Second Phase)*, and *Nuclear Weapons*. In neither of the three proceedings did it openly admit so. In *Norwegian Loans*, its accordance of complete deference can only be established by inference. In *South West Africa (Second Phase)* and *Nuclear Weapons*, it relied on other findings: absence of standing of the applicants in the former, and a *non liquet* in the latter. In these two proceedings, it could have been a self-perceived lack of expertise that drove the ICJ to its decisions. In both instances, states had made assertions to that effect. Additionally, the political controversy among the states on both questions might have played a role as well, as might have considerations of state sovereignty in *Nuclear Weapons*. In turn, the non-reviewability finding in *Norwegian Loans* presumably also rested on the subjective wording of the pertinent provision.

Thus, it appears at first sight that the Court accepted both the institutional expertise- and the sovereignty-based non-reviewability assertion in specific contexts. Yet, it is submitted that on the substance, the importance of this recognition must not be overstated. On the contrary, from the viewpoint of form, the way the ICJ handled the question in these three proceedings even corroborates the conclusion that it is eager to convey an image of self-assertiveness and of an institution unwilling to accept further unwritten limitations.

First, on the substance: The significance of two non-reviewability findings is very limited. The non-reviewability finding in *Norwegian Loans* for self-judging clauses was reversed in the 2008 *Mutual Assistance* judgment, and the non-reviewability finding in *South West Africa (Second Phase)* even earlier in the 1971 *Namibia* opinion.

Second, on the form: It is telling that in all three proceedings in which the ICJ arguably applied a non-reviewability standard, ie, where it considered a question to be beyond its purview, it only did so tacitly. Thus, it never expressly conceded that there are matters beyond its grasp merely by reason of their link to state sovereignty, or their connection to aspects not suitable for determination by a judicial body. This becomes most apparent in *Nuclear Weapons*, where the Court found that the *law* was lacking, not itself. Only in individual opinions did certain judges make a comparable point concerning the Court's abilities. The contrast of these statements with the majority decisions suggests that the majority deliberately remained silent on such claims.

B. Explicit vs Implicit Rejection

Table 5 focuses on the proceedings in which the Court rejected to accord complete deference to the concerned state, and recapitulates whether it did so explicitly or implicitly.

Table 5 Explicit vs implicit ICJ rejection of complete deference claims

Explicit Rejection	Implicit Rejection
• Admission to the UN	• Corfu Channel
• Asylum	• South West Africa (Second Phase)
• Reservations to the Genocide Convention	• Wall in the OPT
• Hostage	
• Nicaragua	
• Oil Platforms	
• Mutual Assistance	
• Diallo	
• Whaling	

Explaining why the ICJ chose to refute the non-reviewability assertion explicitly in most and implicitly in only a handful of proceedings ultimately remains a matter of speculation. Yet, some possible explanations are apparent.

A first potential explanation is based on the two groups of arguments advanced by states to bolster claims for complete deference. As explained above, these arguments rest on the notion and extent of state sovereignty on the one hand, and the limitations of the ICJ's expertise on the other. The first argument appears above all in proceedings involving measures allegedly taken to protect national security interests and involving domestic measures. The second argument appears above all in proceedings involving an evaluation of political determinations, and of scientific determinations.[134] One would assume that the Court's rejection of either argumentative category would be consistent, ie that it would either explicitly or implicitly reject all assertions falling in one category. As Table 6 shows, this is generally the case.

Table 6 Explicit vs implicit ICJ rejection of complete deference claims, sorted by categories

Categories	Explicit Rejection	Implicit Rejection
National Security Interests & Domestic Measures	• Hostage • Nicaragua • Oil Platforms • Mutual Assistance • Diallo	• Corfu Channel • Wall in the OPT
Political & Scientific Determinations	• Admission to the UN • Asylum • Reservations to the Genocide Convention • Whaling	• South West Africa (First Phase)

Yet, the number of proceedings falling in each category is limited. While the table shows a tendency, it would be premature to regard it as more than that. Thus, the categories do not seem to decisively shape the Court's choice of explicit or implicit rejection of the non-reviewability claim.

A second possible explanation for the Court's varying resort to the explicit/implicit rejection of the complete deference plea relates to the merit of the respective non-reviewability argument. As noted in the discussion of *Wall in the OPT*, addressing a non-reviewability claim, even if to disprove it, may confer a certain appearance of legitimacy upon that argument. If the argument had no merit whatsoever, one would presumably not address it in the first place – at least in principle. In those situations, eloquent silence could be a clearer signal than a verbose refutation. From this angle, the fact that the Court paid no visible attention to the assertion that it would be lacking the abilities to deal with the questions brought before it in *Corfu Channel*, *South West Africa (First Phase)* and *Wall in the OPT* could simply mean that the Court wanted to avoid creating the appearance of any merit in this argumentation. Yet, this interpretation cannot explain why the ICJ opted for an explicit rebuttal in the *Hostage* case, where Iran made very little efforts to sustain its plea for complete deference with arguments. Similarly, it cannot explain convincingly why the Court opted for

[134] As already noted above, a precise delimitation is not always possible. Often enough, states have invoked both arguments simultaneously. The *Nuclear Weapons* advisory proceeding is a case in point.

an explicit approach in *Diallo*, when the point that measures allegedly taken to protect national security interests were not beyond its purview had already recently been affirmed implicitly in *Wall* and explicitly in *Mutual Assistance*.

Furthermore, the fact that the Court openly discarded – and thus addressed – the assertion that it should accord complete deference to the respective states in nine of the 12 proceedings where the latter had made such arguments does not necessarily mean that the ICJ saw more merit in their arguments. In itself, an argument may only have merit due to its inherent qualities. However, the *perception* of merit could also derive from other sources – namely, from repeated invocation. The more often a certain point is made, the more convincing it appears to be.[135] Accordingly, it could also be that the Court was anxious to explicitly refute the arguments made for the invocation of complete deference because states had been repeatedly making this sort of assertion, and because this had resulted in conferring a certain apparent legitimacy on it. As argued above,[136] it is the states' perception of the Court that matters most. From this perspective, refuting an argument that constantly reappears in Court proceedings explicitly could be advisable from a policy perspective. In contrast, judicial silence in such a situation could be interpreted by the states as a tacit admission that an argumentative rebuttal is not possible, or at best as an only half-hearted rejection. Ultimately, judicial ignorance might thus confer an even stronger appearance of merit upon that argument. In a world where most inter-state disputes do not reach the Court, leaving such a void could be dangerous. Thus, there are situations in which the explicit rejection of an argument may be stronger than an implicit one.

Finally, one has to keep in mind that 'the' Court is not a monolithic actor, but consists of judges who come and go over time. These individuals come to the ICJ from very different backgrounds and with very different conceptions of the ICJ's role. Thus, lack of perfect consistency in the Court's approach over the decades and situations is not that much of a surprise. Ultimately, each proceeding has to be seen in its distinct context.

C. Non-Reviewability as an Avoidance Technique?

Finally, it remains to be answered whether the ICJ has been resorting to the finding of non-reviewability as an avoidance technique in *Norwegian Loans*, *South West Africa (Second Phase)* or *Nuclear Weapons*. It is submitted here for several reasons that this is not the case.

First, in *South West Africa (Second Phase)* and *Nuclear Weapons*, the ICJ might have arrived at its respective findings based on the non-reviewability consideration. Yet, crucially, it did not make such a finding, but based its decisions on

[135] In psychology, this is known as the 'illusory truth effect'.
[136] Ch 3, section I.

other avoidance techniques: the negative finding on the applicants' standing in the first, and a finding of *non liquet* in the second proceeding.[137] Accordingly, one cannot speak of a use of non-reviewability, and thus of the notion of standard of review, as an avoidance technique in those two proceedings.

In turn, in the *Norwegian Loans* case, the ICJ made a finding of non-reviewability. Yet, here as well, several aspects speak against labelling the resort to the notion of non-reviewability as resort to an avoidance technique – at least, vis-a-vis Norway. Norway had not even argued for the adoption of a non-reviewability standard. Instead, it had explicitly recognised that the Court could evaluate its reciprocal invocation of the *Connally* reservation. Accordingly, the ICJ would not have had to fear any backlash on Norway's part if it had taken the decision to review the latter's invocation of the reservation. Second, the resort to non-reviewability was arguably not outcome-determinative. Norway had submitted several persuasive preliminary objections, and had only relied on the *Connally* reservation as a subsidiary claim.[138] The Court's reliance on that reservation rather seems to be an example of judicial economy.[139]

On the other hand, the non-reviewability finding could be interpreted as the use of an avoidance technique with future proceedings in mind. The ICJ's recognition of a non-reviewable decision-making space for the states relying on a *Connally* reservation could have been intended as a signal that it would most likely not adjudicate the types of disputes covered by such a clause. However, the *Connally* reservation had already been in decline at the time of the judgment.[140] Accordingly, the audience of such a signal would have been limited. Most importantly, however, if the Court had really wanted to make that point, it would have been advisable to do so explicitly, and not as discretely as it did. As outlined above, the second advantage of the resort to the standard of review notion is its candour, ie that it allows the ICJ to lay open its recognition of the limitations of its mandate, and thereby to build trust among the states.[141] Tacit use of an avoidance technique does not provide that advantage.

To sum up, even in the three proceedings in which the Court found the matter to be beyond its purview, it did not resort to this finding as an avoidance technique. Especially the analysis of the *South West Africa (Second Phase)* and *Nuclear Weapons* corroborates the finding that the ICJ is unwilling to acknowledge its institutional limitations openly. It even goes to certain lengths to avoid doing so. Thus, not only does the Court not resort to non-reviewability as an avoidance technique, but deliberately refrains from doing so.

[137] For a discussion of these proceedings see above at ch 3, sections II.B and III.C.

[138] *Norwegian Loans*, Judgment (Preliminary Objections) (n 75), 21–22.

[139] As the ICJ observed, it 'is free to base its decision on the ground which in its judgment is more direct and conclusive', ibid, 25.

[140] With an overview C Stahn, 'Connally Reservation' in R Wolfrum (ed), *Max Planck Encyclopedia of Public International Law* (Oxford University Press, 2012), paras 2–6.

[141] Ch 3, section IV.

In light of the advantages of deferential standards of review as an avoidance technique outlined above, this also makes sense from a judicial policy perspective. As explained, their main advantage is that they allow the ICJ to adopt a nuanced approach and balance out competing demands. Yet, as one of the two extreme forms the standard of review can take, complete deference does not have that advantage. It operates in the same black-or-white logic as the other avoidance techniques the Court has been using, with the same flaws.[142]

D. Final Remarks

This chapter has shown that the ICJ is eager to avoid agreeing with a state that it would be incapable of assessing for itself, and consequently evaluating, a state's determinations and decisions. This may be explained by a desire of self-assertion. From a strategic point of view, clearly signalling that position also has its advantages. For instance, following *Nicaragua*, the states emerged in the decolonisation process turned to the Court in increasing numbers. By asserting its judicial supremacy in that case, the ICJ arguably gained credibility among those doubting whether it would not bow to political might and pressure.[143]

Writing about the *Nuclear Weapons* advisory proceedings, Koskenniemi has observed that the fact '[t]hat the Court has so seldom voiced any doubt about the ability of international law to 'apply' in any given situation, despite the frequency with which respondent parties have objected to legal settlement, is a demonstration of the Court's universalising self-confidence'.[144] Following the above examination, this observation can be paraphrased as follows: The fact that the Court has so seldom acknowledged its institutional incapability to deal with a given situation, despite the frequency with which respondent parties have argued in that way, is a demonstration of the Court's universalising self-confidence (and its desire to manifest that self-confidence, as one might add).

[142] On this, see also ch 3, section IV.

[143] See, for instance, C Gray, 'The Use and Abuse of the International Court of Justice: Cases concerning the Use of Force after Nicaragua' (2003) 14(5) *European Journal of International Law* 867, 885.

[144] M Koskenniemi, 'The Silence of Law/The Voice of Justice' in L Boisson de Chazournes and P Sands (eds), *International Law, the International Court of Justice, and Nuclear Weapons* (Cambridge University Press, 1999), 508.

5

Good Faith

As will be recalled, under the good faith standard of review, the relevant question is whether at the time when the state had taken the disputed decision there was any rational basis to conclude that the reasons for its decision were valid, or that the conditions for the legality of the measure were present. This means that the Court scrutinises the result of the state's initial decision-making process only to a very limited extent. 'Arbitrariness and capriciousness' and 'manifest unreasonableness' represent equivalent standards of review.

Only in three out of the 31 analysed proceedings did the ICJ adopt the good faith standard of review: *ELSI*, *Bosnian Genocide*, and *Mutual Assistance*. Yet, there are seven further cases in which the respondents had – at least at one point – urged the Court to do so: *Rights of US Nationals in Morocco*, *Nottebohm*, *Right of Passage*, *Oil Platforms*, *Obligation to Prosecute or Extradite*, *Whaling* and *Certain Iranian Assets*. Thus, in the clear majority of the proceedings in which a state invoked the good faith standard of review, the ICJ rejected that claim. Both the low number of occurrences of this standard and the high rejection rate illustrate that this standard of review is of limited relevance in the Court's jurisprudence.

The analysis of the three cases in which it adopted the good faith standard of review will also show their particularities. While *ELSI* concerned domestic measures taken by the respondent state, *Mutual Assistance* revolved around national security interests. Yet, categorising these proceedings accordingly would be misleading. In each of the three proceedings in which the Court chose the good faith standard, it had distinct reasons for doing so – reasons that were unrelated to considerations of state sovereignty or institutional expertise. Namely, the decisive factor for the adoption of the good faith standard of review for the Court in *ELSI* and *Mutual Assistance* was the existence of a textual prescription of, respectively preference for, the good faith standard. In turn, in *Bosnian Genocide*, the ICJ applied this standard on its own initiative, arguably as a means to counterbalance its wide applicability finding of the obligation to prevent under the Genocide Convention.[1] After an evaluation of the three cases,

[1] It is out of such considerations that the presentation in this chapter does not follow the categorisation of the proceedings laid out in the introductory chapter.

the chapter's conclusion will address whether the ICJ has resorted to the good faith standard of review as an avoidance technique.

I. A TEXTUAL BASIS FOR THE APPLICATION OF THE GOOD FAITH STANDARD

The first category comprises the *ELSI* and the *Mutual Assistance* cases. The pertinent legal norm in *ELSI* explicitly laid down arbitrariness as standard of review. Correspondingly, the application of that standard was not under dispute. Neither party argued for the application of a different standard of review, nor did any member of the Chamber[2] individually. In the *Mutual Assistance* case, what was at issue was France's reliance on a 'self-judging' clause to justify its non-compliance with an obligation of assistance to Djibouti in a criminal investigation. The text of that provision ('if the State considers') arguably implied the application of a considerable degree of deference, the exact degree of which was disputed among the parties. By applying the good faith standard of review to evaluate whether France could successfully invoke that provision, the Court modified its previous non-reviewability finding in *Norwegian Loans*, also implied in *Nicaragua*.

A. ELSI

The *ELSI* case is the only one in this enquiry in which the relevant norm explicitly determined the applicable standard of review. Invoking public order and 'the general economic public interest', Italian authorities had requisitioned a Sicilian plant owned by two US corporations after these corporations had announced a plan to close it.[3] One question before the Court was whether that requisition violated Article I of the Supplementary Agreement to the bilateral US–Italian Treaty of Friendship. According to that provision, 'nationals, corporations and associations of either High Contracting Party shall not be subjected to arbitrary … measures'. Thereby, Article I called for the application of the good faith standard of review. Not surprisingly, both parties adjusted their argumentation to this. Thus, they directed their efforts to showing that the Italian mayor could (respectively, could under no circumstances) have considered that the requisition of the plant would be justified, and thus that the requisition would (not) be arbitrary.[4]

[2] Set up under Art 26, para 2, of the ICJ Statute.

[3] Order of the Mayor of Palermo, issued on 1 April 1968, reprinted in *ELSI (United States of America v Italy)*, ICJ, Judgment of 20 July 1989, para 30; for the background of the case, see SD Murphy, 'The ELSI Case: An Investment Dispute at the International Court of Justice' (1991) 16(2) *Yale Journal of International Law* 391, 399–406.

[4] The standard of review question was also raised by the parties concerning Art V(2) of the US–Italy Treaty of Friendship, but not decided by the Chamber. Art V(2) prohibited expropriations.

Namely, Italy tried to show that its mayor had ordered the requisition to tackle 'a serious social and economic problem', and because 'the reactions by the employees and the trade unions, with the backing of public opinion, [had been] such as to create fears of "disturbances of public order". In the light of these facts … the Mayor of Palermo [had been] of the opinion that the "features of serious public necessity and urgency" required by law in order to proceed with a requisition [had] actually existed'.[5] Thereby, Italy tried to demonstrate that it had not been implausible for its mayor to believe that the circumstances justifying the requisition had been present. The United States in turn asserted that the 'the planned closing was not a *bona fide* public emergency, nor was the requisition a *bona fide* response'.[6]

The ICJ defined arbitrariness as 'not so much something opposed to a rule of law', but rather 'as something opposed to the rule of law … It is a wilful disregard of due process of law, an act which shocks, or at least surprises, a sense of juridical propriety'.[7] Consequently, as long as the grounds for the requisition were at least remotely connected to legitimate public concerns, the Court would not find a violation of Article I. Applying this standard to the situation at hand, it observed that—

> one must remember the situation in Palermo at the moment of the requisition, with the threatened sudden unemployment of some 800 workers at one factory. It cannot be said to have been unreasonable or merely capricious for the Mayor to seek to use the powers conferred on him by the law in an attempt to do something about a difficult and distressing situation.[8]

This passage makes clear that it was the good faith standard of review that the ICJ applied. It limited its scrutiny to the question whether there had been circumstances which *could* legitimately have motivated the mayor to act the way he had

Italy argued that the mayor of Palermo had exercised a police power when ordering the requisition of the plant. It then cited Christie, who had noted that '[a] State's declaration that a particular interference with an alien's enjoyment of his property is justified by the so-called "police power" does not preclude an international tribunal from making an independent determination of this issue. But if the reasons given are valid and bear some plausible relationship to the action taken, no attempt may be made to search deeper', GC Christie, 'What Constitutes a Taking of Property Under International Law?' (1962) 38 *British Yearbook of International Law* 307, 338; quoted at *ELSI (United States of America v Italy)*, ICJ, Rejoinder of Italy of 18 July 1988, 468. Thereby, Italy explicitly recognised that the Chamber could review the well-foundedness of its invocation of the 'police power' justification, and that it did not have to accept its first-hand assessment as binding. On the other hand, this quote shows that Italy argued for a deferential standard of review nonetheless (arguably reasonableness, as becomes apparent by the formula 'plausible relationship'). However, as the Chamber already held that the requisition did not amount to a 'taking' in the sense of Art V(2) FCN, it did not have to address the question whether it could be justified through 'police powers', and consequently what standard of review would have been appropriate here, *ELSI*, Judgment (n 3), para 119.

[5] *ELSI (United States of America v Italy)*, ICJ, Counter-Memorial of Italy of 16 November 1987, 44; see also *ELSI*, Rejoinder of Italy (n 4), 464–65.

[6] *ELSI (United States of America v Italy)*, ICJ, Memorial of the United States of America of 15 May 1987, 80.

[7] *ELSI*, Judgment (n 3), para 128.

[8] ibid, para 129.

(and not whether the measures had been *objectively* justified). Consequently, the Court applied exactly the standard of review laid down by the applicable norm: the good faith standard of review.[9]

B. Mutual Assistance

The *Mutual Assistance* case is the second case in which the applicable legal norm, Article 2 c) of the Mutual Assistance Convention, bore directly on the applicable standard of review. While this 'self-judging' provision did not lay down a specific standard, it implied at least a certain degree of judicial deference: The concerned state may refuse assistance 'if [it] considers that [doing so] is likely to prejudice its sovereignty, security, *ordre public* or other of its essential interests'.[10]

France had initially even argued that the ICJ should defer completely to its first-hand assessment that it could rely on this provision to reject Djibouti's request for the transmission the files.[11] It was only in the final stage of the oral proceedings that France attenuated this position. There, counsel acknowledged that 'the provisions of a treaty must be interpreted and implemented in good faith, in accordance with the law of treaties'.[12] Thereby, France recognised that its application of this provision purportedly falling within its margin of manoeuvre was not beyond the Court's purview.

Yet, France still emphasised the importance of this margin under Article 2 c). As counsel argued, 'the point is for the requested State to retain for itself a

[9] Note that for Garrido-Muñoz, the Chamber 'seemed more to address the claims of abuse of power put forward by the applicant than to define a general standard of review', A Garrido-Muñoz, 'Managing Uncertainty: The International Court of Justice, "Objective Reasonableness" and the Judicial Function' (2017) 30(2) *Leiden Journal of International Law* 457, 469. Incidentally, this case is also a good example of terminological differences in the scholarly use of the term 'margin of appreciation'. Cannizzaro contends that *ELSI* is an example for the ICJ's use of the notion, E Cannizzaro, 'Proportionality and Margin of Appreciation in the Whaling Case: Reconciling Antithetical Doctrines?' (2016) 27(4) *European Journal of International Law* 1061, 1067; in contrast, Born et al contend that in cases where the treaty standard already predetermines the applicable standard of review, application of that standard by an international court or tribunal 'is not application of either a margin of appreciation or similar concept of deference', G Born, D Morris and S Forrest, '"A Margin of Appreciation": Appreciating Its Irrelevance in International Law' (2020) 61(1) *Harvard Journal of International Law* 65, 132. However, as becomes clear, both sources are based on a different understanding of the term – for Cannizzaro defines the margin of appreciation as the 'measure of discretion about how to implement … international obligations' (1064), without regard to whether there is a textual basis for its application. Thus, the two sources do not so much differ in their reading of the *ELSI* case, but rather in their understanding of the notion of the 'margin of appreciation'.

[10] Own translation, in the original: 's'il 'estime que l'exécution de la demande est de nature à porter atteinte à sa souveraineté, à sa sécurité, à son ordre public ou à d'autres de ses intérêts essentiels.'

[11] See above at ch 4, section I.A.iii.

[12] *Mutual Assistance in Criminal Matters*, ICJ, Oral Proceedings of 29 January 2008, afternoon (CR 2008/7), 29, para 27 (Ascensio).

wide discretion in measuring, by itself, the risk of prejudice to its essential interests. In granting each other this right, States seek to ensure mutual respect for their sovereignty in an especially sensitive area'.[13] In its view, the ICJ *could* review its reliance on that clause, but only through an arbitrariness review.[14] In support, France upheld the arguments already invoked to bolster its prior non-reviewability claim. It pointed to the subjective wording of the provision and to the fact that it would safeguard state interests in a particularly sensitive domain. In contrast, it is noteworthy that it did not argue that the Court would be lacking the expertise to analyse the notion of 'essential interests'.

Djibouti recognised the existence of a margin of manoeuvre under Article 2 c),[15] but rejected complete deference. It asserted that the provision 'does not allow one of the parties to evade its obligations … *ad libitium* by the simple apodictic claim that purported "essential interests" would require acting in such a way'.[16] First, adopting France's initial position would automatically cast aside the ICJ despite the fact that the two parties had conferred jurisdiction upon it to resolve the dispute.[17] Second, doing so would reduce the effectiveness of the obligations enshrined in the Convention to vanishing point.[18] Unlike what France alleged, the Court had, according to Djibouti, not laid down complete deference for a state's invocation of a self-judging clause in *Nicaragua*, nor had it applied such a standard in *Norwegian Loans*.[19]

Instead, under this margin, the respondent would have the obligation to respect the principles of reasonableness and good faith, as *Rights of US Nationals in Morocco*, Judge Lauterpacht's opinion in *Guardianship of Infants* and several investment arbitration decisions would show. Consequently, Djibouti asserted, the Court should evaluate whether the French reliance on the clause was reasonable and had been made in good faith.[20] Accordingly, its task would be to verify whether the motives invoked by France to justify the non-execution of the letter rogatory 'really do exist' and 'are serious, relevant and involve no abuse of the law'.[21] These elements are typical of the reasonableness standard of review.

[13] ibid, 57, para 15 (Belliard).

[14] ibid, 57, paras 16–17 (Belliard).

[15] *Mutual Assistance in Criminal Matters*, ICJ, Oral Proceedings of 22 January 2008, morning (CR 2008/2), 21, para 25 (Condorelli).

[16] *Mutual Assistance in Criminal Matters (Djibouti v France)*, ICJ, Memorial of Djibouti of 15 March 2007, para 149 (own translation. In the original: 'ne permet pas à une des Parties de se soustraire *ad libitum* à ses obligations, telles que prévues par la Convention, au moyen de la simple allégation apodictique que de prétendus "intérêts essentiels" imposeraient d'agir ainsi').

[17] *Mutual Assistance*, Oral Proceedings of 22 January 2008, 18, para 19 (Condorelli).

[18] ibid, 29, para 20 (Condorelli); see also ibid, 45, para 55 (Van den Biesen); *Mutual Assistance in Criminal Matters*, ICJ, Oral Proceedings of 28 January 2008, morning (CR 2008/6), 31, paras 12–13 (Condorelli).

[19] *Mutual Assistance*, Oral Proceedings of 22 January 2008, 20, para 23 (Condorelli); and *Mutual Assistance*, Oral Proceedings of 28 January 2008, 33, para 16 (Condorelli). As noted above, Djibouti's reading of the *Norwegian Loans* case differs from the one adopted here.

[20] With further references to these cases *Mutual Assistance*, Oral Proceedings of 22 January 2008, 22, paras 26–28 (Condorelli).

[21] ibid, 24, para 31 (Condorelli).

Yet, the Court ultimately applied the good faith standard of review.[22] It noted that the competent French judge, when rejecting the request for assistance, had observed that the requested file contained 'declassified "defence secret" documents, together with information and witness statements in respect of another case in progress', whose transmission would be contrary to France's essential interests.[23] Regarding Djibouti's suggestion to transmit only parts of the file, the ICJ observed that France had pointed out that 'that the intelligence service documents and information permeated the entire file'. Thus, it held, the above 'reasons … do fall within the scope of Article 2 (c)'.[24] This fact alone was enough for it to conclude that France's refusal to accede to the request was in conformity with the Convention. Overall, this approach must be qualified as a very superficial evaluation of the essential interests-clause, even under the good faith standard of review. The Court contented itself with the fact that one of the reasons provided for the refusal was covered by the provision.[25]

The ICJ justified this very deferential standard of review exclusively with the wording of Article 2 c). It observed that its terms 'provide a State to which a request for assistance has been made with a very considerable discretion'.[26] Conversely – and significantly – it neither justified the good faith standard with the close nexus to national sovereignty, as France had done, nor did it recognise any institutional limitations on its part for questions of national security.

Judge Keith was the only judge to comment on the standard of review question. He approved of the choice for the good faith standard, pointing to 'the extent of the power conferred by Article 2 (c), the nature of a State's assessment under that provision of its national interests and the need to defer in the usual case to that assessment'.[27] This indicates that for him, unlike the majority, respect for state sovereignty also called for judicial deference. On the other hand, while he agreed with the good faith standard of review, it seems that he would have preferred a more demanding *scope* of review.[28]

[22] *Mutual Assistance in Criminal Matters (Djibouti v France)*, ICJ, Judgment of 4 June 2008, paras 145, 147; Judge Iwasawa in *Certain Iranian Assets* comes to the same conclusion, *Certain Iranian Assets (Islamic Republic of Iran v United States of America)*, ICJ, Judgment (Merits), Separate Opinion of Judge Iwasawa, para 22.

[23] Quoted in *Mutual Assistance*, Judgment (n 22), para 147.

[24] ibid, para 148.

[25] See also S Schill and R Briese, '"If the State Considers": Self-Judging Clauses in International Dispute Settlement' (2009) 13 *Max Planck Yearbook of United Nations Law* 61, 116. Schill and Briese note that 'the precise criteria for ascertaining whether the good faith standard is met, are largely left open in the majority judgment in *Djibouti v France*, where the test applied resembles a "touch and feel"-type test', ibid, 118.

[26] *Mutual Assistance*, Judgment (n 22), para 145.

[27] *Mutual Assistance in Criminal Matters (Djibouti v France)*, ICJ, Judgment, Declaration of Judge Keith, para 10.

[28] See ibid, paras 7–8; on this point, which they term 'honesty in fact', see also MD Nolan and FG Sourgens, 'The Limits of Discretion?: Self-judging Emergency Clauses in International Investment Agreements' in KP Sauvant (ed), *Yearbook on International Investment Law & Policy 2011–2012* (Oxford University Press, 2012), 409–13.

II. GOOD FAITH STANDARD AS COUNTERBALANCING: *BOSNIAN GENOCIDE*

In *Bosnian Genocide*, the Court applied a mixed *de novo*-good faith standard of review. Significantly, what stands behind this choice was not the wording of the norm, nor considerations of legitimacy or expertise. Arguably, instead, the ICJ's partial choice for the good faith standard was motivated by a desire to counterbalance a finding with potentially far-reaching implications: the unlimited territorial reach of the obligation to prevent under the Genocide Convention. The choice of the good faith standard of review in the evaluation whether a state had violated that obligation mitigated this finding.

The case, brought by Bosnia and Herzegovina against Serbia and Montenegro, concerned the civil war that had erupted in the wake of Yugoslavia's dissolution. The applicant state primarily invoked Serbia and Montenegro's violation of Article III of the Genocide Convention during that time. In turn, only its subsidiary claim is relevant for the present enquiry: that the respondent had failed to prevent genocide and thereby violated Article I of the Convention.[29] As the Court found that a genocide had occurred, namely at Srebrenica, it had to answer two further questions in the affirmative to conclude at such a violation: first, if there had been a risk of genocide and if Serbia and Montenegro had or must have known of that risk, and second, if Serbia and Montenegro had had measures at its disposal to prevent it. Remarkably, the ICJ applied the good faith standard of review for the second question on its own initiative. Neither party had invoked a deferential standard of review.[30] Yet, arguably, it did not do so in recognition of its institutional limitations, but in order to balance a particular, far-reaching finding in the case.

Serbia and Montenegro could have claimed that the ICJ ought to defer to its assessment as to the risk of genocide, and justified this with reference to the complexity of the situation,[31] the Court's lack of expertise as a judicial institution, and its own comparative advantage as an actor with superior knowledge

[29] *Convention on the Prevention and Punishment of the Crime of Genocide*, ICJ, Oral Proceedings of 20 April 2006, afternoon (CR 2006/34), 17, para 17 (Condorelli); *Convention on the Prevention and Punishment of the Crime of Genocide*, ICJ, Oral Proceedings of 24 April 2006, morning (CR 2006/37), 60, para 5 (Softić).

[30] Apparently, Bosnia and Herzegovina took the *de novo* standard as basis, as is evidenced by the objective phrasing: In its view, the 'correct question to ask' was whether Serbia and Montenegro *had* had measures at its disposal to prevent the events from unfolding, which it had not taken, *Bosnian Genocide*, Oral Proceedings of 20 April 2006, 15, para 11 (Condorelli). Throughout its written and oral pleadings, Bosnia-Herzegovina purported to show that this was the case, see *Convention on the Prevention and Punishment of the Crime of Genocide (Bosnia and Herzegovina v Serbia and Montenegro)*, ICJ, Memorial of Bosnia and Herzegovina of 15 April 1994, 288; *Convention on the Prevention and Punishment of the Crime of Genocide (Bosnia and Herzegovina v Serbia and Montenegro)*, ICJ, Reply of Bosnia and Herzegovina of 23 April 1998, 848–50; *Bosnian Genocide*, Oral Proceedings of 20 April 2006, 16, paras 14–15 (Condorelli).

[31] See in that connection S Forlati, 'The Legal Obligation to Prevent Genocide: *Bosnia v Serbia* and Beyond' (2011) *Polish Yearbook of International Law* 189, 198.

of the situation at the time. Judge Ranjeva alluded to this point in his separate opinion when he noted that 'one must humbly acknowledge the difficulties encountered by judges in gauging the reality of the threat or risk of genocide when an assessment is required … Judicial monitoring of the categorization of the acts entails the risk that judges may be led to substitute their analysis for that of the State authorities'.[32] Further, the respondent could have asked the Court to defer to its respective assessment as to its options to prevent the genocide and have backed this claim by pointing to the complexity of the decision-making process whether or not, and how, to intervene. Such a claim was later made in the literature.[33] Yet, it made none of these claims.

Both those 'missed opportunities' may be explained by the fact that even under the most deferential standard of review – short of complete deference – Serbia and Montenegro's case was difficult to argue. For one, the Court later noted that the respondent's leaders had been 'fully aware of the climate of deep-seated hatred which reigned between the Bosnian Serbs and the Muslims in the Srebrenica region', and that '*it must have been clear* that there was a serious risk of genocide in Srebrenica'. Further, the ICJ observed that Serbia and Montenegro had had an 'undeniable influence' on the relevant actors, and yet 'has not shown that it took *any* initiative to prevent what happened'.[34] Against this background, even the adoption of the good faith standard of review would not have changed the outcome of the case (and, effectively, did not).

It is not entirely clear what standard of review the ICJ adopted for the first question, namely whether there had been the risk of genocide and the respective awareness of Serbia and Montenegro's part. However, in light of the objective language ('must have been clear', 'what looked likely to happen') and the absence of a deferential standard of review plea by the respondent, it is likely that it adopted the *de novo* standard.

In contrast, the Court adopted the good faith standard for its evaluation of the second question. It held that 'responsibility is … incurred if the state *manifestly* failed to take all measures to prevent genocide which were within its power, and which might have contributed to preventing the genocide'.[35] The use of the term 'manifestly' makes clear that only a qualified failure to act suffices to establish the responsibility of the respective state. This amounts to a deferential standard of review.[36] In light of the required degree of disagreement between the ICJ and the state, this corresponds to the good faith standard.

[32] *Convention on the Prevention and Punishment of the Crime of Genocide (Bosnia and Herzegovina v Serbia and Montenegro)*, ICJ, Judgment (Merits), Separate Opinion of Judge Ranjeva, para 6.

[33] In that sense Forlati, 'The Legal Obligation to Prevent Genocide' (n 31), 204.

[34] *Application of the Convention on the Prevention and Punishment of the Crime of Genocide (Bosnia and Herzegovina v Serbia and Montenegro)*, ICJ, Judgment (Merits) of 26 February 2007, para 438 (emphases added).

[35] ibid, para 430 (emphasis added; the Court resorted to the same formulation at para 438).

[36] See also Forlati, 'The Legal Obligation to Prevent Genocide' (n 31), 203–04.

Crucially, before arriving at this finding, the Court had made clear that the obligation to prevent genocides does not end at a state party's borders.[37] Seen in this light, the ICJ may have wanted to counterbalance the unlimited geographical reach of that obligation by adopting the good faith standard of review for evaluating a state's compliance with it.[38] This interpretation is also supported by the fact that the standard of review was not outcome-determinative, as shown above. This also shows that the Court did not adopt this standard of review in a desire to show deference to the respondent.

Did considerations of institutional expertise and the relative comparative advantage of the state executive also play a role in that finding? Arguably, no. The ICJ explicitly limited the applicability of this standard of review to the obligation to prevent under the Genocide Convention.[39] Had it attributed any merit to the expertise-argument for a deferential standard of review – which would apply for all obligations to prevent, for instance the obligation to prevent trans-boundary harm – it would not have limited the relevance of this standard to the Genocide Convention. This demonstrates that the adoption of the good faith standard in *Bosnian Genocide* is an isolated event, one that can be explained with the high stakes of the specific convention.

III. CONCLUSION FOR GOOD FAITH

Good faith as a standard of review is of limited significance in the ICJ's jurisprudence. In *ELSI*, the pertinent legal norm expressly foresaw good faith as standard of review, and neither party urged the Court to adopt a different standard. This indicates that the ICJ did not adopt the good faith standard in deference to Italy or out of considerations of legitimacy or expertise. Rather, it simply applied the text of the provision as it stood.

In *Bosnian Genocide*, despite the fact that none of the participants had argued for a deferential standard of review for this particular question, the ICJ chose to apply the good faith standard to evaluate whether a party had failed to take all means at its disposal to prevent a genocide. Arguably, it did so to attenuate its broad finding of the applicability of the obligation to prevent, and not out of a concern that it would be lacking the requisite expertise to make its own independent assessment of the facts. Furthermore, it expressly limited the significance of this finding to the Genocide Convention. As a consequence, one

[37] *Bosnian Genocide*, Judgment (Merits) (n 34), paras 183, 430; see also M Milanovic, 'State Responsibility for Genocide: A Follow-Up' (2007) 18(4) *European Journal of International Law* 669, 685.

[38] Forlati makes the same point, Forlati, 'The Legal Obligation to Prevent Genocide: Bosnia v Serbia and Beyond' (n 31), 204. Had the Court laid down a stricter standard of review, arguably, many States would have found themselves in violation of their obligation to prevent in the case of Srebrenica, and, before that, Rwanda.

[39] *Bosnian Genocide*, Judgment (Merits) (n 34), para 429.

may not draw any conclusions as to the standard of review for other obligations to prevent. The adoption of the good faith standard, manifestly intended as a signal towards the community of States, bears little relevance beyond the confines of the particular subject-matter.

In turn, the *Mutual Assistance* case, involving a state's essential interests, is perhaps the only one with potential for generalisation. Yet, the pertinent legal norm was termed as a self-judging clause. In the first and only other case to date in which the ICJ had to decide on the application of such a self-judging norm, *Norwegian Loans*, it settled on complete deference. From this angle, the good faith standard in *Mutual Assistance* appears first and foremost as a gradual *reduction* of judicial deference. Had it not been for the wording of the pertinent provision, it seems likely that the ICJ would have applied the reasonableness or even the *de novo* standard of review, as it did in all other proceedings involving national security interests.

Table 7 summarises the parties' and the ICJ's positions on the standard of review.

Table 7 Good faith – overview of party and ICJ positions on the appropriate standard of review; respondent in dark grey, applicant in light grey, Court in black

Short title	Complete Deference	Good Faith	Reasonableness	*De novo*
ELSI		Italy Court United States		
Mutual Assistance	France	Court	Djibouti	
Bosnian Genocide		Court		Bosnia & Herzegovina Serbia & Montenegro

Did the ICJ resort to the good faith standard as an avoidance technique? A point can be made that it did so in *Bosnian Genocide*. In contrast, *Mutual Assistance* remains a border case.

In *Bosnian Genocide*, the Court did not revert to this standard as a means to avoid the pronouncement that the respondent, Serbia and Montenegro, had violated its obligation to prevent a genocide from occurring. The fact that it arrived at such a pronouncement despite the deferential standard of review it had chosen amply demonstrates this. Yet, by limiting the prospects of success for future proceedings brought against other states for violation of the same obligation, it limited the likelihood of such proceedings. Thereby, it avoided having to find other, potentially more powerful states to be in violation of their obligation to prevent genocides. This is of even greater importance as the obligations under the Genocide Convention are owed *erga omnes partes*. In this respect, the ICJ has affirmed that all states parties to the Genocide Convention have standing to invoke a violation by another state party, thus opening the door wide to further such proceedings.[40] The adoption of the good faith standard drastically lowered the prospects for success of such proceedings, and thus closed again the door it had just opened to a significant degree.

In *Mutual Assistance*, the Court accorded deference to France by applying a deferential standard of review to evaluate its invocation of a national security clause. Thereby, it avoided having to find the respondent to be in violation of its obligations, and avoided to define for itself what would be valid security interests of France. This impression of avoidance is reinforced by the fact that the ICJ applied exactly the standard of review that France had ultimately urged it to adopt, and a more lenient standard than Djibouti had invoked. On the other hand, the Court also applied a stricter standard of review than it had done in its prior jurisprudence. Further, the choice of the good faith standard of review was in line with the approach of other international courts and tribunals concerned with the application of 'self-judging' clauses. Finally, the ICJ did not refer to any institutional considerations as justification for its stance, but exclusively to the wording of the pertinent provision. In conclusion, the case *could* be understood as avoidance vis-a-vis France, but certainly less so towards the international community concerning future proceedings. Ultimately, however, the circumstances of the case suggest that the Court's use of the good faith standard of review is not an instance of avoidance.

[40] *Application of the Convention on the Prevention and Punishment of the Crime of Genocide (The Gambia v Myanmar)*, ICJ, Judgment (Preliminary Objections) of 22 July 2022, paras 106–12; on the question of standing for the invocation of obligations *erga omnes*, see also P Urs, 'Obligations erga omnes and the question of standing before the International Court of Justice' (2021) 34(2) *Leiden Journal of International Law* 505.

6

Reasonableness

UNDER THE REASONABLENESS standard of review, the Court will enquire whether an unprejudiced actor in the position of the state at the time that state had acted *could* (and not *would have needed to*) have come to the same assessment. The ICJ has been using this standard of review in a significant number of proceedings, both explicitly and implicitly. Of the 31 proceedings analysed, it has chosen the reasonableness standard in 12. In contrast, it has opposed the states' call to apply this standard in eight further cases: *LaGrand*, *Oil Platforms*, *Wall*, *Armed Activities*, *Whaling*, *Construction of a Road*, *Certain Activities* and *Jadhav*. While the ICJ's (as is submitted, only partial) use of the reasonableness standard of review in the *Whaling* case has received the most attention, it has been relying on this notion from early on. The *Conditions of Admission to the UN* advisory proceedings is the first example, *Certain Iranian Assets* the most recent one. This does not only show that the Court's use of this particular standard is a regular feature; it is also a constant feature.

At the same time, the ICJ has never adopted the reasonableness standard of review on its own initiative. There is no example where it applied it without the respondent's previous call for judicial deference. By adopting the reasonableness standard, the Court thus conformed to the respective states' basic expectation to accord them deference. This could lend some support to the interpretation that it applied this standard of review out of considerations of expediency, or, put differently, avoidance. On the other hand, the respondents had often urged the Court to go even further, and accord them complete deference or apply the good faith standard of review. Such has been the case in eight proceedings.[1]

[1] In five, the concerned states had at least at some stage pleaded for the recognition of a non-reviewable decision-making space in their favour, and thus for complete deference by the Court: *Admission of a State to the United Nations (Charter, Art 4)*, ICJ, Advisory Opinion of 28 May 1948; *Corfu Channel (United Kingdom v Albania)*, ICJ, Judgment (Merits) of 9 April 1949; *Military and Paramilitary Activities in and against Nicaragua (Nicaragua v United States of America)*, ICJ, Judgment (Merits) of 27 June 1986; *Ahmadou Sadio Diallo (Guinea v the Congo)*, ICJ, Judgment (Merits) of 30 November 2010; *Whaling in the Antarctic (Australia v Japan: New Zealand intervening)*, ICJ, Judgment of 31 March 2014 (note that Japan at some stage also invoked the good faith standard of review). In three cases, the respective respondents had pleaded for the adoption of a good faith standard: *Rights of Nationals of the United States of America in Morocco (France v United States of America)*, ICJ, Judgment of 27 August 1952; *Right of Passage over Indian Territory (Portugal v India)*, ICJ, Judgment (Merits) of 12 April 1960; *Certain Iranian Assets (Islamic Republic of Iran v United States of America)*, ICJ, Judgment (Merits) of 30 March 2023.

By adopting the reasonableness standard, the ICJ thus disappointed these expectations. This is a further demonstration of the fact that it does not automatically adopt the standard of review invoked by the respondent.

Only in four of the 12 proceedings did the Court follow the states in adopting the reasonableness standard of review: *Gabčíkovo-Nagymaros*, *Navigational Rights*, *Pulp Mills* and *Immunities and Criminal Proceedings*. Significantly, these proceedings, with the exception of *Pulp Mills*, were also the only ones in which respondent and applicant had concurred that reasonableness would be the appropriate standard of review. Two explanations come to mind for the ICJ's adoption of the parties' shared position on this point. First, it is possible that the Court accorded decisive importance to the fact that both states agreed on the applicable standard of review.[2] On the other hand, it could also be the case that the parties' agreement on this question was merely an expression of the fact that the reasonableness standard of review was also the legally 'correct' one.

Finally, it will be answered whether the ICJ resorted to the reasonableness standard of review as an avoidance technique, either vis-a-vis the respective respondent, or more broadly vis-a-vis the state community. A point can be made that the Court did so in both respects in proceedings involving national security interests, domestic measures, and scientific determinations. The proceedings in which the ICJ adopted the reasonableness standard in the four categories – national security, domestic measures, political determinations, and scientific determinations – will be evaluated in turn, followed by a conclusion.

I. NATIONAL SECURITY INTERESTS

This category comprises all proceedings in which the respondent states justified their incriminated measures with national security interests, and in which the Court at least partially laid down the reasonableness standard of review. In the first two proceedings, *Corfu Channel* and *Right of Passage*, it only did so implicitly. In contrast, in the three remaining proceedings, *Nicaragua*, *Diallo* and *Certain Iranian Assets*, it did so explicitly. Yet, it found that even under this standard of review, the respective respondents had violated their obligations under international law. This fact makes it less likely that it used this standard as an avoidance technique vis-a-vis the respective respondents. Arguably, however, it thereby sent a signal to the state community as a whole that it was ready to accord them some deference in security matters. One could therefore speak of avoidance vis-a-vis the state community.

[2] Such a pattern was found to exist concerning the ICJ's identification of customary international law, see N Petersen, 'The International Court of Justice and the Judicial Politics of Identifying Customary International Law' (2017) 28(2) *European Journal of International Law* 357, 369–72. He concludes that for the Court, 'consent of the parties to the dispute is arguably the most important consideration to identify a norm of customary international law', ibid, 369.

A. *Corfu Channel*

As outlined above, *Corfu Channel* concerned the right of passage of warships through international straits. Albania argued that there was a right for coastal states to forbid innocent passage to foreign warships in certain circumstances, that it had considered that such circumstances were existing in the case of the passage of the United Kingdom's warships through the Corfu Strait, and that the Court could not question its respective assessment. Accordingly, Albania claimed that it could judge for itself whether there was a threat to its national security, and what measures were appropriate to counter that threat. The ICJ dismissed that argumentation by rejecting a right to prohibit innocent passage in the first place. Yet, it did recognise that states had a right to issue regulations for such passage below the level of prohibitions or prior authorisation requirements.[3] Arguably, for this question, it adopted the reasonableness standard of review.

Specifically, the Court observed that '*in view of these exceptional circumstances* [ie, tensions with Greece invoked by Albania to justify its measures], [Albania] would have been justified in issuing [such] regulations'.[4] It is difficult to discern the standard of review the ICJ applied in this succinct statement, but it is likely that it held at least some degree of deference to be appropriate. The first indicator is the succinctness itself. While the Court chose to address the question of regulations, it only addressed Albania's case superficially. Had it applied the *de novo* standard of review, it would have been logical to devote more attention to this question and address the details of the situation at hand. Not only against this background does it seem that the ICJ adopted the reasonableness standard of review. Several individual opinions lend support to this interpretation, as does a voice in the literature.

In his dissenting opinion, Judge Azevedo concluded that the right of passage for foreign warships through territorial waters 'is subject to a precarious régime which may be modified, *in a reasonable manner*, by the coastal State'.[5] Judge Krylov went even further. He argued that in the absence of international regulation, it would be the right of every costal state to determine the regime of the respective strait. Thus, he concluded, Albania had the right to do so for the Corfu Strait.[6] Finally, Judge *ad hoc* Ečer concluded that in the absence of a definitive rule on the subject, Albania had the right to prohibit the innocent passage of the UK warships since 'the general rule of *in dubio pro reo* must be applied in analogy'.[7] It is likely that these three judges pushed for the recognition of

[3] See above at ch 4, section I.B.

[4] *Corfu Channel*, Judgment (Merits) (n 1), 29 (emphasis added).

[5] *Corfu Channel (United Kingdom v Albania)*, ICJ, Judgment (Merits), Dissenting Opinion by Judge Azevedo, 101 (emphasis added).

[6] *Corfu Channel (United Kingdom v Albania)*, ICJ, Judgment (Merits), Dissenting Opinion by Judge Krylov, 74–75.

[7] *Corfu Channel (United Kingdom v Albania)*, ICJ, Judgment (Merits, Dissenting Opinion by Judge *ad hoc* Ečer, 129.

at least some decision-making space in favour of Albania. Finally, this reading finds some support in the literature. Cannizzaro, drawing a line of continuity from the PCIJ's *Oscar Chinn* judgment, where that court had held that Belgium, the respondent state, 'was the sole judge of this critical situation and of the remedies that it called for – subject of course to its duty of respecting its international obligations',[8] writes that 'the Court seems to have considered that the coastal states had the power to claim a *reasonable* degree of security and, to this purpose, to determine the modalities of the passage of warship'.[9]

B. *Right of Passage*

Right of Passage was the first case before the ICJ in which a state explicitly referred to the 'margin of appreciation'.[10] The case also exhibits important parallels to *Corfu Channel*.[11] Ultimately, the ICJ accorded some assessment-making leeway to India by adopting the reasonableness standard of review.

After an uprising that had led to the overthrow of Portuguese authority in one of Portugal's two enclaves on the Indian Peninsula, India had restricted Portugal's access to both enclaves. Portugal claimed that by doing so, India had violated its right of passage and impeded its exercise of sovereignty. India in turn asserted that this measure had been necessary to uphold public order in its own territory surrounding the enclaves.[12] Otherwise, there would have been a 'very strong probability' of uprisings and clashes between the enclaves' inhabitants and Portuguese personnel at the enclaves' borders and within its own territory.[13]

Portugal conceded that exceptional circumstances could justify a restriction of its right of passage.[14] Yet, the Court could and should question India's assessment as to the reasons brought forward to justify the suspension of its right. In its view, only a 'real danger'[15] could justify a suspension of that right, and '*only*

[8] *Oscar Chinn*, PCIJ, Judgment of 12 December 1934, 79.

[9] E Cannizzaro, 'Proportionality and Margin of Appreciation in the Whaling Case: Reconciling Antithetical Doctrines?' (2016) 27(4) *European Journal of International Law* 1061, 1066 (emphasis added). See also ibid, 1067.

[10] Albeit not with the meaning primarily associated with it today, *Right of Passage over Indian Territory*, ICJ, Oral Proceedings (Merits) of 22 September 1959, afternoon, 314 (Bourquin). Portugal used this term to explain that the exact manner of application of its purported right of passage through Indian territory would vary with the circumstances.

[11] Judge Armand-Ugon also makes that connection, see *Right of Passage over Indian Territory (Portugal v India)*, ICJ, Judgment (Merits), Dissenting Opinion of Judge Armand-Ugon, 85–86.

[12] *Right of Passage*, Judgment (Merits) (n 1), 44.

[13] *Right of Passage over Indian Territory*, ICJ, Counter-Memorial of India of March 1958, para 345; see also *Right of Passage over Indian Territory (Portugal v India)*, ICJ, Rejoinder of India of February 1959, para 634.

[14] *Right of Passage over Indian Territory*, ICJ, Oral Proceedings of 30 September 1959, afternoon, 324 (Bourquin).

[15] *Right of Passage over Indian Territory*, ICJ, Oral Proceedings of 6 October 1959, 597 (Bouquin).

an objective appreciation of the facts' would allow a determination to what degree it could be suspended.[16] This makes clear that Portugal advocated for the *de novo* standard of review. Further, it claimed that India's assertions did not meet that standard. Its assessment as to the risks associated with the passage of Portuguese armed forces through its territory would be exaggerated.[17]

India in turn argued for the application of the good faith standard of review. It claimed that '*[g]ranted the existence of facts involving some possibility of disorder*, the power of appreciating the risks of public order is a power inherent in the sovereignty of India'.[18] Accordingly, for India, as long as there was at least a remote justification for its assessment that its public order would be under threat by the passage of Portuguese armed personnel, the Court should uphold its justification.

The Court recognised that India was due some assessment-making space. While the precise standard of review remains unclear by the terms of the decision alone, ultimately, the better arguments speak for the interpretation that the ICJ opted for the reasonableness standard. It observed that—

> In view of the tension then prevailing in intervening Indian territory, the Court is unable to hold that India's refusal of passage ... was action contrary to its obligation resulting from Portugal's right of passage. Portugal's claim of a right of passage is subject to full recognition and exercise of Indian sovereignty ... India's refusal of passage in those cases was, in the circumstances, covered by its power of regulation and control.[19]

The fact that the ICJ specifically mentioned the prevailing situation at the time ('in the circumstances') shows that it did not blindly accept India's invocation of security concerns.

The language of this decisive section is remarkably similar to that in *Corfu Channel*: 'Albania, in view of these exceptional circumstances, would have been justified in issuing regulations'[20] and 'India's refusal of passage ... was, in the circumstances, covered by its power of regulation'. This similarity in subject-matter and wording suggests that the Court adopted the same approach in the standard of review question as well. As explained above, in *Corfu Chann*el, it had adopted the reasonableness standard of review. Finally, the ICJ explicitly recognised India's territorial sovereignty and its power of regulation. Those domains are historically understood to belong to a state's prerogative of sovereign decision-making.[21] States have regularly been urging the Court to apply a

[16] *Right of Passage over Indian Territory*, ICJ, Reply of Portugal of July 1958, para 388 (emphasis added, own translation. In the original: '*[s]eule une appréciation objective des faits* permettra de déterminer la mesure dans laquelle le passage pourrait être éventuellement suspendu').

[17] *Right of Passage*, Oral Proceedings (Merits) (n 15), 599 (Bourquin).

[18] *Right of Passage*, Rejoinder of India (n 13), para 633 (emphasis added).

[19] *Right of Passage*, Judgment (Merits) (n 1), 45.

[20] *Corfu Channel*, Judgment (Merits) (n 1), 29.

[21] As the Permanent Court had observed in the *Lighthouses* case, 'any grant of legislative powers generally implies the grant of a discretionary right to judge how far their exercise may be necessary

deferential standard of review in these domains. Taken together with the parallel to *Corfu Channel*, this is a final indicator pointing towards the reasonableness standard of review.[22]

C. *Nicaragua* (Treaty Law)

Nicaragua posed the question whether the United States could rely on Article XXI(1)(d) of the US–Nicaragua Treaty of Friendship, according to which that treaty 'shall not preclude the application of measures … necessary to protect [a Party's] essential security interests', to justify the aggressive measures it had taken against Nicaragua. The Court rejected the contention that it had to accept the United States' reliance on that provision as valid without any evaluation on its own.[23] On the other hand, it did accord some credit to the underlying argumentation, and adopted a partially deferential standard of review in some important aspects. Namely, it adopted a mixed reasonableness/ *de novo* standard of review for its evaluation of the conventional security exception. It applied the reasonableness standard for the question whether there had been a risk for an essential security interest, and the *de novo* standard for the question whether the measures taken in reaction had been necessary. Thereby, the ICJ recognised that it could not function as the sole and ultimate decision-maker for the validity of a state's invocation of security interests.

The Court noted that 'whether a measure is necessary to protect the essential security interests of a party *is not… purely a question for the subjective judgment of the party*'.[24] Other commentators have already remarked that this expression implies some degree of deference.[25] This interpretation is further corroborated by another passage in the judgment. Therein, the Court explained that its task was 'to assess whether the risk run by these 'essential security interests' is *reasonable*, and secondly, whether the measures presented as being designed to protect these interests *are* not merely useful but "*necessary*"'.[26] With

or urgent'. Arguably, the power to issue regulations falls in the same category, *Lighthouses Case between France and Greece*, PCIJ, Judgment of 17 March 1934, 4, 22.

[22] Individual statements by the judges appended to the judgment do not shed further light on this question. Judge Spender and Judge *ad hoc* Fernandes both concluded that India's restriction of Portugal's right of passage was not justified. However, they did not arrive at this conclusion by questioning India's assertion that its public order had been under threat, *Right of Passage over Indian Territory (Portugal v India)*, ICJ, Judgment (Merits), Dissenting Opinion of Judge Sir Percy Spender, 110–15; *Right of Passage over Indian Territory (Portugal v India)*, ICJ, Judgment (Merits), Dissenting Opinion of Judge *ad hoc* Fernandes, 140–43.

[23] See above at ch 4, section I.A.i.

[24] *Nicaragua*, Judgment (Merits) (n 1), para 282 (emphasis added).

[25] See for instance C Ragni, 'Standard of Review and the Margin of Appreciation before the International Court of Justice' in L Gruszczynski and W Werner (eds), *Deference in International Courts and Tribunals: Standard of Review and Margin of Appreciation* (Oxford University Press, 2014), 324.

[26] *Nicaragua*, Judgment (Merits) (n 1), para 224 (emphases added).

this statement, the ICJ laid down a differentiated standard of review for the two objects of evaluation: first, the existence of a risk for an essential security interest, and second, the necessity of the measures taken to protect that interest. For the first element, it would accept the state's first-hand assessment that a risk for an essential security interest existed as long as that assessment was reasonable. In contrast, for the necessity of the measures, the Court left no room for deference and chose the *de novo* standard of review. This becomes clear through the wording employed ('are … necessary') and the way the ICJ examined the mining of Nicaraguan harbours and attacks on its infrastructure.

In his separate opinion in *Oil Platforms*, revolving around the identical provision in the US–Iran Treaty of Amity, Judge Kooijmans found this to be 'a rather felicitous choice of words'. For him—

> There seem to be good reasons for such a distinction with regard to the margin of discretion to be left to governmental authorities. The evaluation of what essential security interests are and whether they are in jeopardy is first and foremost a political question and can hardly be replaced by a judicial assessment. Only when the political evaluation is patently unreasonable … is a judicial ban appropriate … the choice of means to be taken in order to protect those interests … lends itself much more to judicial review and thus to a stricter test, since the means chosen directly affect the interests and rights of others. Moreover, the means by which interests may be protected are usually subjected to legal prescriptions that are stricter and more compelling as the interests and rights that may be affected are deemed more important.[27]

Accordingly, Judge Kooijmans justified the Court's deference in the first question with the close nexus to considerations beyond the legal realm, and the strict standard of review in the second with the consideration that any encroachment upon other entities' rights and interests would warrant closer judicial oversight.

D. *Diallo*

As outlined above, the *Diallo* case involved the question whether the DRC had violated its obligations under Article 13 ICCPR by refusing Mr Diallo, a Guinean national, the right to appeal against his expulsion. Under that provision, an alien 'shall, except where compelling reasons of national security otherwise require, be allowed to submit the reasons against his expulsion and to have his case reviewed'. The DRC asserted that the Court could not question its first-hand assessment that the conditions of the exception had been met in Mr Diallo's case. The ICJ, in turn, rejected these assertions.[28]

[27] *Oil Platforms (Iran v United States of America)*, ICJ, Judgment (Merits), Separate Opinion of Judge Kooijmans, para 44.

[28] See already above at ch 4, section I.A.iv.

Instead, it held that—

> *In principle*, it is doubtless for the national authorities to consider the reasons of public order that may justify the adoption of one police measure or another. But when this involves setting aside an important procedural guarantee provided for by an international treaty … [i]t is for the State to demonstrate that the 'compelling reasons' required by the Covenant existed, *or at the very least could reasonably have been concluded to have existed*.[29]

Thereby, the Court explicitly laid down the reasonableness standard of review. However, even under that standard, it concluded that the DRC had violated Art. 13 ICCPR.

This case is remarkable in at least one important aspect: The specific standard of review (beyond the rejection of complete deference) was not outcome-determinative. Given the paucity of the DRC's explanations, it is most likely that the Court would have found the DRC's refusal to grant Mr Diallo the possibility to have his expulsion reviewed unlawful even under the good faith standard of review. To justify its reliance on the security exception, the DRC had only made very broad and largely unsubstantiated statements. It had alleged that 'certain foreign nationals' had engaged in counterfeiting, currency smuggling and had 'destroyed public finances' of the DRC, and that it had taken the decision to expel certain foreign nationals implicated in those activities in this context, including Mr Diallo.[30] However, despite an allegedly close surveillance by special forces, the DRC had not submitted any substantial account of his purported crimes.[31] The DRC thus failed to provide any reasons as to why it could successfully invoke the security exception of Article 13 ICCPR. Against the background of the financial stakes of the case,[32] one may argue that the DRC even committed an abuse of rights when expulsing Mr Diallo and depriving him of effective judicial recourse. Accordingly, by adopting the reasonableness standard of review, the Court adopted a stricter standard than would have been necessary under considerations of judicial economy. Most likely, the result would have been the same under a good faith standard.

This suggests that the ICJ chose to lay down the reasonableness standard for reasons going beyond the individual case. Considering its broad statement as to the decision-making prerogative of states for questions of public order, it is likely that the Court opted for the reasonableness standard as a signal to the state community.

[29] *Diallo*, Judgment (Merits) (n 1), para 74 (emphasis added).

[30] *Ahmadou Sadio Diallo (Guinea v the Congo)*, ICJ, Counter-Memorial of the Congo of 27 March 2008, paras 1.04–1.08.

[31] ibid, paras 1.10–1.11.

[32] Guinea had asked the Court to order the DRC to pay more than $31 billion for the economic damages suffered by Mr Diallo, *Ahmadou Sadio Diallo (Guinea v the Congo)*, ICJ, Application of Guinea of 23 December 1998, 37.

E. *Certain Iranian Assets*

Insofar as is relevant for the purposes of this study, the *Certain Iranian Assets* case, yet another episode in the US–Iran saga before the ICJ, revolved around a virtually identical provision to that at issue in *Nicaragua*, namely Article XX(1)(d) of the US–Iran Treaty of Friendship. Like its counterpart, this provision excluded 'the application of measures … necessary to protect [a Party's] essential security interests' from the treaty's purview. The United States relied on this provision to justify a presidential Executive Order. By virtue of this Order, assets held by Iranian financial institutions within the United States were blocked; subsequently, they became subject to enforcement proceedings in domestic court proceedings. Among others, Iran had brought this Executive Order before the Court as a purported violation of the US–Iran Treaty of Amity.

Unlike in *Nicaragua*, the United States acknowledged from the outset that the ICJ had the ability to examine its invocation of that clause, recognising that the provision was not self-judging.[33] Yet, according to the United States, the Court should grant 'a wide margin of deference' to its appreciation that the clause's conditions had been met.[34] In support, it observed that the provision involved vital state interests,[35] noted that it would be 'a matter of systemic importance going to the interpretation and application of treaties that fundamental, national security exceptions included in a treaty should be honored', and finally pointed to an alleged parallel to the ICJ's standard of review finding in *Mutual Assistance*.[36] Accordingly, whether a situation implicates a party's security interests and whether the interests at stake are essential to it would not be 'questions in the abstract but instead must be viewed from the perspective of the Party invoking the defense – based on … its own perception of those circumstances'.[37] The reference to the *Mutual Assistance* case already made clear that the United States invoked the good faith standard of review, a standard it later also referred to explicitly.[38]

[33] *Certain Iranian Assets (Islamic Republic of Iran v United States of America)*, ICJ, Preliminary Objections of the United States of America of 1 May 2017, para 7.30.

[34] *Certain Iranian Assets*, ICJ, Oral Proceedings of 8 October 2018, afternoon (CR 2018/29), 18, para 49 (Daley); see also *Certain Iranian Assets*, ICJ, Oral Proceedings of 11 October 2018, afternoon (CR 2018/32), 32, para 49 (Grosh).

[35] *Certain Iranian Assets*, ICJ, Oral Proceedings of 21 September 2022, afternoon (CR 2022/18), 39, para 2 (Daley).

[36] *Certain Iranian Assets (Islamic Republic of Iran v United States of America)*, ICJ, Counter-Memorial of the United States of America of 14 October 2019, paras 11.3 and 11.22, respectively; the United States made the same argument in the preliminary objections stage of *Alleged Violations of the 1955 Treaty of Amity*, see for instance *Alleged Violations of the 1955 Treaty of Amity, Economic Relations, and Consular Rights*, ICJ, Oral Proceedings of 14 September 2020, afternoon (CR 2020/10), 69, para 28 (Boisson de Chazournes).

[37] *Certain Iranian Assets*, Counter-Memorial of the United States of America (n 36), para 11.29.

[38] *Certain Iranian Assets (Islamic Republic of Iran v United States of America)*, ICJ, Rejoinder of the United States of America of 17 May 2021, para 7.15; Oral Proceedings of 21 September 2022, 44, para 35 (Daley).

Iran, in turn, pointed to the Court's finding in *Nicaragua* on the applicable standard of review to argue for a stricter standard of review and distinguished Article XX(1)(d) from the pertinent provision in *Mutual Assistance*[39] – a position that ultimately prevailed: The ICJ followed Iran in rejecting the parallel drawn by the United States to *Mutual Assistance*, and confirmed[40] its position taken in *Nicaragua*. Thus, it observed that each party to the treaty only 'enjoy[ed] a *certain* margin of discretion' – and not, as the United States had argued, 'wide discretion'.[41] In consequence, the Court chose a mixed reasonableness/*de novo* standard to review the US invocation of Article XX(1)(d) – a standard under which the United States subsequently lost. None of the judges dissented on the substance of this finding. In turn, Judge *Iwasawa* argued for a slightly more deferential standard of review.[42] According to him, faced with a clause such as the one at issue in this proceeding, 'an international court should determine whether the measure was *rational* in light of a consideration of the *reasonably available alternatives known to that State at the time*'.[43] Arguably, this equates to a consistent reasonableness standard.

F. Conclusion on National Security Interests

The first section of this chapter has shown that the Court has used the reasonableness standard of review in five proceedings revolving around state measures justified with security concerns. While it did so only implicitly in *Corfu Channel* and *Right of Passage*, it explicitly acknowledged the need to pay deference to the states in their security assessments in *Nicaragua*, *Diallo* and *Certain Iranian Assets*. The fact that it openly did so in these three proceedings, even though this acknowledgement was not outcome-determinative, suggests that it did so with the larger audience of states in mind. Arguably, it did so as an avoidance technique.

Thereby, it signalled that it would not delve into a full-fledged evaluation of state measures justified with essential security interests. It did so more openly and broadly in *Diallo*, when it acknowledged that every state has a decision-making prerogative for police measures. One reason for this difference to *Nicaragua*, where the recognition of the state's decision-making prerogative was less broad,

[39] *Certain Iranian Assets (Islamic Republic of Iran v United States of America)*, ICJ, Reply of Iran of 17 August 2020, para 10.26; *Certain Iranian Assets*, ICJ, Oral Proceedings of 10 October 2018, afternoon (CR 2018/31), 37, paras 54–56 (Aughey).

[40] In its judgment on the preliminary objections in *Alleged Violations of the 1955 Treaty of Amity*, the Court likewise announced its adherence to this jurisprudence, *Alleged Violations of the 1955 Treaty of Amity, Economic Relations, and Consular Rights (Islamic Republic of Iran v United States of America)*, ICJ, Judgment (Preliminary Objections) of 3 February 2021, para 112.

[41] *Certain Iranian Assets*, Judgment (Merits) (n 1), paras 106–08 (emphasis added).

[42] *Certain Iranian Assets (Islamic Republic of Iran v United States of America)*, ICJ, Judgment (Merits), Separate Opinion of Judge Iwasawa, paras 23 and 29, respectively.

[43] ibid, para 30 (emphasis added).

could be the fact that in contrast to *Nicaragua*, *Diallo* was concerned with internal measures. The ICJ thereby signalled its readiness in principle to grant leeway for internal security measures, both with respect to the definition of essential security interests and the measures designed to protect them. In turn, the mixed reasonableness/*de novo* standard the Court adopted in *Nicaragua* shows that it is ready to defer to the state for the definition of its essential interests on the one hand, and thus the decision whether or not to take action, but not concerning the decision on *how* to act to protect these interests by external measures on the other hand.

II. DOMESTIC MEASURES

The Court has also occasionally employed the reasonableness standard of review when evaluating the legality of a domestic measure taken by a state. It has done so in three cases: *Rights of US Nationals in Morocco*, *Navigational Rights*, and *Immunities and Criminal Proceedings*. What is noteworthy about the Court's reliance on this standard of review in these cases is first of all that it did so openly in all three. Second, they also highlight the dual function of the reasonableness notion that *Corten* has already pointed out: It preserves a 'margin of appreciation' for the states, yet limits it at the same time.[44] Third, while in two of the three cases, *Navigational Rights* and *Immunities and Criminal Proceedings*, the parties concurred that reasonableness would be the correct standard of review, there is nonetheless some ground to believe that the Court used this standard as an avoidance technique, or one of judicial diplomacy, in *Navigational Rights*.

A. *Rights of US Nationals in Morocco*

At the root of the *Rights of US Nationals in Morocco* case was a decree by the French Resident General in Morocco modifying the previously employed customs calculation method for goods coming into the French Zone of Morocco. The case opposed France and the United States, and inter alia concerned the question whether Article 95 of the General Act of the International Conference of Algeciras prescribed a precise calculation method for these customs. The ICJ laid down a deferential standard of review for its evaluation of the customs authorities' choice of the new calculation method:[45] the reasonableness standard of review.

[44] O Corten, *L'utilisation du "raisonnable" par le juge international: Discours juridique, raison et contradictions* (Bruylant, 1997), para 130.

[45] Judge Cot shares this view, *The "Volga" Case (Russian Federation v Australia)*, ITLOS, Separate Opinion of Judge Cot, ITLOS Reports 50, para 16.

France did not claim that the Court could not question its choice for the new calculation method. However, it initially argued that Article 95 of the Act allowed for two different customs calculation methods, and that economic considerations justified the choice for the second. Under normal economic circumstances, it advanced, both calculation methods would lead to similar results. Yet, because the markets in the French zone had been experiencing shortages, certain products had become more expensive, and importers offering those products could reap 'excessive profits' as a result. The new calculation method would simply remedy that situation. For this reason, the choice for that method would not be arbitrary.[46] This implies that the Court could only declare the calculation method choice to be beyond the range of the permissible under Article 95 if it were arbitrary. This amounts to a plea for the good faith standard of review. France justified this with the need for the local authorities to be able to react to abnormal economic situations, and their power to issue local regulations for that purpose in the first place.

The Court agreed that Article 95 did not lay down a strict rule for the customs calculation method, and recognised that the power to determine the calculation method laid with the customs authorities. At the same time, it held, 'it is a power which must be exercised reasonably and in good faith'.[47] While proof for a certain degree of deference, this statement mixes good faith and reasonableness,[48] and is inconclusive as to the precise standard of review. However, the ICJ also named several factors that the authorities would have to consider when making this determination. These factors were the text of the provision and other trade-related circumstances such as the wholesale cash value in the French Zone.[49] Had the Court opted for the good faith standard, it would not have limited the authorities' margin of manoeuvre in such a detailed manner. Accordingly, its reference to objective circumstances puts the standard of review closer to the reasonableness standard.[50] Thus, the ICJ did recognise a first-hand decision-making and assessment space to the local authorities, but to a lesser degree than urged by France.

B. *Navigational Rights*

The *Navigational Rights* case opposed Costa Rica and Nicaragua over the extent of the former's rights on the San Juan River. According to Article VI

[46] *Rights of Nationals of the United States of America in Morocco (France v United States of America)*, ICJ, Reply of France of 13 February 1952, 31–37.

[47] *Rights of US Nationals in Morocco*, Judgment (n 1), 212.

[48] As noted above, as the Court occasionally does, ch 1, fn 66.

[49] *Rights of US Nationals in Morocco*, Judgment (n 1), 211–12.

[50] Referring to this case in *Mutual Assistance*, France spoke of the 'margin of appreciation' that the Court had allegedly recognised in favour of the customs authorities to calculate the valuation of the imported goods, *Mutual Assistance in Criminal Matters*, ICJ, Oral Proceedings of 25 January 2008, morning (CR 2008/5), 12, para 15 (Ascensio).

of the Treaty of Limits between Costa Rica and Nicaragua of 1858, the Costa Rican bank of the river constitutes the border between the two states, and thus, Nicaragua exercises sovereignty and the power of regulation over the river. At the same time, the provision grants Costa Rica a right of navigation on the river 'con objetos de comercio'.[51] Costa Rica now contested the legality of several regulations Nicaragua had introduced for river navigation. Both parties focused extensively on the question of the applicable standard of review. Nicaragua even claimed a 'margin of appreciation'. The Court ultimately adopted the reasonableness standard of review in recognition of the better-placed argument, as its predecessor had done in *Lighthouses*, and as Nicaragua had emphatically argued for. A second driver for its adoption of this deferential standard of review was the consideration that it is first of all the sovereign's prerogative to decide whether and what measures are necessary on its territory.

First, Nicaragua explicitly invoked its sovereignty as the source of its right to regulate.[52] Regulations adopted for security purposes would be compatible with Costa Rica's right of free navigation as long as they were 'reasonably necessary' to achieve those purposes.[53] Costa Rica retorted that 'the concept of free navigation cannot be rendered nugatory by subordinating it to the will of the territorial sovereign. It cannot be left to unilateral determination by that State'.[54] On the other hand, it agreed with Nicaragua in that the incriminated measures only had to meet the reasonableness standard.[55] Thus, both parties' positions overlapped on this point, as Nicaragua did not fail to notice.[56] In support, both states pointed to the inherent logic of Article VI of the Treaty of Territorial Limits, and to the Barcelona Convention[57] and the International Law Association's 'Berlin Rules', which also refer to the reasonableness requirement for regulation of free navigation on rivers.[58]

The Court in turn concluded '[f]or essentially the reasons given by the Parties', each of Nicaragua's regulations must inter alia '*not be unreasonable*, which means that its negative impact on the exercise of the right in question must not be *manifestly* excessive when measured against the protection afforded

[51] *Navigational and Related Rights (Costa Rica v Nicaragua)*, ICJ, Judgment of 13 July 2009, para 19. The Spanish version of the treaty is the only authoritative one, ibid, para 37.

[52] See for instance *Navigational and Related Rights (Costa Rica v Nicaragua)*, ICJ, Rejoinder of Nicaragua of 15 July 2008, para 4.4.

[53] *Navigational and Related Rights (Costa Rica v Nicaragua)*, ICJ, Counter-Memorial of Nicaragua of 29 May 2007, para 2.1.58.

[54] *Navigational and Related Rights*, ICJ, Oral Proceedings of 9 March 2009, morning (CR 2009/6), 39, para 10 (Caflisch).

[55] ibid, 40, para 13 (Caflisch), see also at 42, para 21.

[56] *Navigational and Related Rights*, ICJ, Oral Proceedings of 12 March 2009, morning (CR 2009/7), 38, para 3 (Reichler).

[57] Barcelona Convention and Statute on the Regime of Navigable Waterways of International Concern, 7 League of Nations Treaty Series 35.

[58] With further references *Navigational and Related Rights*, ICJ, Oral Proceedings of 6 March 2009, morning (CR 2009/5), 10, paras 10–20 (Reichler); *Navigational Rights*, Oral Proceedings of 9 March 2009, 40, paras 15–21 (Caflisch).

to the purpose invoked'.[59] The Court made this point even more openly when it held that '*a court examining the reasonableness of a regulation must recognize that the regulator… has the primary responsibility for assessing the need for regulation and for choosing, on the basis of its knowledge of the situation, the measure that it deems most appropriate to meet that need…* Concrete and specific facts will be required to persuade a court to come to that conclusion [that a regulation is unreasonable]'.[60] Thereby, it explicitly laid down the reasonableness standard of review.

Consequently, the Court refrained from holding a regulation to be in violation of Costa Rica's right of navigation unless it clearly followed no legitimate aim, or unless there were clearly less intrusive, but equally effective measures at Nicaragua's disposal. First, the ICJ showed deference to Nicaragua for its definition of what would constitute legitimate purposes, as is evidenced by the fact that it accepted the requirement for Costa Rican vessels to fly the Nicaraguan flag while on the river.[61] Second, it showed deference towards Nicaragua for its first-hand evaluation of what would be reasonably necessary to reach the purposes it had defined.

These regulations were among others the requirement for Costa Rican vessels to stop at any Nicaraguan post along the river and the requirement of every person aboard to carry an identity document, the obligation for said vessels to obtain a Nicaraguan departure clearance certificate, visa and tourist card requirements for all persons aboard, and the restriction of night-time navigation. Costa Rica contested the reasonableness of some of these measures. Notably, it asserted that the existence of several Nicaraguan army posts along the river would make the stops and the departure authorisation requirements unreasonable.[62]

Nicaragua essentially justified these requirements with environmental and security concerns.[63] The deterrent effect of the stop requirement would be particularly important because of the river's geography, with army posts spread far apart and big stretches of the territory adjacent to the river difficult to access.[64] Furthermore, the clearance certificate requirement would enable verification of the vessels' seaworthiness and capability of safe operation, thus constituting a measure ensuring the safety of navigation.[65] Costa Rica, on the other hand, suggested that there would be less intrusive but still suitable measures available, notably, river patrols.[66] The Court dismissed patrolling as an equally effective

[59] *Navigational Rights*, Judgment (n 51), para 87 (emphasis added).

[60] ibid, para 101 (emphasis added).

[61] ibid, para 132.

[62] *Navigational and Related Rights (Costa Rica v Nicaragua)*, ICJ, Reply of Costa Rica of 15 January 2008, para 3.28.

[63] *Navigational Rights*, Rejoinder of Nicaragua (n 52), para 4.61–4.62 and 4.73, see also ibid, para 4.29.

[64] ibid, para 4.71.

[65] ibid, para 4.81.

[66] *Navigational and Related Rights*, ICJ, Oral Proceedings of 3 March 2009, morning (CR 2009/3), 27, paras 19–20 (Caflisch).

alternative, observing that Costa Rica had failed to bring the specific evidence necessary to enable it to declare unreasonable Nicaragua's choice of measures.[67] Likewise, it saw no viable alternative for the clearance certificate, noting that Costa Rica had not suggested for instance that it could assume the inspection responsibilities for its vessels itself.[68] On the other hand, it held that the requirement to stop at every army point was manifestly excessive, hence unreasonable.[69]

Furthermore, Nicaragua justified the visa and tourist requirements by asserting that it 'ha[d] the same right as every other State, in its discretion, to require foreign nationals … to obtain a valid visa before entering her territory'.[70] Costa Rica noted that this position would result in making its freedom of navigation entirely dependent upon Nicaragua's will.[71] The Court agreed. It recognised that there was a legitimate aim behind the visa requirement, but found that there were clearly less restrictive means available to reach that aim. Namely, Nicaragua could refuse entry to particular individuals at the moment that person identifies him- or herself, or under emergency measures.[72] The requirement to obtain tourist cards, in turn, was found by the Court to follow no legitimate aim in the first place.[73]

Two judges dissented on this point. One of them, Judge Sepúlveda-Amor, concluded that the visa requirement was reasonable because there were no equally effective alternatives. Specifically, he discarded the construction of immigration posts along the bank of the San Juan.[74] He noted 'a sudden inconsistency' between the ICJ's evaluation of this regulation and the others, thereby suggesting that the Court applied a stricter standard of review here than for the other measures, and thus a standard differing from the one it announced.[75]

Finally, Nicaragua justified the prohibition of night-time navigation on the San Juan with law enforcement, environmental protection and safety concerns.[76] In Costa Rica's view, there would be less intrusive, equally effective means at Nicaragua's disposal, like daytime measures, ordering that boats travelling at night carry lights, and installing lights alongside the river.[77] Nicaragua challenged the feasibility of such measures, noting that 'as the sovereign, it is up to Nicaragua in any event to determine what safety measures are required'.[78] Costa Rica's claim would effectively amount to—

[67] *Navigational Rights*, Judgment (n 51), para 106.
[68] ibid, para 109.
[69] 'The Court cannot … see *any* legal justification' for this measure, ibid, para 104 (emphasis added).
[70] *Navigational Rights*, Oral Proceedings of 12 March 2009, 44, para 18 (Reichler).
[71] *Navigational Rights*, Judgment (n 51), para 112.
[72] ibid, para 118.
[73] ibid, para 119.
[74] *Navigational and Related Rights (Costa Rica v Nicaragua)*, ICJ, Judgment, Separate Opinion of Judge Sepúlveda-Amor, paras 14–15.
[75] ibid, para 8, see further paras 9–11.
[76] *Navigational Rights*, Rejoinder of Nicaragua (n 52), paras 4.77, and 4.83.
[77] *Navigational Rights*, Oral Proceedings of 3 March 2009, 31, para 26 (Caflisch).
[78] *Navigational Rights*, Oral Proceedings 6 March 2009, 23, para 39 (Reichler).

> ask[ing] the Court – *sitting here in The Hague and far removed from the San Juan River* – to substitute its own judgment for that of Nicaragua and decide what measure is most appropriate and cost effective to ensure navigational safety *on a river it has never seen. Surely that is not a role the Court wishes to play*. The regulatory measure adopted by Nicaragua is demonstrably reasonable ... The enquiry necessarily stops there.[79]

Thereby, Nicaragua expressly invoked the superior expertise argument, alleging that the Court should leave the primary assessment to itself, given its better knowledge of the local situation. Second, it pointed to its sovereignty over the San Juan as ground for judicial deference. The ICJ acceded to this argumentation, noting that Costa Rica had not provided it with sufficient evidence to question the reasonableness of the prohibition.[80]

Thus, the Court not only signalled the application of a reasonableness standard of review, it also applied this standard in practice. Others see the case in a different light. For one commentator, the ICJ only '*seemed* to recognize the existence of a certain margin of appreciation', yet ultimately applied a 'standard of strict necessity'. This would be evidenced by the fact that it evaluated whether less restrictive means were available for two of the regulations at issue.[81] The underlying assumption of this observation seems to be that any judicial evaluation of a state's necessity assessment is incompatible with a 'margin of appreciation'-type standard of review. This is not the understanding laid down here. As outlined above, the term 'margin of appreciation' does not refer to one specific standard of review, but rather represents a shorthand for varying degrees of deference.[82] While the Court did evaluate Nicaragua's regulations, and thus rejected a non-reviewability standard, it is submitted that the *Navigational Rights* case is still an example for a deferential standard of review – specifically, the reasonableness standard.

C. *Immunities and Criminal Proceedings*

The *Immunities and Criminal Proceedings* case centred on the question whether France had the right to object to the designation of a particular building in Paris as new premises of Equatorial Guinea's embassy, and if so, under which conditions. At the basis of the dispute were criminal investigations in France against the son of Equatorial Guinea's president, Mr Teodoro Nguema Obiang

[79] *Navigational Rights*, Oral Proceedings of 12 March 2009, 43, para 16 (Reichler, emphases added).

[80] *Navigational Rights*, Judgment (n 51), para 128.

[81] Namely for the requirement to stop at any Nicaraguan army post along the river, and for the visa requirement, A Garrido-Muñoz, 'Managing Uncertainty: The International Court of Justice, "Objective Reasonableness" and the Judicial Function' (2017) 30(2) *Leiden Journal of International Law* 457, 469 (emphasis added).

[82] Ch 1, section II.

Mangue. In the course of 2011 and 2012, these investigations had led to various searches and seizures at Avenue Foch 42, and eventually to its confiscation in July 2012. Later that month, Equatorial Guinea made known its intention to France to relocate its embassy's premises to that building. France refused to recognise the premises as the new seat of Equatorial Guinea's embassy. In reaction, Equatorial Guinea brought the dispute before the Court. Criminal proceedings against Mr Teodoro Nguema Obiang Mangue were still pending at the time the ICJ rendered its judgment.

France asserted that it had the right to object to the designation of certain premises as the new seat of a foreign state's embassy. At the same time, it conceded that 'a receiving State must exercise the discretion it enjoys over the sending State's choice of diplomatic premises in a reasonable … manner'.[83] In particular, it argued that it had a right to object '*if it appeared to it* that the circumstances justified such a refusal'.[84] In particular, such would be the case if it *considered* that the designation of the new premises as seat of the embassy would endanger its security or the public order, for instance by compromising criminal procedures.[85] The wording ('if it appeared to it', 'if it considers') makes clear that France advocated for the application of a deferential standard of review – specifically, the reasonableness standard. In this connection, it also invoked its security and public order – subject-matters where the ICJ had already been showing deference to the concerned states in the past, as the proceedings analysed above have shown.

Equatorial Guinea in turn denied that such a right to object to a foreign state's designation of a new seat for its embassy existed in the first place. Yet, were the ICJ to find such right to exist, Equatorial Guinea opined that 'even if a receiving State enjoys discretion over the choice of premises of diplomatic missions in general, such discretion should be exercised in a manner that is reasonable'.[86] In the present case, it asserted, this had not been the case since France's refusal had been arbitrary.[87] Thus, even if both states disagreed on the existence of a right to object, they concurred that if it were to exist, its exercise could be evaluated under the reasonableness standard of review.

[83] *Immunities and Criminal Proceedings (Equatorial Guinea v France)*, ICJ, Judgment (Merits) of 11 December 2020, para 60.

[84] *Immunities and Criminal Proceedings*, ICJ, Oral Proceedings of 18 February 2020, morning (CR 2020/2), 9, para 8 (Alabrune, emphasis added. Own translation, in the original: 'lorsque les circonstances lui paraissent justifier un tel refus').

[85] *Immunities and Criminal Proceedings*, ICJ, Oral Proceedings of 21 February 2020, morning (CR 2020/4), 14, para 13 (Bodeau-Livinec).

[86] *Immunities and Criminal Proceedings*, Judgment (Merits) (n 83), para 51; see also *Immunities and Criminal Proceedings (Equatorial Guinea v France)*, ICJ, Memorial of Equatorial Guinea of 3 January 2017, paras 8.34–8.37; *Immunities and Criminal Proceedings (Equatorial Guinea v France)*, ICJ, Reply of Equatorial Guinea of 8 May 2019, para 2.30.

[87] See for instance *Immunities and Criminal Proceedings*, ICJ, Oral Proceedings of 17 February 2020, morning (CR 2020/1), 40, para 39 (Kamto); *Immunities and Criminal Proceedings*, Reply of Equatorial Guinea (n 86), para 2.31.

The Court shared this opinion. Referring to *Rights of US Nationals in Morocco* and *Mutual Assistance*, it observed that 'the receiving State's power to object to a sending State's designation of the premises of its diplomatic mission is not unlimited. The Court has repeatedly stated that, where a State possesses a discretionary power under a treaty, such a power must be exercised *reasonably and in good faith*'.[88] It then proceeded to the examination whether this had been the case, concluding that 'there existed reasonable grounds' for France's behaviour[89] – namely, the ongoing criminal proceedings.[90] Both the wording of that finding ('reasonable grounds') as well as the reference to the *Rights of US Nationals in Morocco* case make clear that the ICJ applied the reasonableness standard of review.

D. Conclusion of Domestic Measures

This section has analysed the three proceedings in which domestic measures and accordingly a state's power of regulation have been at issue, and in which the Court opted for the reasonableness standard. Three observations can be made at this point. First of all, the ICJ has been more inclined to openly acknowledge the need to accord deference to the states concerning measures on their own territory than this was the case in the first category, measures purportedly taken to protect national security interests. It most openly did so in the *Navigational Rights* case, when it remarked that—

> *a court … must recognize that the regulator … has the primary responsibility for assessing the need for regulation and for choosing, on the basis of its knowledge of the situation, the measure that it deems most appropriate to meet that need…* Concrete and specific facts will be required to persuade a court to come to that conclusion [that a regulation is unreasonable].[91]

This is one of the Court's clearest concessions that there are domains in which the states possess superior expertise, and that they have to be granted some leeway in their first-hand assessments and decisions for that reason. Thereby, it recognised the merit in the expertise-based rationale for judicial deference. Furthermore, it can be concluded that the ICJ also saw some merit in the sovereignty-rationale for judicial deference. Nicaragua explicitly insisted on its sovereignty as a ground for deference, and the Court opted for the reasonableness standard of review '[f]or essentially the reasons given by the Parties'.[92]

[88] *Immunities and Criminal Proceedings*, Judgment (Merits) (n 83), para 73 (emphasis added).
[89] ibid, para 110.
[90] ibid, para 109; see also in this sense *Immunities and Criminal Proceedings (Equatorial Guinea v France)*, ICJ, Judgment (Merits), Dissenting Opinion of Judge Bhandari, para 76.
[91] *Navigational Rights*, Judgment (n 51), para 101 (emphasis added).
[92] ibid, para 87.

In contrast, the limiting function of the reasonableness notion for what would otherwise be the exercise of a discretionary right clearly manifests itself in *Rights of US Nationals in Morocco* and *Immunities and Criminal Proceedings*. The Court referred to the former case in the latter when it noted that 'where a State possesses a discretionary power under a treaty, such a power must be exercised reasonably and in good faith'.[93] Yet, the reasonableness standard also fulfils the function of leaving the concerned states a certain decisional leeway, as is further evidenced by the fact that the ICJ found in both these cases that the measures in dispute were in conformity with international law.

Finally, is has to be noted that Nicaragua and Costa Rica in *Navigational Rights* and France and Equatorial Guinea in *Immunities and Criminal Proceedings* had concurred on the application of the reasonableness standard of review. This makes it somewhat less likely that the Court resorted to this particular standard of review as an avoidance technique in these situations. The two applicants had no interest in judicial avoidance – to the contrary. On the other hand, both cases also implicated central interests of the two respondents: the (visible) preservation of Nicaragua's sovereignty over the San Juan River, and the unimpeded functioning of France's criminal justice system. These stakes could have made the ICJ more inclined to resort to judicial avoidance. Especially the fact that it sanctioned the requirement for Costa Rican vessels to fly Nicaragua's flag while on its section of the river – a measure ostensibly designed as a reaffirmation of its sovereignty and serving no other purpose – suggests that the Court wanted to avoid an open confrontation with Nicaragua. Arguably, one can conclude that the ICJ used the reasonableness standard of review as an avoidance technique in that case: first of all vis-a-vis Nicaragua, and, as its very broad statement about a regulator's 'primary responsibility' shows, towards the audience of states more generally.

III. POLITICAL DETERMINATIONS: *CONDITIONS OF ADMISSION TO THE UN*

There is only one proceeding in which the ICJ resorted to the reasonableness standard of review for political determinations of states: the *Conditions of Admission to the UN* advisory proceedings. As explained above, several states and judges had urged the Court to decline to answer the question whether a UN Member state could make its consent to the admission of another state to the UN dependent on conditions not expressly laid down by Article 4(1) UN Charter. They had argued that the ICJ could not review a state's decision to base its voting decision on such additional criteria, as such a decision would be based on 'political' considerations, and thus only be amenable to a political

[93] *Immunities and Criminal Proceedings*, Judgment (Merits) (n 83), para 73.

appreciation. Yet, the Court issued a substantive answer to the request, and thus declined to adhere to this position.[94]

Yet, while it refused to adopt the consequences that these states and judges had urged it to, it still recognised that there was room for political factors in a state's vote regarding the admission of new members. After the ICJ rejected 'conferring upon Members an indefinite and practically unlimited power of discretion in the imposition of new conditions' for the admission of new Members,[95] it held that the conditions laid down in Article 4(1) entail 'a wide liberty of appreciation'.[96] Consequently, it acknowledged the merit of the argument, if only up to a certain extent. It stated that Article 4(1) 'does not forbid the taking into account of any factor which it is possible *reasonably and in good faith* to connect with the conditions laid down in that Article'.[97] This amounts to the adoption of the reasonableness standard of review. This becomes clear through a further passage in the decision and several individual opinions.

First, after highlighting the exhaustive nature of Article 4(1), the Court observed that 'such circumstances of fact as would enable the existence of the requisite conditions to be verified'[98] could be taken into account. Thereby, the ICJ limited the freedom of assessment of the Member States taking the voting decision. Second, there are the individual opinions of several judges. Jude Azevedo specifically observed that 'elements of expediency … can always be considered when *reasonable* use is made of the wide possibilities opened by Article 4 of the Charter'.[99] In turn, the six judges who dissented all emphasised their preference for the good faith standard of review.[100] Had they been of the opinion that this was the standard adopted by the Court, making this point would have been unnecessary.

The General Assembly had also asked whether a state could subject its consent to the admission of a state to the UN to the condition that other states be admitted simultaneously. The ICJ concluded that even under the reasonableness standard of review, such was in contravention of Article 4.[101] In conclusion, the open-ended content of the Article 4 conditions and the political nature of their evaluation led the Court to recognise some degree of assessment-making

[94] See above at Ch 4, section III.A.i.
[95] *Admission of a State to the UN*, Advisory Opinion (n 1), 63.
[96] ibid, 64.
[97] ibid, 63 (emphasis added).
[98] ibid, 63.
[99] *Admission of a State to the United Nations (Charter, Art 4)*, ICJ, Advisory Opinion of 28 May 1948, Individual Opinion of Judge Azevedo, 81 (emphasis added). It has to be noted, however, that his position is somewhat unclear. Other passages in his opinion seem to point in the direction of the good faith standard of review, see ibid, 79–80.
[100] *Admission of a State to the United Nations (Charter, Art 4)*, ICJ, Advisory Opinion, Dissenting Opinion of Judges Basdevant, Winiarski, Sir Arnold McNair and Read, 91; *Admission of a State to the United Nations (Charter, Art 4)*, ICJ, Advisory Opinion, Dissenting Opinion of Judge Zoričić, 103; *Admission of a State to the United Nations (Charter, Art 4)*, ICJ, Advisory Opinion, Dissenting Opinion of Judge Krylow, 115.
[101] *Admission of a State to the UN*, Advisory Opinion (n 1), 65.

space to the states. Its first substantive decision is thus already the first example for the adoption of a deferential standard of review: Some degree of deference is appropriate when reviewing state decisions based on markedly political considerations.[102]

IV. SCIENTIFIC DETERMINATIONS

Finally, there is the category of first-hand scientific determinations by states. Interestingly, in all three proceedings that implicated such determinations and in which the respondent pleaded for judicial deference, the ICJ acceded to that demand: *Gabčíkovo-Nagymaros*, *Pulp Mills*, and *Whaling*. Yet, it did so more or less tacitly in the two former cases. In contrast, it openly declared that it would accord some deference to Japan's first-hand scientific determinations in *Whaling*. Crucially, however, the Court applied such a deferential standard of review only for the less significant subsumption of Japan's whaling programme under the term 'scientific research'. As will be submitted in chapter seven, contrary to what it had announced, the ICJ applied the *de novo* standard for the central question whether the programme was also 'for purposes of' scientific research.

The implicit recognition of the expertise-based rationale in *Gabčíkovo-Nagymaros* and *Pulp Mills*, in contrast with the largely *pro forma* formal recognition in *Whaling*, is somewhat contradictory. In the first two cases, the Court could have wanted to avoid acknowledging its institutional limitations openly, but was convinced that they existed nonetheless. In the third case, it professed recognition of its institutional limitations, but ultimately accorded little weight to them.

A. *Gabčíkovo-Nagymaros*

As noted above, *Gabčíkovo-Nagymaros* revolved around the question whether Hungary could invoke an ecological state of necessity to justify the interruption and subsequent abandonment of construction works for the joint dam project with Slovakia. In major parts, the case centred on complex scientific facts. Nonetheless, Hungary refrained from urging the Court to defer completely to its respective first-hand assessment,[103] even if, as Desierto has pointed out, 'the

[102] See also Born, Morris and Forrest, for whom the Court's reference to a 'a wide liberty of appreciation' amounts to a 'reference to a margin of appreciation', G Born, D Morris and S Forrest, '"A Margin of Appreciation": Appreciating Its Irrelevance in International Law' (2020) 61(1) *Harvard Journal of International Law* 65, 72.

[103] As counsel for Hungary recognised, 'this argument of necessity is eminently "*justiciable*", in other words, *can be assessed by the Court',* *Gabčíkovo-Nagymaros*, ICJ, Oral Proceedings of 4 March 1997 (CR 97/3), 71, para 6 (Dupuy). This restraint can also be explained by the fact that

claim of unreviewability has historically formed one of the key aspects of the classical usage of necessity'.[104] On the other hand, the consensual referral of the dispute to the ICJ did not stop Hungary from invoking the reasonableness standard of review.[105] The Court ultimately opted for a mixed reasonableness/*de novo* standard.

Hungary highlighted that the risk-assessment for a project such as the one at hand would be 'extremely difficult, with many uncertainties', and that '[r]isks and damage can seldom be proved with 100% certainty … Clearly no one can be absolutely certain about the long-term scientific and technical prognosis for a major project such as this.'[106] Because of this inevitable uncertainty, Hungary argued, the ICJ should merely enquire if it had been 'reasonable in believing in 1989 that there was a substantial likelihood of major risks and damages', and if it had been 'reasonable in believing in 1992 that there was a substantial likelihood of major risks and damage from implementation of the Original Project'.[107]

In further support for this plea, Hungary also referred to the obligation of each state to protect 'the major interests of its territory and its population'. Accordingly, it argued, the ILC had not intended to render the requirements for a successful invocation of the state of necessity so strict as to make the fulfilment of this obligation impossible.[108] Finally, Hungary tried to establish a link to the precautionary principle, arguing that the latter equally called for the application of a deferential standard of review. Accordingly, it argued, 'reasonable apprehension' of future harm would meet the requirements under the state of necessity.[109]

Slovakia initially urged the Court to adopt the *de novo* standard. It challenged Hungary's position on that point, noting that '[i]t has never been the law that a party had only to show that it had a "reasonable belief" that there

Hungary and Slovakia had submitted the dispute to the Court by special agreement. In this light, it would have been contradictory to raise the allegation of lack of expertise to convince the Court to refrain from assessing the matter at all.

[104] With further references DA Desierto, *Necessity and National Emergency Clauses: Sovereignty in Modern Treaty Interpretation* (Brill/Nijhoff, 2012), 212.

[105] Ch 2, section II.D.

[106] *Gabčíkovo-Nagymaros (Hungary v Slovakia)*, ICJ, Counter-Memorial of Hungary of 5 December 1994, paras 1.44 and 1.46; a point repeated during the oral stage, *Gabčíkovo-Nagymaros*, Oral Proceedings of 4 March 1997, 35, para 44 (Wheater).

[107] *Gabčíkovo-Nagymaros*, Counter-Memorial of Hungary (n 106), para 1.47. In the oral proceedings, counsel for Hungary used slightly different words, asserting that the Court should review merely 'whether Hungary's concerns crossed the appropriate threshold of seriousness', *Gabčíkovo-Nagymaros*, ICJ, Oral Proceedings of 3 March 1997 (CR 97/2), 90, para 9 (Crawford); or whether 'Hungary had valid concerns about vital interests', 'valid in the sense that the risks were such that a reasonable government could not be expected to run them', *Gabčíkovo-Nagymaros*, ICJ, Oral Proceedings of 10 April 1997 (CR 97/12), 15, para 12 (Crawford). Ultimately, however, this was no change to the previous position, *cf* ibid, 30, at para 15 (Gorove).

[108] *Gabčíkovo-Nagymaros*, Oral Proceedings of 4 March 1997, 71, para 8 (Dupuy).

[109] *Gabčíkovo-Nagymaros*, ICJ, Oral Proceedings of 5 March 1997 (CR 97/4), 18, para 21 (Crawford); also *Gabčíkovo-Nagymaros*, Oral Proceedings of 10 April 1997, 56, para 2, and 70, para 30 (Sands).

was, for example, a prior material breach, or an impossibility of performance, or a fundamental change of circumstances'. Instead, the party invoking such grounds would have to show that the respective requirements had been met '*in fact*'.[110] Furthermore, Slovakia also asserted that Hungary's uncertainty argument would not be pertinent in the case at hand.[111]

However, Slovakia later attenuated its stance for the 'grave and imminent peril' requirement. While explicitly opposing the good faith standard,[112] it observed that 'the party invoking necessity must have more than unsubstantiated fears that something might happen sometime .... Yes, a reasonable belief is required'.[113] Consequently, Slovakia accepted the reasonableness standard of review for this particular requirement. In justification for its otherwise unchanged invocation of the *de novo* standard, it pointed to the larger significance of the case. Accepting Hungary's plea too readily 'would reduce the binding force of treaties to an empty formula'.[114]

During its work on the codification of the rules on state responsibility, the ILC had also dealt with the appropriate standard of review for the evaluation of a state's invocation of the state of necessity. Several members of the Commission had considered that it would be difficult to establish objectively whether the interest allegedly under peril was 'essential'.[115] Adopting a certain degree of deference towards a state's respective assessment thus seemed logical. Interestingly, one member had even stated that 'in order to mitigate an apparently high level of subjectivity ... and to assist tribunals which might have to interpret it, it might be worthwhile considering introducing into the text a standard of "reasonableness" which would ensure that States exercised at least a minimum of objectivity before concluding that a situation of grave and imminent peril existed'.[116] Ultimately, that proposal was not adopted. Still, it confirms that several ILC members had felt that the state of necessity notion presupposed deference by the reviewing entity to the state invoking it.[117]

[110] *Gabčíkovo-Nagymaros (Hungary v Slovakia)*, ICJ, Reply of Slovakia of 20 June 1995, para 1.35; in its counter-memorial, Slovakia asserted that '[t]here is nothing in the International Law Commission Report that suggests that a state of necessity can be invoked in these circumstances, without *objective* verification, to allow one party to ignore both treaty procedures and treaty obligations', *Gabčíkovo-Nagymaros (Hungary v Slovakia)*, ICJ, Counter-Memorial of Slovakia of 5 December 1994, para 10.39 (emphasis added).

[111] *Gabčíkovo-Nagymaros*, Reply of Slovakia (n 110), para 11.05.

[112] *Gabčíkovo-Nagymaros*, ICJ, Oral Proceedings of 24 March 1997 (CR 97/7), 20 (Tomka).

[113] *Gabčíkovo-Nagymaros*, ICJ, Oral Proceedings of 26 March 1997 (CR 97/10), 12 (McCaffrey).

[114] *Gabčíkovo-Nagymaros*, ICJ, Oral Proceedings of 15 April 1997 (CR 97/15), 61 (Tomka); see also already *Gabčíkovo-Nagymaros*, ICJ, Oral Proceedings of 25 March 1997 (CR 97/9), 59 (McCaffrey); Hungary likewise recognised the importance of this point, *Gabčíkovo-Nagymaros*, Oral Proceedings of 4 March 1997, 70, para 4 (Dupuy).

[115] See, eg International Law Commission, *Yearbook of the International Law Commission* 1980, Vol I, 173, para 2; 174, paras 7 and 13; 175, para 22.

[116] ibid, 178, para 4.

[117] On the other hand, the Commission also spoke of 'what proves in the circumstances to be a *genuinely* "essential" interest of the State'. This suggests more confidence as to the verifiability of

It is against the background of these discussions that one may read an observation contained in the ILC's 1980 report to the UN General Assembly on its work on the codification of the rules governing state responsibility. The Commission felt it necessary to note that—

> the State invoking the state of necessity *is not and should not be the sole judge of the existence of the necessary conditions in the particular case concerned.* Obviously, at the moment when the State adopts the conduct … , only that State itself can decide whether those conditions exist … *But this does not mean that the determination of the existence of the conditions … will be left for good to the unilateral discretion of the State…* The State affected by the conduct … may very well object that the necessary conditions did not exist. This will give rise to a dispute, which will need to be settled.[118]

The Court relied on this report to a significant degree. First, it referred to the ILC report in observing that 'the state of necessity can only be invoked under certain strictly defined conditions'. This arguably goes hand in hand with a strict(er) standard of review. On the other hand, the ICJ also quoted the Commission in observing that 'the State concerned is *not the sole judge* of whether those conditions have been met'.[119] This statement, comparable to the one in *Nicaragua*,[120] implies that while complete deference is inappropriate, so too is the *de novo* standard.

Turning to the case at hand, the Court noted that it had 'no difficulty in acknowledging' that Hungary's concerns for its natural environment constituted an essential interest.[121] By itself, this succinct observation does not allow solid conclusions to be drawn as to the standard of review applied during this evaluation. However, the ICJ's previous references to the ILC's 1980 report, the discussions among the ILC members, which cannot have escaped the Court, and the absence of statements contradicting the reasonableness standard adopted for the same requirement in *Nicaragua* arguably lead to the conclusion that the ICJ implicitly followed along this line. Thus, it applied the reasonableness standard of review for the 'essential interest' requirement.

The Court's standard of review emerges more clearly for two other requirements of the state of necessity. First, it observed that—

> serious though these uncertainties [invoked by Hungary as to the ecological impact of the Gabčíkovo-Nagymaros barrage system] might have been they could not, alone, establish the *objective existence* of a 'peril' in the sense of a component element of a state of necessity … *[T]he mere apprehension of a possible 'peril' could not suffice*

the notion, International Law Commission, *Yearbook of the International Law Commission* 1980, Vol II, Pt II, 49, para 31 (emphasis added).

[118] ibid, 50, para 36 (emphasis added).

[119] *Gabčíkovo-Nagymaros (Hungary v Slovakia)*, ICJ, Judgment of 25 September 1997, para 51 (emphasis added).

[120] See above at section I.C.

[121] *Gabčíkovo-Nagymaros*, Judgment (n 119), ibid, para 53.

> *in that respect*... The Hungarian argument ... could not convince the Court unless it was at least proven that a *real*... 'peril' existed in 1989.[122]

Thereby, the ICJ laid down the *de novo* standard of review for the peril requirement.

In contrast, it conducted the evaluation of the imminence condition under the reasonableness standard. With respect to the Gabčíkovo sector, the Court held that 'it would ... have been difficult ... to see the alleged peril as sufficiently certain and therefore "imminent" in 1989'.[123] The wording employed here – 'would have been difficult', 'sufficiently certain' – carries a sense of deference. It appears therefrom that the ICJ would have accepted Hungary's first-hand assessment even if it was not entirely convinced by it. This equates to the reasonableness standard of review.

Given its finding that there had not been an imminent peril, the Court abstained from addressing the remaining elements of the state of necessity (respectively did not do so in detail).[124] As a result, it is difficult to draw inferences as to its standard of review for those requirements. In conclusion, the Court arguably held that even if limited, some degree of deference was appropriate for its evaluation of a state's invocation of the state of necessity. This applies for the essential interests and the imminence of the peril requirements.[125]

Judge Herczegh was the only judge to dissent from the finding that Hungary could not rely on the state of necessity. He expressly sided with the majority in that the state concerned would not be the sole judge of whether the respective requirements had been met. Yet, he observed, Slovakia's recognition of the peril invoked by Hungary would show that Hungary had not acted *arbitrarily*. For one particular segment of the river dam project, he went on to state that 'the existence of a state of necessity is debatable, but Hungary's anxieties regarding the ecological risks occasioned by the reservoir ... should not have been taken lightly'.[126] Accordingly, he held a more deferential standard of review to be appropriate than the Court majority, presumably a standard amounting to good faith. At the same time, his agreement with the Court's 'sole judge' observation suggests that he also read it as implying a (limited) degree of deference, and thus corroborates the findings made above.

[122] ibid, para 54 (emphasis added).

[123] ibid, para 56, see also at para 57, where the ICJ concluded 'with respect to both Nagymaros and Gabčíkovo [that] the perils invoked by Hungary ... were not sufficiently established in 1989, nor were they "imminent"'.

[124] ibid, paras 57–58.

[125] For a different reading as to the approach chosen by the Court, see S Schill and R Briese, '"If the State Considers": Self-Judging Clauses in International Dispute Settlement' (2009) 13 *Max Planck Yearbook of United Nations Law* 61, 79. The authors argue that the Court accorded no deference to Hungary's assessment that the requirements of the state of necessity were met. It is difficult to retrace their interpretation in detail, and based on the analysis above, a more nuanced reading of the case is proposed.

[126] *Gabčíkovo-Nagymaros (Hungary v Slovakia)*, ICJ, Judgment, Dissenting Opinion of Judge Herczegh, 188–89.

B. *Pulp Mills*

The *Pulp Mills* case opposed Argentina and Uruguay over the latter's construction of two (later one) pulp mills on the bank of the River Uruguay. Argentina inter alia asserted that Uruguay's prior environmental impact assessment had been insufficient, in particular regarding the choice for the remaining plant's location. It criticised that the assessment had not indicated what other locations had been considered, why these had been discarded, and what made the chosen location the most suitable one. Further, in its view, Uruguay had failed to provide any scientific support for its respective decisions.[127] It highlighted that Uruguay had only tried to explain its choice of location in its counter-memorial, claiming before that that choice would be its sovereign decision.[128] As a result, Argentina asserted, Uruguay had breached Articles 40 and 41 of the Statute of the River Uruguay.[129]

Uruguay in turn argued that it was up to itself to determine the necessary elements of the environmental impact assessment.[130] Furthermore, it urged the ICJ to adopt a deferential standard of review. It did so in two ways. Specifically, it tried to convince the Court to accord 'considerable deference'[131] to the views of the experts appointed by the International Finance Corporation (IFC), which had contributed to the financing of the pulp mill. Their experts had concluded that the chosen location for the Botnia plant was well-suited. According to Uruguay, that assessment merited deference because '[t]he process that resulted in the IFC's approval of the Botnia project was deliberate and careful, and its outcome never predetermined'.[132] During the final stage of the oral proceedings, Uruguay clarified this position, asking the Court to adopt the reasonableness standard of review: 'the relevant question is whether the assessments actually undertaken *provided evidence on which it was reasonable to base the decisions … with respect to the likely impact of the plant on the river*'.[133] This would include the choice of location.

[127] *Pulp Mills on the River Uruguay (Argentina v Uruguay)*, ICJ, Memorial of Argentina of 15 January 2007, paras 5.65–5.66.

[128] *Pulp Mills on the River Uruguay*, ICJ, Oral Proceedings of 14 September 2009, morning (CR 2009/12), 20, paras 18–19 (Ruiz Cerutti); ibid, 51, para 36 (Sands); *Pulp Mills on the River Uruguay*, ICJ, Oral Proceedings of 15 September 2009, morning (CR 2009/13), 18, paras 21–23 (Kohen); see further *Pulp Mills on the River Uruguay*, ICJ, Oral Proceedings of 16 September 2009, morning (CR 2009/14), 57, para 7 (Sands).

[129] 1295 United Nations Treaty Series 331.

[130] *Pulp Mills on the River Uruguay (Argentina v Uruguay)*, ICJ, Rejoinder of Uruguay of 29 July 2008, para 5.78.

[131] *Pulp Mills on the River Uruguay*, ICJ, Oral Proceedings of 24 September 2009, morning (CR 2009/19), 37, at para 11 (Reichler).

[132] *Pulp Mills on the River Uruguay (Argentina v Uruguay)*, ICJ, Counter-Memorial of Uruguay of 20 July 2007, para 5.6; an argument Uruguay expanded upon in the oral stage of the proceedings, see *Pulp Mills*, Oral Proceedings of 24 September 2009, 37, paras 12–15 (Reichler).

[133] *Pulp Mills on the River Uruguay*, ICJ, Oral Proceedings of 1 October 2009, afternoon (CR 2009/22), 46, para 12 (Boyle, emphasis added).

In support of that contention, counsel referred to two WTO dispute settlement body reports, *US – Continued Suspension*, and *Argentina – Footwear*. In the latter case, the Appellate Body had observed that panels may not conduct a *de novo* review of a state's decision to take certain measures based on scientific evidence. Instead, they should only evaluate whether the state authorities 'had considered all the relevant facts and had adequately explained how the facts supported the determinations that were made'.[134] In *US – Continued Suspension*, the Appellate Body had held that the scientific basis 'need not reflect the majority view within the scientific community', but rather that these views 'must be considered to be legitimate science'.[135]

The ICJ did neither address this assertion nor the WTO jurisprudence. Instead, it first noted that 'it is for each State to determine … the specific content of the environmental impact assessment required in each case, having regard to the nature and magnitude of the proposed development and its likely adverse impact on the environment as well as to the need to exercise due diligence in conducting such an assessment'.[136] In the following, it was content to observe that 'Uruguay [had] repeatedly indicated that the suitability of the Fray Bentos location [had been] comprehensively assessed and that other possible sites [had been] considered …. [I]n 2003 Botnia [had] evaluated four locations in total … before choosing Fray Bentos'. It further noted that Uruguay had excluded the three alternative sites with reference to environmental and infrastructural considerations.[137] Consequently, the Court limited itself to confirming that Uruguay had at all considered alternative sites and that it had advanced admissible reasons for discarding them as potential location for the plant. It is difficult to define the standard of review the Court applied based on these succinct observations. Two such standards seem possible: reasonableness, or non-reviewability.

On the one hand, the ICJ concluded this portion of its analysis with the observation that it was 'not convinced by Argentina's argument that an assessment of possible sites was not carried out prior to the determination of the final site'.[138] As shown above, Argentina did not only argue that Uruguay had not

[134] *Argentina – Safeguard Measures on Imports of Footwear*, Report of the Appellate Body (14 December 1999) WT/DS121/AB/R, 116–21, and 121.

[135] *US/Canada – Continued Suspension of the Obligations in the EC-Hormones Dispute*, Report of the Appellate Body (16 October 2008) WT/DS320/AB/R, WT/DS321/AB/R, 591. Sulyok, in contrast, making a conclusive argument, describes this case as 'the high-water mark' in terms of the strictness of scrutiny exercised by the WTO Appellate Body, K Sulyok, *Science and Judicial Reasoning: The Legitimacy of International Environmental Adjudication* (Cambridge University Press, 2021), 196, which once more only highlights that what an adjudicative body says the standard of review would be is not always what the standard of review actually adopted is.

[136] *Pulp Mills on the River Uruguay (Argentina v Uruguay)*, ICJ, Judgment of 20 April 2010, para 205.

[137] ibid, para 210.

[138] ibid, para 210.

carried out such an assessment at all, but further that even if it had done so, that assessment was insufficient. The Court's silence vis-a-vis this second assertion could mean that in its view, any evaluation of the quality of Uruguay's first-hand assessment was inappropriate. This would correspond to complete deference. However, if that were really the ICJ's position, it would not have commented on the substance of Uruguay's location assessment at all. Such would have been superfluous, and also too intrusive under the complete deference standard.[139] Accordingly, it is submitted that the Court silently applied the reasonableness standard of review.

Judge *ad hoc* Vinuesa and parts of the literature have likewise concluded that the ICJ laid down a deferential standard of review.[140] In Boyle's view, who served as counsel for Uruguay in the case, the Court—

> was reluctant … to be drawn into reviewing the conclusions of EIAs [environmental impact assessments] conducted in good faith … The Court probably does not want to encourage such challenges and it seems right in principle to give considerable deference to EIAs that are well-reasoned and supported by substantial evidence.[141]

For him, the ICJ's approach—

> appears to leave open the possibility of reviewing the adequacy of an EIA in appropriate cases, and it would not be unreasonable to conclude that the Court did so here but found nothing wrong with the EIA undertaken by Uruguay … On this basis it seems unlikely that an international court will be prepared to set aside an EIA carried out … on the basis of substantial scientific and technical evidence. It may well do so, however, if the EIA is demonstrably inadequate.[142]

Accordingly, in his view, while the ICJ rejected non-reviewability, it still applied a certain degree of deference. Deferring to 'well-reasoned' environmental impact assessments 'supported by substantial evidence' effectively amounts to the reasonableness standard of review. Finally, *Ragni*, referring to *Boyle*, also understands the Court's approach to mean that 'once the State proves it has conducted an evaluation of the possible environmental impact of the project to be authorized, and such evaluation is well-reasoned and supported by substantial evidence … any further review of its decision to grant the permission should, in principle, be excluded'.[143]

[139] See also in this respect *Corfu Channel* and *Right of Passage*, discussed above at sections I.A and B.

[140] *Pulp Mills on the River Uruguay (Argentina v Uruguay)*, ICJ, Judgment, Dissenting Opinion of Judge *ad hoc* Vinuesa, para 54.

[141] A Boyle, 'Developments in the International Law of Environmental Impact Assessments and their Relation to the Espoo Convention' (2011) 20(3) *Review of European Community & International Environmental Law* 227, 231.

[142] ibid, 230.

[143] Ragni, 'Standard of Review and the Margin of Appreciation before the International Court of Justice' (n 25), 330–31.

C. *Whaling*

The third case in this category, *Whaling*, involved the question whether Japan's JARPA II whaling programme could qualify as being 'for purposes of scientific research' and thus be exempt from the prohibition of whaling by virtue of Article VIII ICRW. The Court refused to give any credit to Japan's initially advanced non-reviewability assertion.[144] Yet, later in the proceedings, the respondent also invoked less extreme deferential standards of review: first good faith, and finally reasonableness. The extensive attention this issue received in the proceedings required further clarification from the Court. Specifically, the question was which standards would be appropriate for the sub-questions whether JARPA II constituted *scientific research* and whether it was *for purposes* of such research. The ICJ adopted a differentiated reasonableness/*de novo* standard of review in this respect: reasonableness for the first, and *de novo* for the second sub-question.[145] Mirroring this differentiation, the following sections will outline the general positions of the parties as well as their argumentation and the Court's approach for the first sub-question. The second sub-question will be dealt with in chapter seven.

As Japan asserted, there would not be 'one, uniquely correct, view of what constitutes the "purposes of scientific research"' under Article VIII, but that there would be room for different views.[146] In any case, the Court's evaluation could not take place under a *de novo* standard. Besides being 'clearly inappropriate', such would also be impracticable: The Court would be lacking the full evidentiary basis to substitute its assessment on JARPA II for that of Japan.[147] Further, Japan referred to the *Navigational Rights* case. In its view, this case had demonstrated that 'the Court shows deference to the State's appreciation of the factual and legal conditions in cases … where the State enjoys a large margin of discretion'.[148] This would apply here as well, it asserted, since Article VIII did not authorise whaling, but rather acknowledged the already pre-existing customary freedom to do so.[149] Most importantly, however, Japan relied on the institutional expertise argument. As a court of law, the Court would be

[144] Ch 4, section IV.

[145] Similarly Cannizzaro, for whom the Court resorted to a 'double' standard of review, Cannizzaro, 'Proportionality and Margin of Appreciation in the Whaling Case' (n 9), 1062–63; see also at 1068–69.

[146] *Whaling in the Antarctic (Australia v Japan: New Zealand intervening)*, ICJ, Written Observations of Japan on New Zealand's Written Observations of 31 May 2013, paras 48–49.

[147] *Whaling in the Antarctic*, ICJ, Oral Proceedings of 4 July 2013, morning (CR 2013/15), 18, para 21 (Lowe).

[148] *Whaling*, Written Observations of Japan on New Zealand's Written Observations (n 146), para 54.

[149] ibid, para 51; *Whaling*, Oral Proceedings of 4 July 2013, 15, paras 7–8, and 17, para 15 (Lowe); *Whaling in the Antarctic*, ICJ, Oral Proceedings of 15 July 2013, afternoon (CR 2013/22), 64, para 42 (Lowe).

ill-equipped to decide scientific controversies. In this connection, it also pointed to the 'margin of appreciation' as 'an axiom of international law and relations',[150] which would in particular extend to a state's judgment on questions of scientific necessity.[151]

In the earlier stages of the proceedings, Japan contended that this margin would require the Court to adopt the good faith standard of review.[152] The ICJ's role would be 'to secure the integrity of the process by which the decision is made, and not to review the decision itself'.[153] However, in the final stage of the oral proceedings, it retreated a second time from its previous propositions: It now conceded that the Court could evaluate whether it had '*reasonably* concluded that JARPA II is a programme for the purposes of scientific research'.[154]

Turning to the first sub-question – whether JARPA II constituted scientific research – Japan focused on the expertise-argument:

> [W]hile the definition of scientific research is *not* solely a matter for the determination of each ... State, neither is there one uniquely correct definition, so that the slightest divergence from that definition means that the characterization of a program as 'scientific' puts the State in violation of international law.[155]

Accordingly—

> the Court can ask, could a reasonable State regard [JARPA II] as a properly-framed scientific inquiry. But it can no more impose a line separating science from non-science than it could decide what is and what is not 'Art'. In Japan's view, *the correct question is, 'could a State reasonably regard this as scientific research'*, or, was JARPA II 'supported by coherent reasoning and respectable scientific evidence'.[156]

In contrast, both Australia and New Zealand urged the ICJ to adopt the *de novo* standard of review. They asserted that Article VIII left no margin of discretion at all to the state invoking it, and that consequently, any judicial deference would be inappropriate.[157] Australia further argued that the good faith standard of review would be inappropriate in situations such as this one where resources in the public domain and of collective interest were at stake. Applying such a

[150] *Whaling in the Antarctic (Australia v Japan: New Zealand intervening)*, ICJ, Counter-Memorial of Japan of 9 March 2012, para 9.16.

[151] ibid, para 9.17.

[152] ibid, para 9.7; *Whaling*, Written Observations of Japan on New Zealand's Written Observations (n 146), para 54; *Whaling*, Oral Proceedings of 4 July 2013, 14, para 5, and 21, paras 38–44 (Lowe).

[153] ibid, 24, para 54 (Lowe); note the parallel to the way the ECtHR has been applying the margin of appreciation in recent years, J Gerards, 'Margin of Appreciation and Incrementalism in the Case Law of the European Court of Human Rights' (2018) 18(3) *Human Rights Law Review* 495, 497.

[154] *Whaling in the Antarctic*, ICJ, Oral Proceedings of 15 July 2013, morning (CR 2013/21), 15, para 5; see also at 24, paras 23–24 (Akhavan, emphasis added).

[155] *Whaling*, Oral Proceedings of 15 July 2013, 59, para 17 (Lowe).

[156] ibid, 60, paras 20–21 (Lowe, emphasis added).

[157] *Whaling*, Judgment (n 1), para 60, see also paras 63–64.

standard would amount to allocating these resources to the state exploiting them.[158] Specifically, it opposed Japan's characterisation of the margin of appreciation as an 'axiom of international law and relations'. Rather, it contended that *Oil Platforms* had shown that the Court had 'explicitly rejected this latitudinarian idea'.[159] Consequently, as New Zealand expressed it, '[w]hether Article VIII has been applied properly in a particular case is a question of fact that is open for the judicial determination of this Court in the usual way'.[160] Australia and New Zealand thus argued with the objective language of Article VIII, the missing implication of any Japanese core sovereignty interests, the need to uphold the regime effectiveness of the ICRW, the parallels to oversight mechanisms provided for in the Convention and the Schedule, and the irrelevance of the margin of appreciation in international law.

The Court's rejection of Japan's initial non-reviewability assertion ('whether the killing, taking and treating of whales … is for purposes of scientific research *cannot depend simply on that State's perception*'[161]) incidentally conveys a certain degree of judicial deference, as do the similarly phrased holdings in *Nicaragua* and *Gabčíkovo-Nagymaros*.[162] Arguably, it applied this deference for its evaluation whether JARPA II could be subsumed under the term 'scientific research'. Here, the ICJ announced that it would not 'devise alternative criteria or … offer a general definition' of the term.[163] Instead, it noted that JARPA II—

> describes areas of inquiry that correspond to four research objectives and presents a programme of activities that involves the systematic collection and analysis of data by scientific personnel …. Based on the information before it, the Court thus finds that the JARPA II activities … can *broadly* be characterised as 'scientific research'.[164]

This superficial subsumption and refusal to look at the programme in more detail amounts to the adoption of a deferential standard of review.[165]

A case could be made that the ICJ merely verified whether Japan's initial categorisation of the programme was manifestly unfounded, and thus employed

[158] *Whaling in the Antarctic*, ICJ, Oral Proceedings of 10 July 2013, morning (CR 2013/19), 63, para 15 (Crawford); see also *Whaling*, Judgment (n 1), para 63.

[159] With further references *Whaling in the Antarctic*, ICJ, Oral Proceedings of 26 June 2013, afternoon (CR 2013/8), 45, para 63 (Crawford).

[160] *Whaling in the Antarctic*, ICJ, Oral Proceedings of 8 July 2013, morning (CR 2013/17), 34, para 66 (Finlayson); see also ibid, 24, para 31; see also *Whaling*, Oral Proceedings of 26 June 2013, 46, para 67 (Crawford).

[161] *Whaling*, Judgment (n 1), para 61 (emphasis added).

[162] See above at sections I.C and IV.A, respectively.

[163] *Whaling*, Judgment (n 1), para 86.

[164] ibid, para 127 (emphasis added).

[165] For Cannizzaro, 'the Court seems to have used a loose standard of plausibility' at this stage. As he further notes, '[a]bsent a uniform meaning of this notion at the international law level, the mere existence of elements of scientific research in the programme – a very faint link indeed – was sufficient for the Court to avoid superimposing its own view on that of the acting state', Cannizzaro, 'Proportionality and Margin of Appreciation in the Whaling Case' (n 9), 1063, see also ibid, 1064, where he links this approach to the margin of appreciation doctrine.

the good faith standard of review. Yet, the fact that it analysed the programme's characteristics – even if superficially – points more in the direction of reasonableness. The Court did not provide any justification for the application of a deferential standard of review and its specific choice. However, in light of Japan's arguments, a point could be made that it did so because it considered that its own expertise was insufficient and that it was not its role to decide a scientific question debated among scientists.

It is also worth noting that none of the dissenting judges who took issue with the way the Court established and applied the standard of review opposed the reasonableness standard for this first sub-question.[166] Their disagreement exclusively concerned the evaluation of the second sub-question (whether JARPA II was 'for purposes of' scientific research).

D. Conclusion on Scientific Determinations

In conclusion, the ICJ has applied a somewhat deferential standard of review to evaluate first-hand state determinations and assessments made in the scientific domain in all proceedings implicating such matters. In turn, there is no clear pattern regarding its concrete reliance on that notion. While it explicitly accorded deference to Hungary in the definition of its essential interests in *Gabčíkovo-Nagymaros*, it did so less openly for the scientific elements of the risk analysis for these interests. In *Pulp Mills*, the accordance of deference concerning Uruguay's suitability assessment of the chosen location for its pulp mill under environmental considerations is even more discrete. This makes it less likely that the ICJ resorted to the reasonableness standard of review as an avoidance technique in those two cases. Given that both respondents had pleaded for deference, it would have been logical to apply the reasonableness standard openly, had it been such strategic considerations that had motivated the Court's approach.

In sharp contrast, the ICJ openly recognised the need to defer to a state's scientific assessments in *Whaling*. At the same time however, by adopting a mixed reasonableness/*de novo* standard of review, it showed less deference to Japan than it had announced it would. Thus, in important respects, the Court paid mere lip-service to Japan's contention that it would be lacking the requisite expertise to evaluate Japan's first-hand assessments. This choice could be explained with the attention the states participating in the proceedings had devoted to the standard of review question and the ICJ's scientific expertise

[166] See for instance *Whaling in the Antarctic (Australia v Japan: New Zealand intervening)*, ICJ, Judgment, Dissenting Opinion of Judge Abraham, para 24.

(or rather, purported lack thereof). Despite adopting the reasonableness standard of review with respect to the first sub-question, the Court found Japan to have violated its obligations under the Whaling Convention. This makes it less likely that it resorted to the reasonableness standard as an avoidance technique towards Japan.

On the other hand, the partial adoption of the reasonableness standard of review in *Whaling* helped the ICJ to avoid having to find that the Japanese whaling programme did not even constitute scientific research in the first place. Arguably, it thereby avoided a major embarrassment for Japan. From this perspective, its use of the reasonableness standard of review to evaluate whether JARPA II constituted scientific research could in fact be understood as the use of an avoidance technique vis-a-vis Japan. Finally, and perhaps more importantly, through its express (yet only superficial) adoption of deference, it signalled to the state community that it would refrain from redoing their assessments in scientific matters.

V. CONCLUSION FOR REASONABLENESS

The analysis in this chapter has shown that the ICJ has resorted to the reasonableness standard of review in 12 proceedings, and thus in more than one third of all proceedings in which it took a stance on the standard of review question. This demonstrates that the reasonableness standard is a significant feature of the Court's decision-making practice. Five of those proceedings involved the appreciation of national security state interests (*Corfu Channel, Right of Passage, Nicaragua, Diallo* and *Certain Iranian Assets*). Three further proceedings mainly revolved around domestic measures (*Rights of US Nationals in Morocco*, *Navigational Rights* and *Immunities and Criminal Proceedings*). In turn, one proceeding concerned an appreciation by the ICJ of political (*Admission of a State to the UN*) and three of scientific determinations (*Gabčíkovo-Nagymaros, Pulp Mills* and *Whaling*). Consequently, the ICJ applied the reasonableness standard of review in all four categories of proceedings.

Three particularities merit further attention: first, the Court's *explicit* recognition of state latitude in most of and the terminological repetition in three of these proceedings, second, the generalisable nature of several findings, and third, the fact that in most proceedings, the respondent states had pleaded for an even more deferential standard of review. Finally, the conclusion will address the question whether the ICJ has resorted to the reasonableness standard as an avoidance technique.

First, in most of the proceedings the Court evaluated under this standard, it openly recognised that the respective state was due some first-hand decision-making space (as explained above, *Gabčíkovo-Nagymaros* is a borderline case).

Table 8 Explicit vs implicit adoption of the reasonableness standard of review

<table>
<tr><th>Short title</th><th>Explicit</th><th>Implicit</th></tr>
<tr><td>Admission of a State to the UN</td><td>X</td><td></td></tr>
<tr><td>Corfu Channel</td><td></td><td>X</td></tr>
<tr><td>Rights of US Nationals in Morocco</td><td>X</td><td></td></tr>
<tr><td>Right of Passage</td><td></td><td>X</td></tr>
<tr><td>Nicaragua (treaty law)</td><td>X</td><td></td></tr>
<tr><td>Gabčíkovo-Nagymaros</td><td colspan="2">X</td></tr>
<tr><td>Navigational Rights</td><td>X</td><td></td></tr>
<tr><td>Pulp Mills</td><td></td><td>X</td></tr>
<tr><td>Diallo</td><td>X</td><td></td></tr>
<tr><td>Whaling</td><td>X</td><td></td></tr>
<tr><td>Immunities and Criminal Proceedings</td><td>X</td><td></td></tr>
<tr><td>Certain Iranian Assets</td><td>X</td><td></td></tr>
</table>

Only in three instances did the ICJ grant the first-hand decision-maker latitude merely implicitly: *Corfu Channel*, *Right of Passage* and *Pulp Mills*. The first two of these three decisions originate from the Court's earlier years. The merely implicit adoption of the reasonableness standard of review could suggest that at the time, the Court was still reluctant to acknowledge its limitations. Since then, however, it has been more candid about its restrained role. This is especially the case whenever it has had to deal with essential state interests. In several of those proceedings, it has explicitly recognised that it could not evaluate the state's respective determinations *de novo*, and – likewise explicitly – opted for the reasonableness standard (*Nicaragua, Gabčíkovo-Nagymaros, Navigational Rights, Diallo, Immunities and Criminal Proceedings*).

In these and the remaining other 'reasonableness proceedings', the ICJ thus opted for the open recognition of state latitude and its restrained role of review. The language in *Admission to the UN* and especially *Navigational Rights* is illustrative in this regard. In the former, the Court acknowledged that Article 4(I) of the UN Charter, laying down the conditions for admission of a new state, entails 'a wide liberty of appreciation' for the Member States casting their respective votes.[167] In *Navigational Rights*, it observed that 'a court … must recognize that the regulator … has the primary responsibility for assessing

[167] *Admission of a State to the UN*, Advisory Opinion (n 1), 64.

the need for regulation and for choosing … the measure that it deems most appropriate to meet that need'.[168]

There is also a noteworthy terminological continuity in three of those eight proceedings. This continuity spans over legal domains and decades. At the same time, each of those three quotations has a common base: They concern the application of an exception or exemption clause, often included in treaties as an 'escape valve'. In *Nicaragua*, the Court held that 'whether a measure is necessary to protect the essential security interests of a party [as stipulated in a bilateral treaty] *is not… purely a question for the subjective judgment of the party*'.[169] In *Gabčíkovo-Nagymaros*, it held that 'the State concerned is *not the sole judge*' whether the conditions for the customary state of necessity are fulfilled.[170] Finally, in *Whaling*, it found that whether a whaling programme 'is for purposes of scientific research *cannot depend simply on that State's perception*'.[171] In all these three cases, the respective applicants had asserted that considerations of effectiveness would generally exclude the recognition of any degree of judicial deference. The Court's explicit recognition of deference thus demonstrates that this frequently advanced assertion is not a 'trump all' card. Rather, for the ICJ, it is only one argument against a deferential standard of review. At the same time, the Court has thereby shown its consciousness of the importance of the interests protected by such 'escape valves', and the need for it to tread lightly in the supervision of their application.

Second, the Court's statements in several of the eight proceedings in which it explicitly laid down the reasonableness standard merit further attention. For one, it phrased these respective observations in a generalised manner. Furthermore, in several of them, the standard of review question was not outcome-determinative, ie the result would not have been different under the more lenient good faith or the stricter *de novo* standard of review. This suggests that the ICJ intended those observations as a general signal to all states, and not just to the parties to the proceedings. This can be seen as an attempt to lay open its perspective on its own role for certain questions and subject-matters, and arguably as a use of the standard of review as an avoidance technique for future proceedings.

A first case in point is *Nicaragua*. There, the Court explained that its task was 'to assess whether the risk run by these 'essential security interests' is reasonable and … whether the measures presented as being designed to protect these interests are not merely useful but "necessary"'.[172] As it found that the measures in question had not been necessary, it could have practised judicial economy

[168] *Navigational Rights*, Judgment (n 51), para 101.
[169] *Nicaragua*, Judgment (Merits) (n 1), para 282 (emphasis added).
[170] *Gabčíkovo-Nagymaros*, Judgment (n 119), para 51 (emphasis added).
[171] *Whaling*, Judgment (n 1), para 61 (emphasis added).
[172] *Nicaragua*, Judgment (Merits) (n 1), para 224.

and not have addressed the essential security interest question at all.[173] Yet, it chose to recognise explicitly that the reasonableness standard of review was appropriate for its evaluation of this outcome-irrelevant question. This could be seen as both a means of judicial diplomacy vis-a-vis the United States (which had opposed the involvement of the Court from the beginning), and the state community in general. The ICJ thereby signalled its readiness to grant some deference to a state's security assessments.[174]

The Court's approach in the *Diallo* case can be seen in the same light. Again, its choice of a reasonableness standard of review for the question whether essential security interests could justify the DRC's non-compliance with Article 13 ICCPR was not outcome-determinative. The adoption of the good faith standard would have led to the same result – as would have *de novo*. The ICJ could thus simply have rejected the DRC's plea for complete deference and then have applied a non-disclosed standard of review. Yet, it chose to lay open its (deferential) standard. A reason might be judicial diplomacy vis-a-vis the DRC – by adopting the reasonableness standard, it visibly accorded some weight to the former's concerns for its sovereignty and decision-making prerogative. At the same time however, and perhaps more significantly, the Court thereby also sent a signal to the larger state community.

Finally, the ICJ adopted a particularly broad formulation in the *Navigational Rights* case pointing well beyond the individual case. It observed that 'a court … must recognize that the regulator … has the primary responsibility for assessing the need for regulation and for choosing, on the basis of its knowledge of the situation, the measure that it deems most appropriate to meet that need'.[175] This finding is reminiscent of the *Lighthouses* case, in which the Permanent Court had observed that 'any grant of legislative powers generally implies the grant of a discretionary right to judge how far their exercise may be necessary or urgent'.[176] The PCIJ had justified this with the state institutions' superior knowledge of the facts and superior expertise in appreciating political considerations. The ICJ followed along these lines.[177] Its statement may thus be understood as a signal to the states that it is conscious of its institutional limitations, especially when evaluating domestic measures.

Third, it is notable that the Court only rarely acceded to the standard of review position by the respondent. To the contrary, as a rule, it adopted a *stricter* standard. As a result, it often took the middle ground between applicant and respondent, as Table 9 shows.

[173] Admittedly, that question was logically prior. However, this fact has not hindered the Court from proceeding in such a manner in other proceedings.

[174] The same may be said about the Court's adoption of a reasonableness standard of review for certain questions arising in *Gabčíkovo-Nagymaros* and *Whaling*.

[175] *Navigational Rights*, Judgment (n 51), para 101.

[176] *Lighthouses Case*, Judgment (n 21), 22.

[177] Note, however, that unlike the PCIJ, the ICJ did not refrain from evaluating the respective question for itself – a further illustration of the fact that it has moved from non-reviewability to less deferential standards of review.

Table 9 Reasonableness: overview of party & ICJ positions on the appropriate standard of review; respondent in dark grey, applicant in light grey, other states in white, Court in black

<table>
<tr><th>Short title</th><th>Complete Deference</th><th>Good Faith</th><th>Reasonableness</th><th>De novo</th></tr>
<tr><td>Admission of a State to the UN*</td><td>Various states</td><td></td><td>Court</td><td></td></tr>
<tr><td>Corfu Channel</td><td>Albania</td><td></td><td>Court</td><td>United Kingdom</td></tr>
<tr><td>Rights of US Nationals*</td><td></td><td>France</td><td>Court</td><td></td></tr>
<tr><td>Right of Passage</td><td></td><td>India</td><td>Court</td><td>Portugal</td></tr>
<tr><td>Nicaragua* (treaty law)</td><td colspan="2">United States</td><td colspan="2">Court</td></tr>
<tr><td rowspan="3">Gabčíkovo-Nagymaros</td><td rowspan="3"></td><td rowspan="3"></td><td>Hungary</td><td></td></tr>
<tr><td>Slovakia</td><td></td></tr>
<tr><td colspan="2">Court</td></tr>
<tr><td rowspan="3">Navigational Rights</td><td rowspan="3"></td><td rowspan="3"></td><td>Nicaragua</td><td rowspan="3"></td></tr>
<tr><td>Costa Rica</td></tr>
<tr><td>Court</td></tr>
<tr><td rowspan="2">Pulp Mills*</td><td rowspan="2"></td><td rowspan="2"></td><td>Uruguay</td><td rowspan="2"></td></tr>
<tr><td>Court</td></tr>
<tr><td>Diallo</td><td>DRC</td><td></td><td>Court</td><td>Guinea</td></tr>
<tr><td rowspan="2">Whaling</td><td colspan="3">Japan</td><td>Australia</td></tr>
<tr><td></td><td></td><td>Court</td><td>New Zealand</td></tr>
<tr><td rowspan="3">Immunities and Criminal Proceedings</td><td rowspan="3"></td><td rowspan="3"></td><td>France</td><td rowspan="3"></td></tr>
<tr><td>Equatorial Guinea</td></tr>
<tr><td>Court</td></tr>
</table>

* The position of the respective opponent on the standard of review question cannot be determined with sufficient certainty so as to allow mapping it on this scale.

As Table 9 indicates, there are four exceptions to this rule: *Gabčíkovo-Nagymaros*, *Navigational Rights*, *Pulp Mills*, and *Immunities and Criminal Proceedings*. There, the ICJ concurred with the respondent on the standard of review question. One explanation for the Court's stance in three (the first two and the last) of those instances could be that the respective applicants concurred with the respondents in that the reasonableness standard was appropriate, or at least conceded that such a standard was acceptable. On the other hand, the reason for the ICJ's agreement with the proposed reasonableness standard of review in those four instances could also simply be due to the fact that it held that standard to be the legally correct one.

As the table also shows, the Court has never adopted the reasonableness standard of review without the respondent's prior plea for judicial deference. This could generally suggest that it applies this standard of review as an avoidance technique vis-a-vis those states: Their voiced preference triggers the application of deference by the ICJ. At the same time, the fact that the Court has generally adopted a stricter standard of review than preferred by that state, even if still deferential, shows that it does not regard the respondent's preferences on this question as decisive. This speaks against the impression that it resorts to this standard as a means of unabashed avoidance.

This chapter has shown that the reasonableness standard of review is a recurrent feature in the Court's jurisprudence. The ICJ has especially adopted this standard in proceedings involving essential state interests, domestic measures, and scientific questions. In all proceedings in which it has adopted this standard, the respondent states had previously urged it to accord them some decision-making and assessment leeway. At the same time, the Court has, in general, not adopted this standard of review in complete concordance with the respective states. Rather, it has often taken the reasonableness standard of review as 'middle ground' between the positions of the respective applicants and respondents. Nonetheless, there are some grounds to believe that it resorted to the reasonableness standard of review as a judicial avoidance tool in several instances. First and foremost, this applies vis-a-vis the respective respondents. *Whaling* and *Navigational Rights* are arguably such cases. Finally, in several instances, the ICJ's resort to this notion can also be understood as use of an avoidance technique with future proceedings in mind: as a signal that it is ready to recognise some room of manoeuvre to the states – especially when this concerns their essential interests. *Nicaragua* and *Diallo* are examples for this. Arguably, what the Court has thereby demonstrated is its consciousness that there are certain areas and subject-matters where its institutional expertise and abilities are limited.

7

De Novo

CHAPTER SEVEN DEALS with all instances in which the Court opted for the strictest standard of review: *de novo*. This comprises all instances in which it evaluated the respective state's first-hand determinations without according any particular weight to them, or in which it laid down that standard of review for future proceedings. This choice simultaneously shuts the door to the use of the notion of standard of review as an avoidance technique: As the ICJ abstains from according any weight to the respective state's first-hand assessments and decisions, it has to pass a verdict on every issue itself. Three features make clear that the *de novo* standard of review is the Court's default mode: prevalence, predominantly tacit use, and overall refusal to explain the reasons for its use.

First, prevalence. Of the 31 proceedings in which the Court's stance on the applicable standard of review can be identified, it opted for the *de novo* standard – at least for one of the relevant questions – in 17. Thus, in more than half of the pertinent proceedings, it chose this particular standard of review. This makes it the standard the ICJ most frequently used.

Second, predominantly tacit use. In the clear majority of the proceedings in which it resorted to the *de novo* standard of review, the Court did not waste words to lay open this choice. Even on the four occasions where it openly rejected the non-reviewability standard of review proposed by the concerned states, it then only applied the *de novo* standard implicitly. The *Oil Platforms* case as the sole exception in this regard only serves to prove this rule. The fact that it resorted to this standard of review implicitly on all but one occasion indicates that it does not deem it necessary to report its application of this standard. This silence has to be seen in contrast to those instances in which the ICJ chose a deferential standard of review. Notably, as seen in the previous chapter, it mostly laid open its application of the reasonableness standard of review. One possible way to explain this difference is the consideration that it is not the application of the rule that requires expression, but rather the application of the exception.

Third, overall lack of express justification. Just as the Court has almost never used the *de novo* standard of review explicitly, it has never furnished a justification for its choice of this standard. Again, this could be explained by the fact that it is the deviation from and not the application of the norm that needs explaining. The absence of express justification seems but logical if the ICJ is convinced that the *de novo* standard of review is the default standard.

Following the previous mode of presentation, the presentation of the proceedings in which the Court opted for the *de novo* standard of review is divided into four categories: national security interests, domestic matters, political determinations, and scientific determinations.

The first category, national security interests, will be sub-divided in measures purportedly taken in self-defence, and less aggressive measures, as there is a marked difference in the way the Court determined the applicable standard of review for each. While the Court openly opted for *de novo* in its evaluation of self-defence invocations, it only adopted this standard tacitly in its evaluation of less aggressive state measures justified with other security interests. Presumably, this difference can be explained with the ICJ's desire to uphold the effectiveness of the prohibition of the use of force. This desire made it imperative to communicate the rejection of any degree of deference expressly.

The matters falling into the second category, proceedings involving purportedly domestic matters, are more varied, comprising the conferral of nationality, protection of diplomatic premises, and implementation of international obligations in the field of criminal justice. As will be seen, the *Nottebohm* case was arguably the only one in which the adoption of the *de novo* standard of review was dictated by logic. The *Hostage* case concerned an obligation similar to that in the *Bosnian Genocide* case, in which the ICJ had adopted a mixed *de novo*/good faith standard: an obligation to prevent the occurrence of certain events. In contrast to that case, the Court chose a consistent *de novo* standard in *Hostage*. Presumably, it did so out of a desire to maintain the effectiveness of a basic obligation in the conduct of diplomatic relations: the duty to prevent attacks on diplomatic premises.

In the category of proceedings implicating states' first-hand political determinations, the Court's refusal to adopt a deferential standard of review in *Namibia* merits highlighting. As already mentioned in chapter four, the *Namibia* opinion can be seen as a reversal of the *South West Africa (Second Phase)* judgment. What motivated the ICJ's choice of the *de novo* standard could have been its desire to right the wrong, as it was widely perceived, of that case.

The final category, proceedings implicating states' first-hand determinations in scientific matters, only comprises one[1] case: *Whaling*. That case is also of particular interest. As is submitted here, contrary to what it had announced it would do, the Court applied the *de novo* standard of review for the decisive second sub-question. Possibly, the ICJ announced its resort to the reasonableness standard in an attempt to show its acknowledgement of the limitations of its expertise, and to reap the benefits of such a signal of deference towards the state community. Yet, the fact that it only did so *pro forma* indicates that in reality, it did not accept these limitations.

[1] For better readability, the *de novo* part of *Gabčíkovo-Nagymaros* has already been discussed in ch 6, section IV.A.

I. NATIONAL SECURITY INTERESTS

The first category comprises the six proceedings in which the concerned state invoked its security interests to convince the Court to adopt a deferential standard of review, and in which the ICJ chose the *de novo* standard nonetheless. Three – *Nicaragua*, *Oil Platforms* and *Armed Activities* – concerned the right to self-defence, and the other three – *Wall in the OPT*, *Construction of a Road* and *Jadhav* – other security-related measures. In three proceedings, the concerned states had at least at some stage also asserted that the Court should entirely abstain from evaluating its respective first-hand determinations. In the other three, the respective respondents had directly urged the ICJ to apply the reasonableness standard of review.

A. Self-Defence

In all three cases involving the exercise of the right to self-defence in which the Court took a stance on the applicable standard of review, it opted for the *de novo* standard. In the first of these cases, *Nicaragua* (customary law), the United States as respondent asserted that the application of customary international law would fall outside of the Court's jurisdiction. As a consequence, the United States focused on the conventional security exception, for the application of which it (in part successfully) pleaded for the adoption of the reasonableness standard of review. The ICJ, in contrast, analysed the main issue with regard to customary international law, and implicitly applied the *de novo* standard of review for this task. In the *Oil Platforms* case, the same respondent specifically urged the Court to apply the reasonableness standard to evaluate its reliance on the right to self-defence. This resulted in the ICJ's explicit rejection of judicial deference for the application of this right. In the third of these cases, *Armed Activities*, the Court again applied the *de novo* standard of review, but only tacitly. Presumably, it saw no need to add anything to its finding issued in *Oil Platforms* issued only two years prior – even more so because the adoption of the reasonableness standard would not have led to a different verdict.

One possible explanation for this strict stance pertains to the customary nature of the prohibition of the use of force, to which the right to self-defence constitutes an exception. Pursuing the goal of upholding the effectiveness of a cornerstone rule of public international law meant to counter all claims for judicial deference in the evaluation of the most important exception to that rule. This motivation appears most clearly in *Oil Platforms*.

i. Nicaragua *(Customary Law)*

As explained above, the Court had opted for a mixed reasonableness/*de novo* standard of review for its analysis under Article XXI (1)(d) US–Nicaragua Treaty of Friendship, the conventional security exception.[2] In contrast, it adopted a consistent *de novo* standard for its evaluation whether the US measures could be justified with self-defence.

In this connection, the ICJ observed that its task was to 'establish whether the circumstances required for the exercise of this right of self-defence *are* present and, if so, whether the steps taken by the United States *actually* correspond to the requirements of international law'.[3] First, it examined whether there had been an armed attack by Nicaragua on Honduras and Costa Rica. Here, it noted that while there had been certain incursions into the territory of those two states from 1982 to 1984, the absence of further information on these incidents 'renders it difficult to decide whether they may be treated for legal purposes as amounting, singly or collectively, to an "armed attack" by Nicaragua'.[4] This shows that the Court considered that it was itself that had to decide whether an armed attack had taken place, and not the concerned states.[5]

The notable absence of any element of subjectivity in the subsequent analysis of the other self-defence requirements confirms that the ICJ applied the *de novo* standard of review for the self-defence justification.[6] Presumably, the Court wanted to prioritise the effectiveness of one the core norms of the international legal fabric over deference to the security concerns of the United States. Adopting a deferential standard of review would have undermined this regime.[7]

Among the judges who appended an individual opinion, Judge Schwebel was the only one to take issue with this approach. He would have preferred the reasonableness standard of review not only for the compliance analysis with the Treaty of Friendship,[8] but also in respect to self-defence. Regarding the necessity criterion, Judge Schwebel thus stated that 'such a judgment … requires the Court to pass upon whether or not the United States acts *reasonably* in refusing the belated professions of the Nicaraguan Government's willingness to

[2] Ch 6, section I.C.

[3] *Military and Paramilitary Activities in and against Nicaragua (Nicaragua v United States of America)*, ICJ, Judgment (Merits) of 27 June 1986, para 229 (emphases added).

[4] ibid, para 231.

[5] Note that the Court did refer to the perception of El Salvador, Honduras, Costa Rica, and the United States at the relevant time in the course of its analysis of the 'armed attack'-requirement. However, it merely did so by way of a 'not even'-argument. Since not even these states themselves had considered there had been an armed attack by Nicaragua at the time, the Court thus argued, the conditions for the lawful exercise of (collective) self-defence were not fulfilled, ibid, paras 232–36. There is again a notable absence of any subjectivity in the assessment of necessity and proportionality, see ibid, para 237.

[6] Likewise P Fischer, *Das Irrtumsrisiko bei den Ausnahmen des völkerrechtlichen Gewaltverbotes* (Nomos, 2020), 299–300.

[7] See also in that sense C Ragni, 'Standard of Review and the Margin of Appreciation before the International Court of Justice' in L Gruszczynski and W Werner (eds), *Deference in International Courts and Tribunals: Standard of Review and Margin of Appreciation* (Oxford University Press, 2014), 324; but see Y Shany, 'Toward a General Margin of Appreciation Doctrine in International Law?' (2005) 16(5) *European Journal of International Law* 907, 925–26.

[8] *Military and Paramilitary Activities in and against Nicaragua (Nicaragua v United States of America)*, ICJ, Judgment (Merits), Dissenting Opinion of Judge Schwebel, para 254.

refrain from undermining the governments of its neighbours'.[9] In his view, 'the United States has acted and does *act reasonably – at any rate, not unreasonably* – in deciding that its continuing exertion of armed and other pressures upon Nicaragua is necessary'.[10] Finally, Judge Schwebel observed that 'for the test of proportionality to be met, there by no means must be perfect proportionality',[11] again hinting at the idea that the Court should apply a certain degree of deference vis-a-vis a state's measures in reliance on the self-defence justification.

ii. Oil Platforms

The question of the appropriate standard of review in the *Oil Platforms* case received extensive attention during the merits stage of the proceedings. It was closely linked with the question whether the security exception contained in Article XX(1)(d) of the US–Iran Treaty of Amity had to be interpreted in light of the customary prohibition of the use of force.

According to the United States, which had not accepted the ICJ's jurisdiction for the application of customary international law, doing so would deprive the principle of consensual jurisdiction of all meaning.[12] As a consequence of this position, it laid the focus on the standard of review for the conventional security exception. Nonetheless, it also briefly addressed the standard of review for self-defence, and pleaded for the reasonableness standard.[13] Yet, the United States did so to no avail, as the Court explicitly rejected its plea for deference, and adopted the *de novo* standard of review.

Concerning Article XX, the United States argued for an even more lenient standard of review. It asserted that this provision allocated the 'primary responsibility' to the state invoking it.[14] It also referred approvingly to Schachter, who had observed that 'it must be acknowledged that in many cases a term such as "national defence" allows a very wide margin of appreciation and a court would be exceedingly cautious to avoid imposing its own interpretation on whether a particular act is in the national defence of the State concerned'.[15] The United States claimed that the central terms of the provision, 'necessary' and 'essential security interests', were 'well-understood to have broad meanings

[9] ibid, para 69 (emphasis added).

[10] ibid, para 76 (emphasis added), see also ibid, para 203.

[11] ibid, para 212.

[12] *Oil Platforms (Iran v United States of America), Oral Proceedings*, ICJ, Oral Proceedings of 25 February 2003, morning (CR 2003/11), 17, para 13.12, at 19, paras 13.18–13.19, and at 22, para 13.23; see also *Oil Platforms*, ICJ, Oral Proceedings of 26 February 2003, afternoon (CR 2003/13), 46, paras 22.4–22.5 (Taft).

[13] *Oil Platforms (Iran v United States of America)*, ICJ, Rejoinder of the United States of America of 23 March 2001, paras 5.12–5.13; specifically concerning the proportionality requirement *Oil Platforms*, ICJ, Oral Proceedings of 26 February 2003, morning (CR 2003/12), para 18.58 (Matheson).

[14] *Oil Platforms*, Rejoinder of the United States of America (n 13), para 4.24; see also *Oil Platforms*, Oral Proceedings of 26 February 2003, 29, para 17.42 (Weil).

[15] *Oil Platforms*, Rejoinder of the United States of America (n 13), para 4.25; O Schachter, *International Law in Theory and Practice* (Martinus Nijhoff, 1991), 221–22.

not easily susceptible to judicial scrutiny'.[16] Finally, according to the United States, ruling out deference would deprive Article XX of its effectiveness.[17]

More specifically, the United States argued for the adoption of the good faith standard of review for Article XX.[18] This standard should apply for both its determination at the time that there had been a threat to its essential security interests, and that its measures taken in reaction had been necessary.[19] Later, it modified this position, now advocating for a mixed non-reviewability-reasonableness-good faith-standard. It claimed that the Court could not evaluate a state's determination that the interest invoked had been 'essential', as this determination would be the sovereign and exclusive prerogative of the state concerned.[20] On the other hand, the United States recognised that *Nicaragua* had made clear that the ICJ could review whether there had been a risk for a party's security interests (namely, by resort to the reasonableness standard). Finally, for the necessity requirement, the United States noted that '[t]o ask an international court purely and simply to defer to the assessment of that 'necessity' by state authorities would lead to the abandonment of the judicial function. But purely and simply to substitute the assessment of a court for that of state authorities would be tantamount to creating a 'government of judges' – even less acceptable in the international context than in the domestic context'. Counsel referred approvingly to the fact that other national and international judicial bodies had been resorting to the 'manifest error of assessment' as standard when evaluating decisions based on 'technical' or 'political' appreciations. In justification, the United States pointed to the state authorities' alleged superior technical expertise and more direct political responsibility, and thereby to the fundamental difference between states and courts, arguing that the latter were in some instances structurally unable to appreciate core interests of the former. For these reasons, the ICJ should only review whether the United States had acted in good faith when determining that its attacks on the Iranian platforms were necessary.[21]

[16] *Oil Platforms*, Rejoinder of the United States of America (n 13), para 4.26.

[17] *Oil Platforms*, ICJ, Oral Proceedings, of 5 March 2003, afternoon (CR 2003/18), 22, para 27.11 (Weil).

[18] *Oil Platforms*, Rejoinder of the United States of America (n 13), para 4.25. In that connection, the United States also cited Rosenne with approval, who had observed that the 'primary function, and perhaps [the] sole function [of good faith] is … to allow the decision-making authorities a fair degree of freedom of action in interpreting and applying the terms of the treaty-obligation in a concrete case. In the first instance, the decision-making authorities will be the parties themselves'. However, Rosenne's position on this is more ambiguous than this quotation suggests, for he completes the above sentence with 'or, in the event of their inability to reach agreement, or of actual disagreement between them, duly authorized third-party dispute prevention or dispute-settlement organs', S Rosenne, *Developments in the Law of Treaties 1945–1986* (Cambridge University Press, 1989), 176–77.

[19] *Oil Platforms*, Rejoinder of the United States of America (n 13), para 4.27; see also ibid, para 5.12; and *Oil Platforms (Iran v United States of America)*, ICJ, Counter-Memorial and Counter-Claim of the United States of America of 23 June 1997, paras 3.23–3.38.

[20] *Oil Platforms*, Oral Proceedings of 26 February 2003, 20, paras 17.44–17.45 (Weil).

[21] ibid, 30, paras 17.48–17.52 (Weil); see also ibid, 41, para 18.5 (Matheson): '[T]he Court should afford a wide area of discretion to that party in the application of such measures. This is analogous

Iran in turn advocated for a mixed *de novo*/reasonableness standard of review both for the treaty-based exception clause and the customary law of self-defence. It argued that Article XX(1)(d) had to be interpreted in light of customary international law,[22] and that this would inevitably influence the standard of review. Nonetheless, it also analysed the security exception on its own terms. First, Iran argued that not least the wording of the provision made clear that it would not constitute 'an automatic source of a defence'. Accordingly, the Court would be able to – and even would have to – evaluate whether its invocation was well-founded.[23] Furthermore, Iran made a systemic argument, asserting that as were the requirements mentioned in the first part of Article XX(1)(d), the security interest requirements would be objective ones.[24]

Making the connection to the customary prohibition of the use of force, Iran then argued that bowing to a state's self-assessment to use force to protect essential security interests would gravely undermine the effectiveness of the prohibition.[25] Interestingly, its counsel also directly addressed the avoidance-dimension. He observed that 'no doubt international law has to be applied realistically, and … a court might hesitate before a major power which is invoking essential security interests to justify its behaviour'. Yet, doing so would be inappropriate, because broad state compliance with international law could only be ensured if the most powerful states were also held to account.[26]

Later, Iran adopted a slightly stricter approach, now claiming that the existence of a security interest had also to be analysed by the *de novo* standard as well. Consequently, only the essential character of that interest and the existence of a threat to it should be examined under a reasonableness standard.[27] Iran justified the *de novo* standard for the necessity requirement with a comparison to the necessity requirement under the customary law on self-defence.[28] Counsel stated that '[t]he more peremptory the norm, the less room there is for the margin of appreciation'.[29] On the other hand, it conceded that 'there

to the concepts of 'margin of appreciation' and of 'abuse of the law', which recognize that a court should not simply defer to the subjective judgment of the state taking action, but at the same time should not simply substitute its own judgment for that of a state which determined in good faith that its actions were necessary to protect essential security interests'.

[22] *Oil Platforms (Iran v United States of America)*, ICJ, Reply and Defence to Counter-Claim of Iran of 10 March 1999, paras 7.71–7.77; *Oil Platforms*, ICJ, Oral Proceedings of 19 February 2003, afternoon (CR 2003/8), 176, paras 30–33 (Crawford).

[23] *Oil Platforms*, ICJ, Oral Proceedings of 17 February 2003, afternoon (CR 2003/5), 41, para 31 (Crawford); see also *Oil Platforms*, Oral Proceedings of 19 February 2003, 10, para 16 (Crawford); *Oil Platforms*, ICJ, Oral Proceedings of 3 March 2003, afternoon (CR 2003/16), 15, para 13 (Crawford).

[24] *Oil Platforms*, ICJ, Oral Proceedings of 19 February 2003, morning (CR 2003/7), 53, paras 10–11 (Crawford).

[25] ibid, 37, paras 22–23 (Bothe).

[26] *Oil Platforms*, Oral Proceedings of 17 February 2003, 43, para 34 (Crawford).

[27] *Oil Platforms*, Oral Proceedings of 19 February 2003, 52, para 8 (Crawford); *Oil Platforms*, Oral Proceedings of 19 February 2003, 13, para 22, at 16, para 28, and at 17, para 34 (Crawford); *Oil Platforms*, Oral Proceedings of 3 March 2003, 10, para 2 (Crawford).

[28] *Oil Platforms*, Oral Proceedings of 19 February 2003, 15, para 27, and at 16, para 30 (Crawford).

[29] *Oil Platforms*, Oral Proceedings of 3 March 2003, 16, para 14 (Crawford).

are issues of judgment and appreciation in applying the law of self-defence, for example in the assessment of proportionality'.[30] Read in connection with its other arguments, it seems that Iran recognised the possibility of applying the reasonableness standard of review for this condition.

The ICJ rejected the analytical separation between the treaty-based security exception and the customary law on the use of force, and held that the former had to be interpreted in light of the latter. If a measure constituted a violation of the prohibition of the use of force, it would thus also be unlawful under the treaty provision.[31] Consequently, the Court went on to analyse whether the United States could successfully rely on the customary right of self-defence.[32] It applied the *de novo* standard of review both for the question whether the United States had been the victim of an armed attack by Iran[33] and for the necessity criterion. Regarding the latter, it did so explicitly, explaining that 'the requirement of international law that measures taken avowedly in self-defence must have been necessary for that purpose is *strict and objective, leaving no room for any "measure of discretion"*'.[34] In turn, things are less clear for its position on the proportionality requirement. Yet, the absence of any language hinting at a degree of deference can be taken as an indication that it likewise held the *de novo* standard to be appropriate here.[35]

As a consequence of its linkage of conventional and customary law, the ICJ found it unnecessary to determine the appropriate standard of review for measures taken in reliance on Article XX not constituting a use of force. Yet, from the fact that it cited the relevant passages from *Nicaragua* with apparent approval, one may deduce that it still considered the mixed reasonableness-*de novo* standard adopted in that case to be appropriate.[36]

Four judges addressed the question of the applicable standard of review under Article XX in their separate opinions: Judges Buergenthal, Higgins, Kooijmans, and Simma. For the 'risk for an essential security interest' element, Judges Buergenthal and Kooijmans both opted for the adoption of the reasonableness standard. In turn, for the necessity requirement, Judge Kooijmans sided with Judges Higgins and Simma in openly asserting that the *de novo* standard of review was appropriate. Only Judge Buergenthal disagreed on this second point.

[30] *Oil Platforms*, Oral Proceedings of 19 February 2003, 13, para 22 (Crawford).

[31] *Oil Platforms (Iran v United States of America)*, ICJ, Judgment (Merits) of 6 November 2003, paras 39–42 and 44.

[32] ibid, para 50.

[33] ibid, paras 64, 72.

[34] ibid, para 73 (emphasis added).

[35] ibid, para 77; see also Fischer, who argues that, had the Court wanted to lay down a deferential standard of review, it would have formulated certain passages in the judgment differently, Fischer, *Das Irrtumsrisiko bei den Ausnahmen des völkerrechtlichen Gewaltverbotes* (n 6), 299–301.

[36] With a different reading D Eisenhut, 'Sovereignty, National Security and International Treaty Law: The Standard of Review of International Courts and Tribunals with regard to "Security Exceptions"' (2010) 48(4) *Archiv des Völkerrechts* 431, 436–38. For him, the judgment 'remains mute on the question altogether', ibid, 438.

First, Judge Higgins declared that in her view, '[t]he Court should … have … examined – without any need to afford a "margin of appreciation" – the meaning of "necessary"'.[37] Likewise, Judge Simma saw a need for 'a particularly high demand on the standard of 'necessity'', and concluded that all the requirements of Article XX would 'have to be subjected to extremely careful scrutiny'.[38]

In contrast, Judge Kooijmans opted for a differentiated standard of review. He first criticised the majority's 'nearly exclusive consideration' of the United States attacks in light of customary law.[39] For him, referring to customary law would only have been necessary for the necessity requirement, as on its own, Article XX would only be lacking guidance on this question.[40] In his view, *Nicaragua* had already established the standard of review for the 'risk for an essential security interest' condition – namely, reasonableness. The allegedly political nature of that assessment would justify a more lenient standard.[41] On the other hand, he sided with the majority for the necessity requirement, as his respective examination shows.[42] Consequently, Judge Kooijmans did not so much disagree with the majority on the appropriate standard of review for the self-defence justification. Rather, he disagreed with the fact that the majority had superimposed the customary law analysis over that of the treaty.

In contrast, Judge Buergenthal's degree of disagreement with the Court majority is considerably greater. Siding with the United States, in his view, the ICJ was lacking jurisdiction to interpret the security exception in light of customary law.[43] Regarding Article XX, he argued for the reasonableness standard of review both for the 'risk for an essential security interest' and the necessity requirement. In his opinion, the Court should have inquired 'whether, on the facts before it, a party had *convincing reasons for believing* that the measures were necessary to protect its essential security interests'.[44] For him, that standard of review would be implicit in the language of the provision itself, and be implied in *Nicaragua*.

[37] *Oil Platforms (Iran v United States of America)*, ICJ, Judgment (Merits), Separate Opinion of Judge Higgins, para 48.

[38] *Oil Platforms (Iran v United States of America)*, ICJ, Judgment (Merits), Separate Opinion of Judge Simma, para 11.

[39] *Oil Platforms (Iran v United States of America)*, ICJ, Judgment (Merits), Separate Opinion of Judge Kooijmans, para 22. He quotes Judge Jennings's opinion in the *Nicaragua* case with approval. Judge Jennings had observed that '[t]he question … is not … whether such measures are justified in international law as action taken in self-defence …; the question is whether the measures in question are, or are not, in breach of the Treaty', ibid, para 25 (references omitted).

[40] ibid, paras 47–49.

[41] ibid, para 44.

[42] ibid, paras 54–63. This also becomes clear through his observation that by resorting to the use of force, the United States 'opted for means the use of which must be subjected to strict legal norms, since the prohibition of force is considered to have a peremptory character. The measure of discretion to which the United States is entitled is therefore considerably more limited than if it had chosen, for instance, the use of economic measures', ibid, para 46.

[43] *Oil Platforms (Iran v United States of America)*, ICJ, Judgment (Merits), Separate Opinion of Judge Buergenthal, paras 20–22.

[44] ibid, paras 37–38 (emphasis added).

Reactions in the literature are likewise mixed. For instance, one author advocated the adoption of the reasonableness standard of review also for the customary law requirement of necessity because the respective state assessment would inevitably take place in 'an opaque context'. As long as there was 'some evidence, although not necessarily conclusive evidence' that a reaction was necessary, the ICJ should hold the necessity requirement to be fulfilled: 'If the Court goes beyond this assessment, it will simply substitute the State's subjective assessment of necessity for its own, equally subjective assessment'.[45] In contrast, the same author argued for the adoption of the *de novo* standard of review for the proportionality assessment, since '[u]nlike the assessment of necessity, this determination can be made objectively by reference to facts, i.e., by reference to the extent and intensity of use of force by the other State'.[46] Others have defended the Court's overall choice of the *de novo* standard of review.[47]

Why did the Court opt for the *de novo* standard of review for the self-defence requirements? An answer may be found by taking into account that its entire review of the conventional security exception, and incidentally the customary law on self-defence, was an *obiter dictum*. The question whether the US attacks were justified would have only arisen if there had been a breach of the Treaty of Amity in the first place. This the Court denied by pointing out that the concerned Iranian oil platforms did not serve for commerce between the two states, such that the United States attack on them did not amount to an interference with the freedom of commerce between Iran and the United States in the sense of Article X(1) of the Treaty of Friendship. However, crucially, it only concluded so *after* conducting its self-defence analysis. This suggests that the ICJ had specific motives for dealing with the use of force issue. Presumably, it wanted to uphold the effectiveness of the prohibition in the context of the then-emerging debate about expanding the notion of self-defence. If it wanted to uphold this rule, it necessarily had to reject all calls for a deferential standard of review for its evaluation of such measures.[48]

iii. Armed Activities

Like the United States in *Oil Platforms*, Uganda as the respondent in the *Armed Activities* case urged the ICJ to apply the reasonableness standard of review to

[45] V Heiskanen, 'Oil Platforms: Lessons of Dissensus' (2005) 74(1) *Nordic Journal of International Law* 179, 194–95.

[46] ibid, 197.

[47] Fischer, *Das Irrtumsrisiko bei den Ausnahmen des völkerrechtlichen Gewaltverbotes* (n 6), 394–95.

[48] Hinting in that direction: *Oil Platforms*, Judgment (Merits) (n 31), para 38; explicit: *Oil Platforms*, Judgment (Merits) (n 38), Separate Opinion of Judge Simma, para 6; see also SM Young, 'Destruction of Property (on an International Scale): The Recent Oil Platforms Case and the International Court of Justice's Inconsistent Commentary on the Use of Force by the United States' (2004) 30(2) *The North Carolina Journal of International Law and Commercial Regulation* 335,

evaluate whether its invocation of the right of self-defence was well-founded. And again, that plea was to no avail, even if the Court did not say so explicitly. The case between the DRC and Uganda essentially revolved around the question whether the latter's incursion into the former's territory in the context of the Congolese civil war could be justified under international law, including by resort to the right to self-defence.

Uganda did not go so far as to claim that the ICJ should abstain from evaluating its invocation of its right of self-defence.[49] However, it asserted that '*it must be obvious that the concept of self-defence … involves a necessary power of appreciation* involving reference to contemporary standards of *reasonableness*'. Further, it claimed that 'it is surely necessary to recognise that a State in the position of Uganda must have the benefit of a *margin of appreciation* in relation to the dimensions of the perceived threat and the means of dealing with that threat effectively'.[50] Uganda thereby asked the Court to adopt the reasonableness standard of review, apparently for all elements of the right of self-defence. In the oral stage, its counsel added that because of the need to apply the concept of self-defence 'on the basis of effectiveness and common sense', '*it is surely the view of the victim State* … which must prevail' with respect to the criterion of necessity.[51] Consequently, Uganda justified its invocation of the reasonableness standard with the need to uphold the effectiveness of the right to self-defence.

The DRC opposed this position, and tried to demonstrate objectively that the conditions for the lawful exercise of the right of self-defence had not been fulfilled.[52] While it expressed its readiness to recognise a certain *initial* power of appreciation in favour of the state acting in self-defence, such a power would inevitably end once a third actor had been seized of the matter.[53] In its view, necessity and proportionality were 'strict legal criteria',[54] a formulation implying a strict standard of review. Furthermore, the DRC referred to the *de novo*

342, 370; N Ochoa-Ruiz and E Salamanca-Aguado, 'Exploring the Limits of International Law relating to the Use of Force in Self-defence' (2005) 16(3) *European Journal of International Law* 499, 505; for Eisenhut, the Court's adoption of the *de novo* standard can be explained 'by the special nature of the applied provisions, i.e. the *jus cogens* nature of Article 2(4) UN Charter', Eisenhut, 'Sovereignty, National Security and International Treaty Law' (n 36), 460.

[49] '[T]he wording of Article 51 of the Charter does not preclude … the Court … from making the necessary determinations of fact, and its application depends upon such determinations of fact. The article is not self-executing', *Armed Activities on the Territory of the Congo (the Congo v Uganda)*, ICJ, Rejoinder of Uganda of 6 December 2002, para 296.

[50] ibid, paras 269 and 284 (emphases added).

[51] *Armed Activities*, ICJ, Oral Proceedings of 18 April 2005, morning (CR 2005/7), 34, para 92 (Brownlie, emphasis added).

[52] *Armed Activities on the Territory of the Congo (the Congo v Uganda)*, ICJ, Memorial of the Congo of 6 July 2000, paras 5.26–5.35; and *Armed Activities on the Territory of the Congo (the Congo v Uganda)*, ICJ, Reply of the Congo of 29 May 2002, paras 3.153–3.158, and para 3.172 ('objectivement').

[53] ibid, paras 3.181–3.182.

[54] ibid, para 3.161 (own translation, in the original:' critères juridiques rigoureux').

standard of review adopted by the ICJ in *Oil Platforms*.[55] Finally, its counsel pointed to the danger of arbitrary unilateral qualifications regarding the proportionality requirement.[56]

The Court, in turn, only dealt with the necessity and proportionality of Uganda's actions in a very cursory manner because it found that Uganda had not been the victim of an armed attack by the DRC in the first place. It did not explicitly address the standard of review controversy between the parties. However, its evaluation of the first condition – existence of an armed attack – was clearly based on the *de novo* standard. In the following, it merely observed in passing that 'the taking of airports and towns many hundreds of kilometres from Uganda's border would not seem proportionate to the series of transborder attacks it claimed had given rise to the right of self-defence, nor to be necessary to that end'.[57]

This silence on the standard of review for those two requirements could mean either of three things: implicit recognition of Uganda's claim that a deferential standard of review was appropriate (even if Uganda had ultimately failed to meet even that standard), no position adopted in this respect at all, or implicit rejection of Uganda's position. Several aspects point towards the third interpretation. The first possible reading – implicit agreement with Uganda's deferential standard of review argument – is almost certainly incorrect if one takes into consideration the *Oil Platforms* judgment rendered just a little over two years before. Fourteen of the 17 judges who had sat in that case were still on the bench in *Armed Activities*.[58] If the same judges, who in *Oil Platforms* had opted for the *de novo* standard of review for a state's invocation of self-defence, had intended to deviate from this position now, they would almost certainly have made such a *revirement* explicit.

Rather, the absence of such a statement suggests that the Court did not feel it necessary to respond to the call for deference – presumably, because it had nothing to add to *Oil Platforms*. The indication in paragraph 148 of the judgment points in the same direction. There, the ICJ held that '[t]he prohibition against the use of force is a cornerstone of the United Nations Charter', and 'Article 51 of the Charter may justify a use of force in self-defence only within the strict confines there laid down'.[59] In *Oil Platforms*, the Court had resorted to similar language, which indicates a certain continuity.[60] As in that

[55] *Armed Activities*, ICJ, Oral Proceedings of 12 April 2005, morning (CR 2005/3), 48, para 3 (Klein); *Armed Activities*, ICJ, Oral Proceedings of 25 April 2005, morning (CR 2005/12), 28, para 10 (Klein).

[56] *Armed Activities (Democratic Republic of the Congo v Uganda)*, Oral Proceedings of 12 April 2005, 52, para 17 (Klein), see also at 55, para 22.

[57] *Armed Activities on the Territory of the Congo (the Congo v Uganda)*, ICJ, Judgment of 19 December 2005, para 147.

[58] The two judges *ad hoc* Verhoeven and Kateka in addition to Judge Guillaume, who had replaced Judge Abraham, were the only new members of the bench.

[59] *Armed Activities on the Territory of the Congo*, Judgment (n 57), para 148.

[60] See *Oil Platforms*, Judgment (Merits) (n 31), para 73.

case, given the importance of the prohibition of the use of force and the strict confines for the exception from that prohibition, it seems only logical to apply a strict standard of review for the evaluation of self-defence claims. Consequently, the absence of a statement as to the applicable standard of review can be read as an implicit endorsement of the choice for the *de novo* standard of review in *Oil Platforms*.[61]

B. Other Security-Related Measures

The proceedings falling in this category are more diverse, encompassing both infrastructure works and the denial of consular rights to a detained individual. Yet, in all those instances, the respondent states justified their measures with security interests, and tried to convince the ICJ to apply a deferential standard of review in this respect. The degree of deference invoked translated to non-reviewability in the *Wall* advisory proceedings, and reasonableness in the other two. Contrary to the security-related measures analysed in the previous chapter, and the *Mutual Assistance* case discussed in the chapter before that, these claims were unsuccessful. Accordingly, unlike for the self-defence claim, there is no consistency in the Court's standard of review for other state measures justified with security interests. The three cases where the Court opted for *de novo* – *Wall in the OPT*, *Construction of a Road*, and *Jadhav* – will be presented in turn.

i. Wall in the OPT

The *Wall in the OPT* advisory proceeding concerned the legality of Israel's construction of the wall, and the legal consequences flowing therefrom. A central question before the ICJ was whether the wall and the associated impairments of international human rights and humanitarian law could be justified, either by the terms of the provisions themselves, the state of necessity, or self-defence. Ultimately, this boiled down to whether and to what extent Israeli security concerns could take precedence over these aspects.[62] Accordingly, the proceedings involved questions propitious for standard of review arguments.

[61] None of the judges dissented on this standard of review. Judge Kooijmans found that the measures taken by Uganda in August 1998 had 'not … [been] unnecessary or disproportionate', *Armed Activities on the Territory of the Congo (the Congo v Uganda), Judgment*, ICJ, Judgment, Separate Opinion of Judge Kooijmans, para 33. This negative formulation could point in the direction of a reasonableness standard of review. On the other hand, this has to be contrasted with the strict position Judge Kooijmans took on this question in *Oil* Platforms, see above at section I.A.ii. Therefore, it seems more likely that he agreed with the *de novo* standard of review, and merely dissented on the substance.

[62] As the ICJ noted, 'Israel has argued that the wall's sole purpose is to enable it effectively to combat terrorist attacks launched from the West Bank', *Legal Consequences of the Construction of a Wall in the Occupied Palestinian Territory*, ICJ, Advisory Opinion of 9 July 2004, para 116.

Israel had only submitted a written statement on jurisdiction and propriety, in which it argued for the non-reviewability of the matters. Several other states and the UN Special Rapporteur to the Commission of Human Rights on the situation of human rights in the Palestinian territories occupied by Israel since 1967 commented on the standard of review as well. Finally, certain remarks of the International Committee of the Red Cross (ICRC) and of the International Criminal Tribunal for the former Yugoslavia (ICTY) bear on the standard of review under Article 53 of the Fourth Geneva Convention.

For instance, Madagascar recognised that 'it is difficult to take issue *per se* with the unfettered discretionary freedom of judgment held by a responsible government as to the assessment of the risks and the action to be taken in response to them. Under the Charter, the discretionary power to take action remains within national jurisdiction.'[63] Further, Madagascar referred to the state's right of survival.[64] This notion had gained prominence in the *Nuclear Weapons* opinion, and was at the basis of the Court's finding of *non liquet* there. Arguably, that finding was motivated by the consideration that questions relating to the possession and use of nuclear weapons would be beyond the ICJ's purview.[65] Similarly, Switzerland observed that 'Israel has legitimate security concerns and considerable latitude in selecting and implementing the means required'.[66] Finally, the UN Special Rapporteur to the Commission of Human Rights on the situation of human rights in the Palestinian territories occupied by Israel since 1967 at the time, John Dugard, noted that '[i]t is not possible to adopt an armchair attitude in assessing Israel's response to suicide bombings and Palestinian violence. Israel is entitled to a wide margin of appreciation in its response.'[67]

Palestine in turn observed that international humanitarian law 'ha[d] moved away from Clausewitz's concept of military necessity as *Kriegsraison*, i.e. the idea that the aims of war justify using any means *considered necessary* to achieve them', to 'the modern and much narrower concept of military necessity'.[68] Specifically addressing Article 53 of the Fourth Geneva Convention, according to which an occupying state may not destroy personal property 'except where such destruction is rendered absolutely necessary by military operations', Palestine remarked that '[t]here is no question of a "balance of convenience" or

[63] *Legal Consequences of the Construction of a Wall in the Occupied Palestinian Territory*, ICJ, Oral Proceedings of 24 February 2004, afternoon (CR 2004/4), 6, para 30 (Rambeloson).

[64] ibid, 8, para 41 (Rambeloson).

[65] See above at ch 3, section III.C.

[66] *Legal Consequences of the Construction of a Wall in the Occupied Palestinian Territory*, ICJ, Written Statement by Switzerland of 30 January 2004, para 27.

[67] Commission on Human Rights, 'Question of the Violation of Human Rights in the Occupied Arab Territories, including Palestine: Report of the Special Rapporteur of the Commission on Human Rights, John Dugard, on the situation of human rights in the Palestinian territories occupied by Israel since 1967' (8 September 2003) E/CN.4/2004/6, para 5.

[68] *Legal Consequences of the Construction of a Wall in the Occupied Palestinian Territory*, ICJ, Oral Proceedings of 23 February 2004, morning (CR 2004/1), 45 (Al-Saab, emphasis added).

"*reasonable* necessity": there must be no alternative whatever to the destruction of the property'.[69] Thus, in this regard, Palestine explicitly rejected the reasonableness standard of review, and pleaded for the *de novo* standard. Jordan in turn argued for *de novo* for both the evaluation of the military necessity exceptions and the right of self-defence. In support, it pointed to the standard of review set by the ICJ in the *Oil Platforms* case. In its view, there would be no reason to doubt the transferability of this position to the proportionality requirement.[70]

In contrast, the ICRC's Commentary on the military necessity clause in Article 53 recognises that—

> *it will be for the Occupying Power to judge the importance of such military requirements*. It is therefore to be feared that bad faith in the application of the reservation may render the proposed safeguard valueless ... *The Occupying Power must therefore try to interpret the clause in a reasonable manner: ... the occupying authorities must try to keep a sense of proportion* in comparing the military advantages to be gained with the damage done.[71]

Clearly, this does not constitute an endorsement, but at least a recognition of a certain degree of leeway in favour of the acting state.[72]

Arguably, the Court applied the *de novo* standard of review for the evaluation of Article 12 ICCPR, Article 53 of the Fourth Geneva Convention, and the

[69] *Legal Consequences of the Construction of a Wall in the Occupied Palestinian Territory*, ICJ, Written Statement of Palestine of 29 January 2004, para 445 (emphasis added).

[70] *Legal Consequences of the Construction of a Wall in the Occupied Palestinian Territory*, ICJ, Written Statement of Jordan of 30 January 2004, paras 5.274, and 5.279. On the other hand, in the context of Art 27 of the Fourth Geneva Convention, Jordan noted that 'the Occupying Power may have a measure of discretion in taking security measures'. This points in the direction of a certain degree of concomitant judicial deference. Presumably, Jordan thereby referred to the right of the Occupying Power to define its security interests in the first place, ibid, para 5.157.

[71] OM Uhler, 'Article 53 – Prohibited Destruction' in JS Pictet (ed), *The Geneva Convention of 12 August 1949, Volume IV: Commentary* (1958), 302 (emphasis added).

[72] Note the parallels to the proportionality in attack requirement laid down in Arts 51(5)(b) and 57(2) of the Protocol Additional to the Geneva Conventions of 12 August 1949, and relating to the Protection of Victims of International Armed Conflicts, 1125 United Nations Treaty Series 3, recognised as customary international law applicable in international and non-international armed conflict, J-M Henckaerts and L Doswald-Beck, *Customary International Humanitarian Law: Volume I: Rules* (Cambridge University Press, 2005), 46–49. The commentators of Art 57 in the ICRC's Commentary also recognised the existence of a permissible range of appreciation for military commanders. They held that '[e]ven if this system is based to some extent on a subjective evaluation, the interpretation must above all be a question of *common sense and good faith for military commanders*', J Pictet and C Pilloud, 'Article 57 – Precautions in Attack' in Y Sandoz, C Swinarski and B Zimmermann (eds), *Commentary on the Additional Protocols of 8 June 1977 to the Geneva Conventions of 12 August 1949* (Martinus Nijhoff, 1987), para 2208 (emphasis added). They conclude that 'the provision allows for a *fairly broad margin of judgment*', ibid, para 2210 (emphasis added). The reference to 'common sense' indicates the invocation of the reasonableness standard of review for this type of proportionality assessment. In the *Galić* judgment, Trial Chamber I of the ICTY laid down a similar standard of review. It held that to decide whether an attack had been proportionate under Arts 51(5)(b) and 57(2) of Additional Protocol I, 'it is necessary to examine *whether a reasonably well-informed person* in the circumstances of the actual perpetrator, *making reasonable use of the information available* to him or her, could have expected excessive civilian casualties to result from the attack', *Prosecutor v Stanislav Galić*, ICTY, Judgment and Opinion of 5 December 2003, para 58 (references omitted, emphases added).

elements it reviewed concerning the state of necessity. Yet, it only did so implicitly. In turn, the ICJ did not take a position on the standard of review for the evaluation of the self-defence justification. It summarily rejected its applicability on the basis that the relevant attacks had not emanated from a foreign state, but rather from a territory under Israeli control.[73]

Turning to Article 12 ICCPR, the Court noted that the conditions of paragraph 3 'are not met in the present instance', and declared itself 'not convinced that the specific course Israel has chosen for the wall was necessary to attain its security objectives'.[74] The succinct nature of this and the following observations as well as the lack of detailed reasoning in general[75] makes it difficult to identify the standard of review. Yet, the fact that the ICJ resorted to objective language – conditions '*are* not met', not convinced that the course of the wall '*was* necessary' – indicates that it applied the *de novo* standard of review. This is all the more interesting since the UN Human Rights Committee, on whose jurisprudence the Court based itself,[76] does apply a margin of appreciation to states' national security considerations based on considerations of relative institutional expertise – including for Article 12 ICCPR.[77]

In the same vein, for its evaluation of Article 53 of the Fourth Geneva Convention, the ICJ declared itself 'not convinced that the destructions carried out contrary to the prohibition in Article 53 … were rendered absolutely necessary by military operations'.[78] Once more, the objective language points towards the *de novo* standard of review.

Finally, turning to the state of necessity under customary law, the Court referred to *Gabčíkovo-Nagymaros* to note that it 'can only be invoked under certain strictly defined conditions … and the State concerned is not the sole judge of whether those conditions have been met'.[79] As noted in the analysis of that case, the formulation 'not the *sole* judge' implies a certain degree of judicial deference.[80] In *Wall*, the Court only addressed one element of the state of necessity – one that it did not deal with in *Gabčíkovo-Nagymaros*. Namely, the ICJ concluded that it was 'not convinced that the construction of the wall along the route chosen was the only means to safeguard the interests of Israel against

[73] *Wall in the OPT*, Advisory Opinion (n 62), para 139.

[74] ibid, paras 136 and 137.

[75] For Scobbie, 'a conspicuous feature of this opinion is that, at times, the reasoning is rather abrupt, almost to the point of taciturnity', I Scobbie, 'Words My Mother Never Taught Me: "In Defense of the International Court"' (2005) 99(1) *American Journal of International Law* 76, 80; see also SD Murphy, 'Self-Defense and the Israeli Wall Advisory Opinion: An Ipse Dixit from the ICJ?' (2005) 99(1) *American Journal of International Law* 62, 71–72.

[76] See *Wall in the OPT*, Advisory Opinion (n 62), para 136.

[77] A Legg, *The Margin of Appreciation in International Human Rights Law: Deference and Proportionality* (Oxford University Press, 2012), 158 (referring to *Celepli v Sweden*).

[78] *Wall in the OPT*, Advisory Opinion (n 62), para 135.

[79] ibid, para 140.

[80] Arguably, the Court applied the reasonableness standard of review for the 'essential interest' and the 'imminence' requirement, and the *de novo* standard for the existence of a peril, see ch 6, section IV.A.

the peril which it has invoked'.[81] The reference to the 'strictly defined conditions' along with the objective language yet again points towards an implicit adoption of the *de novo* standard of review for the only means-requirement.

In contrast to the majority, Judge Elaraby apparently accepted the application of a deferential standard of review for the invocation of security needs as justification for the wall. On the one hand, he referred to the fact that such 'military exigencies could arguably be advanced as justification … had Israel proven that it could *perceive* no other alternative for safeguarding its security'. In the same vein, he observed that '[i]t is a fact that the law of belligerent occupation contains clauses which confer on the occupying Power a limited leeway for military necessities and security'.[82]

ii. Construction of a Road

The *Construction of a Road* case was joined with the *Certain Activities* case by the Court.[83] Yet, in the interest of better readability, both cases will be addressed separately in this enquiry. The subject of the former was Costa Rica's construction of a road alongside the San Juan River. Nicaragua claimed that Costa Rica had violated international law, inter alia by having failed to conduct an environmental impact assessment before building the road. Costa Rica in turn maintained, among others, that it had built the road in reaction to Nicaragua's prior occupation of parts of its territory. In its view, a state of emergency exempted it from the requirement to conduct an environmental impact assessment in that situation. Finally, it asserted that such a state of emergency had indeed existed in its case.[84]

Costa Rica recognised that the Court could evaluate the correctness of its assertions,[85] yet pleaded for the application of the reasonableness standard of review – namely, for its assessment at the time that a state of emergency had existed, and that the construction of the road was an appropriate response to that situation. The abundance of different formulations to that effect is contrasted with the relative dearth of justification. Costa Rica merely asserted that 'the starting point in terms of considering the alleged breaches is that Costa Rica, as any other State, is free to make its own appraisal of its own security …

[81] *Wall in the OPT*, Advisory Opinion (n 62), para 140.

[82] *Legal Consequences of the Construction of a Wall in the Occupied Palestinian Territory*, ICJ, Advisory Opinion, Separate Opinion of Judge Elaraby, para 3.2 (emphasis added).

[83] *Certain Activities Carried Out by Nicaragua in the Border Area (Costa Rica v Nicaragua)*, ICJ, Order (Joinder of Proceedings) of 17 April 2013, para 25; *Construction of a Road in Costa Rica along the San Juan River (Nicaragua v Costa Rica)*, ICJ, Order (Joinder of Proceedings) of 17 April 2013, para 20.

[84] *Certain Activities Carried Out by Nicaragua in the Border Area (Costa Rica v Nicaragua) and Construction of a Road in Costa Rica along the San Juan River (Nicaragua v Costa Rica)*, ICJ, Judgment of 16 December 2015, paras 146–48.

[85] *Construction of a Road in Costa Rica along the San Juan River (Nicaragua v Costa Rica)*, ICJ, Counter-Memorial of Costa Rica of 19 December 2013, para 5.15.

needs'. Its decision to construct the road would be a sovereign one, and a 'purely domestic matter'.[86]

First, as Costa Rica asserted, it had had 'a very real and *plausible* concern' that the tensions with Nicaragua would lead to an armed conflict.[87] Further, it described why the obligation to conduct an environmental impact assessment could not be applicable in 'an emergency (*or what is reasonably perceived as such*)'.[88] Finally, its counsel referred to the construction of the road being a 'response to what Costa Rica *legitimately believed to be an emergency situation*', and claimed that '[i]t is difficult to deny that Costa Rica had good reason in the circumstances *to regard itself* as being in a situation of emergency'.[89] The terms employed – plausibility, legitimate belief, reasonable perception, regard itself – all point towards the reasonableness standard of review.

Costa Rica also argued for the adoption of the reasonableness standard for the second aspect: the validity of its assessment that the road was an appropriate response to the emergency. Again, this becomes evident through its repeated reference to its 'perception' at the time it took the decision to construct the road. It stated that there had been 'at the time, *as assessed by Costa Rica, a real risk* that if Nicaragua provoked a military confrontation, Costa Rica would have been unable to ... ensure the evacuation and safety of its inhabitants, and unable to protect its territorial integrity' without the road.[90] Further, citing security needs, it asserted that it had had a '*reasonable perception* of the urgent need for road infrastructure works in the border area'.[91] Seen in this light, Costa Rica continued, its decision to build the road 'was a reasonable and proportionate response to the risk it perceived at that time'.[92] Consequently, Costa Rica used very similar terms – risk as assessed by it, reasonable perception, reasonable response – to describe the standard of review the ICJ should apply: reasonableness.

Nicaragua denied the existence of a general emergency exception in international law per se in the first place. In its view, the recognition of such a legal concept would throw open the doors to abuse.[93] In any case, it asserted, even if

[86] ibid, para 5.3; and *Construction of a Road in Costa Rica along the San Juan River (Nicaragua v Costa Rica)*, ICJ, Rejoinder of Costa Rica of 2 February 2015, 3.40, respectively.

[87] *Certain Activities & Construction of a Road*, Counter-Memorial of Costa Rica (n 85), para 2.22 (emphasis added).

[88] ibid, para 5.18.

[89] *Certain Activities Carried Out by Nicaragua in the Border Area (Costa Rica v Nicaragua) and Construction of a Road in Costa Rica along the San Juan River*, ICJ, Oral Proceedings of 23 April 2015, afternoon (CR 2015/11), 14, para 4 (Brenes, emphasis added), and 52, para 42 (Kohen, emphasis added).

[90] *Certain Activities & Construction of a Road*, Counter-Memorial of Costa Rica (n 85), para 1.15 (emphasis added).

[91] ibid, para 2.3 (emphasis added).

[92] ibid, para 2.37.

[93] *Certain Activities Carried Out by Nicaragua in the Border Area (Costa Rica v Nicaragua) and Construction of a Road in Costa Rica along the San Juan River*, ICJ, Oral Proceedings of 21 April 2015, morning (CR 2015/10), 37, para 20 (McCaffrey); *Certain Activities Carried Out by Nicaragua in the Border Area (Costa Rica v Nicaragua) and Construction of a Road in Costa Rica along*

the existence of an emergency could preclude the wrongfulness of certain measures under international law, the existence of such an emergency 'is not, and cannot be, a self-judging question'.[94] On the other hand, several statements indicate that Nicaragua did not reject Costa Rica's plea for a deferential standard of review outright. For instance, it stated that 'even if Costa Rica *perceived* that there was a grave and imminent peril – *which … it could not, in fact, reasonably have done* – the action it took bore no relation to the perceived peril that allegedly gave rise to the emergency'.[95] Counsel observed that 'even if there had been a bona fide emergency', Costa Rica would have remained under the obligation to conduct an environmental impact assessment beforehand.[96] Consequently, Nicaragua contemplated the possibility that the ICJ would adopt a deferential standard of review for the question whether an emergency had existed.[97] In contrast, it took no position on the standard of review for the second limb of the question, the appropriateness of the road as a response to the alleged emergency.[98]

The ICJ, in turn, focused exclusively on this second limb. It observed that the construction of the road had been projected to take several years, and that the situation purportedly leading to the decision to build the road had already been brought to its attention at the time that Costa Rica had taken that decision. Further, the road would pass through areas where no imminent threat of military confrontation existed, and, serving only parts of the territory in question, be of limited use. Finally, it noted that Costa Rica had issued the decree proclaiming the existence of an emergency only after construction works had begun.[99] All this led the Court to conclude that 'there was no emergency justifying the immediate construction of the road' without an environmental impact assessment.[100] As a consequence of this finding, it did not address the first limb of the question, namely whether an emergency had existed at all, and the question of what standard of review was appropriate in that respect. The absence of any reference to Costa Rica's perception of the necessity to construct the road together with purely objective terms indicate that the ICJ arrived at this finding based on the *de novo* standard of review.

the San Juan River, ICJ, Oral Proceedings of 30 April 2015, morning (CR 2015/16), 13, para 15 (Argüello).

[94] With further references *Construction of a Road in Costa Rica along the San Juan River (Nicaragua v Costa Rica)*, ICJ, Reply of Nicaragua of 4 August 2014, para 6.6; see also at para 6.64.

[95] ibid, para 6.13 (emphasis added, references omitted).

[96] *Certain Activities & Construction of a Road*, Oral Proceedings of 21 April 2015, 39, para 29 (McCaffrey).

[97] See ibid, 46, para 50 (McCaffrey).

[98] Nicaragua merely insisted that the road 'bears no apparent relation to the area in dispute in the *Certain Activities* case, making that dispute appear to be a complete pretext for the rash decision to construct the Road without conducting any prior studies', *Construction of a Road in Costa Rica along the San Juan River (Nicaragua v Costa Rica)*, ICJ, Memorial of Nicaragua of 19 December 2012, para 5.16; see also para 5.19.

[99] *Certain Activities & Construction of a Road*, Judgment (n 84), para 158.

[100] ibid, para 159.

It did not evaluate whether Costa Rica could have *reasonably regarded* the immediate construction of the road as necessary, but merely whether that *had* been the case.

Seen in this light, this case appears to complement the *Gabčíkovo-Nagymaros* case. There, one can identify the standard of review the Court adopted for the evaluation whether an emergency had existed, but not for the evaluation of the concrete measure taken by a state in reaction to this emergency. In *Construction of the Road*, the situation is inverse: The ICJ did not deal with the existence of an emergency, but addressed the suitability of the measures taken in reaction to that purported emergency. While the Court had opted for a mixed reasonableness/*de novo* standard of review for the existence of a 'grave and imminent peril for an essential interest of the State' in *Gabčíkovo-Nagymaros*, it chose the *de novo* standard for the evaluation of the measures taken in *Construction of a Road*. Incidentally, this standard of review for the state of necessity mirrors the standard the Court adopted for the 'essential security interests' clause at issue in *Nicaragua*, and *Oil Platforms*. There as well, it operated a two-prong test, applying the reasonableness standard for the threat to an essential interest requirement, and the *de novo* standard for the necessity requirement.

iii. Jadhav

The final case in this category, *Jadhav*, opposed India and Pakistan over the latter's arrest and subsequent conviction to death of Mr Jadhav, an Indian national, who had allegedly been involved in espionage and terrorism in Pakistan. India claimed that Pakistan had breached Article 36 Vienna Convention on Consular Relations (VCCR) by failing to inform it without delay of his arrest, and him of his rights. In defence, Pakistan made three claims pertinent for the purposes of this enquiry. First, it purported to show that Article 36 VCCR would not apply in cases of espionage. Second, it claimed that there would be a customary law exception for such cases. Third and finally, it stated that the Agreement on Consular Access between Pakistan and India[101] would take precedence over the VCCR.[102] In all three domains, Pakistan made assertions amounting to the invocation of a deferential standard of review.

First, Pakistan alleged that the *travaux préparatoires* showed that espionage and national security questions could constitute 'a justifiable limitation, qualification and/or exception' to a state's right under Article 36 VCCR.[103] In asylum-related cases, the arresting state would 'have to exercise a degree of judgement' whether or not to inform the individual's state of nationality of

[101] 3186 United Nations Treaty Series 54471.
[102] *Jadhav (India v Pakistan)*, ICJ, Judgment of 17 July 2019, para 68.
[103] *Jadhav (India v Pakistan)*, ICJ, Counter-Memorial of Pakistan of 13 December 2017, para 296.

the arrest.[104] The same would apply in prima facie espionage cases. A judicial body evaluating a state's alleged non-compliance with Article 36 VCCR would thus have to recognise a degree of judgment to the arresting state, and limit its evaluation to whether there was sufficient evidence to conclude prima facie that there was a case of espionage. While it remains unclear to what degree of deference Pakistan's claim corresponds, there is a strong indicator pointing towards the reasonableness standard.

This indicator can be found in its second claim: the existence of a customary law exception from the right to consular access for prima facie espionage cases. Pakistan claimed that there had been such an exception at the time the VCCR had been adopted, and that it had survived its entry into force.[105] This exception would apply in cases where individuals are '*reasonably suspected* of espionage'.[106] This makes clear that Pakistan invoked the reasonableness standard of review at this point. Most likely, it thought of the same standard concerning the application of the alleged treaty-based VCCR exception. In justification, Pakistan stressed the national security nexus, and referred to the proclaimed need for effective domestic law enforcement.[107]

Third and finally, the respondent alleged that the Agreement on Consular Access would take precedence over the VCCR. According to point (vi) of that agreement, '[i]n case of arrest, detention or sentence made on political or security grounds, each side may examine the case on its merits'. Pakistan asserted that Mr Jadhav's arrest fell 'squarely within the national security qualification contained in [that provision]; accordingly, Pakistan was entitled to consider consular access to Commander Jadhav "on the merits" and to consider the question of consular access in the particular circumstances of this case'.[108] Here again, it invoked the reasonableness standard of review, alleging that the agreement would address all cases where 'an individual [was] *reasonably suspected* of espionage'.[109]

India in turn contested the existence of any exception to Article 36 VCCR, treaty-based or customary. Furthermore, were a judicial body to adopt a deferential standard of review regarding the applicability of such an exception, this would 'enabl[e] [states] to jettison Article 36 by unilaterally making allegations of espionage'.[110] Allegations would be all there could be at the stage where the obligation to grant consular access arises – namely, before going to trial. Accordingly, the recognition of such an exception would

[104] ibid, para 300.

[105] *Jadhav*, Judgment (n 102), para 87.

[106] *Jadhav*, ICJ, Oral Proceedings of 19 February 2019, morning (CR 2019/2), 53, para 109 (4) (Qureshi, emphasis added).

[107] *Jadhav*, Counter-Memorial of Pakistan (n 103), paras 287–95, and 311–25.

[108] ibid, paras 385.3–385.4.

[109] *Jadhav*, Oral Proceedings of 19 February 2019, 54, para 109 (6) (Qureshi, emphasis added).

[110] *Jadhav*, ICJ, Reply of India of 17 April 2018, para 113; see also at para 104; reaffirmed in *Jadhav*, ICJ, Oral Proceedings of 18 February 2019, morning (CR 2019/1), 28, para 92 (Salve).

inevitably lead to a deferential standard of review, and make Article 36 'a dead letter'.[111] Commenting on the case at hand, India noted that Pakistan had not demonstrated 'that giving consular access prior to extracting a confession would have so imperilled its national security or so hampered the investigation, that consular access was denied'.[112] With regard to the Agreement on Consular Access, it pointed to the indeterminacy of key terms of the pertinent provision:

> The phrases 'political' and 'national security' are amorphous and indefinite in their import. If both countries can unilaterally … reject its application on such subjective conditions, Article 36 would have lost its meaning … All that Pakistan would have to do to wriggle out of Article 36 is to add a ground that can provide a hook to later claim 'political' considerations in the arrest, even if it does not show up in the final charges and conviction, and on that basis deny consular access.[113]

Only Judge Robinson acceded to Pakistan's standard of review argument in relation to point (vi) of the Agreement on Consular Access. For him, emphasis in that provision should be laid on the word 'may'. That word would show that the parties had afforded each other the discretion to decide whether or not to grant consular access in cases of arrests made on political or security grounds. In Judge Robinson's view, this would encompass espionage-related arrests.[114]

The ICJ in turn rejected Pakistan's assertions on an interpretational level. As a consequence, it did not have to address the law-application stage, where the standard of review question would have arisen. Yet, certain comments the Court made also bear on this question. It rejected Pakistan's first claim by holding that the VCCR does not refer to espionage.[115] At that stage, it also incidentally rejected Pakistan's standard of review argument. It noted that Article 36 VCCR's purpose was to—

> 'facilitat[e] the exercise of consular functions relating to nationals of the sending state'… It would run counter to the purpose of that provision if the rights it provides could be disregarded when the receiving State alleges that a foreign national in its custody was involved in acts of espionage.[116]

Thus, the ICJ argued that the exception Pakistan claimed to exist – and the application of a deferential standard of review for its evaluation – would undermine the effectiveness of the protection Article 36 VCCR accords.

[111] ibid, 27, para 86 (Salve).
[112] ibid, 30, para 102 (Salve).
[113] *Jadhav*, Reply of India (n 110), para 151; reasserted in *Jadhav*, Oral Proceedings of 18 February 2019, 33, para 120 (Salve).
[114] *Jadhav (India v Pakistan)*, ICJ, Judgment, Declaration of Judge Robinson, para 6, see further at para 9. However, Judge Robin's acceptance of Pakistan's standard of review argument still amounted to a pyrrhic victory, for this led him to conclude that the 2008 agreement represented a limitation to the VCCR, not authorised by Art 73(2) VCCR.
[115] *Jadhav*, Judgment (n 102), para 73.
[116] ibid, para 74.

Second, for Pakistan's customary law assertion, the Court succinctly observed that Article 36 VCCR expressly regulated questions of consular access, and that accordingly, it was this provision and not customary law that was pertinent for the case.[117] Third and finally, it rejected Pakistan's claim relating to the Agreement on Consular Access. Pointing to its preamble, the ICJ noted that the parties had manifested their desire 'of *furthering* the objective of humane treatment of nationals of either country arrested, detained or imprisoned in the other country'.[118] Against this background, had it been their intention to restrict the right of consular access, they would have done so explicitly.[119] At the same time, the Court repeated that 'any derogation from Article 36 … for political or security grounds may render the right related to consular access meaningless'.[120]

C. Conclusion on National Security Interests

The above analysis has yielded a clear pattern for the evaluation of self-defence claims, where the Court consistently applies the *de novo* standard. There is no exception to this rule. Arguably, the ICJ does so out of a desire to uphold the effectiveness of the prohibition of the use of force. This desire, manifested time and again, not least through a very restrictive interpretation of the right to self-defence – the strict applicability finding in *Wall* comes to mind – would be incompatible with the application of any degree of deference and corresponding accordance of leeway to the states.

In several respects, the picture is less clear for the other measures justified with national security interests. First of all, the ICJ only resorted to the *de novo* standard of review implicitly in those proceedings. Second, and more importantly, its choice of this strictest standard of review for national security matters has to be contrasted with those instances in which it opted for a more lenient standard, notably *Corfu Channel*, *Right of Passage*, *Nicaragua*, *Diallo* and *Certain Iranian Assets*. Accordingly, there is a clear and consistent pattern in the standard of review question for the first sub-category (self-defence), but not for the second (other national security-related measures). This difference could be explained by the less fundamental nature of the rules of international law implied in this second sub-category, and correspondingly, by a lesser need for the Court to protect these rules and ensure their effectiveness.

[117] ibid, paras 89–90. On the related question whether international treaties contain an implicit national security exception, see already S Rose-Ackerman and B Billa, 'Treaties and National Security' (2008) 40 *International Law and Politics* 437.
[118] Emphasis added.
[119] *Jadhav*, Judgment (n 102), para 94.
[120] ibid, para 95.

II. DOMESTIC MEASURES

Five proceedings in which the ICJ arguably adopted the *de novo* standard of review revolved around domestic measures, broadly understood, spanning from the conferral of nationality, matters allegedly indissolubly linked to a national revolution, measures pertaining to the organisation of the state's criminal justice system, and border control measures. In all five proceedings, the respective respondents pointed to the domestic nature of the measures under review and the allegedly close connection to their national sovereignty to justify their plea for judicial deference.

First of all, the Court expressly rejected non-reviewability in *Nottebohm*, even if the respondent, Liechtenstein, had not pleaded for deference to this extent. At the same time, that case was the only one in this enquiry in which the adoption of the *de novo* standard of review was dictated by logic. In *Hostage*, the ICJ also held explicitly that it could review Iran's behaviour, and thus openly rejected Iran's plea for complete deference.

Besides its express rejection of non-reviewability in those two proceedings, its stance on the substantive standard of review can only be inferred in the remaining three proceedings, *LaGrand*, *Obligation to Prosecute or Extradite* and *Certain Activities*. As a consequence of its implicit approach, it furnished no justification for its strict stance.

A. *Nottebohm*

The *Nottebohm* case involved a claim of diplomatic protection by Liechtenstein against Guatemala on behalf of Mr Nottebohm, a former German national who had been granted Liechtenstein nationality during World War Two. The essential question was whether Liechtenstein's claim was at all admissible. For this to be the case, it did not matter per se whether the conferral of nationality had been lawful, but only whether Mr Nottebohm's naturalisation could have effect vis-a-vis Guatemala.[121]

Liechtenstein asserted that while the ICJ could evaluate a state's conferral of nationality, it could only verify that it had taken place 'validly and in good faith under the law of the State granting it'.[122] As long as this was the case, Liechtenstein advanced, that conferral had to be recognised, including by the Court and Guatemala. As justification, it asserted that the matter fell within

[121] *Nottebohm (Liechtenstein v Guatemala)*, ICJ, Judgment (Second Phase) of 6 April 1955, 21. The ICJ recognised that 'it is for every sovereign State ... to settle by its own legislation the rules relating to the acquisition of its nationality, and to confer that nationality by naturalization granted by its own organs in accordance with that legislation. It is not necessary to determine whether international law imposes any limitations on its freedom of decision in this domain', ibid, 20.

[122] *Nottebohm (Liechtenstein v Guatemala)*, ICJ, Memorial of Liechtenstein (Second Phase) of 14 May 1952, para 23; *Nottebohm*, ICJ, Oral Proceedings (Second Phase) of 14 February 1955, afternoon, 334 (Sauser-Hall).

its domestic jurisdiction because there would be no rules of international law restricting the grant of nationality as such,[123] making 'each State the sole master of its decisions'.[124] Guatemala recognised as well that there was no specific international law governing the matter, but asserted that nonetheless, the Court could enquire whether there had been any abuse of rights on the part of Liechtenstein from the perspective of international law.[125] Accordingly, both states invoked what amounts to the good faith standard of review.

The ICJ first expressly held that it *could* review the granting of nationality to an individual. Whether a naturalisation could produce effects under international law as desired by the granting state could not only depend on that state's perspective. Were it otherwise, any situation where two states make contradictory statements that an individual is their national would pose an unsolvable problem to a judicial body tasked with answering this question.[126] Going further and by logical implication, that body would also have to reject the application of *any* degree of judicial deference for such situations. Under the good faith or a reasonableness standard of review, the possibility would still remain that both states may consider an individual to be only their national, and thus both be 'right' at the same time. Situations such as this one require the judicial body to decide conclusively about the correctness of the states' respective assertions, and thus ultimately to apply the *de novo* standard of review.

The situation in the *Nottebohm* case was not one of such conflicting claims. Nonetheless, the Court applied the *de novo* standard of review. It held that the decisive criterion for whether a naturalisation could produce the international effects desired by the respective state was whether the nationality was 'real and effective'. Nationality had to 'correspond with the factual situation', and be based upon a 'genuine connection' between the individual and the state.[127] Consequently, the ICJ held, it had to 'ascertain … whether the factual connection between Nottebohm and Liechtenstein … appears to be sufficiently close, so preponderant in relation to any connection which may have existed between him and any other State, that it is possible to regard the nationality conferred upon him as real and effective'.[128] The analysis that followed is characterised by an objective and independent analysis of the pertinent facts, and correspondingly by a notable absence of any express readiness to adopt a deferential standard

[123] *Nottebohm (Liechtenstein v Guatemala)*, ICJ, Reply of Liechtenstein (Second Phase) of 14 July 1954, para 18; see also the reference to certain statements at the 1930 Hague Conference, *Nottebohm*, Memorial of Liechtenstein (Second Phase) (n 122), para 24 (with further references).

[124] *Nottebohm*, Oral Proceedings (Second Phase) (n 122), 89 (Sauser-Hall, own translation. In the original: 'chaque État est seul maître de ses décisions.').

[125] *Nottebohm (Liechtenstein v Guatemala)*, ICJ, Counter-Memorial of Guatemala (Second Phase) of 20 April 1954, para 16, see also at para 18; affirmed in *Nottebohm (Liechtenstein v Guatemala)*, ICJ, Rejoinder of Guatemala (Second Phase) of 2 November 1954, para 16; and *Nottebohm*, ICJ, Oral Proceedings (Second Phase) of 7 March 1955, morning, 406–407 (Rolin).

[126] *Nottebohm*, Judgment (Second Phase) (n 121), 21.

[127] ibid, 22–23.

[128] ibid, 24.

of review in favour of Liechtenstein.[129] This shows that the Court opted for the *de novo* standard of review.

B. *Hostage*

Given the absence of any exchange between the parties on the merits during the proceedings, the obviousness of Iran's violation of international law and the ICJ's correspondingly succinct application of law to the facts, it is difficult to establish what standard of review the Court adopted to review Iran's behaviour in the 1980 *Hostage* case. It could have adopted a deferential standard of review when evaluating whether Iran had done everything in its power to protect the diplomatic premises of the United States, its diplomatic agents and its consular officers under Articles 22 and 29 Vienna Convention on Diplomatic Relations (VCDR), and Articles 31(3) and 40 VCCR. Yet, as is submitted here, it chose not to.

The ICJ began by noting that in light of the United States' repeated calls for help, Iran had been positively aware of the attacks on the United States' diplomatic premises and of the need for urgent action. Furthermore, the Court observed that Iran also had had the means at its disposal to protect the premises, yet that it had not taken any such steps.[130] Thus, the ICJ 'inevitably' had to conclude that Iran had 'completely failed' to meet its obligations.[131] Arguably, the Court would have found that it had violated its obligation to prevent the attacks even under the good faith standard of review. Out of judicial economy, it could thus have skipped the preliminary step of defining the appropriate standard of review, such a definition being outcome-irrelevant.

Yet, unlike in the later *Bosnian Genocide* case, the Court did not use the '*manifest* failure' standard for its evaluation of Iran's compliance with its obligation to prevent. This suggests that it implicitly adopted the *de novo* standard of review. The absence of any subjective wording also points in this direction. Taken together, these two points indicate that the ICJ adopted the *de novo* standard of review to evaluate Iran's compliance with its obligation to prevent the attacks on the United States' diplomatic premises and its staff in the *Hostage* case.

C. *LaGrand*

The *LaGrand* case revolved around the execution of two German nationals, the LaGrand brothers, in the United States. Germany as the applicant claimed that the United States had violated the VCCR by neither notifying the two brothers

[129] ibid, 24–26.
[130] See *United States Diplomatic and Consular Staff in Tehran (United States of America v Iran)*, ICJ, Judgment of 24 May 1980, paras 17–19, and 63–66.
[131] ibid, para 68.

of their right to consular assistance, nor Germany of their arrest and subsequent conviction. With one of the LaGrands having already been executed and the other to follow on the next day, Germany initiated proceedings before the ICJ. Hours before the scheduled execution, the Court requested the United States to 'take all measures at its disposal to ensure that Walter LaGrand [would] not be executed pending the final decision'.[132] Yet, the United States moved forward with his execution as planned. This raised the issue of whether the United States had indeed taken 'all measures at its disposal' to delay the execution. The debate that ensued among the parties also turned around the standard of review question: Whose prerogative was it to decide what measures had been at the United States' disposal? If it were that of the United States, to what extent could the Court evaluate that assessment?

The United States argued that transmission of the Order to various national authorities was all that had been feasible. Thus, it 'did in fact comply … in that it took every step *reasonably available to it*, given the extreme circumstances in which it had to act'.[133] Thereby, the United States invoked the reasonableness standard of review. In other words, it asked the Court to limit the enquiry to whether it had reasonably concluded at the time that it had done everything that appeared to be feasible to comply with the Order. Given the 'extraordinarily short time' to act and the 'complex and disputed factual and legal issues' involved, it claimed that '[a]ssessing the bases for further action – not to mention undertaking required consultation with senior officials and effective coordination among them … simply was not possible'.[134] In this connection, its counsel also emphasised the link to 'matters uniquely within the core sovereign functions of States'.[135] Specifically, it purported to show that asking the Governor of Arizona to defer the execution 'was simply not feasible', '[w]ith less than three hours available, and the relevant State Department officials in East Asia'. Furthermore, sending such a request to the Governor would have raised thorny questions of constitutional and international law.[136]

Germany countered all contentions that the United States should benefit from a deferential standard of review. It pointed out that 'the operative part of the … Order contain[ed] no ambiguity or discretion whatsoever', and that '[t]he discretion left to the United States *concerned exclusively the selection of the instruments* of municipal law necessary to reach the result'.[137] Later, counsel conceded that 'the strictness of the obligations which they engender

[132] *LaGrand (Germany v United States of America)*, ICJ, Order (Provisional Measures) of 3 March 1999, para 29(1)(a).

[133] *LaGrand*, ICJ, Oral Proceedings of 14 November 2000, afternoon (CR 2000/29), 45, para 7.3 (Matheson).

[134] *LaGrand*, ICJ, Counter-Memorial of the United States of America of 27 March 2000, para 119.

[135] *LaGrand*, ICJ, Oral Proceedings of 17 November 2000, afternoon (CR 2000/31), 33, para 7.4 (Matheson).

[136] *LaGrand*, Oral Proceedings of 14 November 2000, 50, para 7.22 (Matheson).

[137] *LaGrand*, ICJ, Memorial of Germany of 16 September 1999, para 4.166 (emphasis added).

will depend, *inter alia*, on the degree of urgency and the balance of interests at stake'. However, given that this case involved 'a question of life and death', any deference would be inappropriate. Thus, Germany posed the question whether the United States 'could … have done anything but what it did'.[138] The objective formulation makes clear that it opted for the *de novo* standard of review.[139]

The ICJ ultimately held that the United States had not taken 'all measures at its disposal' and that as a result, it had failed to comply with the Order.[140] Yet, it is not readily apparent what standard of review it applied to reach this result. First, it noted that 'due to the extremely late presentation of the request for provisional measures, there was certainly very little time for the United States authorities to act'.[141] This could speak for the adoption of an at least somewhat deferential standard of review. However, after analysing *in concreto* the measures taken, the Court noted that there would have been further such options for the United States. It concluded that the measures taken were 'certainly less than could have been done'.[142] The absence of any reference to the notion of reasonableness coupled with the objective language hints at the *de novo* standard.

Indeed, it seems more plausible that this is the stance the ICJ ultimately adopted. Later in the judgment, it stated that it would have taken into account the time pressure and the so far unresolved question of the binding character of its orders at the remedies stage, had Germany requested a remedy.[143] This shows that the Court would have had regard to two of the factors invoked by the United States in support of a deferential standard of review – but not during its evaluation of the United States' compliance. This leaves little, if any, room to justify the application of a deferential standard of review.

D. *Obligation to Prosecute or Extradite*

The *Obligation to Prosecute or Extradite* proceedings were the culmination of Belgium's attempt to ensure that Hissène Habré, the former Chadian president, would be held criminally accountable for gross human rights violations, including torture, during his time in office. Prior attempts to bring him to justice in Senegal, where he had taken up residence, had remained

[138] *LaGrand*, ICJ, Oral Proceedings of 16 November 2000, afternoon (CR 2000/30), 44, para 5 (Dupuy).

[139] See ibid, 48, paras 9–11, and at 50, paras 15–16 (Donovan).

[140] *LaGrand (Germany v United States of America)*, ICJ, Judgment of 27 June 2001, para 115.

[141] ibid, para 111.

[142] ibid, para 112. Only Judge Oda objected to this finding based on the merits. For him, the United States *had* taken all measures at its disposal to comply with the order, *LaGrand (Germany v United States of America)*, ICJ, Judgment, Dissenting Opinion of Judge Oda, para 35.

[143] *LaGrand*, Judgment (n 140), para 116.

unsuccessful. Faced with Senegal's refusal to extradite him to Belgium and an alleged lack of effort to investigate, Belgium filed a claim before the ICJ, invoking a breach by Senegal of the Convention against Torture (CAT). The question was whether Senegal had respected its obligations under Articles 6(2) and 7(1) CAT. According to Article 6(2), a state in whose territory a person suspected to be responsible for torture is present 'shall immediately make a preliminary inquiry into the facts'. Under Article 7(1), the same state 'shall ... if it does not extradite [that person], submit the case to its competent authorities for the purpose of prosecution'.

As noted above, Senegal urged the Court to apply the good faith standard of review.[144] In support, it argued that—

> [h]ow a State fulfils an international obligation, particularly in a case such as that before the Court, where the State must take internal measures of application, is to a very large extent left to the discretion of that State. Belgium cannot therefore imply that there is a specific way in which Senegal should comply with the 1984 Convention, which, in any case, does not contain any provision contradicting the overriding principle of freedom under international law.[145]

Further, it pointed to the scale of the challenged associated with Habré's prosecution[146] and to the independence of its judicial authorities. Accordingly, in Senegal's view, the ICJ should defer to some extent to its assessment what measures had been feasible and appropriate on the way to Habré's prosecution. A violation could, accordingly, only be found to exist if it were proven that Senegal had not made that assessment and acted upon it in good faith.[147]

The ICJ addressed Senegal's compliance with its obligations under Articles 6(2) and 7(1) in turn. First, regarding the obligation to conduct a preliminary enquiry under the former provision, it held that the choice of how to conduct that enquiry is left to the state. However, based on an assessment of the CAT's object and purpose, the Court set a minimum standard for this enquiry. It observed that Senegal had so far not established the facts regarding Habré's alleged crimes, and found that Senegal had thus not immediately exercised its jurisdiction as stipulated by Article 6(2).[148] Accordingly, it rejected applying the good faith standard of review: mere good faith efforts to comply with Article 6(2) were not sufficient.

Turning to Senegal's obligation to initiate prosecutions against Habré under Article 7(1), the ICJ noted that the competent national authorities 'remain

[144] Ch 2, section II.B, and *Obligation to Prosecute or Extradite (Belgium v Senegal)*, ICJ, Counter-Memorial of Senegal of 23 August 2011, para 250.

[145] ibid, para 235.

[146] See, inter alia, ibid, para 228; *Obligation to Prosecute or Extradite*, ICJ, Oral Proceedings of 16 March 2012, morning (CR 2012/5), 32, paras 35–37 (Gaye).

[147] *Obligation to Prosecute or Extradite*, ICJ, Oral Proceedings of 21 March 2012, morning (CR 2012/7), 26, paras 42–43 (Thiam).

[148] *Obligation to Prosecute or Extradite (Belgium v Senegal)*, ICJ, Judgment of 20 July 2012, paras 83–88.

responsible for deciding on whether to initiate proceedings, thus respecting the independence of States parties' judicial systems'.[149] Concerning the time frame for performance of this obligation, it held that 'it is necessarily implicit in the text that it must be implemented *within a reasonable time*, in a manner compatible with the object and purpose of the Convention'.[150] However, it then went on to observe that in light of the CAT's object and purpose, 'proceedings should be undertaken without delay', and all measures necessary for implementation of the obligation under Article 7(1) must be taken 'as soon as possible'.[151] The objective language ('without delay', 'all measures necessary') points towards the *de novo* standard of review.

Accordingly, with resort to the object and purpose of the CAT, the ICJ declined to adopt a deferential standard of review to evaluate Senegal's compliance with its obligations under Articles 6(2) and 7(1) of the Convention. As Belgium did not fail to observe,[152] the Court would also have concluded that Senegal had violated those obligations under the reasonableness standard of review. The Committee against Torture had indeed laid down this standard in the *Suleymane Guengueng* case.[153] Arguably, the same result would have been reached under the good faith standard. Therefore, the *de novo* standard of review was not outcome-determinative in this instance. This makes it plausible that the ICJ set its strict standard of review out of considerations going beyond the individual case. Presumably, it did so to strengthen the CAT regime, comparably to its approach taken in *Oil Platforms*. In both cases, what was at issue was the effective implementation of a *ius cogens* norm.[154]

Judge Cançado Trindade also referred to this point in his separate opinion, noting that '[t]he absolute prohibition of grave violations of human rights (such as torture) entails obligations … endowed *with a necessarily objective character*'.[155] This formula evidences his conviction that the obligations under Articles 6(2) and 7(1) must be reviewed under the *de novo* standard of review. As one commentator observed, '[t]he Court demonstrated that in interpreting [obligations to prosecute human rights offences], it was important … not to defer too strongly [to] the judgment of state governments'.[156]

[149] ibid, para 90.
[150] ibid, para 114 (emphasis added).
[151] ibid, paras 115 and 117, respectively.
[152] *Obligation to Prosecute or Extradite*, ICJ, Oral Proceedings of 13 March 2012, morning (CR 2012/3), 19, paras 38–39 (Wood).
[153] *Suleymane Guengueng et al v Senegal*, Committee against Torture, Communication no 181/2001, para 9.5.
[154] In this case, the prohibition of torture, *Obligation to Prosecute or Extradite*, Judgment (n 148), para 99; in *Oil Platforms*, the prohibition of the use of force.
[155] *Obligation to Prosecute or Extradite (Belgium v Senegal)*, ICJ, Judgment, Separate Opinion of Judge Cançado Trindade, para 49 (emphasis added).
[156] C Gall, 'Coming to Terms with a New Role: The Approach of the International Court of Justice to the Interpretation of Human Rights Treaties' (2014) 21(1) *Australian International Law Journal* 55, 73.

E. *Certain Activities*

Six years after *Navigational Rights*, Costa Rica's right of free navigation as stipulated by Article VI of the Treaty of Limits between Costa Rica and Nicaragua of 1858 again became the subject of ICJ proceedings in *Certain Activities*. Among others, Costa Rica claimed that Nicaragua had violated the aforementioned right by prohibiting navigation on the river to a Costa Rican national and his passengers for whom he had paid transport. Furthermore, it alleged that Nicaragua's treatment of a riparian farmer and his uncle, who had been detained and purportedly been subjected to humiliating treatment before being allowed to continue their journey on the river, constituted a violation of that right.[157]

Nicaragua did not contest that these two incidents had taken place.[158] Yet, it insisted that according to the 2009 *Navigational Rights* judgment, Costa Rica's right of navigation was not unqualified, but subject to specific conditions. In Nicaragua's view, its authorities could and had to determine whether individuals traveling on the river met these requirements, and could thus rely on that right in the first place.[159] In that regard, counsel asserted, the Nicaraguan authorities 'must … be left some *margin of appreciation* in making these determinations, which must be made quickly, on boats bobbing in the water, and in the context of the officers' responsibility to control immigration and protect Nicaraguan territory'.[160] Consequently, Nicaragua justified its invocation of the margin of appreciation, and thus of a deferential standard of review, with the need to make rapid assessments on the spot in less than perfect conditions but with special vigilance, since these assessments implicated Nicaragua's immigration control and security. Addressing the two incidents, Nicaragua asserted its authorities had been acting within that margin because the Costa Rican individuals had not been able to prove that they could benefit from the right of free navigation.[161]

However, the ICJ found that 'Nicaragua did not provide a convincing justification … for the conduct of its authorities in these two incidents', and concluded that it had violated Costa Rica's right of free navigation.[162] This succinct statement contains no reference to the standard of review. This leaves two possibilities. Either the Court implicitly rejected the Nicaraguan invocation of a deferential standard of review, and applied the *de novo* standard,

[157] *Certain Activities Carried Out by Nicaragua in the Border Area* and *Construction of a Road in Costa Rica along the San Juan River*, ICJ, Oral Proceedings of 15 April 2015, morning (CR 2015/4), 16, para 22, and at 17, para 24 (Del Mar).

[158] *Certain Activities & Construction of a Road*, Judgment (n 84), para 135.

[159] *Certain Activities Carried Out by Nicaragua in the Border Area* and *Construction of a Road in Costa Rica along the San Juan River*, ICJ, Oral Proceedings of 29 April 2015, afternoon (CR 2015/15), 42, para 18 (McCaffrey).

[160] ibid, 43, para 20 (McCaffrey, emphasis added).

[161] ibid, 42, para 19 (McCaffrey).

[162] *Certain Activities & Construction of a Road*, Judgment (n 84), para 136.

or it accepted Nicaragua's plea as well-founded in the abstract, yet concluded *in concreto* that Nicaragua was still in breach even under this deferential standard. The better arguments speak for the former reading.

As shown above, in *Navigational Rights*, the ICJ had adopted the reasonableness standard of review.[163] This might suggest that it silently opted for the same standard in this case, likewise concerned with the application of the right of free navigation. On the other hand, the previous judgment, and the Court's respective approach in the standard of review question, concerned the extent to which Nicaragua as the sovereign over the river could limit the exercise of that right. In contrast, the present case posed the question who could benefit from the said right in the first place. The identification of rights-holders is a distinct step from the determination under what circumstances their exercise of that right can be limited. Deferring to Nicaragua's first-hand assessment not only for the regulation of that right, but also for the identification of the rights-holders, would amount to double deference, as it were. This would have further restricted the effectiveness of Costa Rica's right under Article VI. Absent explicit statements to that effect, it is not to be presumed lightly that the Court wanted to proceed that way. Arguably, therefore, the ICJ silently laid down and applied the *de novo* standard of review.

F. Conclusion on Domestic Matters

As diverse as they are, the five proceedings analysed under the header of 'domestic measures' all implied a state's exercise of sovereignty as construed by them on their territory or vis-a-vis their nationals. The respective respondents had all pleaded for the adoption of a deferential standard of review – namely non-reviewability in one, good faith in two, and reasonableness in the remaining two proceedings. They justified their claims with express invocations of their national sovereignty – yet to no avail.

As explained, the *Nottebohm* case was the only case in which the adoption of the *de novo* standard was inherently logical. In three of the other cases, *LaGrand*, *Obligation to Prosecute or Extradite*, and *Certain Activities*, the Court seems to have been motivated by a desire to uphold the effectiveness of the respective norms and obligations – namely, compliance with its provisional measures, the prohibition of torture, and a treaty right to travel on the territory of the neighbouring state. This rationale was articulated most clearly by a judge in *Obligation to Prosecute or Extradite* and in the literature discussing that case. In the *Certain Activities* case, the *de novo* standard of review was the judicious complement to the prior choice of the reasonableness standard in *Navigational Rights*. As explained, had the Court accorded deference to Nicaragua not only in the limitation of the right of navigation, but also

[163] Ch 6, section II.B.

in respect to the identification of the rights-holders, this would have significantly undermined the effectiveness of that right of navigation in the first place. Thus, and as it also became clear in the analysis of the self-defence sub-cluster, considerations of norm effectiveness often appear to have motivated the ICJ's choice of the *de novo* standard of review.

III. POLITICAL DETERMINATIONS

There are two proceedings revolving around what may be coined 'political determinations'. The first, *Asylum*, concerned Colombia's grant of asylum to an alleged political offender in its embassy in Peru. The second, *Namibia*, represents the culmination of a series of proceedings involving South Africa's administration of the Mandate Territory of South West Africa.

Both in *Asylum* as well as in an earlier stage of the *South West Africa* case, Colombia and South Africa had argued for an absence of judicial oversight. In *Namibia*, so to speak the continuation of the *South West Africa* dispute by other means, South Africa took a less extreme position, and instead advocated for the good faith standard of review. At the same time, it is one of the proceedings in which the concerned state relied most vocally on the expertise argument for its plea for judicial deference.[164] The Court took no express position on this argument as such. Instead, it contented itself with explicitly rejecting the consequences South Africa had attached to it, namely application of the good faith standard of review. It proceeded in the same manner in *Asylum*: open rejection of the standard of review proposed by the concerned state, and subsequent merely implicit choice of the *de novo* standard.

A. *Asylum*

The Court's rejection of the non-reviewability standard proposed by Colombia[165] did not answer the question whether another, less but still deferential standard of review would be appropriate. The ICJ answered in the negative, and opted for the *de novo* standard. First, in its analysis of whether Haya de la Torre had been accused of common crimes (Article 1(1) Havana Convention), it analysed the relevant Peruvian criminal law independently of what the parties had advanced on this question. It did not refer to either the host or the asylum state's respective assessment at this stage.[166] It proceeded in the same way concerning the urgency requirement under Article 2(2). Consequently, it rejected according any weight to the Colombian ambassador's appreciation

[164] The other one is the *Whaling* case.
[165] Ch 4, section III.A.ii.
[166] *Asylum (Colombia v Peru)*, ICJ, Judgment of 20 November 1950, 281–82.

at the time. Instead, the ICJ stressed that 'the only important question to be considered here is the *objective existence of the facts*'[167] – and not mere perceptions, even if reasonable or made in good faith. This makes clear that the Court adopted the *de novo* standard of review for both questions. And once more, it gave no justification for this stance.

B. *Namibia*

If only indirectly, South Africa's compliance with its obligation under Article 2(2) of the Mandate for South West Africa – 'to promote to the utmost the material and social well-being and the social progress of the inhabitants', already at the centre in the *South West Africa* case – was once more at issue in the *Namibia* advisory proceedings. Faced with South Africa's continued presence in the territory despite the UN General Assembly's termination of the mandate five years prior, the UN Security Council had requested an advisory opinion from the Court on the consequences of that presence. Among other grounds, the General Assembly had justified the termination of the mandate with South Africa's violation of its obligations under Article 2(2), which South Africa denied.

As noted above, South Africa had already made certain standard of review assertions in the second phase of the *South West Africa* proceedings.[168] In the alternative to its principal non-reviewability claim, it had urged the Court to apply the good faith standard to review its compliance with Article 2(2). In support, it had pointed to the allegedly discretionary nature of its power of legislation and administration over the territory. Any judicial interference with its exercise of this right would necessarily be limited.[169] Furthermore, South Africa had invoked the ICJ's exclusively judicial function. Absent tangible *legal* criteria for whether a certain policy promotes the well-being of the inhabitants according to Article 2(2), such an evaluation could only be performed based on 'social, ethnological, economic and political considerations'. Such a function would, 'in its very nature, not [be] a judicial one', and therefore, the Court should refrain from assuming such a task.[170] Additionally, South Africa had also explicitly qualified the reasonableness standard of review as inappropriate, arguing that Article 2(2) had not specifically granted the ICJ such powers of review.[171]

[167] ibid, 287 (emphasis added); in contrast, it seems that Judge Read would have preferred to apply a reasonableness standard of review for this question, *Asylum (Colombia v Peru)*, ICJ, Judgment, Dissenting Opinion by Judge Read, 329.

[168] Ch 4, section III.B and C.

[169] *South West Africa (Ethiopia v South Africa; Liberia v South Africa)*, ICJ, Counter-Memorial of South Africa of 10 January 1964, 390.

[170] ibid, 391.

[171] *South West Africa (Ethiopia v South Africa; Liberia v South Africa)*, ICJ, Rejoinder of South Africa of 22 December 1964, 159.

In the *Namibia* proceedings, South Africa came back to this position, now as principal claim. It asserted that in principle, the mandate system conferred 'full power of administration and legislation' upon the Mandatory state. Article 2(2) merely established a goal, leaving the Mandatory discretion and the exclusive choice of methods. In support for this contention, its counsel cited the *Lighthouses* case, where the Permanent Court had observed—

> that any grant of legislative powers generally implies the grant of a discretionary right to judge how far their exercise may be necessary … it is a question of appreciating political considerations and conditions of fact, a task which the Government, as the body possessing the requisite knowledge of a political situation, is alone qualified to undertake.[172]
>
> Accordingly whatever the Court might think of the merits of a particular legislative or administrative act, practice or policy, if it was devised and performed or practised in the exercise of the mandatory's discretion, seriously and honestly applied, as being in its view the best means of pursuing the objective … it could not constitute a violation of Article 2.

Such, its counsel continued, would be 'logically inherent in all cases where courts have to decide on the legality or otherwise of the exercise of a discretionary power'. Here, South Africa referred to municipal law, observing that municipal courts 'have repeatedly affirmed the *incapacity to substitute their own discretion for that of the authority* in which the discretion has been confided'.[173]

Instead, it asserted, when reviewing the exercise of a discretionary right, as any court of law, the ICJ could merely perform a review of abuse of power.[174] South Africa had already spelled out what this review should resemble in the *South West Africa* proceedings seven years earlier:

> [I]f the evidence … should establish that Respondent's policies are so unreasonable, inhumane or unscientific, or fail so lamentably to measure up to universally accepted standards, that no governmental authority honestly applying its mind to the problems of the Territory could come to the conclusion that they are the most suitable method for 'promoting to the utmost' then an inference of *mala fides* in the sense under discussion might be justified. But anything falling short thereof would not be sufficient.[175]

Judge Tanaka, no longer on the bench, had agreed with this position in *South West Africa*, and expressed his preference for the good faith standard. He had justified this position by noting that—

> investigation of the degree of expediency is not a matter for courts of law to deal with. The appropriateness of the exercise of a discretionary power by the Mandatory

[172] *Legal Consequences for States of the Continued Presence of South Africa in Namibia (South West Africa)*, ICJ, Oral Proceedings of 26 February 1971, morning, 329–30 (footnotes omitted).

[173] ibid, 331 (emphasis added, reference omitted). See already, almost identically, *South West Africa*, Counter-Memorial of South Africa (n 169), 392 (foonotes omitted); *South West Africa*, Rejoinder of South Africa (n 171), 158.

[174] *Namibia*, Oral Proceedings of 26 February 1971, 331 (Van Heerden).

[175] *South West Africa*, Rejoinder of South Africa (n 171), 171.

> does not belong to matters subject to the jurisdiction of a court of law … The political obligations are in themselves incompatible with judicial review.[176]

Judge *ad hoc* Van Wyck had made similar statements.[177]

The Court, however, categorically rejected South Africa's good faith standard of review claim, observing that 'the question of intent or governmental discretion is not relevant; nor is it necessary to investigate or determine the effects of those measures upon the welfare of the inhabitants'.[178] The Court did not lay open the concrete standard of review it applied. However, there are several indications from which one may conclude that it adopted the *de novo* standard of review. For one, the language in the judgment is free of any wording typically expressing deference – instead, the findings are couched in objective terms.[179] Furthermore, that reading finds support in the individual statements of President Sir Zafrulla Khan and Vice-President Ammoun, who, siding with the majority, explicitly advocated for the *de novo* standard.

President Sir Zafrulla Khan noted that 'it is not enough that the administration should believe in good faith that the policy it proposes to follow is in the best interests of all sections of the population. *The supervisory authority* must be satisfied that it is in the best interests of the indigenous population of the Territory'.[180] Clearly, he held it necessary that the 'supervisory authority' should conduct its own assessment independently of the mandatory – amounting to the *de novo* standard of review. Similarly, Vice-President Ammoun remarked that—

> the international judge cannot be denied the right of determining in all circumstances whether proper use has been made of the discretionary power; *whether, in the opinion of the international tribunal*, it has been exercised with a view to the promotion of the well-being and social progress of the population, or whether the mandatory State has done its utmost to fulfil its obligations.[181]

Incidentally, such a standard also made sense from a policy perspective. The Court's use of an avoidance technique in the 1966 judgment[182] had led to bitter criticism and a weakening of the Court. Against this background, it seemed advisable for the ICJ to assert itself, and squarely tackle the question

[176] *South West Africa (Ethiopia v South Africa; Liberia v South Africa)*, ICJ, Judgment (Second Phase), Separate Opinion of Judge Tanaka, 283.

[177] See *South West Africa (Ethiopia v South Africa; Liberia v South Africa)*, ICJ, Judgment (Second Phase), Separate Opinion of Judge *ad hoc* Van Wyk, 150–52.

[178] *Legal Consequences for States of the Continued Presence of South Africa in Namibia (South West Africa)*, ICJ, Advisory Opinion of 21 June 1971, para 129.

[179] See, e.g. ibid, paras 130–31.

[180] *Legal Consequences for States of the Continued Presence of South Africa in Namibia (South West Africa)*, ICJ, Advisory Opinion, Declaration of President Sir Zafrulla Khan, 62–63 (emphasis added).

[181] *Legal Consequences for States of the Continued Presence of South Africa in Namibia (South West Africa)*, ICJ, Advisory Opinion, Separate Opinion of Vice-President Ammoun, 88 (emphasis added).

[182] Ch 3, section II.B.

of apartheid. By necessary implication, this called for the application of the most demanding standard of review. From this perspective, the Court's *de novo* standard of review in *Namibia* could be explained by its desire to make good its widely perceived failure five years earlier.

C. Conclusion on Political Determinations

At first sight, few inferences can be drawn from the Court's stance in *Asylum*. Yet, the succinctness in the law application stage demonstrates once again that absent cogent justification invoked for the application of a deferential standard of review, the ICJ shows no inclination to apply such a standard. Faced with Colombia's plea for complete deference, unsupported by any conclusive argumentation, it merely rejected this claim explicitly, without explaining in the following why *any* degree of deference would be inappropriate.

The choice for the *de novo* standard of review in the *Namibia* advisory opinion in turn can be explained in part with the particular circumstances and history of the matter. The Court's widely perceived failure in *South West Africa* and the influx of new members elected to the bench since then made repetition of the non-reviewability finding unlikely. At the same time, there was some merit in South Africa's argument that the ICJ would be lacking expertise to fully oversee its respective first-hand assessments and decisions in a domain inextricably linked to the political. The Court's refusal to engage with this extensively argued position could be seen as a signal of self-assertion: As advanced above, eloquent silence can at times be a clearer signal than a verbose refutation.[183] Yet, the members of the bench did not completely remain silent on this question, as the declaration of Sir Zafrulla Khan and the separate opinion of Vice-President Ammoun show. To this, one has to add Judge Jessup's dissenting opinion in the second stage of South West Africa. Therein, he had concluded that the 'task which … confronted this Court … is not beyond its capabilities'.[184]

IV. SCIENTIFIC DETERMINATIONS: *WHALING*

The *Whaling* case is not only the case in which the question of the applicable standard of review received the most attention thus far. Together with *South West Africa* and *Namibia*, it is also the case in which the respondent most volubly relied on the expertise argument to argue for a deferential standard of review. The case revolved around the question of whether Japan's whaling programme

[183] Ch 4, section V.B.

[184] *South West Africa (Ethiopia v South Africa; Liberia v South Africa)*, ICJ, Judgment (Second Phase), Dissenting Opinion of Judge Jessup, 438.

was exempt from the whaling ban as a scientific research programme. While the Court refused to give any credit to Japan's initial non-reviewability plea, it adopted the reasonableness standard of review to assess whether JARPA II was a programme constituting 'scientific research'.[185] Determining the standard of review the ICJ adopted for the second sub-question, namely whether JARPA II was also a programme 'for purposes of' scientific research, is a less straightforward exercise.[186] It is submitted here that despite its assertions to the contrary, it silently applied the *de novo* standard. Consequently, while giving the impression of having acceded to the expertise-argument, in reality, it only paid lip-service to the underlying considerations.

As explained above, Japan had made several general arguments for a 'margin of appreciation' in its favour.[187] At the same time, it also made specific points to justify the application of a deferential standard of review for this second sub-question, and again relied heavily on the expertise argument. Specifically, it claimed a 'margin of appreciation' for the programme's design choices, its necessity, scientific objectives, and choice and extent of lethal methods.[188] As 'the "organ" of "international law"', the ICJ '*[could] not decide between opposing scientific views*' – such as relating to the use lethal methods, and the determination of the sample sizes.[189] It would be difficult to see 'how the Court might interfere in scholarly discussions between experts, given that they cannot agree amongst themselves, and that no reasonable person could ever claim to discern an indisputable truth'.[190] Faced with this scientific controversy, Japan invited the Court to limit its review to the question whether Japan had reasonably considered that JARPA II was 'for purposes of' scientific research – in other words, to apply the reasonableness standard of review.

As noted above, the Court's rejection of Japan's non-reviewability assertion ('whether the killing, taking and treating of whales … is for purposes of scientific research *cannot depend simply on that State's perception*'[191]) implies a certain degree of deference.[192] In the same vein, at the outset of its analysis of the second sub-question, the Court announced that it 'need not pass judgment on

[185] See above at ch 6, section IV.C.

[186] As Gros notes, 'the objective standard of review applied by the Court is difficult to grasp on many levels … [T]he Court did not clearly qualify the standard with regard to the degree of intrusion or deference it implies in reviewing the contested decision. … [T]he Court gives the impression of having used different standards of review simultaneously', G Gros, 'The ICJ's Handling of Science in the Whaling in the Antarctic Case: A Whale of a Case?' (2015) 6(3) *Journal of International Dispute Settlement* 578, 605.

[187] Ch 6, section IV.C.

[188] *Whaling in the Antarctic*, ICJ, Oral Proceedings of 4 July 2013, afternoon (CR 2013/16), 51, para 37 (Pellet).

[189] *Whaling in the Antarctic*, ICJ, Oral Proceedings of 16 July 2013, morning (CR 2013/23), 22, para 18 (Pellet, references omitted).

[190] ibid, 22, para 18, and 23, para 20 (Pellet).

[191] *Whaling in the Antarctic (Australia v Japan: New Zealand intervening)*, ICJ, Judgment of 31 March 2014, para 61 (emphasis added).

[192] Ch 6, section IV.C.

the scientific merit or importance' of JARPA II's research objectives, '[n]or is it for the Court to decide whether the design and implementation of a programme are the best possible means of achieving its stated objectives'. Instead, it would only 'consider whether the elements of a programme's design and implementation are reasonable in relation to its stated scientific objectives'.[193] Before analysing the sample sizes, it reiterated that 'the purpose of such an inquiry is not to second-guess the scientific judgments made by individual scientists or by Japan, but rather to examine whether Japan … has demonstrated a reasonable basis for annual sample sizes'.[194]

The accumulation of these statements is conspicuous, even when compared with the other proceedings in which the ICJ adopted the reasonableness standard of review. The Court went to great lengths to convince Japan (and the larger public) that it would not act as a *de novo* decision-maker. The fact that it had regard to objective elements in the subsequent evaluation (such as the scale of lethal sampling, and actual and target sample sizes) led some commentators to speak of an 'objective reasonableness' standard.[195] Yet, as is argued here, this avowed standard stands in marked contrast with the standard the ICJ actually chose: *de novo*.

The Court dedicated over 30 pages to the evaluation of JARPA II. First, it noted that Japan had not analysed the feasibility of non-lethal methods before granting the whaling permit.[196] It then turned to the scale of the use of lethal methods, noting that JARPA II envisaged a much higher use of lethal sampling than the predecessor programme, despite similar research objectives. This, in the Court's view, indicated that the sample sizes 'were not driven by strictly scientific considerations'.[197] It went on to criticise that for two of the three whale species, the target sample number fell short of what would be necessary to reach the proclaimed research objectives.[198] The ICJ also found the lack of explanation (respectively, the lack of a *consistent* explanation) for the chosen research periods to be 'problematic'.[199] Furthermore, it noted 'scant analysis and justification for the underlying decisions that generate the overall sample size'.[200] Finally, it emphasised the discrepancy between the planned and the actual sample size.[201] All this led the Court to conclude that JARPA II's design and implementation were not reasonable in relation to the research objectives.[202]

[193] *Whaling in the Antarctic*, Judgment (n 191), para 88. The Court even repeated that statement, and thereby emphasised its (alleged) stance of judicial deference, see para 172.

[194] ibid, para 185.

[195] See for instance SR Tully, '"Objective Reasonableness" as a Standard for International Judicial Review' (2015) 6(3) *Journal of International Dispute Settlement* 546.

[196] *Whaling*, Judgment (n 191), para 141.

[197] ibid, para 156.

[198] ibid, para 179.

[199] ibid, para 193.

[200] ibid, para 198.

[201] ibid, para 212.

[202] ibid, para 227.

What becomes immediately apparent from this is that the ICJ conducted a particularly detailed examination of JARPA II. This also by far surpasses in intensity the evaluation whether it 'broadly' constituted scientific research. If the standard of review there may be qualified as reasonableness (even if on the verge of good faith), the approach here is to the least on the other side of the reasonableness spectrum. It is so demanding that it resembles the *de novo* standard to the point of becoming indistinguishable from it. For instance, given that the Court reached a negative conclusion on JARPA II despite the fact that involved experts had considered the sample sizes to be reasonable in relation to the research objectives,[203] it seems that it applied a stricter standard of review than the one announced.

This categorisation finds support in Japan's prior statements, the opinions of three judges, and in the literature. For instance, Japan had argued in the oral proceedings that 'the question of how far non-lethal means … provide for a partial or complete alternative to lethal takes is certainly another question to be addressed in a *de novo* review'.[204] Yet, the Court examined precisely this aspect.[205]

Among the four judges who issued a dissenting opinion, Judge Owada was the most critical. He was also the one to enunciate most clearly his observation that the standard of review which the ICJ applied was in reality not reasonableness, but *de novo*.[206] Likewise, Judge Abraham noted that despite its avowed adherence to the reasonableness standard of review, the Court proceeded 'on a path which [led] it to depart from its role and to assess the scientific value of JARPA II'. It would not be its function 'to decide whether JARPA II was designed as well as it might have been …, but only to decide if this is indeed a programme pursuing scientific aims'.[207] Yet, in his view, the Court did the former, thereby 'attempting to function as a sort of scientific committee'.[208] In contrast, Judge Bennouna welcomed the 'objective reasonableness' standard of review.[209] Yet, his criticism implies that this was not the standard the ICJ applied. As he pointed out, despite contrary statements, the Court did engage in a detailed analysis of JARPA II in a 'whole arduous and complex discussion'[210] – which indicates that for him, the standard applied was actually non-deferential.

[203] See *Whaling in the Antarctic (Australia v Japan: New Zealand intervening)*, ICJ, Judgment, Dissenting Opinion of Judge Abraham, paras 47–48.

[204] *Whaling in the Antarctic*, ICJ, Oral Proceedings of 4 July 2013, morning (CR 2013/15), 18, para 23 (Lowe).

[205] *Whaling*, Judgment (n 191), paras 128–44.

[206] *Whaling in the Antarctic (Australia v Japan: New Zealand intervening)*, ICJ, Judgment, Dissenting Opinion of Judge Owada, para 38.

[207] *Whaling*, Judgment (n 203), Dissenting Opinion of Judge Abraham, paras 33 and 38, respectively.

[208] ibid, para 48.

[209] *Whaling in the Antarctic (Australia v Japan: New Zealand intervening)*, ICJ, Judgment, Dissenting Opinion of Judge Bennouna, 342.

[210] ibid, 345.

Several voices in the literature also conclude that the Court effectively applied the *de novo* standard of review. For instance, Gros distinguishes the test applied here from the 'reasonable regulator test' employed for instance in the context of the WTO. He concludes that the ICJ did not apply such a test, and thus left no margin of assessment to Japan.[211] Garrido-Muñoz in turn draws attention to the Court's finding that for one particular research objective, there had been 'no *strict* scientific necessity to use lethal methods'.[212] For him, this also points in the direction of the *de novo* standard of review.[213]

The four dissenting judges to have taken issue with the standard of review adopted by the majority conceded that the question of Japan's compliance with Article VIII ICRW was open to some form of judicial review. They mostly even said so explicitly.[214] Judges Abraham, Owada and Yusuf put forward considerations of relative institutional expertise to explain why they would have preferred the adoption of what amounts to the good faith standard of review.[215] Judge Owada made this point most vocally when he observed 'in all frankness that this Court, as a court of law, is not professionally qualified to give a scientifically meaningful answer' on the question whether JARPA II could be subsumed under Article VIII.[216] It is also interesting to note that the concern that the Court would be overstepping its judicial mandate and stray beyond the field of its expertise was also shared by judges constituting the majority. Namely, Judge Xue observed that it would be inappropriate for the Court to assess the merits of JARPA II, because such would only be open to scientific review.[217]

[211] Gros, 'The ICJ's Handling of Science in the Whaling in the Antarctic Case' (n 186), 608–09 (with further references); see also already explicitly at 605; similarly K Sulyok, *Science and Judicial Reasoning: The Legitimacy of International Environmental Adjudication* (Cambridge University Press, 2021), 113.

[212] *Whaling*, Judgment (n 191), para 211 (emphasis added).

[213] A Garrido-Muñoz, 'Managing Uncertainty: The International Court of Justice, "Objective Reasonableness" and the Judicial Function' (2017) 30(2) *Leiden Journal of International Law* 457, 469–70; see further Palmer, who speaks of a 'demanding and rigorous' standard of review, G Palmer, 'A Victory for Whales' (2014)(May) *New Zealand Law Journal* 124, 125. Note, however, that other voices in the literature conclude that the ICJ did adopt the reasonableness standard of review for this sub-question as well. See for instance J Pauwelyn, 'Defences and the Burden of Proof in International Law' in L Bartels and F Paddeu (eds), *Exceptions and Defences in International Law* (Oxford University Press, 2020), 105–06.

[214] *Whaling*, Judgment (n 206), Dissenting Opinion of Judge Owada, para 20; *Whaling*, Judgment (n 203), Dissenting Opinion of Judge Abraham, para 23; *Whaling*, Judgment (n 209), Dissenting Opinion of Judge Bennouna, 342.

[215] Explicitly *Whaling*, Judgment (n 206), Dissenting Opinion of Judge Owada, para 25; opting for 'clear unreasonableness' *Whaling*, Judgment (n 203), Dissenting Opinion of Judge Abraham, para 35; *Whaling in the Antarctic (Australia v Japan: New Zealand intervening)*, ICJ, Judgment, Dissenting Opinion of Judge Yusuf, para 21.

[216] *Whaling*, Judgment (n 206), Dissenting Opinion of Judge Owada, para 24.

[217] *Whaling in the Antarctic (Australia v Japan: New Zealand intervening)*, ICJ, Judgment, Separate Opinion of Judge Xue, paras 14–15. She only agreed with the majority on the fact that JARPA II was not 'for purposes of scientific research' because she accorded decisive importance to the fact that once funding considerations came into play in the determination of the sample size – as had been

In terms of the standard of review debate, *Whaling* was indeed 'a whale of a case'.[218] The Court applied the concept explicitly for the first time, yet, at least in partial contradiction to what it announced it would do, ultimately adopted a mixed reasonableness/*de novo* standard of review. By adopting a deferential standard of review for the first sub-question, namely whether JARPA II constituted 'scientific research', and a concealed *de novo* standard for the determinative second sub-question, the ICJ only half-heartedly recognised its institutional limitations as a court of law.

V. CONCLUSION FOR *DE NOVO*

The analysis of the 14 proceedings in this chapter[219] in which the Court has adopted the *de novo* standard of review to evaluate a state's compliance with its obligations under international law has shown two things: first, that the ICJ generally does not deem it necessary to explain that it applies the *de novo* standard of review. Furthermore, there is a near-constant, conspicuous absence of justification for its adoption of this standard. This dearth of justification particularly catches the reader's eye in those proceedings in which the respective states and participants had extensively argued for or at least had extensively dwelled on the possibility of the adoption of a deferential standard of review. Such was for instance the case in *Nicaragua*, *Obligation to Prosecute or Extradite*, *Jadhav* and *Namibia*.

This silence also stands in marked contrast to the explicit approach the ICJ has taken to reject the standard of review on the other end of the spectrum: complete deference. There, it has apparently considered that it was appropriate or even necessary to reject the proposed non-reviewability standard explicitly in most instances.[220] The Court has apparently not seen the same need to lay open its choice of the *de novo* standard of review. This contrasted reading reinforces the conclusion outlined in the introduction to this chapter: that the *de novo* standard is the ICJ's default standard of review. Accordingly, the Court is far from routinely according deference to the concerned states. As the above proceedings have shown, this applies with particular force to measures allegedly taken in self-defence, measures for which it has never adopted a deferential standard of review. The fact that there are proceedings in all four subject-matter categories in which the Court at least partially opted

the case here, in her view – that programme could no longer be considered to be for such purposes, ibid, paras 27–28.

[218] Gros, 'The ICJ's Handling of Science in the Whaling in the Antarctic Case' (n 186).

[219] To this list, one has to add the partial adoption of the *de novo* standard in *Gabčíkovo-Nagymaros*, *Bosnian Genocide* and *Certain Iranian Assets*, discussed in the previous chapters in the interest of better readability.

[220] Ch 4, section V.B.

for the *de novo* standard of review also shows that it is far from applying a generalised doctrine of judicial deference in those categories as well.

The respective stances taken by the participants and the Court in the proceedings are shown in Tables 10–13, which are clustered.

Table 10 *De novo* – overview of party and ICJ positions on the appropriate standard of review in proceedings relating to national security interests

<table>
<tr><th>NATIONAL SECURITY</th><th>Complete Deference</th><th>Good Faith</th><th>Reasonableness</th><th>De novo</th></tr>
<tr><td>Nicaragua* (customary law)</td><td>United States</td><td></td><td></td><td>Court</td></tr>
<tr><td rowspan="3">Oil Platforms</td><td colspan="3">United States</td><td></td></tr>
<tr><td></td><td></td><td colspan="2">Iran</td></tr>
<tr><td></td><td></td><td></td><td>Court</td></tr>
<tr><td rowspan="2">Wall in the OPT**</td><td rowspan="2">Israel</td><td rowspan="2"></td><td rowspan="2">Other actors</td><td>Palestine</td></tr>
<tr><td>Court</td></tr>
<tr><td>Armed Activities*</td><td></td><td></td><td>Uganda</td><td>Court</td></tr>
<tr><td rowspan="2">Construction of a Road</td><td rowspan="2"></td><td rowspan="2"></td><td>Costa Rica</td><td rowspan="2">Court</td></tr>
<tr><td>Nicaragua</td></tr>
<tr><td rowspan="2">Jadhav</td><td rowspan="2"></td><td rowspan="2"></td><td rowspan="2">Pakistan</td><td>India</td></tr>
<tr><td>Court</td></tr>
</table>

For this and the following tables: respondents in dark grey, applicants in light grey, other actors/states in white, and Court in black.
* The position of the respective opponent on the standard of review question cannot be determined with sufficient certainty so as to allow mapping.
** Israel and Palestine are shown as respondent and applicants respectively. Although not technically correct, this captures the contradictory nature of the *Wall* proceedings, not least evidenced by the fact that the ICJ accorded extra time for Palestine in the oral stage.

Table 11 *De novo* – overview of party and ICJ positions on the appropriate standard of review in proceedings relating to domestic matters

<table>
<tr><th>DOMESTIC MATTERS</th><th>Complete Deference</th><th>Good Faith</th><th>Reasonableness</th><th>De novo</th></tr>
<tr><td rowspan="2">Nottebohm</td><td rowspan="2"></td><td>Liechtenstein</td><td rowspan="2"></td><td rowspan="2">Court</td></tr>
<tr><td>Guatemala</td></tr>
<tr><td>Hostage*</td><td>Iran</td><td></td><td></td><td>Court</td></tr>
<tr><td rowspan="2">LaGrand</td><td rowspan="2"></td><td rowspan="2"></td><td rowspan="2">United States</td><td>Germany</td></tr>
<tr><td>Court</td></tr>
<tr><td>Obligation to Prosecute or Extradite*</td><td></td><td>Senegal</td><td></td><td>Court</td></tr>
</table>

Table 12 *De novo* – overview of party and ICJ positions on the appropriate standard of review in proceedings relating to political determinations

POLITICAL DETERMINATIONS	Complete Deference	Good Faith	Reasonableness	*De novo*
Asylum*	Colombia			Court
Namibia*		South Africa		Court

* Although Colombia was the applicant in *Asylum* and not the respondent, Colombia was the de facto respondent regarding the question relevant for this study.

Table 13 *De novo* – overview of party and ICJ positions on the appropriate standard of review in proceedings relating to scientific determinations

<table>
<tr><th>SCIENTIFIC DETERMINATIONS</th><th>Complete Deference</th><th>Good Faith</th><th>Reasonableness</th><th>De novo</th></tr>
<tr><td rowspan="3">Whaling</td><td colspan="3" rowspan="3">Japan</td><td>Australia</td></tr>
<tr><td>New Zealand</td></tr>
<tr><td>Court</td></tr>
</table>

As mentioned in the introduction, the sole proceeding in which the ICJ explicitly opted for the *de novo* standard of review was the *Oil Platforms* case. And, as shown in the analysis of that case, the Court's explicit reference to *de novo* has to be seen against the background of the discussions surrounding the dispute at the time – namely, the debate about the extension of the right to self-defence. Arguably, the ICJ's explicit choice of the *de novo* standard of review is its contribution to that debate.

Besides that case, *Whaling* merits particular attention. There, the Court asserted to have applied a deferential standard of review for both sub-questions. Yet, that appearance is deceiving, for it is contradicted by the actual stance the ICJ took for the central sub-question – whether the Japanese whaling programme was 'for purposes of' scientific research as understood by Article VIII ICRW. Why did the ICJ act in such a contradictory manner? One answer could be that it wanted to send a signal of acknowledgement towards Japan and especially the larger community of states. Its explicit reference to the 'objective reasonableness' standard of review could be seen as the recognition of some merit in the expertise-argument in the domain of science on which Japan relied heavily. Thereby, the Court signalled its cognisance of its limitations in the evaluation of such matters. This way, it could have tried to reap the benefits connected with the use of a deferential standard of review as an avoidance technique for future proceedings, as outlined above.[221] Namely, it could have tried to build up trust among the states that it would not transgress the unwritten boundaries of its mandate and expertise.

[221] See ch 3, section IV.

Yet, the fact that the ICJ ultimately resorted to the *de novo* standard of review indicates that as was the case in *Namibia*, it attached little merit to the expertise-based claim for judicial deference. Curiously, its approach had been the opposite in *Gabčíkovo-Nagymaros*, and *Pulp Mills*. There, it had resorted to the reasonableness standard, presumably out of considerations of expertise – but only (somewhat) implicitly so. This change in approach could be explained with a change in perception of the ICJ's role of the judges on the bench. If this reading is correct, the Court would have expanded its purview, contrary to what it professed in *Whaling*.

Finally, a word about judicial avoidance in connection with the *de novo* standard of review. Its use rules out resorting to the standard of review notion as an avoidance technique. Certainly, not every instance of judicial deference can be qualified as the ICJ's use of an avoidance technique – far from it. In contrast, every use of the *de novo* standard is a refusal by the Court to employ this particular avoidance technique. There are several proceedings analysed in this chapter in which the rationales underlying judicial avoidance had been applicable. Besides *Oil Platforms*, *Wall* and *Jadhav* readily come to mind. The fact that the ICJ refused to practice judicial avoidance in those proceedings by adopting a deferential standard of review – against the expressive position of the concerned states, and in some instances also against the presumable preferences of the larger community of states – amply demonstrates that it has resorted to this notion as an avoidance technique in far fewer proceedings than it could have. Consequently, to speak of an 'avoiding Court' in that sense would be a clear misrepresentation.

8

Conclusion

THIS BOOK HAS examined the role and importance of the standard of review notion before the ICJ from both a conceptual and an empirical perspective. First, it has turned to the standard of review notion as such. Relying on the works of Lauterpacht, it has set out to show that the standard of review notion has shared roots with the non-justiciability doctrine in the international order. Both notions rest on the claim that states are in some matters better placed than the Court to 'call the shots'. These matters can be grouped into four domains: essential interests, domestic measures, 'political' decisions, and scientific determinations. According to this claim, the ICJ as a judicial institution would be unable to apprehend these matters as would be required for a proper fulfilment of its role. As a consequence, it should decline to adjudicate in proceedings involving such decisions and assessments, respectively reduce its control density vis-a-vis the states. With the non-justiciability doctrine having been constantly rejected by the ICJ, it seems that the standard of review invocation, based on the same conception of the Court's role and abilities, is just old wine in new skins, and merits no other response from the Court.

Yet, the book has argued, such a reading would be premature. The standard of review notion has distinct potential for the ICJ: as a judicial avoidance technique allowing it to dispose of thorny questions in a way that enables it to rebalance the fragile equilibrium between living up to its mandate as foreseen by the UN Charter and avoiding antagonising those on whose support it heavily depends, the states. Dealing with this institutional reality often enough requires the Court to act strategically, including by practising avoidance. Studying the Court's past use of other such avoidance techniques, the enquiry demonstrates that the standard of review notion holds distinct advantages for the ICJ's institutional stability and credibility in comparison to these other techniques, in both the long and the short run. This notion is more balanced, its use can be made transparent, and it can be employed as part of an incremental approach aiming at durably strengthening the Court's role in the settlement of inter-state disputes.

Against this background – legal uninventiveness of the standard of review notion, but important practical potential – the book has then examined the way the ICJ determines its standard of review for state behaviour. It has done so by studying in depth all 31 Court proceedings in which the appropriate control density was an issue and in which the ICJ took a position on this, mapping the Court's stance in each of them on a four-tier standard of review scale, and grouping them in four subject-matters in order to uncover patterns, commonalities and parallels in its jurisprudence. It is tempting to conclude from certain landmark cases that the ICJ has so far refused to apply a deferential standard of review, let alone used it as a judicial avoidance technique. Certainly, it prominently adopted the non-deferential *de novo* standard in *Oil Platforms*. Yet, the empirical analysis in this book has proven that the real picture is more complex. Even if not systematically, the ICJ has regularly laid down a deferential standard of review when evaluating state behaviour.

In this connection, several aspects are worth highlighting. First, the Court's predominant, albeit far from continuous use of the *de novo* standard of review – a finding contrasted against the respective practices of the dispute settlement organs in investment arbitration, international trade law, and European Union law. Second, its tendency to adopt a deferential standard of review only when prompted to do so by the concerned states. Third, even then, that standard is usually stricter than pleaded for by the states. Fourth, there is no clear pattern for the ICJ's use of the standard of review notion in three of the four analysed categories (national security, domestic matters, and political determinations). Only the evaluation of measures allegedly taken in self-defence stands out in this respect, albeit as an instance of rejection of deference. In turn, there is an early tendency of deference in the fourth domain, scientific appreciations. Thus, the book shows that it is difficult to speak of a Court doctrine of deferential standards of review. Fifth and finally, the last section recapitulates that it is likely that the ICJ has been resorting to deferential standards of review in a strategic manner on several occasions.

I. *DE NOVO* AS THE COURT'S DEFAULT, BUT FAR FROM CONSTANT STANDARD OF REVIEW

The first of the following tables, Table 14, summarises the standard of review the ICJ adopted in the 31 proceedings that formed the object of enquiry. As the table shows, the Court adopted complete deference as standard of review in three, good faith equally in three, reasonableness in 12, and *de novo* in 17 proceedings. In five of the analysed proceedings, it adopted a mixed standard of review, combining *de novo* and reasonableness (*Nicaragua, Gabčíkovo-Nagymaros, Whaling* and *Certain Iranian Assets*), respectively good faith (*Bosnian Genocide*), standards of review. Finally, in one further proceeding, *Reservations to the Genocide Convention*, it is unclear which substantive standard of review the ICJ opted for, besides rejecting complete deference.

Table 14 Overview – standard of review adopted by the ICJ in the analysed proceedings

Short title	Complete Deference	Good Faith	Reasonableness	*De novo*
1948, Admission of a State to the UN			X	
1949, Corfu Channel			X	
1950, Asylum				X
1951, Reservations to the Genocide Convention	rejected	substantive standard unclear		
1952, Rights of US Nationals in Morocco			X	
1955, Nottebohm				X
1957, Norwegian Loans	X			
1960, Right of Passage			X	
1966, South West Africa (Second Phase)	X			
1971, Namibia				X
1980, Hostage				X
1986, Nicaragua			X	X
1989, ELSI		X		
1996, Nuclear Weapons	X			
1997, Gabčíkovo-Nagymaros			X	X
2001, LaGrand				X
2003, Oil Platforms				X
2004, Wall in the OPT				X
2005, Armed Activities				X
2007, Bosnian Genocide		X		X
2008, Mutual Assistance		X		
2009, Navigational Rights			X	
2010, Pulp Mills			X	
2010, Diallo			X	
2012, Obligation to Prosecute or Extradite				X
2014, Whaling			X	X
2015, Certain Activities				X
2015, Construction of a Road				X

(continued)

Table 14 *(Continued)*

Short title	Complete Deference	Good Faith	Reasonableness	*De novo*
2019, Jadhav				X
2020, Immunities and Criminal Proceedings			X	
2023, Certain Iranian Assets			X	X

As Table 14 illustrates, the ICJ chose the *de novo* standard of review in over half of the analysed proceedings. This number alone does not prove conclusively that this standard of review is the Court's default standard. Yet, as chapter seven has shown, two further factors point in this direction: the Court's predominantly tacit use of this standard, and overall lack of explanation for its choice. The ICJ has not deemed it necessary to lay open its use of the *de novo* standard in all but one proceeding, *Oil Platforms*. Nor has it deemed it necessary to explain the reasons for its choice of this strictest standard. This stands in marked contrast to those occasions on which the Court resorted to a deferential standard of review, and where it mostly laid open its adoption of such a standard. This pattern could be explained by the consideration that it is the deviation from the rule that needs explaining, and not its application. In any case, this shows that the Court is far from applying a generalised doctrine of deferential standards of review.

Yet, as Table 14 also illustrates, it has been resorting to deferential standards of review at least partially in more than half of the proceedings as well (18). This shows that these instances are not isolated. Instead, it demonstrates that the ICJ regularly applies deferential standards of review – mostly, the reasonableness standard.

This conclusion – regular choice of a deferential standard of review, yet absence of a generalised systematic approach in this regard – profits from being put into perspective by looking at the respective decision-making practice of the WTO dispute settlement system, in investment arbitration and of the ECJ.

Turning first to the WTO dispute settlement mechanism, scholars have contended that it has overall been privileging a moderately deferential standard of review, situated between reasonableness and *de novo*.[1] This moderately deferential standard has been described as a 'compromise', allowing states to choose their regulatory aims with relative liberty, while the means employed to reach them are subjected to a more demanding scrutiny.[2] The relative consistency

[1] With further references M Oesch, *Standards of Review in WTO Dispute Resolution* (Oxford University Press, 2003), 137.

[2] V Vadi, *Proportionality, Reasonableness and Standards of Review in International Investment Law and Arbitration* (Edward Elgar Publishing, 2018), 321–22; *Gattini*, in turn, speaks of the WTO Appellate Body's 'marked self-restraint and deference to the states', A Gattini, 'Judicial Discretion' in R Wolfrum (ed), *Max Planck Encyclopedia of Public International Law* (Oxford University Press, 2012), para 19.

noted in the WTO dispute settlement mechanism's decision-making practice is facilitated by certain of its key features – the uniformisation of jurisprudence through the Appellate Body, a relatively constrained set of subject-matters and relevant legal norms, and the personal continuity at the Appellate Body.

In turn, the overall picture concerning the standard of review determination in investment arbitration is mixed. This is even more unsurprising than it is for the ICJ, given the distinct features setting it apart from the latter as well as WTO dispute settlement and the ECJ. Most notably, investment arbitration panels are constituted *ad hoc* for each dispute and are made up of individuals coming from a variety of professional backgrounds, there is no doctrine of precedent, and the relevant legal norms vary greatly. Accordingly, the emergence of a generalised approach towards the standard of review is more difficult, if not unlikely. In the past, investment tribunals have thus been employing a wide range of deferential standards of review.[3] However, this does not mean that at least the basic choice for deference is the default rule. While Fahner concludes that the number of arbitral awards explicitly in favour of the application of one form of a deferential standard of review or another exceeds those explicitly against, he adds the caveat that this does not necessarily mean that investment arbitration tribunals apply a deferential standard of review as a generalised practice.[4] In turn, an earlier study, empirically examining whether arbitrators exercise judicial restraint more generally, observed that they had overall privileged an 'unrestrained approach', assuming 'far-reaching authority to oversee states intensively in relation to legislative and executive decision-making'.[5] However, on the basis of the sizable portion of awards explicitly adopting a deferential standard of review already, one may confidently conclude that deferential standards of review do have an important place in investment arbitration, even if not in a systematic manner.

The ECJ, finally, also applies deferential standards of review vis-a-vis the Member States, and increasingly so in recent years, as Schulte and Zglinski both conclude. Zglinski observes that '[w]hat started off as a sporadic phenomenon, has become a doctrine increasingly cherished by the ECJ. The margin of appreciation has turned into an important element of free movement adjudication'.[6] Schulte notes the presence of certain jurisprudential patterns in the ECJ's standard of review determination, but deplores the absence of a refined, coherent and consistent jurisprudence in this respect.[7] Zglinski, in turn, identified

[3] See for an overview JH Fahner, *Judicial Deference in International Adjudication: A Comparative Analysis* (Hart, 2020), 78–79.

[4] ibid, 83.

[5] G van Harten, *Sovereign Choices and Sovereign Constraints: Judicial Restraint in Investment Treaty Arbitration* (Oxford University Press, 2014), 17.

[6] J Zglinski, *Europe's Passive Virtues* (Oxford University Press, 2020), 96; with specific data at 42–45; similarly H Schulte, *Zur Übertragbarkeit der Margin-of-appreciation-Doktrin des EGMR auf die Rechtsprechung des EuGH im Bereich der Grundfreiheiten* (Nomos, 2018), fn 1118.

[7] Schulte, *Zur Übertragbarkeit der Margin-of-appreciation-Doktrin des EGMR auf die Rechtsprechung des EuGH im Bereich der Grundfreiheiten* (n 6), 357.

a very limited number of factors (out of those announced by the ECJ itself) that actually drive its application of deferential standards of review: notably, the implication of public health, games of chance, public policy or morality and security, and road safety.[8] In several of these domains, the better placed-contention comes into play, in the variant of the superior expertise/democratic legitimacy branch. Insofar, there is an important parallel to the ICJ. Interestingly, the ECJ has so far, as Schulte contends, never explained the adoption of a deferential standard of review with reference to the better placed-contention.[9] This is a noteworthy difference to the ICJ, which has acknowledged the underlying concerns on several occasions.[10]

In summary, the overall decision-making practice regarding standards of review is quite heterogenous in between these judicial fora, with all four – perhaps somewhat less so in the WTO system – ostensibly trying to preserve a certain margin for how they determine the applicable standard of review in each case. Against the backdrop of the very different institutional realities, the starkly differing caseload, subject-matters before them as well as procedural situations, this does not come as a surprise. From this short overview, one can deduce two findings: first, that Japan's assertion in the *Whaling* case referred to at the very beginning of this book that the 'margin of appreciation' 'must be an axiom of international law and relations'[11] is certainly not correct from an empirical point of view, and second, that the ICJ is not a statistical outlier among international courts and tribunals – rather to the contrary, it appears to be in good company.

II. RARELY AUTONOMOUS ADOPTION OF A DEFERENTIAL STANDARD OF REVIEW

Second, the empirical analysis shows that the Court has only very rarely adopted a deferential standard of review without being urged to do so by the respective respondent or otherwise concerned state(s) in the first place. There is only one exception to this rule: *Bosnian Genocide*. However, as argued, that case is particular for several reasons, and most likely, the ICJ chose the good faith standard of review on its own initiative in order to counterbalance its parallel, far-reaching finding of the unlimited geographical reach of the obligation to prevent under the Genocide Convention. Considerations of institutional expertise presumably played no role in this connection. Thereby, *Bosnian Genocide* rather serves as an exception proving the rule.

[8] Zglinski, *Europe's Passive Virtues* (n 6), 92–95.

[9] Schulte, *Zur Übertragbarkeit der Margin-of-appreciation-Doktrin des EGMR auf die Rechtsprechung des EuGH im Bereich der Grundfreiheiten* (n 6), 368.

[10] For instance, in *Diallo* and *Navigational Rights*, see above at ch 6, sections I.D and II.B, respectively.

[11] *Whaling in the Antarctic (Australia v Japan: New Zealand intervening)*, ICJ, Counter-Memorial of Japan of 9 March 2012, 9.16.

The observation that the Court does not apply a deferential standard of review unless particularly asked for further confirms that *de novo* is its default standard. It does not conclude by itself that either its legitimacy or its expertise is insufficient to evaluate a certain set of facts on its own without any regard to the concerned state's initial perspective.

III. MOSTLY STRICTER STANDARD OF REVIEW THAN INVOKED BY THE RESPONDENTS

Third, even in those 18 proceedings in which the Court adopted a deferential standard of review, it mostly adopted a stricter standard than that invoked by the respective respondents. There are only six occasions on which it settled for their proposed standard: *South West Africa (Second Phase), ELSI, Nuclear Weapons, Navigational Rights, Pulp Mills* and *Immunities and Criminal Proceedings*. Yet, only in *South West Africa (Second Phase), Nuclear Weapons* and *Pulp Mills* did the Court adopt this standard without the applicants' or otherwise opposed states' express agreement. Finally, there is only one case in which it adopted a more lenient standard than that invoked by the concerned state: *Norwegian Loans*.

In the other 12 instances, the Court ultimately adopted a stricter standard of review than that invoked by the concerned state(s), even if at least partially deferential. To these instances, one has to add the 12 proceedings in which it adopted a consistent *de novo* standard, and where it discarded the plea for a deferential standard of review altogether. Finally, there is the *Reservations to the Genocide* advisory opinion, in which the ICJ rejected the complete deference contention advanced by several states. This is recapitulated in Table 15.

Consequently, the ICJ only followed the concerned state(s)' standard of review proposal (or went even beyond it) in seven proceedings, whereas it adopted an at least partially stricter standard of review in 24 proceedings. It is thus far less willing to defer to the respective subsumptions of the concerned states than they would prefer.[12] An explanation for this stance could be that in the ICJ's view, the reasons invoked for the application of a deferential standard of review – intrusion into state sovereignty, or lack of expertise – do not carry as much weight as the states making these claims had believed.

[12] Certainly, a state could already view it as a success if the ICJ adopts a deferential standard of review at all in its favour, if only for individual questions. From this point of view, all these 18 proceedings where it did so represent such successes. Yet, the plea for a deferential standard of review is only a means to an end: winning the case. While the concerned states ultimately prevailed in all seven proceedings where the Court followed or even went beyond their standard of review proposal, they only did so in three of the other eleven proceedings where the ICJ opted for a deferential standard of review, namely *Rights of US Nationals in Morocco, Right of Passage*, and *Mutual Assistance*. Consequently, while the states at least partially succeeded in convincing the Court to apply a deferential standard of review in 18 proceedings, they only prevailed in 10 of them. Of those 10 proceedings, two stand apart, as the Court discarded them based on other grounds: *South West Africa (Second Phase)*, and *Nuclear Weapons* (Ch 4, sections III.C and I.C, respectively).

Table 15 Overview – respondent state and ICJ positions on the appropriate standard of review

<table>
<tr><th>Short title</th><th>Complete Deference</th><th>Good Faith</th><th>Reasonableness</th></tr>
<tr><td>Admission of a State to the UN</td><td>Several states</td><td></td><td>Court</td></tr>
<tr><td>Corfu Channel</td><td>Albania</td><td></td><td>Court</td></tr>
<tr><td>Rights of US Nationals</td><td></td><td>France</td><td>Court</td></tr>
<tr><td>Norwegian Loans</td><td>Court</td><td>Norway</td><td></td></tr>
<tr><td>Right of Passage</td><td></td><td>India</td><td>Court</td></tr>
<tr><td rowspan="2">South West Africa (Second Phase)</td><td colspan="2">South Africa</td><td rowspan="2"></td></tr>
<tr><td>Court</td><td></td></tr>
<tr><td>Nicaragua (treaty law)</td><td colspan="2">United States</td><td>Court</td></tr>
<tr><td>ELSI</td><td></td><td>Italy
Court</td><td></td></tr>
<tr><td>Nuclear Weapons</td><td>Several states
Court</td><td></td><td></td></tr>
<tr><td>Gabčíkovo-Nagymaros</td><td></td><td></td><td>Hungary
Court</td></tr>
<tr><td>Bosnian Genocide*</td><td></td><td>Court</td><td></td></tr>
<tr><td rowspan="2">Mutual Assistance</td><td colspan="2">France</td><td rowspan="2"></td></tr>
<tr><td></td><td>Court</td></tr>
<tr><td>Navigational Rights</td><td></td><td></td><td>Nicaragua
Court</td></tr>
<tr><td>Pulp Mills</td><td></td><td></td><td>Uruguay
Court</td></tr>
<tr><td>Diallo</td><td>DRC</td><td></td><td>Court</td></tr>
<tr><td rowspan="2">Whaling</td><td colspan="3">Japan</td></tr>
<tr><td></td><td></td><td>Court</td></tr>
<tr><td>Immunities and Criminal Proceedings</td><td></td><td></td><td>France
Court</td></tr>
<tr><td>Certain Iranian Assets</td><td></td><td>United States</td><td>Court</td></tr>
</table>

Respondent in dark grey, opponent states in advisory proceedings in white, Court in black. Half-filled boxes mean that the Court adopted a mixed deferential/*de novo* standard of review.

* Serbia and Montenegro forwent the opportunity to plead for the application of a deferential standard of review.

Besides this interpretation based on the standard of review argument's persuasiveness, another explanation is also conceivable. States often make a standard of review claim as a claim of last resort. Asserting that the Court ought to accord special weight to their perspective on the measures at issue is often the best strategy left in situations in which they cannot convincingly claim that these are lawful from an objective *ex post* view in the first place. This is evidenced first of all by the fact that in most proceedings in which the respondents lost on their standard of review claim, they also lost their case. Colombia's position in *Asylum* and Greece's in *Interim Accord* are illustrative examples in this respect. Concerning Colombia's invocation of complete deference in the *Asylum* case, Peru did not fail to notice that '[i]t is without doubt due to … initial irregularities that the Colombian government saw itself pressed to advance this extreme contention'.[13] The former Yugoslav Republic of Macedonia in turn qualified Greece's invocation of a 'margin of appreciation' in the form of the reasonableness standard in the *Interim Accord* case[14] as 'the best the Respondent [could] come up with'.[15] Had the ICJ applied the standard of review invoked by the two respondents, it would effectively have sanctioned their behaviour, even if clearly unlawful. From this perspective, adopting a stricter standard of review may often have imposed itself to arrive at a just verdict.

IV. SUBJECT-MATTER AS A FACTOR FOR THE ADOPTION OF A DEFERENTIAL STANDARD OF REVIEW

Throughout the empirical chapters, the proceedings have been grouped in four categories, based on their characterising aspects: national security interests, domestic matters, political determinations, and scientific determinations. While the former two are inextricably linked to considerations of state sovereignty, the latter two are based on the consideration that states possess superior institutional expertise in these domains in comparison to the Court as a judicial institution.

As the empirical analysis has shown, it is difficult to speak of a Court doctrine of deferential standards of review. In the first three categories, the ICJ has regularly resorted to the *de novo* standard. What is more, there is a clear pattern for a subset of the national security measures: measures justified with

[13] *Asylum (Colombia v Peru)*, ICJ, Counter-Memorial by Peru of 21 March 1950, 156 (own translation, in the original: 'C'est, sans aucun doute, en raison de ces irrégularités du début que le Gouvernement de Colombie s'est trouvé acculé à soutenir cette prétention extrême').

[14] See for instance *Interim Accord of 13 September 1995 (Macedonia v Greece)*, ICJ, Rejoinder of Greece of 27 October 2010, para 6.30; *Interim Accord of 13 September 1995*, ICJ, Oral Proceedings of 25 March 2010, morning (CR 2011/9), 34, para 40 (Crawford).

[15] *Interim Accord of 13 September 1995*, ICJ, Oral Proceedings of 22 March 2011, morning (CR 2011/6), 46, para 78 (Murphy).

the right of self-defence. Here, the ICJ has explicitly and consistently rejected the application of any deferential standard of review.

In turn, there are also instances of deference in all four categories (except for the forementioned sub-category of self-defence). This shows that the ICJ has not generally discarded the underlying arguments altogether – neither national sovereignty, nor deficient institutional expertise. Regarding scientific determinations, the Court has even resorted at least to a mixed reasonableness standard in each proceeding, and thus always applied at least a limited degree of deference. However, the fact that there are only three proceedings falling in this category – *Gabčíkovo-Nagymaros, Pulp Mills* and *Whaling* – cautions against drawing far-reaching conclusions from this. Tables 16–20 mapping the ICJ's approach in the respective categories will illustrate these points.

A. National Security

Table 16 comprises all proceedings implicating national security interests included in this study. As can be seen, the Court opted for complete deference and good faith in one proceeding each, for reasonableness at least partially in five proceedings, and for *de novo* at least partially in seven:

Table 16 Overview – ICJ's standard of review choice in proceedings relating to national security interests

National Security	Complete Deference	Good Faith	Reasonableness	*De novo*
Corfu Channel			X	
Right of Passage			X	
Nicaragua (treaty & customary law)			X	X
Nuclear Weapons	X			
Oil Platforms				X
Wall in the OPT				X
Armed Activities				X
Mutual Assistance		X		
Diallo			X	
Construction of a Road				X
Jadhav				X
Certain Iranian Assets			X	X

The proceedings in which it opted for complete deference and good faith, *Nuclear Weapons* and *Mutual Assistance*, are particular. The former revolved around the possession and use of nuclear weapons, a cornerstone in the security architecture of many states, including the most powerful ones. The latter dealt with the application of a 'self-judging clause', presupposing an important degree of judicial deference. Apart from these two proceedings, the Court opted for a relatively strict standard of review. It is especially noteworthy that it consistently chose the *de novo* standard in proceedings revolving around the right to self-defence. It even did so explicitly in *Oil Platforms*.

For all other security-related measures, the ICJ only adopted the *de novo* standard implicitly. Interestingly enough, however, it mostly laid open its (partial) application of the reasonableness and the good faith standards (*Nicaragua, Mutual Assistance, Diallo* and *Certain Iranian Assets*). Thus, it predominantly used the *de novo* standard tacitly, but mostly resorted to the reasonableness and good faith standards openly. This can be seen as an attempt by the Court to signal its general willingness to defer to the security-assessments of states – even if effectively, this is not always true. This same phenomenon can be observed in domestic matters and in *Whaling*, and will be further analysed below.

B. Domestic Matters

Second, there is the category of domestic matters. The ICJ chose complete deference and good faith in one proceeding each, reasonableness in three, and *de novo* in five.

Table 17 Overview – ICJ's standard of review choice in proceedings relating to domestic matters

Domestic Matters	Complete Deference	Good Faith	Reasonableness	*De novo*
Rights of US Nationals in Morocco			X	
Nottebohm				X
Norwegian Loans	X			
Hostage				X
ELSI		X		
LaGrand				X
Navigational Rights			X	
Obligation to Prosecute or Extradite				X
Certain Activities				X
Immunities and Criminal Proceedings			X	

Again, the two proceedings in which it adopted the two most deferential standards of review – complete deference and good faith – represent particular cases. The Court reversed the non-reviewability finding in *Norwegian Loans* later in *Mutual Assistance*, and *ELSI* was particular because of the explicit reference to arbitrariness in the pertinent norm. Thus, again, one can speak of a rather strict standard of review for domestic matters, with *de novo* occurrences representing the majority. Comparable to what was the case for national security measures, the Court chose to make its resort to the reasonableness standard of review explicit, but its use of the *de novo* standard implicit on every occasion. Again, this could be explained with a willingness by the ICJ to merely pretend that it is ready to accommodate the states' sovereignty concerns.

C. Political Determinations

In the five proceedings falling in this category, the ICJ opted for complete deference and reasonableness once each, and twice for *de novo*, with the substantial standard of review left unclear in *Reservations to the Genocide Convention*. Yet, it reverted on its choice of complete deference in *South West Africa (Second Phase)* only five years later in *Namibia*. Effectively, it thus adopted the reasonableness standard once, and the *de novo* standard twice. Accordingly, the Court privileged a relatively strict standard of review for the proceedings falling in this category.

Table 18 Overview – ICJ's standard of review choice in proceedings relating to political determinations

Political Determinations	Complete Deference	Good Faith	Reasonableness	*De novo*
Admission of a State to the UN			X	
Asylum				X
Reservations to the Genocide Convention	rejected	substantial standard unclear		
South West Africa (Second Phase)	X			
Namibia				X

D. Scientific Determinations

Finally, in the three proceedings revolving around state first-hand determinations in the domain of science, the ICJ always opted at least for a partial reasonableness standard of review. Remarkably, it applied the reasonableness standard only implicitly in *Pulp Mills*, and somewhat indirectly in *Gabčíkovo-Nagymaros*. In turn, it explicitly professed to apply the reasonableness standard unreservedly in *Whaling*, yet effectively only did so for the subordinate of the two sub-questions. This gives a somewhat contradictory impression. In the first two proceedings, the Court saw the limitations of its expertise, yet refused to acknowledge them openly. In the third proceeding, it purported to recognise these limitations and adopt its review intensity accordingly, yet effectively only did so in part.

Table 19 Overview – ICJ's standard of review choice in proceedings relating to scientific determinations

Scientific Determinations	Complete Deference	Good Faith	Reasonableness	*De novo*
Gabčíkovo-Nagymaros			X	X
Pulp Mills			X	
Whaling			X	X

Again, it is illustrative to compare the ICJ's choice of an at least partial reasonableness standard of review in science-heavy matters with the standards of review adopted in this domain by the WTO and investor-state dispute settlement bodies, and by the ECJ. In the WTO system, the standard of review in science intensive matters is most acute in disputes under the Agreement on the Application of Sanitary and Phytosanitary Measures (SPS Agreement), which allows Member States to introduce trade-restrictive measures to protect inter alia human and animal health.[16] Several scholars contend that the initial standard of review adopted by panels and the Appellate Body when evaluating SPS measures was bordering *de novo*, but was later geared towards a more deferential one.[17] Following this more recent approach, panels and the Appellate Body are called to apply a more deferential two-tier standard of review when examining an SPS measure. In the first stage, it is enquired whether the contested measure is based on solid scientific evidence rather than the 'best' or 'correct' scientific evidence. In contrast, in the second stage, the state's reasoning for its contested measure based on this scientific evaluation

[16] 1867 United Nations Treaty Series 493.

[17] Regarding this initial standard of review, see for instance J Peel, 'Of Apples and Oranges (and Hormones in Beef): Science and the Standard of Review in WTO Disputes under the SPS Agreement' (2012) 61(2) *International and Comparative Law Quarterly* 427, 437–39; R Becroft, *The Standard of Review in WTO Dispute Settlement: Critique and Development* (Edward Elgar, 2012), 52–56; more nuanced Oesch, *Standards of Review in WTO Dispute Resolution* (n 1), 121–24 and 139–42; with a different reading L Gruszczynski, 'Standard of Review of Health and Environmental Regulations by WTO Panels' in G van Calster (ed), *Research Handbook on Environment, Health and the WTO* (Elgar, 2013), 740–43, 749–56, viewing *US – Continued Suspension* as 'an anomaly in an otherwise rather consistent line of cases that subscribed to a fairly intrusive standard of review', at 756–57.

is amenable to a more intensive scrutiny.[18] The first stage equates to a reasonableness standard of review, as defined above, while the second stage comes closer to a *de novo* standard. Arguably, one may therefore speak of a mixed reasonableness/*de novo* standard of review in WTO SPS disputes, a standard equivalent to that of the ICJ in proceedings involving scientific assessments.

Investment tribunals have likewise adopted a (somewhat) deferential approach when confronted with scientific assessments invoked by host states as justification for a contested regulation. Scholars have argued that the prevailing method for investment tribunals is to focus on the quality of the process leading to the emergence of the invoked scientific knowledge in terms of transparency and openness, or of the regulatory process in general. Accordingly, investment tribunals are privileging a procedural over a substantive approach, which also equates to a certain degree of deference.[19] In this connection, *Vadi* observes that '[w]ith regard to public policy-related disputes, arbitral tribunals usually refrain from second-guessing decisions adopted by local scientific authorities, especially when such measures appear to be reasonable'.[20] Accordingly, the standard of review employed by investment tribunals appears somewhat more lenient than that of the Court.

Finally, with regard to the ECJ, *Zglinski* tentatively concludes that it also applies a deferential standard of review when confronted with scientific uncertainties while reviewing a Member State's respective first-hand assessment. However, the exact degree of deference appears to be more variable, ranging from complete deference to a review closer to *de novo*.[21]

In sum, there is thus a notable overlap in the standard of review-setting practice of several international adjudicative bodies when it comes to evaluating state measures justified with or based on scientific knowledge: The ECJ, the WTO as well as investor-state arbitration dispute settlement bodies and the ICJ all employ at least a moderate degree of deference when examining such measures. While the exact degree of deference varies to a certain extent, not only between these bodies, but also in their respective case law, this leads to the preliminary conclusion that several major international courts and tribunals and dispute settlement mechanisms recognise their inherent epistemic limitations vis-a-vis the states.[22]

[18] With further references to WTO case law K Sulyok, *Science and Judicial Reasoning: The Legitimacy of International Environmental Adjudication* (Cambridge University Press, 2021), 192–202.

[19] See for instance ibid, 232–40, speaking of a 'a high measure of deference to host states' scientific claims', 234.

[20] Vadi, *Proportionality, Reasonableness and Standards of Review in International Investment Law and Arbitration* (n 2), 349.

[21] Zglinski, *Europe's Passive Virtues* (n 6), 86–87.

[22] See also Sulyok, *Science and Judicial Reasoning* (n 18), 317–19, 324–28, who speaks of 'essentially similar solutions for the cross-cutting challenge of science-intensive judicial review', 327; Vadi and Gruszczynski argue that international investment tribunals and WTO panels 'both concentrate on reasonableness rather than correctness of specific scientific claims', thus presenting 'some notable convergences', V Vadi and L Gruszczynski, 'Standard of Review and Scientific Evidence

V. STRATEGIC USE OF DEFERENTIAL STANDARDS OF REVIEW

Fifth and finally, there remains the question of whether the Court has made strategic use of deferential standards of review. The fact that it has resorted to the *de novo* standard of review *implicitly* in all but one proceeding in which it chose this standard, and to deferential standards of review *explicitly* in most proceedings in which it chose such a standard could be a first indicator in that sense. The explicit choice of the *de novo* standard could send a signal to the states deemed too assertive, while implicit adoption of a deferential standard of review would have fewer advantages as compared to an explicit one.

Ultimately, there is ground to believe that the ICJ has, on several instances, been resorting to deferential standards of review as an avoidance technique. At times, it has only given the *impression* of laying down a deferential standard of review in what could be interpreted as an attempt to reap the advantages of resorting to such a standard without incurring the disadvantages. On the other hand, there are also situations in which resort to a non-deferential standard of review may be preferable for the Court also from a strategic point of view. Finally, one could speak of a decremental use of the standard of review notion. Each point will be addressed in turn.

A. Deferential Standards of Review as an Avoidance Technique

First, there are several proceedings in which the Court arguably resorted to deferential standards of review as a technique 'to dispose of cases or issues within cases where a decision seems unnecessary, inappropriate, or perhaps simply too controversial'.[23] Such can be said both of its use of the good faith and of the reasonableness standard of review.[24] In turn, it most likely did not resort to the most deferential standard, complete deference, as an avoidance technique.

The adoption of a deferential standard of review resulted in the concerned state winning the case in eight instances.[25] In four additional proceedings where the ICJ adopted at least a partial deferential standard, the respondent prevailed on the respective sub-question, even while ultimately losing the case.[26]

in WTO Law and International Investment Arbitration' in L Gruszczynski and W Werner (eds), *Deference in International Courts and Tribunals: Standard of Review and Margin of Appreciation* (Oxford University Press, 2014), 169.

[23] WJ Davey, 'Has the WTO Dispute Settlement System Exceeded Its Authority? A Consideration of Deference shown by the System to Member Government Decisions and its Use of Issue-Avoidance Techniques' (2001) 4(1) *Journal of International Economic Law* 79, 96.

[24] Of course, this is not to suggest that every instance where the ICJ opted for a deferential standard of review amounts to the use of this notion as an avoidance technique.

[25] *Norwegian Loans, Rights* of *US Nationals in Morocco, Right of Passage, ELSI, Mutual Assistance, Navigational Rights, Pulp Mills*, and *Immunities and Criminal Proceedings*.

[26] *Gabčíkovo-Nagymaros* (notably the identification of an essential interest), *Nicaragua* (identification of an essential security interest), *Diallo* (identification of compelling reasons of national security), and *Whaling* (definition of science).

Thus, there are only four proceedings in which the adoption of a deferential standard of review had no concrete beneficial consequences for the concerned state.[27] Especially in this last category, a point can be made that the Court resorted to a deferential standard of review as a forward-looking avoidance technique with future proceedings in mind. This is arguably also the case in some of the proceedings in which the concerned state benefitted directly from the ICJ's choice of a lenient standard of review.

For instance, the sweeping and generalised observation about the regulator's decision-making prerogative and concomitant application of the reasonableness standard of review in *Navigational Rights* has all the characteristics of an avoidance technique for the present case, and points beyond it at the same time. First of all, Nicaragua as the respondent benefitted from the Court's choice of the reasonableness standard. By adopting this standard of review, the ICJ avoided a finding against Nicaragua on several of Costa Rica's claims. Further, it thereby set higher hurdles to finding a violation of international law in possible future proceedings involving a state's power of regulation, and thereby (incidentally) reduced the likelihood of such – often thorny – questions coming before it.

Similarly, in *Nicaragua* and *Diallo*, the ICJ explicitly recognised a decision-making prerogative to the United States and the DRC in their definition of their essential security interests. While this finding ultimately did not help the two states concerned, it spared the Court from concluding that their claimed security interests were not legitimate ones in the first place, and thus disposed of this sub-question.[28] Arguably, especially in the *Diallo* case, the likelihood of such a finding would have been considerable under a more demanding standard of review. This would have resulted in a highly embarrassing situation for the DRC and would have increased the likelihood of a hostile reaction from it. In *Nicaragua*, the recognition of a decision-making leeway to the United States might have been an attempt to temper its reaction – as the aftermath of the case has shown, a fruitless attempt.

Finally, the Court's resort to the good faith standard of review in *Bosnian Genocide* can be categorised as a forward-looking avoidance technique. Even under this standard, the respondent lost on the sub-question. Yet, the choice of this particularly lenient standard for the evaluation of a state's compliance with its obligation to prevent genocides, and the concomitant low chances of success for new applicants, make it unlikely that the ICJ will again be seised of such proceedings in the future. By laying down this highly deferential standard of review, the Court thus significantly reduced the risk of having to adjudicate again on the behaviour of states when faced with a risk of a genocide.

[27] *Admission of a State to the UN, Corfu Channel, Bosnian Genocide*, and *Certain Iranian Assets*.

[28] Note, however, that the same was not the case in *Certain Iranian Assets*, where the United States lost on the question of the presence of essential security interests even under the reasonableness standard.

B. Only Purported Use of a Deferential Standard of Review

In some instances, the Court asserted that it would apply a deferential standard of review, yet proceeded with the application of the *de novo* standard nonetheless. At first glance, this gives the impression that the ICJ is ready to accord a decision-making space to the states when evaluating such measures and matters, when in reality, it is far less deferential in these domains than it claims to be.

This was the case in *Whaling*, in which it professed to apply the reasonableness standard of review to evaluate whether Japan's whaling programme was 'for purposes of' scientific research, yet effectively applied the *de novo* standard for that second sub-question. It thereby only appeared to acknowledge its limitations in terms of institutional expertise in the domain of science. The same can be said for the Court's overall evaluation of security-related measures and domestic measures. Most instances in which the ICJ chose a deferential standard of review in those two categories are clearly flagged. In turn, those occasions on which it resorted to the *de novo* standard are not. Thereby, the Court gives the impression of acceding to the contention that respect for national sovereignty excludes full judicial oversight in such matters. Consequently, in these domains, the ICJ regularly makes rhetorical concessions, without however doing so on the substance with equal consistency.

By doing so, on paper, the Court recognises the appropriateness of a deferential standard of review for these types of measures, and the states' respective decision-making prerogative. Yet, at the same time, it regularly takes the liberty to decide the matter at hand by adopting a non-deferential standard of review. This can be described as strategic ambiguity: The ICJ signals its acknowledgement of the states' concerns for their sovereignty and its consciousness of its own limitations, yet practices intensive scrutiny whenever this seems more appropriate to it.

C. A Strict Standard of Review can also be Advantageous for the ICJ

The book does not argue that adopting a deferential standard of review (or avoidance more generally) as a basic rule is the solution to every problem that international courts and tribunals face. The fate of the WTO Appellate Body shows this only too well, and for the IACtHR, the opposite approach – applying a strict standard of review from the outset – has been argued to have been instrumental for the standing it has today.[29] Even at the level of individual proceedings, the rejection of deference and subsequent adoption of the *de novo*

[29] On the IACtHR, see G Candia Falcón, 'Standard of Review: Inter-American Court of Human Rights' in R Wolfrum (ed), *Max Planck Encyclopedia of Public International Law* (Oxford University Press, 2012), paras 7–13.

standard of review may sometimes be preferable for the Court. The *Namibia* advisory opinion and the *Nicaragua* judgment are illustrative in this respect. In the former proceedings, the rejection of the application of a deferential standard of review has to be seen in the context of the *South West Africa* judgment. Adopting the *de novo* standard in *Namibia* arguably helped restore at least some of the trust the ICJ had lost through its avoidance practised in *South West Africa*. In the same vein, the adoption of the *de novo* standard for the evaluation of the United States' self-defence claim in *Nicaragua* led to a finding against the United States. This conviction resulted in making the Court 'a hero to the states of the developing world, and ushered in a period of increased activity on its docket'.[30] While this is not to say that the hope for such an outcome led the Court's hand, this example shows that considerations of judicial policy do not invariably speak for the adoption of a deferential standard of review. Rather, at times, they speak for the (clear) rejection of any degree of deference. In any case, by avoiding the development of a doctrine of deferential standards of review, the ICJ has preserved the flexibility to adopt its respective approach on a case-by-case basis, enabling it to react to the circumstances at hand.

D. Resort to Standards of Review as Part of a Strategy of Incrementalism

Finally, it is noteworthy that the three instances in which the Court adopted the most deferential standard of review, complete deference, all date back to before 1996. In turn, two-thirds of the proceedings in which it adopted the *de novo* standard date back to the last 20 years. This could be exclusively due to the substance of these proceedings, or to a case selection bias. Nonetheless, this phenomenon could also suggest that the ICJ is gradually scaling back the degree of deference it accords to the states. This could be part of a larger strategy of incrementalism.[31] Such a strategy would follow what parts of the literature recommend for newly established international courts and tribunals[32] – a description which, in some regards, can be used for the ICJ even today, given its dependency on state consent.

[30] SD Murphy, 'The United States and the International Court of Justice: Coping with Antinomies' in CPR Romano (ed), *The Sword and the Scales: The United States and International Courts and Tribunals* (Cambridge University Press, 2009), 97.

[31] As noted above in ch 3, section IV, the notion of deferential standards of review is particularly well-suited for such an approach. Besides the scholarship referred to there, see also with further references on judicial incrementalism S Dothan, *Reputation and Judicial Tactics: A Theory of National and International Courts* (Cambridge University Press, 2015), 131–36.

[32] See for instance KJ Alter, 'Agents or Trustees? International Courts in their Political Context' (2008) 14(1) *European Journal of International Relations* 33; MR Madsen, 'The Protracted Institutionalization of the Strasbourg Court: From Legal Diplomacy to Integrationist Jurisprudence' in J Christoffersen and MR Madsen (eds), *The European Court of Human Rights between Law and Politics* (Oxford University Press, 2011); A Schwartz, 'An Agent-based Model of Judicial Power' (2019) 9(1) *Journal of Law (Journal of Legal Metrics)* 21; but see S Caserta, 'Regional International Courts in Search of Relevance: Adjudicating Politically Sensitive Disputes in Central America and the Caribbean' (2017) 28(1) *Duke Journal of Comparative & International Law* 59.

Scholars have been arguing that other courts and tribunals have had success with such an incremental approach. For instance, *Donoho* has asserted that the margin of appreciation doctrine was an instrumental tool in the ECtHR's incremental rise.[33] From this perspective, according greater deference in earlier years and gradually scaling back this approach as the need for defensive behaviour declines could be a viable strategy for the Court as well. At the national level, *Kavanagh* has pointed out that constitutional courts might consider it advisable to apply a deferential standard of review in a particular case to gain the institutional standing to be able to be less deferential on a future occasion.[34] From this perspective, the scaled-back use of deferential standards of review could suggest that the ICJ is becoming more self-confident.[35]

* * *

In connection with the *Whaling* case, it has been said that—

> it is likely that [the standard of review] becomes a crucial issue and takes an important place in the arguments of litigants. The Court will therefore probably be required in the near future to clarify its position with regard to the theory of the margin of appreciation and to describe the intensity of its scrutiny.[36]

It will be interesting to see if this prognosis holds true. However, it is not this future that has been the subject of this book. Rather, it has shown that the standard of review notion has already been part and parcel of the ICJ's decision-making practice in the over 75 years of its existence.

[33] DL Donoho, 'Autonomy, Self-Governance, and the Margin of Appreciation: Developing a Jurisprudence of Diversity within Universal Human Rights' (2001) 15(2) *Emory International Law Review* 391, 465; see also on this point Y Shany, 'Toward a General Margin of Appreciation Doctrine in International Law?' (2005) 16(5) *European Journal of International Law* 907, 922.

[34] A Kavanagh, 'Deference or Defiance? The Limits of the Judicial Role in Constitutional Adjudication' in G Huscroft (ed), *Expounding the Constitution: Essays in Constitutional Theory* (Cambridge University Press, 2008), 206.

[35] In this sense Murphy, 'The United States and the International Court of Justice' (n 30), 97.

[36] G Gros, 'The ICJ's Handling of Science in the Whaling in the Antarctic Case: A Whale of a Case?' (2015) 6(3) *Journal of International Dispute Settlement* 578, 620.

Bibliography

Akande D, 'Nuclear Weapons, Unclear Law? Deciphering the Nuclear Weapons Advisory Opinion of the International Court' (1998) 68(1) *British Yearbook of International Law* 165.

Alexy R, *A Theory of Constitutional Rights* (Oxford University Press, Reprint 2010).

Allan TRS, 'Human Rights and Judicial Review: A Critique of "Due Deference"' (2006) 65(3) *Cambridge Law Journal* 671.

Alter KJ, 'Agents or Trustees? International Courts in their Political Context' (2008) 14(1) *European Journal of International Relations* 33.

—— 'Judicialization of International Relations' in B Badie, D Berg-Schlosser and L Morlino (eds), *International Encyclopedia of Political Science* (Sage, 2011), 1378–82.

—— 'The ICJ in Comparison: Understanding the ICJ's Limited Influence' (2021) 21(3) *Melbourne Journal of International Law* 1.

Alvarez-Jimenez A, 'The ICJ's Marshall Islands (Mis)judgments on Nuclear Disarmament' (2017) 45(1) *Syracuse Journal of International Law and Commerce* 1.

Amerasinghe CF, *Evidence in International Litigation* (Martinus Nijhoff, 2005).

Arai-Takahashi Y, *The Margin of Appreciation Doctrine and the Principle of Proportionality in the Jurisprudence of the ECHR* (Intersentia, 2002).

Arato J, 'The Margin of Appreciation in International Investment Law' (2014) 54(3) *Virginia Journal of International Law* 545.

Asche J, *Die Margin of Appreciation: Entwurf einer Dogmatik monokausaler richterlicher Zurückhaltung für den europäischen Menschenrechtsschutz* (Beiträge zum ausländischen öffentlichen Recht und Völkerrecht, Veröffentlichungen des Max-Planck-Instituts für ausländisches öffentliches Recht und Völkerrecht vol 267, Springer, 2018).

Bahmaei M-A and Sabzevari H, 'Self-Judging Security Exception Clause as a Kind of Carte Blanche in Investment Treaties: Nature, Effect and Proper Standard of Review' (2023) 13(1) *Asian Journal of International Law* 97.

Becker MA, 'The dispute that wasn't there: judgments in the Nuclear Disarmament cases at the International Court of Justice' (2017) 6(1) *Cambridge International Law Journal* 4.

Becroft R, *The Standard of Review in WTO Dispute Settlement: Critique and Development* (Edward Elgar, 2012).

Bedjaoui M, 'Expediency in the Decisions of the International Court of Justice' (2001) 71(1) *British Yearbook of International Law* 1.

Benzing M, *Das Beweisrecht vor internationalen Gerichten und Schiedsgerichten in zwischenstaatlichen Streitigkeiten* (Beiträge zum ausländischen öffentlichen Recht und Völkerrecht vol 215, Springer, 2010).

Bernstorff J von and others, 'Courts as Rhetorical Actors: A Rhetorical Analysis of Judicial Conflict Avoidance' (2021) 81(4) *Zeitschrift für ausländisches öffentliches Recht und Völkerrecht* 1001.

Bertelsen S, 'A margin for the margin of appreciation: Deference in the Inter-American Court of Human Rights' (2021) 19(3) *International Journal of Constitutional Law* 887.

Bianchi A, 'Choice and (the Awareness of) its Consequences: The ICJ's "Structural Bias" Strikes Again in the Marshall Islands Case' (2017) 111 *AJIL Unbound* 81.

Bickel AM, *The Least Dangerous Branch: The Supreme Court at the Bar of Politics*, 2nd edn (Yale University Press, 1986).

Bjorge E, 'Been There, Done That: The Margin of Appreciation and International Law' (2015) 4(1) *Cambridge Journal of International and Comparative Law* 181–90.

Bodansky D, 'Non Liquet' in R Wolfrum (ed), *Max Planck Encyclopedia of Public International Law* (Oxford University Press, 2012).

Bohanes J and Lockhart N, 'Standard of Review in WTO Law' in DL Bethlehem and others (eds), *The Oxford Handbook of International Trade Law* (Oxford University Press, 2009), 378–436.
Boklan D and Bahri A, 'The First WTO's Ruling on National Security Exception: Balancing Interests or Opening Pandora's Box?' (2020) 19(1) *World Trade Review* 123.
Born G, Morris D and Forrest S, '"A Margin of Appreciation": Appreciating Its Irrelevance in International Law' (2020) 61(1) *Harvard Journal of International Law* 65.
Boyle A, 'Developments in the International Law of Environmental Impact Assessments and their Relation to the Espoo Convention' (2011) 20(3) *Review of European Community & International Environmental Law* 227.
Brady ADP, *Proportionality and Deference under the UK Human Rights Act: An Institutionally Sensitive Approach* (Cambridge University Press, 2012).
Briese R and Schill S, 'Djibouti v France: Self-Judging Clauses before the International Court of Justice' (2009) 10 *Melbourne Journal of International Law* 308.
Broude T, Haftel YZ and Thompson A, 'Legitimation Through Modification: Do States Seek More Regulatory Space in Their Investment Agreements?' in D Behn, OK Fauchald and M Langford (eds), *The Legitimacy of Investment Arbitration: Empirical Perspectives* (Cambridge University Press, 2022), 531–54.
Brownlie I, 'The Justiciability of Disputes and Issues in International Relations' (1967) 42 *British Yearbook of International Law* 123.
Burke-White W and von Staden A, 'Investment Protection in Extraordinary Times: The Interpretation and Application of Non-Precluded Measures Provisions in Bilateral Investment Treaties' (2008) 48(2) *Virginia Journal of International Law* 307.
—— 'The Need for Public Law Standards of Review in Investor-State Arbitrations' in SW Schill (ed), *International Investment Law and Comparative Public Law* (Oxford University Press, 2010), 689–720.
—— 'Private Litigation in a Public Law Sphere: The Standard of Review in Investor-State Arbitrations' (2010) 35(2) *Yale Journal of International Law* 283.
Burri T, 'The Kosovo Opinion and Secession: The Sounds of Silence and Missing Links' (2010) 11(8) *German Law Journal* 881.
Button C, *The Power to Protect: Trade, Health and Uncertainty in the* WTO (Studies in International Trade Law vol 2, Hart, 2004).
Caflisch L, 'Vattel and the Peaceful Settlement of International Disputes' in V Chetail and P Haggenmacher (eds), *Vattel's International Law from a XXIst Century Perspective/Le Droit International de Vattel vu du XXIe Siècle* (Brill/Nijhoff, 2011), 257–66.
Candia Falcón G, 'Standard of Review: Inter-American Court of Human Rights' in R Wolfrum (ed), *Max Planck Encyclopedia of Public International Law* (Oxford University Press, 2012).
Cannizzaro E, 'Proportionality and Margin of Appreciation in the Whaling Case: Reconciling Antithetical Doctrines?' (2016) 27(4) *European Journal of International Law* 1061.
Carrubba CJ and Gabel, Matthew, Hankla, Charles, 'Judicial Behavior under Political Constraints: Evidence from the European Court of Justice' (2008) 102(4) *American Political Science Review* 435.
Casas M, 'Functional Justiciability and the Existence of a Dispute: A Means of Jurisdictional Avoidance?' (2019) 10(4) *Journal of International Dispute Settlement* 599.
Caserta S, 'Regional International Courts in Search of Relevance: Adjudicating Politically Sensitive Disputes in Central America and the Caribbean' (2017) 28(1) *Duke Journal of Comparative & International Law* 59–97.
Charney JI, 'Disputes Implicating the Institutional Credibility of the Court: Problems of Non-Appearance, Non-Participation, and Non-Performance' in LF Damrosch (ed), *The International Court of Justice at a Crossroads* (Brill/Nijhoff, 1987), 288–309.
Chesterman S, 'The International Court of Justice, Nuclear Weapons and the Law' (1997) 44(2) *Netherlands International Law Review* 149.
Christie GC, 'What Constitutes a Taking of Property Under International Law?' (1962) 38 *British Yearbook of International Law* 307.

Christoffersen J, *Fair Balance: Proportionality, Subsidiarity and Primarity in the European Convention on Human Rights* (International Studies in Human Rights vol 99, Brill/Nijhoff, 2009).

Coleman A, 'The International Court of Justice and Highly Political Matters' (2003) 4(1) *Melbourne Journal of International Law* 29.

Commission on Human Rights, 'Question of the Violation of Human Rights in the Occupied Arab Territories, including Palestine: Report of the Special Rapporteur of the Commission on Human Rights, John Dugard, on the situation of human rights in the Palestinian territories occupied by Israel since 1967' (8 September 2003) E/CN.4/2004/6.

Contreras P, 'National Discretion and International Deference in the Restriction of Human Rights: A Comparison Between the Jurisprudence of the European and the Inter-American Court of Human Rights' (2012) 11(1) *Northwestern Journal of International Human Rights* 28.

Cook G, *A Digest of WTO Jurisprudence on Public International Law Concepts and Principles* (Cambridge University Press, 2015).

Corten O, *L'utilisation du 'raisonnable' par le juge international: Discours juridique, raison et contradictions* (Éditions de l'Université de Bruxelles, Collection de droit international vol 34, Bruylant, 1997).

Cot J-P, 'Eloge de l'Indécision: La Cour et la Compétence Universelle' (2002) 35(1–2) *Revue belge de droit international* 546.

Council of Europe – European Court of Human Rights, 'Annual Report 2022 of the European Court of Human Rights' (2023), www.echr.coe.int/documents/d/echr/annual_report_2022_eng-2.

Cram I, 'Protocol 15 and articles 10 and 11 ECHR – The partial triumph of political incumbency post-Brighton?' (2018) 19 *International and Comparative Law Quarterly* 1.

Crawford JR, 'Military and Paramilitary Activities in and against Nicaragua Case (Nicaragua v United States of America)' in R Wolfrum (ed), *Max Planck Encyclopedia of Public International Law* (Oxford University Press, 2012).

—— '"Dreamers of the Day": Australia and the International Court of Justice' (2013) 14(2) *Melbourne Journal of International Law* 520.

Croley SP and Jackson JH, 'WTO Dispute Procedures, Standard of Review, and Deference to National Governments' (1996) 90(2) *American Journal of International Law* 193.

D'Argent P, 'Article 65' in A Zimmermann and others (eds), *The Statute of the International Court of Justice: A Commentary*, 3rd edn (Oxford University Press, 2019).

D'Aspremont J, 'The Multidimensional Process of Interpretation: Content-Determination and Law-Ascertainment Distinguished' in A Bianchi, D Peat and M Windsor (eds), *Interpretation in International Law* (Oxford University Press, 2015), 111–30.

Davey WJ, 'Has the WTO Dispute Settlement System Exceeded Its Authority? A Consideration of Deference shown by the System to Member Government Decisions and its Use of Issue-Avoidance Techniques' (2001) 4(1) *Journal of International Economic Law* 79.

Delaney EF, 'Analyzing Avoidance: Judicial Strategy in Comparative Perspective' (2016) 66(1) *Duke Law Journal* 1.

Desierto DA, *Necessity and National Emergency Clauses: Sovereignty in Modern Treaty Interpretation* (International Litigation in Practice vol 3, Brill/Nijhoff, 2012).

Devaney JG, *Fact-Finding Before the International Court of Justice* (Cambridge University Press, 2016).

Dixon J, Jr. 'The Connally Amendment: The Conflict Between Nationalism and an Effective World Court' (1964) 53(1) *Kentucky Law Journal* 164.

Donoho DL, 'Autonomy, Self-Governance, and the Margin of Appreciation: Developing a Jurisprudence of Diversity within Universal Human Rights' (2001) 15(2) *Emory International Law Review* 391.

Dothan S, *Reputation and Judicial Tactics: A Theory of National and International Courts* (Comparative Constitutional Law and Policy vol 9, Cambridge University Press, 2015).

—— 'Judicial Deference Allows European Consensus to Emerge' (2018) 18(2) *Chicago Journal of International Law* 393.

—— 'Margin of Appreciation and Democracy: Human Rights and Deference to Political Bodies' (2018) 9(2) *Journal of International Dispute Settlement* 145.

'Draft Report of the Rapporteur of Committee IV/1, Doc. 875, IV/1/74, June 9, 1945', *Documents of the United Nations Conference on International Organization, San Francisco, 1945: Volume XIII: Commission IV, Judicial Organization.*

Du MM, 'Standard of Review under the SPS Agreement after EC-Hormones II' (2010) 59(2) *International and Comparative Law Quarterly* 441.

Dyevre A, 'Uncertainty and international adjudication' (2019) 32(1) *Leiden Journal of International Law* 131.

Ehlermann C-D and Lockhart N, 'Standard of Review in WTO Law' (2004) 7(3) *Journal of International Economic Law* 491.

Eisenhut D, 'Sovereignty, National Security and International Treaty Law: The Standard of Review of International Courts and Tribunals with regard to "Security Exceptions"' (2010) 48(4) *Archiv des Völkerrechts* 431.

Eskridge W and Baer L, 'The Continuum of Deference: Supreme Court Treatment of Agency Statutory Interpretations from *Chevron* to *Hamdan*' (2008) 96 *The Georgetown Law Journal* 1083.

Fahner J, 'The Margin of Appreciation in Investor-State Arbitration: The Prevalence and Desirability of Discretion and Deference' in N Lavranos and RA Kok (eds), *Hague Yearbook of International Law* (Brill/Nijhoff, 2013), 422–95.

—— *Judicial Deference in International Adjudication: A Comparative Analysis* (Studies in International Law vol 78, Hart, 2020).

—— 'The Limited Utility of Deference in International Dispute Settlement' (2022) 21(2) *The Law and Practice of International Courts and Tribunals* 467.

Falk R, 'Nuclear Weapons, International Law, and the World Court: An Historic Encounter' (1996) 71(3) *Die Friedens-Warte* 235.

Fallon RH, Jr. 'Legitimacy and the Constitution' (2005) 118(6) *Harvard Law Review* 1787.

Farnelli GM, 'Consistency in the ICJ's Approach to the Standard of Proof: An Appraisal of the Court's Flexibility' (2022) 21(1) *The Law and Practice of International Courts and Tribunals* 98.

Fischer P, *Das Irrtumsrisiko bei den Ausnahmen des völkerrechtlichen Gewaltverbotes* (Kölner Schriften zum Friedenssicherungsrecht vol 13, Nomos, 2020).

Fitzmaurice G, 'The Law and Procedure of the International Court of Justice, 1951–4: Questions of Jurisdiction, Competence and Procedure' (1958) 34 *British Yearbook of International Law* 1.

Fitzmaurice M and Tamada D (eds), *Whaling in the Antarctic: Significance and Implications of the ICJ Judgment* (Queen Mary Studies in International Law 23, Brill/Nijhoff, 2016).

Forlati S, 'The Legal Obligation to Prevent Genocide: *Bosnia v Serbia* and Beyond' [2011] *Polish Yearbook of International Law* 189.

Foster CE, 'Adjudication, Arbitration and the Turn to Public Law 'Standards of Review': Putting the Precautionary Principle in the Crucible' (2012) 3(3) *Journal of International Dispute Settlement* 525.

Fouchard F, 'Allowing "leeway to expediency, without abandoning principle"? The International Court of Justice's use of avoidance techniques' (2020) 33(3) *Leiden Journal of International Law* 767.

Franck TM, 'Word made Law: The Decision of the ICJ in the Nuclear Test Cases' (1975) 69(3) *American Journal of International Law* 612.

Fukunaga Y, 'Margin of Appreciation as an Indicator of Judicial Deference: Is It Applicable to Investment Arbitration?' (2019) 10(1) *Journal of International Dispute Settlement* 69.

Gall C, 'Coming to Terms with a New Role: The Approach of the International Court of Justice to the Interpretation of Human Rights Treaties' (2014) 21(1) *Australian International Law Journal* 55.

Gardiner RK, *Treaty Interpretation*, 2nd edn (Oxford International Law Library, Oxford University Press, 2015).

Garrido-Muñoz A, 'Managing Uncertainty: The International Court of Justice, "Objective Reasonableness" and the Judicial Function' (2017) 30(2) *Leiden Journal of International Law* 457.

Gattini A, 'Judicial Discretion' in R Wolfrum (ed), *Max Planck Encyclopedia of Public International Law* (Oxford University Press, 2012).

Gerards J, 'Pluralism, Deference and the Margin of Appreciation Doctrine' (2011) 17(1) *European Law Journal* 80.

—— 'Margin of Appreciation and Incrementalism in the Case Law of the European Court of Human Rights' (2018) 18(3) *Human Rights Law Review* 495.

Goldmann M and Sonnen M, 'Soft Authority Against Hard Cases of Racially Discriminating Speech: Why the CERD Committee Needs a Margin of Appreciation Doctrine' (2016) 7(1) *Goettingen Journal of International Law* 131.

Goodman R and Jinks D, 'How to Influence States: Socialization and International Human Rights Law' (2004) 54(3) *Duke Law Journal* 621.

Graham L, 'Strategic Admissibility Decisions in the European Court of Human Rights' (2020) 69(1) *International and Comparative Law Quarterly* 79.

Gray C, 'The Use and Abuse of the International Court of Justice: Cases concerning the Use of Force after Nicaragua' (2003) 14(5) *European Journal of International Law* 867.

Gros G, 'The ICJ's Handling of Science in the Whaling in the Antarctic Case: A Whale of a Case?' (2015) 6(3) *Journal of International Dispute Settlement* 578.

Gross L, 'Bulgaria Invokes the Connally Amendment' (1962) 56(2) *American Journal of International Law* 357.

Gruszczynski L, 'Standard of Review of Health and Environmental Regulations by WTO Panels' in G van Calster (ed), *Research Handbook on Environment, Health and the WTO* (Elgar, 2013), 731–58.

—— 'Saving Regulatory Space for States Through the Standard of Review' in G Kajtár, B Çalı and M Milanović (eds), *Secondary Rules of Primary Importance in International Law: Attribution, Causality, Evidence, and Standards of Review in the Practice of International Courts and Tribunals* (Oxford University Press, 2022), 65–82.

Gruszczynski L and Werner W (eds), *Deference in International Courts and Tribunals: Standard of Review and Margin of Appreciation* (Oxford University Press, 2014).

—— 'Introduction' in L Gruszczynski and W Werner (eds), *Deference in International Courts and Tribunals: Standard of Review and Margin of Appreciation* (Oxford University Press, 2014), 1–15.

Guzman AT, *How international Law Works: A Rational Choice Theory* (Oxford University Press, 2008).

—— 'Determining the Appropriate Standard of Review in WTO Disputes' (2009) 42(1) *Cornell International Law Journal* 45.

—— 'Rethinking International Law as Law' (2009) 103 *Proceedings of the Annual Meeting (American Society of International Law)* 155.

Hahn MJ, 'Vital Interests and the Law of GATT: An Analysis of GATT's Security Exception' (1991) 12(3) *Michigan Journal of International Law* 558.

Hannum H, 'The Advisory Opinion on Kosovo: An Opportunity Lost, or a Poisoned Chalice Refused?' (2011) 24(1) *Leiden Journal of International Law* 155.

Heiskanen V, 'Oil Platforms: Lessons of Dissensus' (2005) 74(1) *Nordic Journal of International Law* 179.

Helfer LR, 'Adjudicating Copyright Claims Under the TRIPs Agreement: The Case for a European Human Rights Analogy' (1998) 39(2) *Harvard Journal of International Law* 357.

Helfer LR and Slaughter A-M, 'Toward a Theory of Effective Supranational Adjudication' (1997) 107(2) *Yale Law Journal* 273.

—— 'Why States Create International Tribunals: A Response to Professors Posner and Yoo' (2005) 93(3) *California Law Review* 899.

Henckaerts J-M and Doswald-Beck L, *Customary International Humanitarian Law: Volume I: Rules* (Cambridge University Press, 2005).
Henckels C, 'Indirect Expropriation and the Right to Regulate: Revisiting Proportionality Analysis and the Standard of Review in Investor-State Arbitration' (2012) 15(1) *Journal of International Economic Law* 223.
—— 'The Role of the Standard of Review and the Importance of Deference in Investor-State Arbitration' in L Gruszczynski and W Werner (eds), *Deference in International Courts and Tribunals: Standard of Review and Margin of Appreciation* (Oxford University Press, 2014), 113–34.
—— *Proportionality and Deference in Investor-State Arbitration* (Cambridge Studies in International and Comparative Law, Cambridge University Press, 2015).
Higgins R, 'The International Court and South West Africa: The Implications of the Judgment' (1966) 42(4) *International Affairs* 573.
—— 'Policy Considerations and the International Judicial Process' (1968) 17(1) *International and Comparative Law Quarterly* 58.
Hillebrecht C, *Saving the International Justice Regime: Beyond Backlash against International Courts* (Cambridge University Press, 2021).
Huneeus A, 'Compliance with Judgments and Decisions' in C Romano and others (eds), *The Oxford Handbook of International Adjudication* (Oxford University Press, 2014), 437.
Idleman SC, 'A Prudential Theory of Judicial Candor' (1995) 73 *Texas Law Review* 1307.
International Law Commission, 'Yearbook of the International Law Commission 1980, Volume I (Summary Records of the Meetings of the Third-Second Session, 5 May–25 July 1980)'.
—— 'Yearbook of the International Law Commission 1980, Volume II, Part II (Annual Report of the Commission to the General Assembly)'.
Ioannidis M, 'Beyond the Standard of Review: Deference Criteria in WTO Law and the Case for a Procedural Approach' in L Gruszczynski and W Werner (eds), *Deference in International Courts and Tribunals: Standard of Review and Margin of Appreciation* (Oxford University Press, 2014), 91–112.
Itzcovich G, 'One, None and One Hundred Thousand Margins of Appreciations: The Lautsi Case' (2013) 13(2) *Human Rights Law Review* 287.
Janis MW, 'Somber Reflections on the Compulsory Jurisdiction of the International Court' (1987) 77(1) *American Journal of International Law* 144.
Jenks CW, *The Prospects of International Adjudication* (Stevens & Sons, 1964).
Jennings RY, 'Recent Cases on "Automatic" Reservations to the Optional Clause' (1958) 7(2) *International and Comparative Law Quarterly* 349.
John A, 'Inarticulate and Unconscious: Non-Justiciability before the International Court of Justice' (2021) 20(1) *The Law and Practice of International Courts and Tribunals* 77.
Jones HL, 'Why Comply: An Analysis of Trends in Compliance with Judgments of the International Court of Justice since Nicaragua' (2012) 12(1) *Chicago-Kent Journal of International and Comparative Law* 57.
Jovanović S, *Restriction des compétences discrétionnaires des Etats en droit international* (Publications de la Revue générale de droit international public vol 43, A Pedone, 1988).
Kahn PW, 'Nuclear Weapons and the Rule of Law' (1999) 31 *NYU Journal of International Law and Politics* 349.
Kattan V, '"There was an elephant in the court room": Reflections on the role of Judge Sir Percy Spender (1897–1985) in the South West Africa Cases (1960–1966) after half a century' (2018) 31(1) *Leiden Journal of International Law* 147.
Kavanagh A, 'Deference or Defiance? The Limits of the Judicial Role in Constitutional Adjudication' in G Huscroft (ed), *Expounding the Constitution: Essays in Constitutional Theory* (Cambridge University Press, 2008), 184–216.
Kazazi M, *Burden of Proof and Related Issues: A Study on Evidence before International Tribunals* (Studies and Materials on the Settlement of International Disputes vol 1, Kluwer, 1996).

King J, *Judging Social Rights* (Cambridge Studies in Constitutional Law vol 3, Cambridge University Press, 2012).

Kolb R, *Interprétation et création du droit international: Esquisses d'une herméneutique juridique moderne pour le droit international public* (Collection de droit international vol 63, Bruylant, 2006).

—— 'Article 2(2)' in B Simma and others (eds), *The Charter of the United Nations: A Commentary*, 3rd edn (Oxford University Press, 2012).

Koskenniemi M, 'The Silence of Law/The Voice of Justice' in L Boisson de Chazournes and P Sands (eds), *International Law, the International Court of Justice, and Nuclear Weapons* (Cambridge University Press, 1999), 488–510.

Krisch N, 'Capitulation in The Hague: The Marshall Islands Cases' (2016), www.ejiltalk.org/capitulation-in-the-hague-the-marshall-islands-cases/.

Kulick A, 'Let's (Not) (Dis)Agree to Disagree!? Some Thoughts on the "Dispute" Requirement in International Adjudication' (2020) 19(1) *The Law and Practice of International Courts and Tribunals* 79.

Lanovoy V, 'Standards of Review in the Practice of International Courts and Tribunals' in G Kajtár, B Çalı and M Milanović (eds), *Secondary Rules of Primary Importance in International Law: Attribution, Causality, Evidence, and Standards of Review in the Practice of International Courts and Tribunals* (Oxford University Press, 2022), 42–64.

Lapa V, 'The WTO Panel Report in Russia – Traffic in Transit: Cutting the Gordian Knot of the GATT Security Exception?' (2020) 69 *Questions of International Law* 5.

Larson A, 'The Facts, the Law, and the Connally Amendment' (1961) 10(1) *Duke Law Journal* 74.

Lauterpacht H, 'The Doctrine of Non-Justiciable Disputes in International Law' (1928) 24 *Economica* 277.

—— *The Function of Law in the International Community* (Oxford University Press, First Published 1933, Reprint 2011).

Legg A, *The Margin of Appreciation in International Human Rights Law: Deference and Proportionality* (Oxford Monographs in International Law, Oxford University Press, 2012).

Llamzon AP, 'Jurisdiction and Compliance in Recent Decisions of the International Court of Justice' (2007) 18(5) *European Journal of International Law* 815.

Madsen MR, 'The Protracted Institutionalization of the Strasbourg Court: From Legal Diplomacy to Integrationist Jurisprudence' in J Christoffersen and MR Madsen (eds), *The European Court of Human Rights between Law and Politics* (Oxford University Press, 2011), 43–60.

—— 'Rebalancing European Human Rights: Has the Brighton Declaration Engendered a New Deal on Human Rights in Europe?' (2018) 9(2) *Journal of International Dispute Settlement* 199.

Madsen MR, Cebulak P and Wiebusch M, 'Backlash against international courts: explaining the forms and patterns of resistance to international courts' (2018) 14(2) *International Journal of Law in Context* 197.

Mantilla Blanco S and Pehl A, *National Security Exceptions in International Trade and Investment Agreements: Justiciability and Standards of Review* (Springer Briefs in Law, Springer, 2020).

McGarry B, 'Nicaragua's Impacts on Optional Clause Practice' in E Sobenes Obregon and B Samson (eds), *Nicaragua Before the International Court of Justice: Impacts on International Law* (Springer, 2018), 179–211.

McGoldrick D, 'The Boundaries of Justiciability' (2010) 59(4) *International and Comparative Law Quarterly* 981.

—— 'A Defence of the Margin of Appreciation and an Argument for its Application by the Human Rights Committee' (2016) 65(1) *International and Comparative Law Quarterly* 21.

Menkes MJ, 'The Legality of US Investment Sanctions against Iran before the ICJ: A Watershed Moment for the Essential Security and Necessity Exceptions' (2019) 56 *Canadian Yearbook of international Law/Annuaire canadien de droit international* 328.

Milanov M, 'A Lauterpachtian Affair: Security Exceptions as "Self-Judging Obligations" in the Case Law of the International Court of Justice and Beyond' (2021) 22(4) *The Journal of World Investment & Trade* 509.

Milanovic M, 'State Responsibility for Genocide: A Follow-Up' (2007) 18(4) *European Journal of International Law* 669.

Miles CA, 'Provisional Measures and the "New" Plausibility before the International Court of Justice' (2018) 88 *British Yearbook of International Law*.

Murphy SD, 'The ELSI Case: An Investment Dispute at the International Court of Justice' (1991) 16(2) *Yale Journal of International Law* 391.

—— 'Self-Defense and the Israeli Wall Advisory Opinion: An Ipse Dixit from the ICJ?' (2005) 99(1) *American Journal of International Law* 62.

—— 'The United States and the International Court of Justice: Coping with Antinomies' in CPR Romano (ed), *The Sword and the Scales: The United States and International Courts and Tribunals* (Cambridge University Press, 2009), 46–98.

Murphy WF, *Elements of Judicial Strategy* (Phoenix Books vol 551, University of Chicago Press, 1964).

Nolan MD and Sourgens FG, 'The Limits of Discretion?: Self-judging Emergency Clauses in International Investment Agreements' in KP Sauvant (ed), *Yearbook on International Investment Law & Policy 2011–2012* (Oxford University Press, 2012), 363–418.

Nollkaemper A, 'The Court and its Multiple Constituencies' in M Milanovic and M Wood (eds), *The Law and Politics of the Kosovo Advisory Opinion* (Oxford University Press, 2015), 219–39.

Ochoa-Ruiz N and Salamanca-Aguado E, 'Exploring the Limits of International Law relating to the Use of Force in Self-defence' (2005) 16(3) *European Journal of International Law* 499.

Odermatt J, 'Patterns of avoidance: political questions before international courts' (2018) 14(2) *International Journal of Law in Context* 221.

Oesch M, *Standards of Review in WTO Dispute Resolution* (International Economic Law vol 5, Oxford University Press, 2003).

Olleson S, "Killing Three Birds with One Stone"? The Preliminary Objections Judgments of the International Court of Justice in the Legality of Use of Force Cases' (2005) 18(2) *Leiden Journal of International Law* 237.

Orakhelashvili A, *The Interpretation of Acts and Rules in Public International Law* (Oxford Monographs in International Law, Oxford University Press, 2008).

Paine J, 'Standard of Review: Investment Arbitration' in R Wolfrum (ed), *Max Planck Encyclopedia of Public International Law* (Oxford University Press, 2012).

Palmer G, 'A Victory for Whales' [2014] *New Zealand Law Journal* 124.

Pauwelyn J, 'Defences and the Burden of Proof in International Law' in L Bartels and F Paddeu (eds), *Exceptions and Defences in International Law* (Oxford University Press, 2020), 88–107.

Peel J, 'Of Apples and Oranges (and Hormones in Beef): Science and the Standard of Review in WTO Disputes under the SPS Agreement' (2012) 61(2) *International and Comparative Law Quarterly* 427.

Pellet A, 'Kosovo – The Questions Not Asked' in M Milanovic and M Wood (eds), *The Law and Politics of the Kosovo Advisory Opinion* (Oxford University Press, 2015), 268–79.

Perelman C, *Le raisonnable et le déraisonnable en droit: Au-delà du positivisme juridique* (Bibliothèque de philosophie du droit vol 29, Librairie générale de droit et de jurisprudence, 1984).

Perez AF, 'The Passive Virtues and the World Court: Pro-Dialogic Abstentation by the International Court of Justice' (1997) 18(3) *Michigan Journal of International Law* 399.

Petersen N, 'The International Court of Justice and the Judicial Politics of Identifying Customary International Law' (2017) 28(2) *European Journal of International Law* 357.

Petersmann E-U, 'Judicial Standards of Review and Administration of Justice in Trade and Investment Law and Adjudication' in L Gruszczynski and W Werner (eds), *Deference in International Courts and Tribunals: Standard of Review and Margin of Appreciation* (Oxford University Press, 2014), 19–37.

Pictet J and Pilloud C, 'Article 57 – Precautions in Attack' in Y Sandoz, C Swinarski and B Zimmermann (eds), *Commentary on the Additional Protocols of 8 June 1977 to the Geneva Conventions of 12 August 1949* (Martinus Nijhoff, 1987).

Pinchis-Paulsen M, 'Trade Multilateralism and U.S. National Security: The Making of the GATT Security Exceptions' (2020) 41(1) *Michigan Journal of International Law* 109.
Posner EA and Yoo JC, 'Judicial Independence in International Tribunals' (2005) 93(1) *California Law Review* 1.
Prodromou Z, *The Public Order Exception in International Trade, Investment, Human Rights and Commercial Disputes* (International Arbitration Law Library vol 56, Wolters Kluwer, 2020).
Prott LV, 'Avoiding a Decision on the Merits in the International Court of Justice' (1976) 7(3) *Sydney Law Review* 433.
Proulx V-J, 'The Marshall Islands Judgments and Multilateral Disputes at the World Court: Whither Access to International Justice?' (2017) 111 *AJIL Unbound* 96.
Ragni C, 'Standard of Review and the Margin of Appreciation before the International Court of Justice' in L Gruszczynski and W Werner (eds), *Deference in International Courts and Tribunals: Standard of Review and Margin of Appreciation* (Oxford University Press, 2014), 319–36.
Ranganathan S, 'Nuclear Weapons and the Court' (2017) 111 *AJIL Unbound* 88.
Ratner SR, 'Belgium's War Crimes Statute: A Postmortem' (2003) 97(3) *American Journal of International Law* 888.
Riddell A and Plant B, *Evidence before the International Court of Justice* (Reprint 2011, British Institute of International Comparative Law, 2009).
Roberts A, 'The Next Battleground: Standards of Review in Investment Treaty Arbitration' (2011) 16 *International Council for Commercial Arbitration Congress Series* 170.
Romano CPR, 'The Proliferation of International Judicial Bodies: The Pieces of the Puzzle' (1999) 31 *International Law and Politics* 709.
Rosas A, 'Standard of Review: Court of Justice of the European Union' in R Wolfrum (ed), *Max Planck Encyclopedia of Public International Law* (Oxford University Press, 2012).
Rose-Ackerman S and Billa B, 'Treaties and National Security' (2008) 40 *International Law and Politics* 437.
Rosenne S, *Developments in the Law of Treaties 1945–1986* (Cambridge University Press, 1989).
—— *The Law and Practice of the International Court, 1920–2005: Volume I, The Court and the United Nations*, vol 1, 4th edn (Martinus Nijhoff, 2006).
Salmon J, 'Le concept du "raisonnable" en droit international public', *Le Droit international, unité et diversité: Mélanges offerts à Paul Reuter* (A. Pedone, 1981), 447–78.
Schachter O, *International Law in Theory and Practice* (Developments in International Law vol 13, Martinus Nijhoff, 1991).
Schill S, 'International Investment Law and Comparative Public Law – an Introduction' in SW Schill (ed), *International Investment Law and Comparative Public Law* (Oxford University Press, 2010), 3–38.
—— 'Deference in Investment Treaty Arbitration: Re-conceptualizing the Standard of Review' (2012) 3(3) *Journal of International Dispute Settlement* 577.
Schill S and Briese R, '"If the State Considers": Self-Judging Clauses in International Dispute Settlement' (2009) 13 *Max Planck Yearbook of United Nations Law* 61.
Schulte C, *Compliance with Decisions of the International Court of Justice* (International Courts and Tribunals vol 3, Oxford University Press, 2004).
Schulte H, *Zur Übertragbarkeit der Margin-of-appreciation-Doktrin des EGMR auf die Rechtsprechung des EuGH im Bereich der Grundfreiheiten* (Internationales Recht der Gegenwart vol 3, Nomos, 2018).
Schultz T and Ridi N, 'Comity and International Courts and Tribunals' (2017) 50(3) *Cornell International Law Journal* 577.
Schwartz A, 'An Agent-based Model of Judicial Power' (2019) 9(1) *Journal of Law (Journal of Legal Metrics)* 21.
Scobbie I, 'Words My Mother Never Taught Me: "In Defense of the International Court"' (2005) 99(1) *American Journal of International Law* 76.
Scott JB, 'The Reports to the Hague Conferences of 1899 and 1907' (Oxford 1917).

Shachor-Landau C, 'The Judgment of the International Court of Justice in the Aerial Incident Case between Israel and Bulgaria' (1960) 8(3) *Archiv des Völkerrechts* 277.

Shany Y, 'Toward a General Margin of Appreciation Doctrine in International Law?' (2005) 16(5) *European Journal of International Law* 907.

—— *Assessing the Effectiveness of International Courts* (International Courts and Tribunals, Oxford University Press, 2014).

—— *Questions of Jurisdiction and Admissibility before International Courts* (Hersch Lauterpacht Memorial Lectures vol 10, Cambridge University Press, 2016).

—— 'All Roads Lead to Strasbourg? Application of the Margin of Appreciation Doctrine by the European Court of Human Rights and the UN Human Rights Committee' (2018) 9(2) *Journal of International Dispute Settlement* 180.

Shirlow E, 'Deference and Indirect Expropriation Analysis in International Investment Law: Observations on Current Approaches and Frameworks for Future Analysis' (2014) 29(3) *ICSID Review* 595.

—— *Judging at the Interface: Deference to State Decision-Making Authority in International Adjudication* (Cambridge University Press, 2021).

St Macdonald RJ, 'The Margin of Appreciation in the Jurisprudence of the European Court of Human Rights', *Le droit international à l'heure de sa codification: études en l'honneur de Roberto Ago, Vol. III* (Giuffrè, 1987), 187–208.

Stahn C, 'Connally Reservation' in R Wolfrum (ed), *Max Planck Encyclopedia of Public International Law* (Oxford University Press, 2012).

Steinberg RH, 'Judicial Lawmaking at the WTO: Discursive, Constitutional, and Political Constraints' (2004) 98(2) *American Journal of International Law* 247.

Stiansen Ø and Voeten E, 'Backlash and Judicial Restraint: Evidence from the European Court of Human Rights' (2020) 64(4) *International Studies Quarterly* 770.

Sulyok K, *Science and Judicial Reasoning: The Legitimacy of International Environmental Adjudication* (Cambridge Studies on Environment, Energy and Natural Resources Governance vol 9, Cambridge University Press, 2021).

Sweeney JA, 'A "Margin of Appreciation" in the Internal Market: Lessons from the European Court of Human Rights' (2007) 34(1) *Legal issues of economic integration* 27.

Tomuschat C, 'Article 36' in A Zimmermann and others (eds), *The Statute of the International Court of Justice: A Commentary*, 3rd edn (Oxford University Press, 2019).

Traore SB and Leta PAA, 'La marge nationale d'appreciation dans la jurisprudence de la Cour africaine des droits de l'homme et des peuples: entre effeurements et remises en cause' (2021) 31(3) *Swiss Review of International and European Law* 317.

Tully SR, '"Objective Reasonableness" as a Standard for International Judicial Review' (2015) 6(3) *Journal of International Dispute Settlement* 546.

'U.S. Withdrawal From the Proceedings Initiated by Nicaragua in the International Court of Justice' *New York Times* (19 January 1985), www.nytimes.com/1985/01/19/world/text-of-us-statement-on-withdrawal-from-case-before-the-world-court.html.

Uhler OM, 'Article 53 – Prohibited Destruction' in JS Pictet (ed), *The Geneva Convention of 12 August 1949, Volume IV: Commentary* (1958).

UN General Assembly, 'Declaration on Principles of International Law concerning Friendly Relations and Co-operation among States in accordance with the Charter of the United Nations' (24 October 1970) A/RES/2625(XXV).

United Nations, 'Official Records from the 206th Meeting of the Security Council' (1 October 1947) UN Doc. S/PV.206, undocs.org/en/S/PV.206.

Urs P, 'Obligations erga omnes and the question of standing before the International Court of Justice' (2021) 34(2) *Leiden Journal of International Law* 505.

Vadi V, *Proportionality, Reasonableness and Standards of Review in International Investment Law and Arbitration* (Elgar International Investment Law, Edward Elgar Publishing, 2018).

Vadi V and Gruszczynski L, 'Standard of Review and Scientific Evidence in WTO Law and International Investment Arbitration' in L Gruszczynski and W Werner (eds), *Deference in*

International Courts and Tribunals: Standard of Review and Margin of Appreciation (Oxford University Press, 2014), 152–72.
van Harten G, *Sovereign Choices and Sovereign Constraints: Judicial Restraint in Investment Treaty Arbitration* (Oxford University Press, 2014).
Vanberg G, *The Politics of Constitutional Review in Germany* (Political Economy of Institutions and Decisions vol 1, Cambridge University Press, 2009).
Vattel E de, *Le Droit des gens, ou Principes de la loi naturelle appliqués à la conduite et aux affaires des nations et des souverains: Translation of the Edition of 1758* (The Classics of International Law, Carnegie Institution of Washington, 1916).
von Staden A, 'The democratic legitimacy of judicial review beyond the state: Normative subsidiarity and judicial standards of review' (2012) 10(4) *International Journal of Constitutional Law* 1023.
Wang C, 'Invocation of National Security Exceptions under GATT Article XXI: Jurisdiction to Review and Standard of Review' (2019) 18(3) *Chinese Journal of International Law* 695.
Waters TW, 'Misplaced Boldness: The Avoidance of Substance in the International Court of Justice's *Kosovo* Opinion' (2013) 23 *Duke Journal of Comparative & International Law* 267.
Weisburd AM, 'Use of Force: Justiciability and Admissibility' in M Weller (ed), *The Oxford Handbook of the Use of Force in International Law* (Oxford University Press, 2015), 329–46.
Weller M, 'Modesty Can Be a Virtue: Judicial Economy in the ICJ Kosovo Opinion?' (2011) 24(1) *Leiden Journal of International Law* 127.
Wilde R, 'Kosovo (Advisory Opinion)' in R Wolfrum (ed), *Max Planck Encyclopedia of Public International Law* (Oxford University Press, 2012).
Wolfrum R, 'Preamble' in B Simma and others (eds), *The Charter of the United Nations: A Commentary*, 3rd edn (Oxford University Press, 2012).
Wouters J, 'The Judgement of the International Court of Justice in the Arrest Warrant Case: Some Critical Remarks' (2003) 16(2) *Leiden Journal of International Law* 253.
Young SM, 'Destruction of Property (on an International Scale): The Recent Oil Platforms Case and the International Court of Justice's Inconsistent Commentary on the Use of Force by the United States' (2004) 30(2) *The North Carolina Journal of International Law and Commercial Regulation* 335.
Yourow HC, *The Margin of Appreciation Doctrine in the Dynamics of European Human Rights Jurisprudence* (International Studies in Human Rights vol 28, Kluwer Law International, 1996).
Zarbiyev F, 'Judicial Activism in International Law – A Conceptual Framework for Analysis' (2012) 3(2) *Journal of International Dispute Settlement* 1.
Zglinski J, *Europe's Passive Virtues* (Oxford Studies in European Law, Oxford University Press, 2020).

Index

www.ingramcontent.com/pod-product-compliance
Ingram Content Group UK Ltd.
Pitfield, Milton Keynes, MK11 3LW, UK
UKHW020802290926
15470UKWH00003B/914

9 781509 971305